MEDIA AND COMMUNICATION RESEARCH METHODS

An Introduction to Qualitative and Quantitative Approaches

Fourth Edition

Arthur Asa Berger
San Francisco State University

Los Angeles | London | New Delhi
Singapore | Washington DC

Los Angeles | London | New Delhi
Singapore | Washington DC

FOR INFORMATION:

SAGE Publications, Inc.

2455 Teller Road

Thousand Oaks, California 91320

E-mail: order@sagepub.com

SAGE Publications Ltd.

1 Oliver's Yard

55 City Road

London EC1Y 1SP

United Kingdom

SAGE Publications India Pvt. Ltd.

B 1/I 1 Mohan Cooperative Industrial Area

Mathura Road, New Delhi 110 044

India

SAGE Publications Asia-Pacific Pte. Ltd.

3 Church Street

#10-04 Samsung Hub

Singapore 049483

Printed in the United States of America

Library of Congress Cataloging-in-Publication Data

Names: Berger, Arthur Asa, 1933-

Title: Media and communication research methods: an introduction to qualitative and quantitative approaches/ Arthur Asa Berger, San Francisco State University.

Description: Fourth Edition. | Thousand Oaks: SAGE Publications, Inc., 2016. | Revised edition of the author's Media and communication research methods, 2014. | Includes bibliographical references and index.

Identifiers: LCCN 2015028126 | ISBN 978-1-4833-7756-8 (pbk.: alk. paper)

Subjects: LCSH: Mass media—Research—Methodology. | Communication—Research—Methodology.

Classification: LCC P91.3 .B385 2016 | DDC 302.23072/1—dc23 LC record available at http://lccn.loc.gov/2015028126

This book is printed on acid-free paper.

Acquisitions Editor: Matthew Byrnie

Editorial Assistant: Janae Masnovi

Production Editor: Bennie Clark Allen

Copy Editor: Paula L. Fleming

Typesetter: C&M Digitals (P) Ltd.

Proofreader: Rae-Ann Goodwin

Cover Designer: Anupama Krishnan

Marketing Manager: Ashlee Blunk

Certified Sourcing
www.sfiprogram.org
SFI-00453

15 16 17 18 19 10 9 8 7 6 5 4 3 2 1

Brief Contents

Detailed Contents

Preface to the Fourth Edition

S hortly after I purchased my smartphone, a Nexus 4, Google came out with a newer model. In the technology world, devices such as smartphones and tablets and apps are constantly being updated. The new models offer improvements, sometimes of considerable importance. For example, the operating system on my phone has been updated so taking photos no longer depletes the phone's batteries. Digital gizmos need to keep changing to incorporate new developments, and so do books. One thing that I've learned over the years is that a textbook is never really finished. As soon as you publish a book, any number of new topics suggest themselves as new devices are invented, new apps appear, and things happen that need to be covered. The publishing industry is changing rapidly as well, as publishers increasingly put out electronic books in addition to and perhaps, in the near future, instead of DTBs—"dead-tree books."

In this fourth edition of my book you will find the following:

- New images and quotations

- A new chapter on discourse analysis

- An expanded discussion of social media

- Updated statistics, references, and bibliographies

- An enhanced treatment of ethics and research

- Discussion of the Facebook experiment and the ethics surrounding it

- The application of rhetorical concepts to a Kenneth Cole fashion advertisement

- A paradigmatic analysis of James Bond film *Skyfall*

- An expanded discussion of analyzing research articles

- An explanation and discussion of ethnomethodology by Dirk vom Lehn

- New material on intertextuality from M. M. Bakhtin

- A discussion of neuropsychoanalysis

- Daniel Kahneman on thinking in *Thinking Fast and Slow*

- An abbreviated American Psychological Association style sheet

I have deleted some material included in the third edition, here and there, to make room for new material, and I've been selective in what I added to the book. I was guided in this task by suggestions from a number of scholars who reviewed the third edition. I hope you will find the fourth edition of *Media and Communication Research Methods* useful, interesting, and maybe even entertaining—and that it will help you become an informed media and communication researcher.

Acknowledgments

I would like to express my appreciation to my first editor, Margaret Seawell, for suggesting I write this book and to my current editor, Matt Byrnie, for asking me to write a new edition. I appreciate his continued support and helpfulness. I wish to thank the following professors who were kind enough to review the fourth edition and make suggestions, many of which I adopted:

Melissa Boehm, Montana State University Billings

Nickesia Gordon, Barry University

Maggie Griffith Williams, University of Illinois at Chicago

Linda Moerschell, State University of New York at Potsdam

I am also grateful to Felianka Kaftandjieva, a Bulgarian scholar, who wrote the first part of the chapter on statistics and offered many useful suggestions for the chapter on surveys. Al Kielwasser was kind enough to send me his syllabus for the course he teaches on media research at San Francisco State University, which was very useful. I want to thank Dirk Vom Lehn, author of a book on Harold Garfinkel, for his boxed insert on ethnomethodology. I also want to thank my copy editor, Paula Fleming, and my production editor, Bennie Clark Allen, for their assistance. I've published 11 books with SAGE over the years, and I am happy to have had such a long and rewarding relationship with a publishing house of such distinction.

At this moment he wished to be a man without qualities. But this is probably not so different from what other people sometimes feel too. After all, by the time they have reached the middle of their life's journey few people remember how they have managed to arrive at themselves, at their amusements, their point of view, their wife, character, occupation and successes, but they cannot help feeling that not much is likely to change any more. It might even be asserted that they have been cheated, for one can nowhere discover any sufficient reason for everything's having come about as it has. It might just as well have turned out differently. The events of people's lives have, after all, only to the least degree originated in them, having generally depended on all sorts of circumstances such as the moods, the life or death of quite different people, and have, as it were, only at the given point of time come hurrying towards them—Something has had its way with them like a flypaper with a fly; it has caught them fast, here catching a little hair, there hampering their movements, and has gradually enveloped them, until they lie, buried under a thick coating that has only the remotest resemblance to their original shape.

—Robert Musil, *The Man Without Qualities* (1965, p. 151)

Introduction

In this introduction, I describe myself as "The Man Without Quantities" or, in comic book lingo, Data-Free Man. In the past, I have sometimes described myself as The Secret Agent and at other times as Decoder Man. So you are getting, if you think about it, three "superheroes" for the price of one.

The Secret Agent   Decoder Man

❖ ROUND UP THE USUAL SUSPECTS

There are, psychologists tell us, people who have multiple identities or multiple personalities. I have an analogous problem, although *problem* probably isn't the right word: I tend to see things not "from both sides now," as the song goes, but sometimes from 5 or 10 "sides," points of view, or disciplinary perspectives. I suggest that doing this, using a multidisciplinary perspective, often offers us better ways of making sense of phenomena such as television commercials, common objects, fashions, popular culture, and humor than a single or unitary perspective does.

In a sense, when I find something I wish to analyze, I say to myself, "Round up the usual disciplines," and begin, often using a number of complementary perspectives. These disciplines include the following:

- *Semiotic theory*, which deals with signs and how we find meaning in phenomena such as films, songs, fashions, advertisements, and so on

- *Aesthetic theory*, which deals with how lighting, color, cutting, sound, music, camera shots, and related matters generate ideas, feelings, and emotions in audiences

- *Psychoanalytic theory*, which deals with unconscious elements in our thinking and behavior

- *Sociological theory*, which deals with institutions and groups and matters such as race, gender, religion, and class

- *Political theory*, which concerns itself with power, control, and resistance in groups and societies

- *Anthropological theory*, which focuses on culture and the enculturation process by which people are taught to fit into their cultures

- *Literary theory*, which investigates how literary works (of all kinds) generate their effects, the various artistic devices writers use, and the role that "readers" play

- *Philosophical theory*, which concerns itself with matters such as how we know about the world, the status of knowledge, ethical issues, and principles of reasoning and logic

- *Historiography theory*, which studies change over time—what happened, how it happened, and theories and suggestions about why it happened

- *Comparative theory*, which deals, when considering media, with how a given text (such as the film *Skyfall*) or other phenomena are perceived and the role that a given text plays in different societies and cultures

These methods are at the heart of a new subject or "metadiscipline" (some people say I never met a discipline I didn't like, but I swear it's not true) called cultural studies, which, as I see things, developed out of an old one—popular culture. Cultural studies eliminates the boundaries between elite arts and popular arts, but what it represents, I would suggest, is really a formalization (and perhaps an elaboration) of what people who had been studying the mass media and popular culture were already doing. Or should have been doing. In the late 1960s, for example, I used to teach a course called "The Arts, Popular Culture, and Society."

There are, I suggest, a number of focal points one might consider when doing cultural criticism. These are shown in Figure 0.1.

Figure 0.1   Focal Points Model

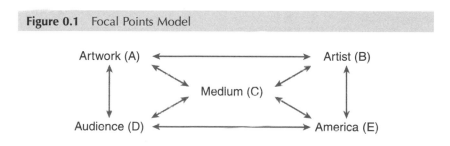

In this model, everything is connected to everything else, which is meant to suggest that each of the focal points may have an influence on each or all of the others. When we write about popular culture, mass communication, or media culture, we may focus on a text, such as a film or television program, but we also might want to concern ourselves with the creator(s) of the text, the audience of the text, and what impact the text might have on society and culture (the "effects" of the text). Communication researchers generally focus on one or more aspects of the communication process, such as sources, messages, channels/media, encoding and decoding, audiences/receivers, feedback, barriers and obstacles to communication, and communication contexts.

❖ APPLYING THE FOCAL POINTS MODEL TO MEDIA

In doing our research, we can direct attention to each of the focal points and deal with one or all of the topics listed in Table 0.1, which suggest some of the avenues of exploration possible in media and communication research.

Table 0.1   Topics for Exploration in Media and Communication Research

Artwork/ Text	Audience	America	Artist	Medium
Apply critical techniques to the work	Focus on cultures and subcultures	Study social functions of media	Investigate kinds of artists	Use transportation theories
Consider the work's genre	Analyze uses and gratifications	Relate national character to the work	Analyze demographics of artists	Study effects on audiences
Deal with intertextual connections	Conduct demographic analysis	Study changes in society due to the work	Analyze psychographics of artists	Study effects on America
Analyze style of the work	Conduct psychographic analysis	Explain role of subcultures	Study critical beliefs of artists	Study effects on artists
Make content analysis of the work	Relate to taste cultures	Tie to postmodernism and media	Study gender and creativity	Tie to effects on the work or other works
Study psychology of the work's creation and the work itself	Make comparative study of audiences	Compare to other countries	Consider impact of fads and fashions	Study impact of new media

In addition, we can deal with various combinations of the focal points in our research, such as the following:

Art and the Audience   Art/Artist and Audience

Art and the Artist   Art/Artist and Media

Art and the Media   Art/Artist and Society

Art and America   Art/Artist/America and Media

In short, we can use any number of combinations of focal points, depending on what we want to investigate.

❖ HOW I BECAME A MAN WITHOUT QUANTITIES

In 1984, a colleague and I were having a chat. We were standing in one of the corridors of the expensive and very plush (although, in certain ways, remarkably dysfunctional) building that houses one of California's premier communication research schools. During the course of our conversation, my colleague, a noted quantitative researcher, said, "Arthur, did you ever think about the fact that you are data-free?"

"Data-free?" What could that mean?

I recognized, suddenly in an epiphany, that I was a man without quantities. During the course of my academic career, I have argued that the dynamics of the McDonald's corporation and its fast-food outlets were similar to the methods of evangelical religions; that television commercials showing "muscle" cars crashing through roadside signs and similar barriers represented, symbolically, the deflowering of virgins; and that our passion for using deodorants to remove body odor was tied, ultimately, to Puritanism, perfectionism, and a fear of death. I have also hypothesized, in an article in *Rolling Stone*, that traditional white or "American" bread reflected our lack of ideology in America, where political parties often compromise on important issues. (Nowadays, there is a revolution in American bread, and we're seeing hard-crusted breads in many American bakeries and stores, a trend that reflects, I suggest, the fact that our politics is also getting more ideological.) I have also written about the importance of language in shaping people's consciousness. For example, a masculine identity is part of so many words dealing with women, such as *women, she, her, female, menstruate*, and *menopause*. (The science that explains the power of language to shape consciousness is, of course, *semantics*.) All of these arguments I made without using statistics or "data" in the sense that quantitative researchers use data. (Recall my "usual suspects.")

❖ DATA MAN VERSUS DATA-FREE MAN

Let us assume, using the perspective found in comic books, that we have two heroes, both of whom are researchers—Data Man and

Data-Free Man. There are considerable differences in the way our two heroes see and make sense of the world, which I have sketched out in this chart of complementary opposites.

Data Man	Data-Free Man
Information	Interpretation
The mean	The meaning
$N = \infty$	$N = 1$
Quantitative	Qualitative
Ingenuity in design	Ingenuity in analysis
Focus on audience	Focus on artwork (text)
Statistics	Concepts from various domains
Quantifiable subjects	Subjects useful for theorizing
Certainty but triviality	Uncertainty but significance
Getting data a problem	Getting ideas a problem
American pragmatic tradition	European philosophical tradition
Counts all grains of sand in the universe	Sees the universe in a grain of sand

This chart oversimplifies things, of course, but it does show how different the orientation of quantitative and qualitative scholars can be.

Quantitative researchers often use sophisticated statistical methods, but they sometimes (maybe often?) are forced to deal with relatively trivial matters—ones that lend themselves to quantification. Qualitative researchers, at the other extreme, often deal with important social, political, and economic matters and use concepts and theories from psychoanalytic thought, Marxist thought, semiotic thought, and the like—which may yield interesting ideas but are highly speculative and do not give certainty. This polarity is a gross simplification, but thinking about these two extremes can help us see the "middle ground" more clearly.

For Data Man, designing research so that one gets good data (and not the wrong data) is very difficult. For Data-Free Man, applying the right concepts correctly and "not going off the deep end" is the problem. The optimal situation is to figure out how to compare statistics and quantitative data with qualitative and theoretical material. The best scholars do this. They occupy some middle ground between the two extremes I've sketched out. But it isn't easy being both Data Man and Data-Free Man at the same time.

Consider economics, probably the most scientific of the social sciences. Economists, using the same data—statistics from various governmental agencies, for example—often disagree about what they mean. So you can't escape from some kind of interpretation and "going beyond" one's data. (And that's assuming that the data are accurate and correct.)

❖ KINDS OF QUESTIONS RESEARCHERS ASK

The questions we ask shape, in large measure, the research methods we use and our findings. Here are some questions you can use in planning your research and writing about it.

Types of Research Questions	Examples
Broad, diagnostic overview questions	"How do you interpret?" "How do you make sense of . . . ?"
Action or decision questions	"What should be done about . . . ?" "What would you do in this situation?"
Synthesis questions	"How does this relate to . . . ?" "What connections can you make between this and . . . ?"
Priority or ranking questions	"What's the most important aspect of . . . ?" "What's the central issue in . . . ?"
Justification questions	"Why do you believe?" "What support or evidence do you have for . . . ?"
Clarification questions	"What do you mean by . . . ?" "How do you define . . . ?"
Hypothetical questions	"If X were the case, what would it mean?" "What if . . . ?"
Application questions	"How can we use this concept to explain . . . ?" "How can you apply this concept?"
Summarizing questions	"What have we learned from . . . ?"

❖ CONCLUSIONS OF A MAN WITHOUT QUANTITIES, WHO IS ALSO A PRACTICING THEORETICIAN

I am, as I have explained, a man without quantities, and since I am "data-free" and have no statistics to "massage," I cannot, so the logic of quantitative researchers suggests, do research. A number of years ago, when I told a colleague of mine that I had written a book called *Media Research Techniques*, he laughed and said, "What do you know about research, Arthur?"

Since I've published more than 100 articles and more than 70 books (this book is the fourth edition of my 35th book, it turns out), if I don't do research, I must at the very least have a really fantastic imagination. Maybe being data-free is actually a kind of postmodernist stance? Maybe qualitative scholars should best be seen as fiction writers? Fiction writers use stories to convey truths about people—and isn't truth what we're after? I may be data-free, a man without quantities, but I like to think that I, and other qualitative researchers, have qualities—imaginative, literary, artistic, ethical, and otherwise—and that these qualities count for something. But I am not as data-free as I pretend.

If you wish to get in touch with me, thanks to the magic of email, you can do so easily now at arthurasaberger@gmail.com . . . but please, don't expect me to help you with your homework.

❖ INTRODUCTION: APPLICATIONS AND EXERCISES

1. Find two articles on media and society—one that Data Man would enjoy and one Data-Free Man could relate to—and compare them. Which one do you find more compelling? Which is more interesting? Which has more important implications? Explain your answer.

2. The theme of this introduction, "The Man Without Quantities," is based on a famous novel by Robert Musil, *The Man Without Qualities* (1965). Let me add another paragraph that comes after the material I quoted earlier:

   > And then they only dimly remember their youth when there was something like a force of resistance in them—this other force that tugs and whirrs and does not want to linger anywhere, releasing a storm of aimless attempts at flight. Youth's scorn and its revolt against the established order, youth's readiness for everything that is heroic, whether it is self-sacrifice or crime, its fiery seriousness and its unsteadiness—all this is nothing but its fluttering attempts to fly. Fundamentally it merely means that nothing of all that a young man undertakes appears to be the result of an unequivocal inner necessity, even if it expresses itself in such a manner as to suggest that everything he happens to dash at is exceedingly urgent and necessary. (pp. 151–152)

What response do you have to this passage? Do you think Musil is correct about people becoming stuck like flies on flypaper? Does he understand young people? Would you describe him as a pessimist or a realist? Explain your answers.

3. Examine the focal points model in Figure 0.1. Which of the focal points or which combination of them interests you the most? Explain your answer.

4. Investigate communication models and then try your hand at creating a model that deals with the media, communication, and society. What problems did you encounter in creating your model?

Part I

Getting Started

Our conceptions arise through comparison. "Were it always light we should not distinguish between light and dark, and accordingly could not have either the conception of, nor the word for light. . . ." "It is clear that everything on this planet is relative and has independent existence only in so far as it is distinguished in its relations to and from other things. . . ." "Since every conception is thus the twin of its opposite, how could it be thought of first, how could it be communicated to others who tried to think it, except by being measured against its opposite."

—Sigmund Freud, "The Antithetical Sense of Primal Words" (1910/1963a, p. 47)

All research methods involve compromises with reality. Researchers prefer more than one method whenever possible, because human thought and behavior are too complex for any one method to capture fully. Also, when different methods converge on the same insight, the researcher can feel greater confidence in its soundness. . . . The most limiting aspect of research, however, does not stem from inherent compromise but from human nature. That is, the person using a method—rather than the method itself—most determines both the benefits and problems that the method will generate. These limitations come largely from the inappropriate matching of a method to a problem. Sometimes, too, researchers forget or ignore the compromises that a method entails and present findings as more robust and reliable than warranted.

—Gerald Zaltman, *How Customers Think: Essential Insights Into the Mind of the Market* (2003)

1

What Is Research?

CHAPTER 1 FOCUS QUESTIONS

- Why does the author say that we all do research all the time?
- What is the difference between scholarly and everyday research?
- What role does cultural studies play in research?
- What did Nietzsche say about the role of interpretation?
- What is the difference between diachronic and synchronic research?
- What role do binary oppositions play in the way the mind works?
- What are the two systems that shape our thinking and behavior according to Daniel Kahneman?
- What's the difference between "dry" and "wet" Japanese?
- How does qualitative research differ from quantitative research?
- What are the five aspects of communication?

A certain look comes over the faces of some of my students when they hear the word *research*. Their eyes glaze over, and their faces take on a pained expression as if they had a migraine or a bad stomachache. They see the required course on research as some kind of an ordeal they must survive before being allowed to take the courses they want and go on to live a normal life.

❖ WE ALL DO RESEARCH, ALL THE TIME

Yet curiously, many students in my internship courses, when they describe what they do in their internships—that is, when they are out there in the "real world"—talk about looking for information and data, finding material on this or that subject, getting names and addresses—in other words, **research**. It turns out that research is one of the most valuable courses students take, as far as practical use is concerned, but there's something about the term *research* that generates lumps in throats and expressions of pain.

What is research? Literally it means "to search for, to find" and comes from the Latin *re* (again) and from *cercier* (to search). In French, the term *chercher* means "seek." In the most general sense, research means looking for information about something.

Like Molière's character Monsieur Jourdain, who didn't realize he was always speaking prose, most of us do what could be called "research" all the time—even though we may not think of what we are doing as research. For example, when people decide to buy a computer, they generally try to get some information about the brand and models of the computers they are thinking of buying. They may look in computer magazines, they may check in *Consumer Reports*, and they may ask their friends who have computers about the particular kind of computer they have. This is research.

Let me offer another example. In one of my classes, during a break, several of my students were discussing a professor. "What's he like?" asked one student. "Oh, he's easy," someone said. "He gives you a preliminary exam, and then in the real exam, he always asks one of the questions in the preliminary exam. I'd take him." This was information of value to the student who was thinking of taking a course with that professor. This is research.

So we are always doing research, even though we don't think of what we are doing as such. We do this research because we have choices to make about matters such as what we want to buy, what we want to take at college (and with whom we want to take the courses), and where we want to live. Even when we have limited budgets, generally speaking, we still have choices to make.

A SHORT THEATRICAL PIECE ON RESEARCH

Grand Inquisitor:	*Who is John Q. Public?*
Arthur:	Nobody! It's just a name we use for the ordinary American.
Grand Inquisitor:	*Why is his middle initial* Q?
Arthur:	That's an interesting question. You can find out if you do a bit of research.
Grand Inquisitor:	*Is John Q. Public related to Joe Sixpack?*
Arthur:	Some people think they're both the same person. You can find out if you do some research.
Grand Inquisitor:	*Why do people do research?*
Arthur:	To find the answer to questions that interest them or problems they want to solve, like what does the *Q* in John Q. Public stand for. Or should I attend college, and if so, which college, and what should I major in? Or should I get married to X? Or what kind of car should I get?
Grand Inquisitor:	*When do people do research?*
Arthur:	All the time.
Grand Inquisitor:	*How do you do research?*
Arthur:	That's the $64,000 question.

❖ SCHOLARLY RESEARCH IS DIFFERENT FROM EVERYDAY RESEARCH

A number of differences between everyday research and scholarly research need to be considered. Scholarly research is, generally speaking, more systematic, more objective, more careful, and more concerned about correctness and truthfulness than everyday research. Notice that

I've not said anything about data and numbers and statistics. That's because a great deal of research doesn't involve such matters.

Think, for example, of what historians do. There are, of course, some quantitative historians who do use statistics, but for the most part, historians read documents (e.g., speeches, letters, diaries, news reports) and, on the basis of their reading, try to describe what happened and why it happened; they focus on economic, political, and social considerations. Because there's no way to be certain about why things happened (and in some cases even what happened), there are lots of controversies in history, and different historians offer conflicting explanations of, say, the significance of the American Revolution or the causes of the American Civil War.

❖ CULTURAL STUDIES AND RESEARCH

Or take **cultural studies**, a rather amorphous multidisciplinary field that investigates everything from elite fiction to comics, television, films, music, and everyday life. Scholars who write in these fields usually base their analyses on the concepts, ideas, and theories of philosophers, psychologists, social scientists, linguists, and others with a more theoretical bent. Many cultural studies scholars base their analyses on concepts taken from thinkers such as Karl Marx, Sigmund Freud, the Russian scholar Mikhail Bakhtin, and the French scholars Roland Barthes and Jean Baudrillard.

In their book *Media and Cultural Studies: Key Works* (2001), editors Meenakshi Gigi Durham and Douglas M. Kellner explained how cultural studies approaches help us better understand the role of popular culture and the media and other forms of communication. They discuss the role that the media and culture play in socializing people to accept the rules, conventions, and codes found in their cultures and the ways that they indoctrinate people into political and socioeconomic systems. Pop culture, the media, and advertising, among other things, play an important role in providing role models, gender models, and lifestyle models for people to imitate. The narratives found in pop culture or **mass**-mediated culture help shape the sensibilities of those exposed to these narratives, as they are found in texts such as jokes, commercials, comic books, films, television shows, and popular fiction.

Durham and Kellner (2001) wrote the following:

With media and culture playing such important roles in contemporary life, it is obvious that we must come to understand our cultural environment if we want control over our lives. Yet there are many approaches to the study of media, culture, and society in separate disciplines and academic fields. . . . We would advocate the usefulness of a wide range of theoretical and methodological approaches to the study of media, culture, and society, yet we do not believe that any one theory or method is adequate to engage the richness, complexity, variety, and novelty displayed in contemporary constellations of rapidly proliferating cultural forms and new media. (p. 1)

It is because of the complexity of studying media, communication, and culture that I offer chapters on research methodologies that can be combined, in many cases, to offer more complete and more interesting analyses of the topics investigated than single-disciplinary approaches.

Because interpretations of these theorists differ and the applications of their ideas vary, we find considerable controversy in cultural studies and in other humanistic disciplines. But we also find controversy in the social sciences, such as economics, sociology, and political science, where a great deal of the research involves numbers. Economics is generally considered the most rigorous of the social sciences as far as gathering hard data is concerned, but we discover that given the same data, economists often differ on how they interpret these data.

Friedrich Nietzsche

❖ NIETZSCHE ON INTERPRETATION

The philosopher Friedrich Nietzsche believed that everything boils down to interpretation. As he wrote in his *Will to Power* (1987),

> Against positivism, which halts at phenomena—There are only *facts.*—I would say: No, facts is precisely what there is not, only interpretations. We cannot establish any fact "in itself": perhaps it is folly to want to do such a thing.
>
> "Everything is subjective," you say; but even this is interpretation invented and projected behind what there is.—Finally, is it necessary to posit an interpreter behind the interpretation? Even this is invention, hypothesis. . . . In so far as the word "knowledge" has any meaning, the world is knowable; but it is *interpretable* otherwise, it has no meaning behind it, but countless meanings. (p. 481)

Nietzsche suggested we cannot know facts, only perspectives. There is, he said, "no limit to the ways the world can be interpreted." He focused on what he called "perspectivism," a notion that informs much postmodern theory—a topic to be discussed in more detail in Chapter 9. Nietzsche may have overestimated the importance of interpretation, but it is correct to say that, in the final analysis, after social scientists have collected their data, they have to interpret these data, and sometimes there is more than one way to interpret the data.

Everyday Research	Scholarly Research
Intuitive	Theory based
Common sense	Structured
Casual	Systematic
Spur of the moment	Planned
Selective (often)	Objective
Magical thinking	Scientific thinking
Flawed thinking at times	Logical to the extent possible
Focus is personal decisions	Focus is knowledge about reality

As the preceding table shows, there is a considerable difference between what I've described as everyday research and scholarly research. In our everyday research, we are often very casual in our methods, and sometimes, when we want to convince ourselves that something we want to do should be done, we are very selective as well. That is, we neglect information that might convince us that a course of action we want to take is wrong. This is known as "selective inattention," which can be understood to mean ignoring information that wouldn't support your research or your wishes.

Sometimes our everyday research is tied to "magical thinking," which can be defined as believing that "wishing makes it so" or, for example, that we can, through force of will, cause something to happen. Perhaps you know someone who hopes to become a movie star without taking acting classes or being rejected at audition after audition.

Our everyday research generally involves personal matters — things we might want to do or products we might want to purchase. In many cases, we make our decisions based on advertising or something else that has an emotional appeal, which colors our decisions. We want to do something and look for information to support our desire. So the research we do, on the personal level, at times is not a matter of seeking truth but of finding support and justification.

Scientific thinking is the opposite; it seeks truth and accepts information that runs counter to one's wishes and desires. It is logical and bases its conclusions on rigorous thinking and honesty. Of course, people trying to be scientific and systematic and honest sometimes make mistakes, too, but the emphasis is on honesty, accepting the results one finds, and careful and logical reasoning. Much everyday research exists to justify prior decisions, whereas scientific research is disinterested and honest, accepting what it finds and not stacking the deck to get a desired result.

I can remember reading about some interesting "everyday" research a copywriter named Martin Solow conducted. He was invited to a gathering at a friend's house and asked his hosts about how they decided which products to purchase. Inevitably, they told him they paid no attention to advertising and bought most of their products based on what was recommended in *Consumer Reports*. He described how he conducts his research in his article "The Case of the Closet Target" (1988):

> I excuse myself and ask, since it is a large house, for a roadmap to the bathroom. Once in the large bathroom, the door safely locked, I open the medicine cabinet and survey the contents: Colgate toothpaste, L'Oreal hairspray; Trac II shaving cream and the new Gillette Trac II razor; Ban Roll-on Deodorant (for him, I guess) and Arid Extra-Dry (for her—or maybe vice-versa); Bayer aspirins. (p. 428)

The moral of this story is that we often deceive ourselves and think we are making or have made rational decisions about products we buy when, in reality, we've been influenced by the numerous advertisements and commercials to which we've been exposed. When people say, "I am aware of advertising but not influenced by it," they are fooling themselves.

❖ PROBLEM OF CERTAINTY

Although it is a big generalization, it's fair to say that we seldom (perhaps never) get certainty from our research. Even when we have statistics, the way we interpret these statistics is open to disagreement. This explains why scholarly disciplines are full of disputes and why scholars seem to spend so much time arguing with other scholars (who disagree with their findings or their methodologies or both).

Just because we can't be certain of our interpretations of **data** or **texts** (the term used for works of elite and popular art, such as operas, plays, poems, films, television programs, paintings, and comic books), doesn't mean that anything goes and we can offer interpretations without giving good reasons for them.

It is our research, I would suggest, that supplies us with the "reasons" we use when we argue about how to interpret a film or a bunch of statistics. It's best to think of academics as spending their careers trying to prove that their way of looking at whatever portion of the world they look at is correct. They do this by writing articles and books in which they explain their ideas and theories and offer support for them. They also critique scholars with different methodologies and points of view. Thinking doesn't make it so, however. You have to have some kind of **evidence** that a reasonable person can accept. And that evidence comes from research. How good that research is (is it reliable?) and how well the research is used are another matter.

❖ DIACHRONIC AND SYNCHRONIC RESEARCH

At the heart of all research is the matter of comparisons. In diachronic or historical studies, we focus on *change over time*, and in synchronic or comparative studies, we study *change over distance*, to put things in rather simplistic terms. This takes us to de Saussure (1915/1966) and his notion that concepts take their meaning differentially. De Saussure used the term *diachronic* for linguistic study that has a historical focus and the term *synchronic* for linguistic research that is comparative.

As de Saussure wrote (1915/1966),

> Certainly all sciences would profit by indicating more precisely the co-ordinates along which their subject matter is aligned. Everywhere distinctions should be according to the following illustration, between ... *the axis of simultaneities* ... which stands for the relations of coexisting things and from which the intervention of time is excluded; and ... *the axis of successions* ... on which only one thing can be considered at a time but upon which are located all the things on the first axis together with their changes. (pp. 79–80)

The axis of simultaneity involves comparison in space, and the axis of successions involves change over time. Those are the two general perspectives on which research tends to locate itself.

In experimental research, the comparison is between a *control* group, to whom nothing is done, and an *experimental* group, to whom something is done. The thing that is done to the experimental group is called an *independent variable*. Then, the two groups are measured to see whether the experimental group was affected by the independent variable. For example, a study of the impact of televised **violence** on people would have two groups of people: The experimental group is exposed to televised violence (the independent variable), and the control group is not exposed to televised violence. Then both are tested to see whether the televised violence has had a significant effect.

The following diagram shows the historical and comparative orientations. The horizontal axis is comparative (differences between one place and another), and the vertical axis is historical (change over time).

Time
X (Before)

Place (Here) A ⎯⎯⎯⎯⎯⎯⎯⎯⎯⎯⎯⎯⎯⎯⎯⎯⎯➤ B (There)

Y (After)

So we usually find that comparisons are at the heart of most research, just as they are at the heart of thinking and communicating, if de Saussure was correct. The A to B axis is comparative at a given moment in time (for example, the way people do things in the United States and the way people do things in some other country), and the X to Y axis is comparative historically, between an earlier time and a later time (for example, the way we did things earlier and the way we do things now).

When we try to make sense of the world and the information we have obtained (because concepts take their meaning differentially) we are always asking, one way or another, "Compared to what?" Another way of putting this is that facts don't speak for themselves; they have to be put into context and their significance explained. That is where the research report comes in, and the way the report is written plays an important part in how others accept the report. The medium may not be the message, but the way information is conveyed—that is, the quality of your thinking and writing—has a significant impact on how your research is received.

❖ THE WAY THE HUMAN MIND WORKS

Let us return to the way people view the world. According to the humorist Robert Benchley (1920), the world is divided into two groups of people: those who divide the world into two groups of people and those who don't. This division is whimsical and doesn't really tell us very much. In part, that is because we are given a statement about a group of people and then a negation.

The human mind, de Saussure (1915/1966) argued, makes sense of the world essentially by forming **binary oppositions** such as rich and poor, happy and sad, healthy and ill, and tall and short. These oppositions establish relationships in various areas, and it is through *relationships* that we find meaning.

Facts, by themselves, tell us little. Thus, to say that John Q. Public, who is married and has two children, earns $21,000 a year (a factoid) gives us some information about John Q. Public, but not very much. If we get another fact, that according to the federal government a family of four with an income of $22,500 in America in 2012 is living below the poverty line, then we can see that John Q. Public and his family are living in poverty. We have here some information—how much John Q. Public makes—and a concept—level of poverty—and we can see a relationship between the concept and the information we have.

De Saussure's (1915/1966) great insight is that **concepts** are relational. As he wrote in his book *Course in General Linguistics*, "Concepts are purely differential and defined not by their positive content but negatively by their relations with the other terms of the system. *Their most precise characteristic is in being what the others are not*" (italics added; p. 117). In other words, "In languages there are only differences" (p. 120) and, more particularly, oppositions. As he explained, language is based on oppositions. Relationships, then, help us make sense of the world, and the most important relationship, de Saussure argued, is that of binary oppositions.

Let me suggest some of the more important binary oppositions that we deal with in our everyday lives and, where appropriate, the thinkers who have made these oppositions part of our fund of knowledge.

Important Binary Oppositions	
Qualitative	Quantitative
The one	The many (Plato)
Active	Passive
Nature	History
Bourgeois	Proletarian (Marx)
Digital	Analog
Gesellschaft	Gemeinschaft (Tönnies)
Raw	Cooked (Lévi-Strauss)
Potentiality	Actuality
I	Thou (Buber)
Ascetic	Hedonistic
Acid	Alkali
Idealism	Materialism
Thesis	Synthesis (Hegel)
Good	Evil
Sacred	Profane (Durkheim, Eliade)
Young	Old
Id	Superego (Freud)
Yin	Yang

(Continued)

(Continued)

Important Binary Oppositions	
Existence	Essence (Kierkegaard)
Dionysian	Apollonian (Nietzsche)
Electronic	Mechanical
Rigid	Flexible
Superficial	Profound
Wet	Dry (Lifton)
Classical	Romantic
Ethical	Aesthetic
Free	Enslaved
Democratic	Totalitarian
Hierarchy	Equality
Fast thinking	Slow thinking (Kahneman)
Western	Eastern
Free market	Command market
Beginning	End
Capitalism	Communism (Marx)

Note: The names in parentheses stand for thinkers who have dealt with these concepts in their work.

These oppositions, and a few dozen others, have shaped our consciousness and profoundly affected our history. In a sense, one can argue that much of history involves confrontations between people believing in one or the other side of certain oppositions in this list and some kind of final resolution of the dialectic between them.

❖ OVERT AND COVERT OPPOSITIONS

In many cases, oppositions are hidden in texts and have to be elicited. Let me offer an example. I will quote the first paragraph from an article by Robert Jay Lifton and then show the bipolar oppositions found in that paragraph.

Lifton's (1974) article "Who Is More Dry? Heroes of Japanese Youth" starts as follows:

> In postwar Japan, especially among young people, it is good to be "dry" (or *durai*) rather than "wet" (or *wetto*). This means—in the original youth language, as expanded by the mass media—to be direct, logical, to the point, pragmatic, casual, self-interested, rather than polite, evasive, sentimental, nostalgic, dedicated to romantic causes, or bound by obligation in human relations; to break out of the world of cherry blossoms, haiku, and moon-viewing into a modern era of bright sunlight, jazz, and Hemingway (who may be said to have been the literary god of dryness). Intellectual youth, of course, disdain these oversimplified categories. But they too have made the words *durai* and *wetto* (typical examples of postwar Japanized English) part of their everyday vocabulary, and they find dry objects of admiration in an interesting place: in American films about cowboys and gunmen. (p.104)

This passage yields a considerable number of oppositions, listed here:

Dry (Durai)	Wet (Wetto)
Young people	(Old people)
Direct	Polite
Logical	Evasive
To the point	Sentimental
Pragmatic	Dedicated to romantic causes
Self-interested	Obligated to society
Sunlight loving	Moon viewing
Hemingway	Haiku
Cowboys, gunmen	"Samurai"

I put *old people* in parentheses because they are not mentioned but are logically present as the "wet" people in Japan, and I put *samurai* in quotations because they are not mentioned in this paragraph but are dealt with, in some detail, later on in Lifton's article.

What we see from this little exercise is that de Saussure's (1915/1966) statement about concepts having meaning differentially is correct. Wet is the opposite of dry, and when we see the term *wet*, it has its meaning because of its relationship with its opposition, *dry*. Thus we get "wet, not dry" and "dry, not wet" when we think of either term.

Oppositions, I should point out, are different from negations. *Healthy* and *unhealthy* is a negation. *Healthy* and *sick* is an opposition; both terms have meaning, and one term is not simply the negation of the other. (There are some scholars who argue that de Saussure's ideas about the mind finding meaning through polar oppositions is an over-simplification, but their arguments are somewhat arcane, and we need not bother with them.)

❖ THINKING FAST AND SLOW

Daniel Kahneman, a psychologist at Princeton University, offers a wide-ranging analysis of how the human mind works in his book *Thinking Fast and Slow* (2011). In this book he argued that there are two opposi-tional systems working in our minds, **System 1** (fast) and **System 2** (slow). He wrote,

> *System 1* operates automatically and quickly, with little or no effort and no sense of voluntary control.
>
> *System 2* allocates attention to the effortful mental activities that demand it, including complex computations. The operations of System 2 are often associated with the subjective experience of agency, choice, and concentration.
>
> The labels of *System 1* and *System 2* are widely used in psychology, but I go further than most in this book, which you can read as a psycho-drama with two characters.
>
> When we think of ourselves, we identify with System 2, the conscious, reasoning self that has beliefs, makes choices, and decides what to think about and what to do. Although System 2 believes itself to be where the action is, the automatic System 1 is the hero of this book. I describe System 1 as effortlessly originating impressions and feelings that are the main sources of the explicit beliefs and deliberate choices of System 2. The automatic operations of System 1 generate surprisingly complex pat-terns of ideas, but only the slower System 2 can construct thoughts in an orderly system of steps. I also describe circumstances in which System 2 takes over, overruling the freewheeling impulses and associations of System 1. You will be invited to think of the two systems as agents with their individual abilities, limitations, and functions. (pp. 20–21)

Kahneman (2011) then spent 400 pages showing how System 1 and System 2 shape our thinking and discussed many experiments that deal with the way people think and the way they can be influ-enced by any number of factors. For example, he discussed what are called "narrative fallacies," showing how flawed stories of the past shape our view of the world and our expectations of the future:

> Narrative fallacies arise inevitably from our continuous attempt to make sense of the world. The explanatory stories that people find compelling are simple; are concrete rather than abstract; assign a larger role to talent, stupidity, and intentions than to luck; and focus on a few striking events that happened rather than on countless events that failed to happen. (p. 199)

What we learn, here, is that we are continually relying too much on System 1 and our intuitions and gut feelings often lead us astray. Kahneman showed how professors of statistics make mistakes in deciding on the size of their samples due to their reliance on System 1 thinking and how voters also are affected by System 1 thinking. At the conclusion of the book, he pointed out that we must find a way to counter the "cognitive minefield" produced by System 1 and find a way to get System 2 involved, which is not always easy since System 2 takes effort and is stressful. It's easier to identify these minefields when we see others wandering around in them than it is to see the minefields in which we ourselves are caught, but it is the minefields we are in that are most important to us. Those are the ones we must find a way to deal with.

❖ QUANTITY AND QUALITY IN MEDIA RESEARCH

The stage is now set to discuss the basic opposition in media and communication research (and research of all kinds)—the difference between qualitative and quantitative research. I mentioned some of these oppositions in my introduction, but let us return to them again.

The term *quality* comes from the Latin word *qualitas*, which means "Of what kind?" Quality, when it comes to texts carried by one or more of the media, involves matters such as the text's properties, degree of excellence, and distinguishing characteristics. There is an element of evaluation and judgment and taste connected to the term *quality*.

Quantity is a different matter. The term *quantity* comes from the Latin word *quantitas* meaning "How great?" or, for our purposes, "How much?" or "How many?" When we think of quantitative research in the media and communication, we think of numbers, magnitude, and measurement. Of course, the problem that quantitative researchers often face is that they count only certain things, not everything, and it may be the case that something that cannot be quantified is of great importance in one's research.

Thus, quantitative researchers are sometimes accused of being too narrow, basing their research on what they can count, measure, and observe and neglecting other matters. Qualitative researchers, however, are often accused of "reading into" texts things that are not there or of having opinions or making interpretations that seem odd, excessive, or even idiosyncratic. (The term *idios* means private, and idiosyncratic interpretations of media and texts are highly personal and not defensible.)

Let us look at the two modes of research in terms of the oppositions connected to each of them. These oppositions are somewhat reductionist (that is, I've oversimplified them to make a point), but they direct our attention to important elements in the two kinds of research.

Qualitative Research	Quantitative Research
Evaluates	Counts, measures
Uses concepts to explicate	Processes data collected
Focuses on aesthetics in texts	Focuses on incidences of X in texts
Theoretical	Statistical
Interprets	Describes, explains, and predicts
Leads to an evaluation	Leads to a hypothesis or theory
Interpretation can be attacked	Methodology can be attacked

It is instructive to look at the kinds of investigations made by qualitative and quantitative scholars in the media. A number of years ago, I received a flyer from the Qualitative Studies Division of the Association for Education in Journalism and Mass Communication (AEJMC) calling for papers for the organization's annual conference. The flyer read (in part) as follows:

Entries may include studies employing any type of qualitative research approach. Essays, analyses, and literature reviews on topics within the interests of the division are also invited. Subjects falling within the Qualitative Studies Division's interests include, but are not limited to, the following:

Popular Culture

Philosophy of Communication

Literary or Textual Analysis of Communications Context

Performance Studies of Mass Communicators

Mythic/Ideological Studies

Media Criticism

Empirical or Theoretical Work in Cultural Studies

Production/Organization Studies of Mass Media

The flyer listed a number of other topics. I offer this list because it gives a good idea of the range of interests of qualitative methodologists, many of which will be dealt with in this book.

Under quantitative methodologies, I include experiments, content analysis, surveys, and questionnaires—techniques that lend themselves to statistical manipulations to gain information.

❖ MEDIA AND COMMUNICATION

For our purposes, we can focus on five aspects of **communication:**

1. *Intrapersonal.* This area covers things such as talking to ourselves, thinking about how we will respond to situations we expect to arise, and writing in a journal or diary. We are communicating with ourselves.

2. *Interpersonal.* Here, the communication takes place between ourselves and a relatively small number of people. This area includes conversations between two people and conversations with friends at dinner parties. There is interaction among all parties involved.

3. *Small group.* In small-group communication, a person might be teaching a class or talking to a relatively small group of people. The group is large enough that ordinary interpersonal communication cannot take place.

4. *Organizational.* This area deals with how organizations communicate to members of the organization and to other interested parties.

5. *Mass media.* Here we are dealing with radio, television, film, and other media. The communication flows from a sender of messages to a large number of receivers of messages. A great deal of the content of the mass media takes the form of texts—narratives or stories found in radio programs, television programs, films, songs, and music videos. (We also find narratives in personal conversations and many other areas.)

The development of **social media** sites such as Facebook, Twitter, and Pinterest, and video sites such as YouTube and Vimeo means that people now have the capacity to create messages and images that can be seen by huge numbers of people. The fact that most smartphones have decent-resolution cameras and video-taking capabilities has made everyone with a smartphone a potential photo journalist, and sometimes these photos and video uploads go "viral," which means huge numbers of people see them.

Social media

Source: Marina Zlochin/iStock/Thinkstock.

Different research methods lend themselves to each of these areas of communication. For example, if you are interested in the narratives carried by the mass media, you will use qualitative or interpretative techniques such as semiotics or ideological analysis, but if you are interested in the effects of the media, you will probably use quantitative techniques such as content analysis or surveys. In some cases, you might wish to use a number of techniques at the same time.

❖ WHY A BOOK THAT TEACHES BOTH METHODOLOGIES?

There is a logic to teaching both methodologies, for quite often it makes sense to do both a qualitative and a quantitative study research project. Take, for example, a television series about the police. The qualitative researcher might study the metaphors in the dialogue and the narrative structure of the shows in the series, whereas the quantitative researcher might study how many violent incidents occur per minute in the series. It is quite possible that the amount of violence in the series affects the qualitative interpretation of the text or vice versa.

It's reasonable to expect, then, that if a text is so violent it creates psychological distress and a sickening feeling in audiences, quite likely viewers, and perhaps critics, will give negative aesthetic evaluations. It may be that physiological or ethical considerations will shape evaluations of the text and decisions about whether to look at other episodes. In some cases, the intensity of the violence in a given scene (a qualitative measure) may be more important than the amount of violence (a quantitative measure) in the text as a whole. This is why we need to have a repertoire of analytic and measurement techniques: A diversity of techniques allows us to obtain the full array of information we need or want. It's better to have many arrows (that is, research techniques) in one's quiver than just one.

❖ CONSIDERING RESEARCH TOPICS

Here are some things to consider before undertaking a research project:

- Is the problem important enough to bother with?
- Is your hypothesis reasonable and testable?
- Are there ethical problems involved in the research? (For example, will it violate people's privacy? If so, should it be done?)
- Do you have the skills to do the research? For example, do you know enough about statistics to be able to deal with your data (if they require statistical analysis, that is)?
- Is the topic sufficiently narrow and focused so that you can do it in the time and with the funds you have at your disposal?
- Is your methodology the best one to deal with your hypothesis or subject being investigated?
- Does your college or university have library and computer resources that are adequate for your research?

❖ WHAT IS RESEARCH? APPLICATIONS AND EXERCISES

1. Find an article in the *New York Times* based on a scholarly article that deals with social science research on media. Analyze the article and answer the following questions:

(a.) What methodology was used in the research?

(b.) How important is the topic?

(c.) What conclusions were reached?

(d.) Are the conclusions supported by the data? Are the conclusions credible?

(e.) Can one generalize from the research?

(f.) Do the findings have any policy implications?

2. Find the scholarly article on which the *New York Times* article was based and compare the two articles in terms of how accurately the newspaper article conveyed what was in the scholarly article. Did it leave out anything important? Was the news report biased in any way?

3. Investigate smartphones. What have scholars found about the impact smartphones have on American culture and society? Deal with topics such as smartphones and the socialization of young people and smartphones and politics. On a personal level, which smartphone do you think is "best" for the typical student? What brand and model of smart phone do you have, and why did you decide to purchase it? If you could afford to purchase any cell phone, which brand and model would you choose?

❖ CONCLUSIONS

If we look at research as an attempt to find out about things and people and the complexities of communication, research becomes fascinating. Because of the way the human mind works, we are, in a sense, always doing research—but not always doing scientific and scholarly research. This book offers an introduction to scientific and scholarly research. It functions as a primer and describes the more commonly used techniques for analyzing media and communication.

A number of years ago, I was asked by a German publisher to write a book with both a historical and a comparative perspective—on techniques used by women who seduce men. This led to a fascinating search to find material I could use and to a book about women who might be called superstar seductresses, covering everyone from Lilith to Madame de Pompadour, from Cleopatra to Monica Lewinsky.

Who says research can't be fun?

❖ FURTHER READING

Bakhtin, M. M. (1981). *The dialogic imagination: Four essays* (M. Holquist, Ed.; C. Emerson & M. Holquist, Trans.). Austin: University of Texas Press.

Baudrillard, J. (1996). *The system of objects* (J. Benedict, Trans.). London, UK: Verso.

Becker, H. S. (1998). *Tricks of the trade: How to think about your research while you're doing it.* Chicago, IL: University of Chicago Press.

Berger, A. A. (1995). *Cultural criticism.* Thousand Oaks, CA: SAGE.

Berger, A. A. (1998). *Media research techniques* (2nd ed.). Thousand Oaks, CA: SAGE.

Berger, A. A. (2010). *The cultural theorist's book of quotations.* Walnut Creek, CA: Left Coast Press.

Bernard, H. R. (1994). *Research methods in anthropology: Qualitative and quantitative approaches* (2nd ed.). Walnut Creek, CA: AltaMira.

Creswell, J. W. (2013). *Qualitative inquiry and research design: Choosing among five approaches* (3rd ed.). Thousand Oaks, CA: SAGE.

Clemens, R. (2016). *Using social media for qualitative research: A theoretical and practical guide.* Thousand Oaks, CA: SAGE.

Durham, M. G., & Kellner, D. M. (2001). *Media and cultural studies: Key works.* Malden, MA: Blackwell.

Flick, U. (2014). *An introduction to qualitative research* (5th ed.). Thousand Oaks, CA: SAGE.

Poindexter, P. M., & McCombs, M. E. (1999). *Research in mass communication: A practical guide.* New York, NY: Bedford/St. Martins.

Priest, S. H. (2009). *Doing media research* (2nd ed.). Thousand Oaks, CA: SAGE.

Rubin, R. B., Rubin, A. M., & Piele, L. J. (1990). *Communication research: Strategies and sources* (2nd ed.). Belmont, CA: Wadsworth.

Sparks, G. G. (2015). *Media effects research: A basic overview* (5th ed.). Boston, MA: Cengage.

Strauss, A., & Corbin, J. M. (1998). *Basics of qualitative research: Grounded theory procedures and techniques* (2nd ed.). Thousand Oaks, CA: SAGE.

Surber, J. P. (1998). *Culture critique: An introduction to the critical discourses of cultural studies.* Boulder, CO: Westview Press.

Wimmer, R. D., & Dominick, J. R. (2003). *Mass media research: An introduction* (7th ed.). Belmont, CA: Wadsworth.

My Illustrious Friend and Joy of My Liver!

The thing you ask of me is both difficult and useless. Although I have passed all my days in this place, I have neither counted the houses nor have I inquired into the number of the inhabitants; and as to what one person loads on his mules and the other stows away in the bottom of his ship, that is no business of mine. But, above all, as to the previous history of this city, God only knows the amount of dirt and confusion that the infidels may have eaten before the coming of the sword of Islam. It were unprofitable for us to inquire into it. O my soul! O my lamb! Seek not after the things which concern thee not. Thou camest unto us and we welcomed thee: go in peace.

—Reply of a Turkish official to an
Englishman's questions, quoted in
Austen H. Layard, *Discoveries in the Ruins of
Nineveh and Babylon* (1853; see Barzun & Graff, 1957)

2

The Research Process

CHAPTER 2 FOCUS QUESTIONS

- What are the two "basic" search strategies?
- What are some of the most important sources of information?
- How does one read analytically? What tips are offered?
- What are the most important points made in the article about social media?
- What is the difference between primary and secondary research sources?
- What steps should one take in analyzing the methodologies of research articles?

Woody Allen has a wonderful line in one of his standup routines in which the writer F. Scott Fitzgerald brings Allen a book he has just written, *Ivanhoe*. "It's a good book," Allen says to him, "but you didn't have to write it. Sir Walter Scott has already written it." The point of this little story is it doesn't make sense to reinvent the wheel, to do research on some topic that's already been investigated—unless you wish to replicate the study.

❖ SEARCH STRATEGIES

One of the most important problems we face when thinking about doing research involves determining what topic we want to do our research on and how to conduct that research. We should always do research on a topic that interests us—that way, research becomes something positive and pleasant, something that satisfies our curiosity, rather than a chore.

There are two general search strategies:

1. Going from the specific to the general

2. Going from the general to the specific

In the first approach, we have something rather specific in mind for our project, and we search for material of a rather general nature to give us a sense of context and to collect material that might be helpful to us. Thus, if you are doing research on professional wrestling in television, you might investigate topics such as the history of wrestling, sports in society, or media and sports.

In the second approach, we have some area we are interested in studying and look around for information that will help us narrow our subject down to a manageable size—that is, information that will help us to focus. It is particularly important that as a student doing a research project you find narrow enough subjects to investigate, because your time will be limited (and you probably will have no funds for assistance). If you are interested in violence and television, for example, you have to find a narrower focus, such as the amount of violence on a selected animated cartoon program or violence in professional football, to deal with the subject adequately.

Once we have narrowed our focus so that we can manage the research adequately, it makes sense to find out what has already been written on the topic we are researching by doing a search of academic literature on that topic. Before the development of the Internet and search engines such as Google and Bing, this involved going to a good library and searching through the books and journals there. Now, in the age of the Internet, when libraries now are full of computers and librarians are experts in information retrieval, it may not be necessary to go to a library to conduct a search for academic writings that will be of use in conducting our research, since we can find a great deal of information using the Internet.

❖ SOURCES OF INFORMATION

Here are some important sources we can use:

Google Scholar, which lists articles and books on a wide range of topics

Google, the most widely used search engine

Bing, Microsoft's search engine

Wikipedia. At the end of Wikipedia articles, you'll generally find links to the articles and books used by the writer(s) of the Wikipedia article.

Here are some other sources of information that may be of use to you in doing your research:

- *Computer-based central catalogs* (formerly card catalogs). These list all the books in the library and often tell whether they are available or not. You can also use these catalogs to look for books on particular subjects or books written by an author of interest to you.

- *Bibliographic databases.* Here, I have in mind resources such as the *Reader's Guide to Periodical Literature,* the *National Newspaper Index,* the *Social Sciences Index,* and the *Business Periodicals Index.*

- *Indexes to specific periodicals.* The best known of these indexes is probably the *New York Times Index,* which lists articles from the *New York Times.* Because this paper is a newspaper of record, the index can be used to find lengthy articles on many subjects of interest to media and communication researchers. The *New York Times* devotes a great deal of attention to advertising and the media.

- *Abstracts collections.* Various fields have collections of abstracts, such as *Biological Abstracts, Historical Abstracts, Linguistics and Language Behavior Abstracts, Psychological Abstracts,* and *Communications Abstracts.*

- *Guides to research.* These publications are generally selective and offer what editors consider to be the most important source material in a given area. Some typical guides are *Philosophy: A Guide to the Reference Literature, Guide to Reference Books,* and *A Guide to English and American Literature.*

- *Dictionaries.* The most authoritative dictionary is probably the *Oxford English Dictionary,* but there are numerous other, smaller dictionaries that are useful. And there are dictionaries in specific fields, such as James Watson and Ann Hill's (1997) *Dictionary of Communication and Media Studies* and Ellis Cashmore and Chris Rojek's (1999) *Dictionary of Cultural Theorists.*

- *Encyclopedias.* Many encyclopedias, such as the *Encyclopedia Britannica,* are available online by subscription. Some specialized encyclopedias are devoted to communication, television, and the mass media.

- *Yearbooks.* Many subjects have yearbooks that often combine important theoretical articles and those that present significant new research. The *Communication Yearbook* is such a reference.

- *Statistical sources.* Every year the federal government publishes a huge volume, the *Statistical Abstract of the United States,* and the United Nations publishes two volumes, the *Statistical Yearbook* and the *Demographic Yearbook.* Private publishers also issue books of statistics on both broad and narrowly focused topics.

- *The Internet.* The Internet enables students to access mind-boggling amounts of information using search engines such as Google and Bing and other sources such as Nexis, Vu-Text, Lexis, and other online databases. Some useful Internet sources for statistical information include the following:

  http://www.amazon.com (Amazon bookstore)

  http://www.barnesandnoble.com

  http://www.census.gov (Census Bureau)

  http://www.census.gov/compendia/statab/ (statistical abstract of the United States)

  http://fedstats.sites.usa.gov (federal government statistics)

Online bookstores such as Amazon.com and Barnesandnoble.com are useful because they can be accessed for information about books on all kinds of subjects. They sometimes also provide reviews of the books and links to books on related subjects.

As you can see from this list, many sources of statistical data are available to researchers. By using search engines and other websites, you can obtain all kinds of other information.

Libraries, which are increasingly computerized nowadays, generally have the information people are looking for; the problem is finding it. And that's where diligence and ingenuity are needed. It's also a good idea to use the services of reference librarians, who frequently can be of great help. We can find out, if we conduct a good library search, whether research we are planning on doing, or research very similar to what we had in mind, has been done. It doesn't make sense to do all the work involved with studying X or Y or Z if someone has done so already—unless, that is, you wish to replicate the research and test whether it was done correctly.

So, generally speaking, scholars do a library search to find out what has already been done. This library search has another value: It sometimes helps our research by leading us to articles and books dealing with research of a similar nature. We can learn, then, from other people's work—and, in some cases, their mistakes.

We generally make library searches to gain as much information as we can about a given subject before narrowing down the focus for our particular research project. Because research demands a good deal of resourcefulness and energy, and in some cases is so difficult, we have to find manageable topics to deal with. Library searches can also be used to help provide readers of your research with background information to give them a sense of context.

If you have the chance to wander around the stacks during a library search, you sometimes find books that you didn't know existed that can be extremely helpful. The stacks are generally designed so works on related subjects are found together, and if you wander up and down the aisles, you'll come across useful books from related fields that you may not have discovered when checking through your library's computer system. Thus, researchers do library searches for a number of reasons.

❖ HOW TO READ ANALYTICALLY

Once we've found some scholarly articles and books we think will be useful, we should read them analytically—in an effort to see their strengths and weaknesses and to determine whether they will be of use in conducting our research. I list some of the more important considerations to keep in mind when reading analytically. There is a difference between reading an article or book strictly for its content and reading that book or article analytically; the latter involves making a critical assessment of the style and content of the text being analyzed. Here are some suggestions that will help you read analytically. We must recognize that scholars in every discipline often differ in their approaches to research and their beliefs that generate this research. Thus, for example, Marxist economists differ considerably from capitalist economists and focus their attention on different matters. They may interpret the same data quite differently, based on their theoretical orientations. Also, there is a difference between quantitative articles, which contain data, and qualitative articles, which use different approaches to gaining information and generally don't include quantitative data.

In this section, I will be making use of psychiatrist David Brunskill's article "Social Media, Social Avatars and the Psyche: Is Facebook Good for Us?" (2013). I will be using selections from his article as examples of the various topics I deal with in my discussion of reading analytically. In some cases, it is difficult to decide where a passage belongs, as far as reading analytically is concerned, since it may be applicable to several topics. I wish to thank the editors of *Australasian Psychiatry* for giving me permission to quote from the article.

Find the thesis statement.

Scholarly articles, and articles in general, are about something and usually have some thesis to prove, some proposition that is to be defended. Once you find the thesis statement, you can look at the evidence offered to support that thesis and see whether you think it is credible. You should keep in mind that when you write a paper, you should have a thesis that you are defending.

> *Abstract Objective: This paper aims to explore how social media users represent themselves online and to consider whether this process has inherent potential to impact upon the psyche of the individual.*

> ***************

> *The following observations have been made: going online results in a state of disinhibited and dissociated personhood and this state is the foundation on which a distinct e-personality has been described as a virtual whole which is greater than the sum of its parts and, despite not being real, is full of life and vitality, existing as it does alongside traditional offline personality, but with the liberating advantages of being unfettered by either old rules or the wider social contract.*

Look for conclusions.

After the authors state their objectives, they generally state their conclusions and then explain how they reached their conclusions in the body of their articles.

> **Conclusions:** *Advanced thinking around social media may exist on an organizational level, but on an individual level there exists a need to catch up, as the psychological dimensions of going online are significant and deserve consideration. Inherent to the experience of using social media is the self-selection of favorable material to represent the individual. This process is cumulative, and effectively creates a socially-derived and socially-driven, composite online image ('social avatar'). Humans notably select their best aspects for presentation to others and the social avatar reflects this tendency, effectively facilitating the creation of a "gap" between online image (representation) and offline identity (substance). The creation of a social avatar should therefore be an important and conscious consideration for all users of social media, not just those individuals already struggling with the task of integrating the multiple facets which make up modern personal identity. Social avatars appear to be an important factor in understanding the inherent potential for social media to affect the psyche/contribute to psychopathology within the individual.*

Look at the methodology employed.

Generally speaking, scholars evaluate articles based on the methodologies employed by the writers of articles. These methodologies—the approaches scholars make to their research—are crucial. How do authors support their arguments? What assumptions do they make? Are the methods they use valid? Could they have used other methodologies that would have been better? I deal with analyzing methodologies in more detail later in this chapter.

> *It has also been proposed that five psychological forces (Grandiosity, Narcissism, Darkness, Regression and Impulsivity) vie to assert themselves as the material from which the e-personality is built and that they—in a twenty-first century confirmation of the Freudian id—cause a transformation (and fracture) of personality, known as the Net Effect.*

Look for important theories and concepts.

Scholarly articles generally contain both theories and concepts. The theories generally shape the research carried out to determine something about the theory. I make a distinction between theories, such as psycho-analytic theory, and concepts, which are elements in the theory, such as obsessive–compulsive disorder (OCD). Thus, if people wash their hands two hundred times a day, we can describe this as an example of obsessive–compulsive disorder: behavior which, according to psycho-analytic theory, has a number of possible causes, such as trauma and genetics. You should look carefully at how the theory is explained and how it is used.

We can see this clearly in the following list:

Theory: Psychoanalytic theory

Concept: Obsessive-compulsive disorder

Behavior: Wash hands 200 times a day (or similar kinds of behaviors)

The concepts and the way they are defined are parts of theories and explain particular behaviors.

The way in which the human user represents the self in cyberspace is fascinating, complex and with respect to our human nature, ultimately revealing. In seeking to explore the phenomenon of self-representation online, the term "avatar" is a key concept to recognize and understand. . . . The term avatar has been firmly highjacked and expanded in definition to include one's personal manifestation in a virtual world—the image you create for yourself as well as the psychological character of persona you present to others.

****

Image is defined as a symbolic representation and a conception created in the minds of people, especially the general public. It is accorded increasing importance in society and has become established as central and influential to many aspects of modern life, including the online experience.

If data are used, look at how they are used.

How does the article use data to support its theories and concepts? On the night of the 2012 presidential election, the Republican nominee Mitt Romney believed he was going to be elected president, based on data that his campaign staff had secured. But the data his staff used were not accurate and Romney discovered he lost the election by a considerable margin. Nate Silver, whose "FiveThirtyEight" column in *The New York Times* predicted that Romney would lose, did so on the basis of surveys of individual states, which were more accurate than the national surveys Romney's advisers used (Silver, 2012). My point here is that you can't always be sure that data are accurate, and even when they are, there are often many ways to interpret that data. This explains why economists with different political attachments can interpret the same data in such different ways.

Look for arguments made by the author.

For all practical purposes, articles in scholarly journals are arguments about some topic. The article presents the author's discussions of some matter of interest, generally backed by data that lead to some conclusion. We have already seen that some data are not accurate. It is also possible that author's logical argument has problems, which then would lead to conclusions that are not valid. Whenever you see *all* or *every* in an article, you are dealing with very strong generalizations whose validity would be destroyed by a single contrary instance. That explains why authors of scholarly articles often qualify their generalizations, but even qualified generalizations may not be correct. You have to ask yourself why does the author (or the authors) believe something or not believe something else? It's a good idea to take a piece of paper, write down the thesis statement and list the components of the article's "argument" and see whether they lead to the conclusion the author reaches.

> *In order to explore any specific psychological aspects of going online (such as the effects of social media upon the psyche), it is first necessary to consider the forces which might govern and influence our online behaviors; both those specific to the medium and also those related to the individual user. Fundamental to understanding this process is the long-standing recognition that the online setting is a medium which exerts a disinhibiting influence (Table 2). On an individual level, it has been proposed that five interlocking factors can help observers to understand how individuals manage who they are in cyberspace (Table 3). Thus it appears likely that the personality of the individual is another important consideration (i.e. an individual's use of cyberspace—as in many other areas of life—is likely to reflect the characteristics of their personality). Building on this notion, it has been further hypothesized that individuals with specific personality traits/clusters may potentially express themselves in a characteristic fashion online (Table 4), although the need for significant further research into this aspect is noted. Finally, and importantly, the case has also been made that the medium itself has the*

*power to fundamentally change the personality of the user. Although it
seems clear that going online and the use of social media have the potential to affect the psyche, outlining a cohesive and unifying explanatory
mechanism for how they can do so is both a challenge of terminology and
of process.*

Look at the sources used by the author.

Are the sources credible? Are they reliable? Are they up-to-date? Do
they support the thesis being argued in the paper? This does not mean
every source used must be contemporary. If one is doing research that
involves psychoanalytic theory, it is reasonable to quote Freud and
other theorists, from the 19th century to the present.

Note: The author has 22 references. I show a few of them below.

References

1. *Te Kaunihera, Tapuhi-Aotearoa/Nursing Council of New Zealand.
   Social media and electronic communication guidelines, http://nursing
   council.org.nz/Publications/Standards-and-guidelines-for-
   nursesGuidelinesSocialMedia.pdf (2012, accessed 19 April 2013).*

2. *Kiss,* J. Facebook hits 1 billion users per month. The Guardian, 4
   *October 2012, http://www.guardian.co.uk/technology/2012/oct/04/
   facebook-hits-billion-users-a-month (2012, accessed 19 April 2013)*

3. *Aboujaoude,* E. Problematic *Internet use: An overview.* World
   Psychiatry 2010; 9:85–90.

4. *Aboujaoude,* E. Virtually you—*the dangerous powers of the
   e-personality. 1st ed. New York: W. W. Norton & Company, 2011.*

Look for contrasts and comparisons.

As I explained earlier, our minds think in terms of oppositions. As
Jonathan Culler explained in *Ferdinand de Saussure* (1986), the linguist
Roman Jakobson said that binary oppositions are the fundamental
process by which people find meaning; that is, the human mind
works to understand what a concept means by finding oppositions.
Thus, *rich* means what it does because it is the opposite of *poor*, and
healthy is the opposite of *sick*—not its negation, *unhealthy*. We look for
real oppositions and not negations. As we will see in Chapter 3 on
semiotics, concepts take their meaning from being the opposite of

other concepts. Thus, we should focus attention on the way the authors of articles use contrasts and comparisons in their writing, and we should pay attention to whether the contrasts and comparisons are correct.

> *Identity refers to the individual characteristics which define a person, or by which a person can be recognized. Unlike image, identity is therefore more of an essence that a representation.*

Look at the examples offered.

We should pay attention to the examples authors use and make sure that they are useful and correct. Are the examples relevant? Are they interesting? Do they support the author's arguments? Let me offer a far-fetched example. If an author is writing about the Oedipus complex and psychoanalytic theory and uses, as an example, people washing their hands 200 times a day, we can see that there is something wrong, since we know this behavior is an example of obsessive-compulsive disorder. My point is that sometimes authors use inappropriate examples. If we find this in an article, we have reason to doubt its usefulness.

> *That the Internet can serve as a tool which can enhance well-being is accepted; likewise, obvious advances in communication are clearly enjoyed by many. However, problems related to social media continue to emerge and appear to both match the pace of technological advance, and also reflect the dark side of human behavior. Posted material designed to be damaging and offensive to others can be varied, inventive and designed for maximum impact (as an example of subversive – likely pathological – online behavior, the use of anonymity to troll memorial Internet groups in order to deface online obituaries seems hard to beat). Cyber-bullying, unwanted/inappropriate contact, the posting of inappropriate/distressing information and problems related to the concept of addiction have all been identified as online behaviors which can have a negative impact in the general population.*

Look for threads.

Generally speaking, you can find threads—topics that come up repeatedly—in articles. What role do these threads play in the article? Do they help readers by reminding them what has been established? Do they have some other function?

Look for insights.

I define an insight as establishing connections that you've not recognized before between things. An insight is valuable because it helps explain things; to some degree, we can say that the quality of the insights provided in an article affects our estimation of the research's value. Can you apply the insights you've found in articles to your proposed research?

> *The Internet's facilitation of shifts in personal identity and behavior does appear to have been largely insidious, leading to the observation that for all the change wrought by the virtual world, the subtle reconfiguring of our psychological landscape that has taken place along the way appears lost on us, and the very significant and often negative psychological transformations that have ensued have gone largely unexplored.*

> *Examples of negative psychological effects can therefore be readily identified and perhaps an obvious place to find them is with respect to individuals who already struggle to integrate aspects of their personal identity. Specific concerns have been identified which range from the concrete (the Internet has been incorporated into delusions by some individuals), to the abstract (the creation of a social avatar creates compartmentalization and reinforcement of pre-existing pathological divisions within the self). Compartmentalization has been traditionally defined in pathological terms as keeping separate parts of one's personality that should be kept together. Whilst it may alternatively be conceived of as an everyday defense mechanism—serving to increase efficiency in a world with complex and competing demands on our time and emotions—such compartments will clearly need to be periodically processed and integrated in order for an authentic psychological self to thrive.*

Consider the style of writing.

Term papers, research reports, and all writing done in academic settings should use appropriate styles of writing. One should avoid conversational and informal styles in academic writing. But just because you are writing an academic paper doesn't mean it has to be dull and boring. You must also avoid awkward and unclear passages in your writing and observe the rules of grammar.

I chose the paper on social media because it deals with a topic of interest to many people and because the author writes in an accessible style. Brunskill offers definitions of the terms he uses and avoids the kind of jargon one finds in many academic papers. You should remember that people reading your papers and research reports will be asking these questions, so you must keep them in mind when you do your research and write it up.

❖ DOING A LITERATURE REVIEW

A literature review is a particular kind of library search. A literature review summarizes the major findings of scholars and researchers who have conducted research in the area you are interested in investigating. To do a literature search, you comb through the materials available in the library, in databases, and on the Internet for articles, research reports, journals, and books on your subject, and you offer a summary of what has been done in the particular area you are investigating.

This literature search does two things: First, it offers a sense of context for your readers so that they can see how your research fits into the scheme of things. Second, it shows readers where you got your information and lets them assess how current it is and how reliable it might be.

❖ PRIMARY AND SECONDARY RESEARCH SOURCES

Primary research involves firsthand observation and study by a researcher. For example, you survey a group of people on some topic and then see what the data reveal. **Secondary research** uses research performed by others to come to some conclusion about a topic or make some kind of an argument. This kind of research is essentially a form of editing, in which quotations (and sometimes summaries, paraphrases, and syntheses of the material) from various scholars are collected to produce an essay or article that makes its argument. In primary research, we *do* the actual research; in secondary research, we *use* the research that others have done.

In the *MLA Handbook*, Joseph Gibaldi (1995) described the difference between primary and secondary research as follows:

> Primary research is the study of a subject through firsthand observation and investigation, such as analyzing a literary or historical text, conducting a survey, or carrying out a laboratory experiment. Primary sources include statistical data, historical documents, and works of literature and art. Secondary research is the examination of studies that other researchers have made of a subject. Examples of secondary research are books and articles about political issues, historical events, scientific debates, or literary works. (p. 2)

Students generally use a good deal of secondary research in their papers and research projects, using ideas and findings of other researchers.

In a sense, what is done in such papers is an appeal to authority; the authority of the "experts" quoted is used to make some argument. At times, quotations from theorists such as Marx, Freud, Aristotle, and Plato can also be used to justify and support contentions. In fields such as literature, media and communication, the arts, and cultural studies in general, many **interpretations** of texts and other phenomena are based on concepts from famous philosophers, thinkers, and scholars that can be applied to whatever is being studied. How well they are applied then becomes the question.

In other cases, arguments are made on the basis of evaluations and interpretations made by scholars and critics about a given work of art or "text." Critics often disagree with one another about how to interpret a particular text, and the researcher has the problem of trying to figure out which critics are correct (and also *when* they are correct) and which are wrong (and *when* they are wrong). I say this because critics are sometimes correct about some aspects of a text and wrong about other aspects. In part, critics' disagreements are tied to the incredible complexity of creative works. In my work, I've had a great deal of fun applying (and maybe, in some cases, misapplying) ideas from Freud and Marx and various philosophers to all kinds of different texts, objects, and practices.

It has been said that there is no disputing taste. We all have the right to our opinions about films, television programs, and other texts, but that doesn't mean that our opinions are always correct or always as good as those of others. It is the quality of the argument you make about a text that counts, not the strength or intensity of your opinion.

Using Journals for Research in Media and Communication.

It is now possible to find many useful scholarly journals in libraries. If they aren't in your library, you can access them using the Internet. Below I offer some journals that might be useful to you in doing your research. This listing suggests only some possibilities for you to consider. Many of these journals, incidentally, are covered by *Communication Abstracts,* a bimonthly publication that provides approximately 1,500 abstracts of articles each year.

An abstract is a summary of the most important points in an article. If you find something in the abstract that seems useful and interesting, you can then go to the magazine and read the entire article.

American Anthropologist

American Behavioral Scientist

American Educational Research Journal

American Journal of Psychology

American Journalism

American Political Science Review

Canadian Journal of Communication

Central States Speech Journal

Communication

Communication Education

Communication Quarterly

Communication Research

Communications and the Law

Critical Studies in Mass Communication

Human Communications Research

InterMedia

Journal of Advertising

Journal of Applied Communication Research

Journal of Broadcasting and Electronic Media

Journal of Communication

Journal of Communication Inquiry

Journal of Marketing Research

Journal of Media Law and Practice

Journalism History

Journalism Quarterly

Mass Comm Review

Media, Culture and Society

Political Communication and Persuasion

Public Culture

Public Opinion Quarterly

Public Relations Journal

Quarterly Journal of Speech

Reference and Research Book News

Signs: Journal of Women in Culture and Society

Telecommunication Journal

Thalia: Studies in Literary Humor

Theory and Society

Western Journal of Communication

Written Communication

There are also numerous business or trade periodicals about media, communication, and broadcasting that you can use to get information on topics of interest to you. Many of these trade journals have a great deal of data in them that you can sometimes use or adapt for your own purposes. Below I offer some useful Internet addresses that may aid you in your research.

BOX 2.1   USEFUL INTERNET ADDRESSES

http://www.amazon.com (bookstore)

http://www.barnesandnoble.com (bookstore)

http://www.cios.org (Communication Institute for Online Scholarship—CIOS)

http://www.cios.org/www/afjourn.htm (journals list from CIOS)

http://www.ipl.org (Internet Public Library)

http://www.iTools.com/research-it/ (research source)

http://www.library.uiuc.edu/cmx/ (Communications Library, University of Illinois)

http://www.loc.gov (Library of Congress)

http://www.moviedatabase.com (movie database)

http://www.mmds.com/af/fr-bottom.asp (to find the meaning of acronyms)

http://www.nytimes.com (*New York Times*)

http://www.nara.gov (National Archives & Records Administration)

http://www.netlibrary.com (2,000 books, periodicals, journals, and articles)

http://www.onelook.com (dictionaries)

http://www.wsj.com (*Wall Street Journal*)

http://www.wsu.edu/~brians/errors/errors.html (common errors in English)

http://www.yahoo.com/Reference (research source)

This wealth of resources means you have to exercise some judgment in deciding where to search. The *Library of Congress Subject Headings* identifies alternative subject headings and may be of help to you with this problem. As you can see, there's a solution for almost every problem you face doing research; you just have to know where to look for it or find the right person to ask for help—such as a reference librarian.

BOX 2.2   WEB SEARCH ENGINES

Web search engines keep a catalog of pages they have investigated. When you ask about some topic, the search engine scans its catalog looking for relevant web pages.

Excite	http://www.excite .com
Google	http://www.google.com
Hotbot	http://www.hotbot.com
WebCrawler	http://www.webcrawler.com
Yahoo!	http://www.yahoo.com

Web Meta-Search Engines

Meta-search engines send requests for information to a number of search engines simultaneously, which means their searches take more time than those of regular search engines. They often summarize the data they receive or present only a few matches, and thus they may miss important information.

Dogpile	http://www.dogpile.com
MetaCrawler	http://www.metacrawler.com
SavvySearch	http://www.savvysearch.com

❖ SEARCHING ON THE INTERNET (OR "FIND THE INFO IF YOU CAN!")

Libraries are wonderful places to do research because when you go into the stacks looking for a book, you often find other books of interest. The Internet is also very useful because you can access all kinds of information very quickly. Below I offer some suggestions for searching for material on the Internet. In some cases, you will have to change around the wording of your searches to find the information you want.

You might want to think of finding information using the Internet as a game called "Find the Info If You Can." There's a good chance that the information is out there, somewhere on the Internet; finding it is the problem. It is customary to indicate the location of the information you use and the date you accessed it in papers and reports you write.

1. Use search engines such as Google, Yahoo!, and Bing for information on any topic you can think of. You can then click on some of the sites that the search engines provide for more information. The first thing I do when there is something I want to find out about (and that millions of other people do, every day) is go to Google to see what it has to offer. Here is what I found when I investigated media and communication research on Google in 2012 and in 2015:

	2012	2015
Media and communication research	38,200,000	288,000,000
Media research	172,000,000	1,960,000,000

I was curious about how many pages dealt with my own book *Media and Communication Research Methods* and found that typing "Media and Communication Research Methods Berger" into Google on May 5, 2015, yielded 266,000 sites. We can see there's been an enormous change in the number of sites that deal with media and communication research over the last few years. This means you have to learn how to narrow your searches.

2. Use Google Scholar for academic material. Most articles on the site aren't free, but you can find them very quickly there and then get them at your library or use your library's electronic access to the journals in which the articles appeared.

3. Use Google Books to read books that Google has scanned and that can be accessed on the Internet. You can access 35,000 online books at the University of Pennsylvania's Online Book Page (http://digital.library.upenn.edu/books/) and via other online book services.

4. Use Wikipedia for a list of search engines and databases that you can access. It lists many sites that will be helpful to you, such as EBSCO, which lists research databases.

5. Organizations such as the Kaiser Family Foundation (http://www.kff.org) and Pew Research Center (http://pewresearch.org) have a great deal of information about the media, public opinion, and related matters.

6. Amazon.com, Barnes & Noble, and other Internet booksellers have lists of books on most subjects you want to get information about. On Amazon.com you can look inside many of these books (you can read some passages in the books and look at their indexes, bibliographies, etc.) for more information.

7. Many, if not most, scholarly journals can be read on the Internet. Your library probably has ways of accessing them, so you can look at scholarly journals related to your search. The advantage of getting information in journals is that the information is much more current than you find in books, since it takes around a year to publish a book from the time it is accepted by a publisher.

The most important scholarly journals are "peer reviewed." That means the editor of the journal sends out articles, without telling who wrote them, to a number of scholars with expertise in the subject of the article. The reviewers don't know who wrote the article, and the writer(s) of the article don't know to whom it was sent. If the reviewing scholars think the article should be published, the editor generally will publish it. Sometimes the reviewing scholars want changes, and other times they think an article isn't worth publishing at all; they explain their decisions in reviews they write about the article. Editors use "peer review" to make sure that articles are judged impartially and to ensure that the articles are worth publishing.

❖ ANALYZING METHODOLOGY IN RESEARCH ARTICLES

You can look at research articles not only in terms of their findings but also in terms of their methodologies. We can learn both from the mistakes in others' methods and from the ingenious methods described in many research articles. First, however, you have to be able to identify the methodology that was used.

Suppose you were doing research about some subject based on survey research. This methodology, which I will discuss in more detail in Chapter 13, involves giving surveys to gather information from a carefully selected group of people who are thought to be representative of some larger population, such as the audience for television programs in a city or state or country.

In examining journal articles that employ survey research, you should do the following things to evaluate the quality of the research.

This list is adapted from materials supplied to me by my colleague Chaim Eyal, who often teaches courses in research in my department.

1. Identify the method or methods used in the research.

2. Determine the research question(s) or hypothesis(es).

3. Identify the independent and dependent variables.

4. Consider the sample size: $N = ?$

5. Evaluate the sampling method that was used.

6. Ask yourself how the survey was conducted.

7. Make note of the major results and conclusions.

Just because an article is full of statistics and other data doesn't mean that the research it describes was carried out correctly or that the findings are valid.

In analyzing other kinds of research, we follow a similar routine:

1. What topic was investigated?

2. What methods were used?

3. What were the conclusions or findings?

4. What problems (if any) did you find with the methods used?

5. How valid are the findings, and how useful is the research?

Sometimes we can adapt research methods worked out by someone else to deal with a particular problem for topics we are interested in, so it is always good to look at research articles in terms of both what they say and what methodologies they employ.

❖ THE RESEARCH PROCESS: APPLICATIONS AND EXERCISES

1. Using the library and the Internet's access to scholarly journals, find articles that deal with the following topics:

   The relation between modernism and postmodernism

   Suicide rates in various countries

   International tourism (how many people go to the top 10 countries)

Advertising expenditures in the United States, France, Germany, Japan, China, and Brazil

The cultural significance of James Bond movies

2. Apply Chaim Eyal's list of questions and other things you've learned from this book to ask about research to an article that uses survey research.

❖ CONCLUSIONS

Research can be very enjoyable if you have a topic that interests you. Thanks to the Internet, you can do a great deal of research using a computer or smartphone. You can often find books and articles in libraries as well as librarians who can help you with your research. University libraries also have large numbers of popular magazines, scholarly journals, government publications, and books that you can use in your research and, in some cases, for your own reading pleasure.

❖ FURTHER READING

Agosti, M. (Ed). (2008). *Information access through search engines and digital libraries*. Berlin, Germany: Springer.

Bent, M. J. (2015). *Practical tips for facilitating research*. London, UK: Facet.

Fink, A. (2014). *Conducting research literature reviews: From paper to the Internet* (4th ed.). Thousand Oaks, CA: SAGE.

Fielding, N. G., Lee, R. M., & Blank, G. (Eds.). (2008). *The SAGE handbook of online research methods*. London, UK: SAGE.

Gibaldi, J. (2009). *Handbook for writers of research papers* (7th ed.). New York, NY: Modern Language Association.

Gross, R. (Ed.). (1993). *The independent scholar's handbook*. Berkeley, CA: Ten Speed Press.

Hart, C. (1998). *Doing a literature review: Releasing the social science research imagination*. Thousand Oaks, CA: SAGE.

Mann, T. (1987). *A guide to library research methods*. New York, NY: Oxford University Press.

Muijs. D. (2018). *Doing research with secondary data*. Thousand Oaks, CA: SAGE.

Pelley, G., Bracken, C. C., & Babin, E. (2015). *Communication research methods: A strategic communication science approach to applied research methods*. New York, NY: Routledge.

Semonche, B. P. (Ed.). (1993). *News media libraries*. Westport, CT: Greenwood.

Weinberg, S. (1996). *The reporter's handbook: An investigator's guide to documents and techniques* (3rd ed.). New York, NY: St. Martin's.

Part II

Methods of Textual Analysis

Language is a system of signs that express ideas, and is therefore comparable to a system of writing, the alphabet of deaf-mutes, military signals, etc. But it is the most important of these systems.

A science that studies the life of signs within society is conceivable; it would be part of social-psychology and consequently of general psychology; I shall call it semiology (from Greek, sēmeîon "sign"). Semiology would show what constitutes signs, what laws govern them. Since the science does not yet exist, no one can say what it would be; but it has a right to existence, a place staked out in advance. . . . By studying rites, customs, etc. as signs, I believe that we shall throw new light on the facts and point up the need for including them in a science of semiology and explaining them by its laws.

—Ferdinand de Saussure, *Course in General Linguistics* (1966, p. 16)

3

Semiotic Analysis

- What are the two parts of a sign according to Saussure?
- How do people use blonde hair to "lie" with signs?
- Why do semioticians argue that society is the primary reality?
- What are the components of Peirce's trichotomy?
- What is the difference between denotation and connotation?
- What important points does Rapaille make in his analysis of culture codes?
- What is the difference between a syntagmatic and paradigmatic text analysis?
- What does Ekman say about facial expressions? What do we learn from them?
- What components comprise a paradigmatic analysis of *Skyfall*?

Semiotics—the science of signs—is a vast subject that can, at times, be extremely complicated. Some of the writings of semiotic theorists are quite difficult. Yet it is possible to explain enough of the basic principles of semiotics in this brief chapter (and offer an example or two of applied semiotic analysis) so that you can learn enough about semiotics to make your own semiotic analyses. Those of you interested in semiotics can, of course, pursue the matter in greater depth by reading some of the books on semiotics mentioned in the bibliography at the end of this chapter. Let me offer one of many definitions of the term *sign*, as defined by prominent sociosemiotician Mark Gottdiener (1997) in his book *The Theming of America: Dreams, Visions, and Commercial Spaces*:

> The basic unit of semiotics is the *sign* defined conceptually as something that stands for something else, and, more technically, as a spoken or written word, a drawn figure, or a material object unified in the mind with a particular cultural concept. The sign is this unity of word-object, known as a *signifier* with a corresponding, culturally prescribed content or meaning, known as a *signified*. Thus our minds attach the word "dog," or the drawn figure of a "dog," as a signifier to the idea of a "dog," that is, a domesticated canine species possessing certain behavioral characteristics. If we came from a culture that did not possess dogs in daily life, however unlikely, we would not know what the signifier "dog" means. . . . When dealing with objects that are signifiers of certain concepts, cultural meanings, or ideologies of belief, we can consider them not only as "signs," but *sign vehicles*. Signifying objects carry meanings with them. (pp. 8–9)

You will find that semioticians have analyzed facial expressions, hairstyles and hair colors, teeth, fashions in clothing and eyeglasses and jewelry, body piercing, and just about anything you can think of to determine how they generate meaning and what they reflect about society and culture. I analyze several signs in this chapter.

A SHORT THEATRICAL PIECE ON SEMIOTICS

Grand Inquisitor:	*I've been observing students. Tell me about long hair. What does it mean?*
Arthur:	Long hair used to mean counterculture, but now it's lost its meaning. Even squares have long hair now . . . and earrings, too.
Grand Inquisitor:	*What about purple hair and green hair?*
Arthur:	That's usually the sign of a punk.

Grand Inquisitor:	*What about women with shaved hair? Are they war criminals?*
Arthur:	Not now. They're just trying to be cool.
Grand Inquisitor:	*But don't their heads get cold in the winter? And why do so many men wear beards all of a sudden? Even baseball players.*
Arthur:	American society has become increasingly **desexualized**. Men wear beards to affirm their masculinity. Or to hide weak chins.
Grand Inquisitor:	*Do you see that cloud over there? It looks like a camel.*
Arthur:	You're right. It does look like a camel.
Grand Inquisitor:	*Maybe it's more like a weasel.*
Arthur:	It is backed like a weasel.
Grand Inquisitor:	*Or like a whale.*
Arthur:	Very like a whale.

❖ SAUSSURE'S DIVISION OF SIGNS INTO SIGNIFIERS AND SIGNIFIEDS

The Swiss linguist Ferdinand de Saussure (1857–1913) is the founder of semiology, and the American philosopher Charles Sanders Peirce (1839–1914) is the founder of semiotics—both sciences are involved

Ferdinand de Saussure

with how to interpret **signs.** In recent years, in part to make life simpler for ourselves, we have taken to using the term *semiotics* to stand for both methods of analyzing signs. But what is a sign? I will explain Saussure's theories first and then deal with Peirce's.

For Saussure, the important thing to remember about signs is that they are made up of sounds and **images,** what he called *signifiers,* and the concepts these sounds and images bring to mind, what he called *signifieds.* As he wrote,

I call the combination of a concept and a sound-image a *sign,* but in current usage the term generally designates only a sound-image, a word, for example. . . . I propose to retain the word *sign [signe]* to designate the whole and to replace *concept* and *sound-image* respectively by *signified [signifie]* and *signifier [signifiant];* the last two terms have the advantage of indicating the opposition that separates them from each other and from the whole of which they are parts. As regards *sign,* if I am satisfied with it, this is simply because I do not know of any word to replace it, the ordinary language suggesting no other. (1966, p. 67)

The relationship Saussure talked about is shown in the chart that follows:

SIGN	
Signifier	*Signified*
Sound-image	Concept

Example: Word *tree*   Large stemmed plant . . .

Words are signs, but so are many other things, such as facial expressions, body language, clothes, haircuts—you name it. To a semiotician, *everything* can be taken for a sign. Semiotics is, you will see, an imperialistic science. One problem with signs, however, is that they can be used for deception. That beautiful blonde woman you see sitting at the bar turns out to be neither a woman nor a blonde but a man, a transvestite who is deceiving with signs.

Blonde hair (not dyed blonde hair)

❖ SEMIOTICS OF BLONDENESS

Blonde hair is the most popular color used by women who dye their hair. As the saying goes, "Many a blonde dyes by her own hands." In the United States we think that "blondes have more fun." But there are different ways to interpret what blonde hair means, for it is also associated with coldness or innocence. D. H. Lawrence said that in American novels, blonde women are often portrayed as cold, unobtainable, and frigid while dark-haired women are shown as passionate and sexually exciting. In his book *Desexualization in American Life*, sociologist Charles Winick (1995) wrote that "for a substantial number of women, the attractiveness in blondeness is less an opportunity to have more fun than the communication of a withdrawal of emotion, a lack of passion" (p. 169). He suggested that this was why Marilyn Monroe was so popular: She didn't come across as a temptress but, instead, as an innocent. For Winick, a brunette who dyes her hair blonde looks like a blonde but thinks like a brunette.

We can cite dyed blonde hair as an example of "lying" with signs.

Umberto Eco (1976), a prominent Italian semiotician (and author of the novel *The Name of the Rose*) has explained that if signs can be used to tell the truth, they can also be used to lie:

> Semiotics is concerned with everything that can be taken as a sign. A sign is everything which can be taken as significantly substituting for something else. This something else does not necessarily have to exist or actually be somewhere at the moment in which a sign stands for it. Thus semiotics is in principle the discipline studying everything which can be used in order to lie. If something cannot be used to tell a lie, conversely it cannot be used "to tell" at all. (p. 7)

Think, for example, of brunettes who dye their hair blonde, of short men wearing elevator shoes, of bald men wearing wigs, and women dressing like men—they are all, semiotically speaking, lying with signs.

Ferdinand de Saussure (1966) said there was something very important to remember about signs: The relation between signifier and signified is based on convention, is arbitrary. The relationship that exists between the word *tree* and the large-stemmed plant for which the word *tree* stands is not natural but historical, tied to conventions and choices that people made. He distinguished symbols from signs by saying that symbols, which he saw as a subcategory of signs, are not completely arbitrary. As he wrote,

> One characteristic of the symbol is that it is never wholly arbitrary; it is not empty, for there is the rudiment of a natural bond between the signifier and the signified. The symbol of justice, a pair of scales, could not be replaced by just any other symbol, such as a chariot. (p. 68)

Symbols have enormous significance in our lives and play an important role in our thinking and behavior.

❖ SEMIOTICS AND SOCIETY

A relationship between signifiers and signifieds based on conventions has important implications, for it means that we need society and its institutions to teach us how to interpret signifiers. As Jonathan Culler wrote in the revised edition of his book *Ferdinand de Saussure* (1986),

For human beings, society is a primary reality, not just the sum of individual activities . . . and if one wishes to study human behavior, one
must grant that there is a social reality. . . . Since meanings are a social
product, explanation must be carried out in social terms. . . . Individual
actions and symptoms can be interpreted psychoanalytically because
they are the result of common psychic processes, unconscious defenses
occasioned by social taboos and leading to particular types of repression and displacement. Linguist communication is possible because we
have assimilated a system of collective norms that organize the world
and give meaning to verbal acts. Or again, as Durkheim argued, the
reality crucial to the individual is not the physical environment but the
social milieu, a system of rules and norms, of collective representations,
which makes possible social behavior. (pp. 86–87)

What semiotic theory tells us, by implication, is that we are social
animals and that the way we make sense of the world is connected to
the social milieu in which we are brought up. The notion that society
doesn't exist and that only individuals exist is something we learn,
ironically, from society. We learn more about this matter shortly in the
discussion of **culture codes.**

C. S. Peirce, who gave the study of signs, semiotics, its name

❖ PEIRCE'S TRICHOTOMY: ICON, INDEX, AND SYMBOL

Peirce had a different system. He believed there were three kinds of
signs: icons, indexes, and symbols. **Icons** signify by resemblance,
indexes signify by cause and effect, and **symbols** signify on the basis
of convention. As Peirce wrote,

Every sign is determined by its objects, either first by partaking in the characters of the object, when I call a sign an *Icon*; secondly, by being really and in its individual existence connected with the individual object, when I call the sign an *Index*; thirdly, by more or less approximate certainty that it will be interpreted as denoting the object, in consequence of a habit (which term I use as including a natural disposition), when I call the sign a *Symbol*. (cited in Zeman, 1977, p. 36)

Their relationships are shown in the following chart:

	Icons	Indexes	Symbols
Signify by:	Resemblance	Cause and effect	Convention
Example:	Photograph	Fire and smoke	Cross
Process:	Can see	Can figure out	Must learn

There's a considerable difference, then, between Saussure's science of signs and Peirce's, although both were interested in signs and both theories have been very influential. Peirce said a sign "is something which stands to somebody for something in some respect or capacity" (cited in Zeman, 1977, p. 27). He also argued that the universe is "perfused with signs, if it is not composed exclusively of signs" (cited in Sebeok, 1977, p. vi). If everything in the universe is a sign, semiotics is the "master" science!

These two interpretations of signs can be looked on as being at the foundation of the science of semiotics. There are, of course, many other aspects to semiotic thought, but with these two understandings of the sign, we can start making applied semiotic analyses. They allow us to understand how people find meaning in things. Thus, we can use semiotics to analyze and understand how meaning is generated in print advertisements, television and radio commercials, photographs, buildings, television programs, and films. The media are full of signs, both visual and acoustic, that semioticians analyze. Great filmmakers and creative artists of all kinds subconsciously understand the importance of signs, even if they've never studied semiotics. They've learned about signs the hard way—through their failures and their successes.

❖ ALLIED CONCEPTS

A number of other concepts are useful in making semiotic analyses, the more important of which are explained here.

Denotation. **Denotation** refers to the literal meaning of a term or object. It is basically descriptive. A denotative description of a Big Mac is a sandwich sold by McDonald's that weighs x number of ounces and comes with certain sauces and so on. Or let's take a Barbie Doll. The denotative meaning of a Barbie Doll is a toy doll, first marketed in 1959, that is 11.5 inches high, 5.25 inches in the bust, 3.0 inches at the waist, and 4.25 inches at the hips.

Connotation. **Connotation** deals with the cultural meanings that become attached to a term. The connotative meanings of a Big Mac come from the fact that it stands for certain aspects of American culture—fast foods, uniformity, our lack of time, our lack of interest in cooking, the mechanization of food, and so on. The connotative meanings of a Barbie Doll deal with her significance as a courtesan figure and as a consumer icon that teaches young girls to be consumers. The following chart shows the differences between denotation and connotation.

Denotation	Connotation
Literal	Figurative
Signifier	Signified
Evident	Inferred
Describes	Suggests meaning

Metaphor. **Metaphor** refers to communicating by analogy. Thus, one might say, "My love is a red rose." A great deal of our thinking, as I shortly point out, is metaphoric.

Simile. **Simile** is a weaker subcategory of metaphor, which uses *like* or *as.* For example, "My love is *like* a rose" is a simile. Metaphor is based on identity ("my love = a red rose"), whereas simile is based on similarity ("my love is *like* a red rose").

Metonymy. **Metonymy** deals with communicating by association. We make sense of a lot of things by association, by making connections between things we know about and other things. For example, we learn that Rolls-Royce automobiles are very expensive, and this associates Rolls-Royces with wealth (and perhaps good taste).

Synecdoche. **Synecdoche** is a subcategory of metonymy in which a part is used to stand for the whole or vice versa. We use, for example, *the White House* to stand for the American presidency and *the Pentagon* to stand for the American military.

Metaphor and metonymy (and their subcategories) are commonly known as "figures of speech." We encounter them in poetry and other literary works, but they are also found in advertising and many other genres in the media. It turns out that metaphors play an important role in our everyday lives. Thus, George Lakoff and Mark Johnson (1980) have argued that metaphor is basic to our thinking:

> Most people think they can get along perfectly well without meta-phor. We have found, on the contrary, that metaphor is pervasive in everyday life, not just in language but in thought and action. Our ordinary conceptual system, in terms of which we both think and act, is fundamentally metaphoric in nature. (p. 3)

Sometimes, to make life more complicated, we find that something can function both metaphorically and metonymically. For example, a snake can function metaphorically as a **phallic symbol** and, at the same time, metonymically as a reference to the Garden of Eden.

Intertextuality. **Intertextuality** deals with the relation between texts and is used to show how texts borrow from one another, consciously and sometimes unconsciously. Thus, the famous Macintosh commercial "1984" was intertextually related to George Orwell's famous dystopian novel *1984* and the biblical story of David and Goliath. Parody, in which a text makes a humorous imitation of another text, is one of the more common examples of intertextuality. Think, for example, of Woody Allen's spoof of science fiction films, *Sleeper.* Many texts borrow stylistic elements from other texts or even use characters from other texts. The theory comes from the work of a Russian semiotician, Mikhail Bakhtin, who wrote in his book *The Dialogic Imagination: Four Essays* (1981):

> The word in living conversation is directly, blatantly, oriented toward a future answer-word. It provokes an answer, anticipates it and structures itself on the answer's direction. Forming itself in an atmosphere of the already spoken, the word is at the same time determined by that which has not been said but which is needed and in fact anticipated by the answering word. Such is the situation in any living dialogue. (p. 280)

He offered an example in his discussion of texts from the Middle Ages, quoting an authority on literature in this period who wrote (1988),

> The history of medieval literature and its Latin literature in particular "is the history of the appropriation, re-working and imitation of someone else's property. . . . or, as we would say, of another's lan-guage, another's style, another's word. (p. 69)

If we apply Bakhtin's ideas to texts, rather than words in conversa-tion, we understand how intertextuality works. All texts are influenced by texts that preceded them, even if the persons creating the texts are not aware that they are (to various extents) "borrowing" plots, themes, language, or anything else. This is because, in part, we share a common cultural heritage.

Codes. In spy stories, codes refer to ways of interpreting messages written in ways that are not easily understood or easy to "crack." When you know the code, you can "unlock" the meaning in the message. In semiotic thought, we use **codes** to refer to structured behavior and argue that much human behavior can be seen as coded, as having secret or covert structures not easily understood or recognized.

Culture can be seen as collections of codes. To understand culture, you have to "decode" the behavior of people in the culture or subculture. Semiotics helps us interpret the meaning of forms and kinds of communication whose meaning, or in some cases whose most significant meaning, is not evident. For example, as we grow up, we learn certain codes about how to cook meat. We don't boil porterhouse steaks or pork chops. We also have codes about what starches to eat with steaks: We usually have baked potatoes or French fries, but not boiled potatoes or rice (unless we're Asian). We learn any number of codes but don't think about them; because almost everyone's behavior is shaped by them, they become invisible.

Language and speaking. Language, from a semiotic standpoint, is a social institution: We learn languages by being raised in a given community (or subculture) where the language is spoken. Saussure (1966) made an important distinction between language and speaking:

> But what is language [*langue*]? It is not to be confused with human speech [*langage*], of which it is only a definite part, though certainly an essential one. It is both a social product of the faculty of speech and a collection of necessary conventions that have been adopted by a social body to permit individuals to exercise that faculty. (p. 9)

What individuals do, Saussure calls speaking (*parole*). Thus, we have three different phenomena to consider, shown in the following chart:

Langue	Langage	Parole
Language	*Speech*	*Speaking/individual act*
Institution (social) rules and conventions	Individual/social act	Individual use of rules

The term *speaking* can also include matters such as haircuts, clothes, facial expression, and other forms of individual communication. Once we understand body language, for example, we can understand the meaning of a particular gesture a person makes (for example, turning away from you while you're talking to him or her).

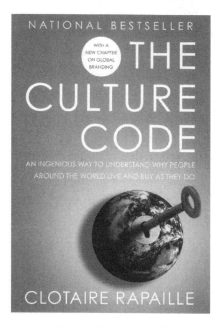

Cover of *Culture Code*

Source: Jacket Cover copyright © 2006 by Broadway Books, a division of Random House, Inc., from *The Culture Code: An Ingenious Way to Understand Why People Around the World Live and Buy as They Do* by Clotaire Rapaille. Used by permission of Broadway Books, a division of Random House, Inc.

❖ CLOTAIRE RAPAILLE ON CULTURE CODES

Let me expand a bit on the discussion of codes. French scholar and marketing expert Clotaire Rapaille dealt with codes in his book *The Culture Code: An Ingenious Way to Understand Why People Around the World Live and Buy as They Do* (2006). Rapaille placed a great deal of importance on what he called "imprints": combinations of experiences and accompanying emotions. As he explained, "Once an imprint occurs, it strongly conditions our thought processes and shapes our future actions. Each imprint helps make us who we are. The combination of imprints defines us" (p. 6). These imprints influence us at the unconscious level. His work, he wrote, involved searching for our imprints so he could decode "elements of our culture to discover the emotions and meanings attached to them" (pp. 10–11). He suggested that most imprinting is done by the age of 7 because "emotion is the central force for children under the age of seven" (p. 21). As he put it, he went in search of the codes "hidden within the unconscious of every culture."

His book deals with the imprintings and codes found in different cultures. In it, he offered an example of decoding cultures in his discussion of cheese:

> The French Code for cheese is ALIVE. This makes perfect sense when one considers how the French choose and store cheese. They go to a cheese shop and poke and prod the cheeses, smelling them to learn their ages. When they choose one, they take it home and store it in a cloche (a bell-shape cover with little holes to allow air in and keep insects out). The American Code for cheese, on the other hand, is DEAD. Again, this makes sense in context. Americans "kill" their cheese through pasteurization (unpasteurized cheeses are not allowed into the country), select hunks of cheese that have been prewrapped—mummified if you will—in plastic (like body bags), and store it, still wrapped airtight, in a morgue known as a refrigerator. (p. 25)

Rapaille's choice of language is most telling and amusing. Americans mummify their cheeses and store them in morgues. The important point to keep in mind here is that from Rapaille's and a semiotic perspective, cultures can be seen as full of different codes that the semiotician must learn how to decode.

❖ SEMIOTICS IN SOCIETY: A REPRISE

We are now ready to use these concepts to analyze images, objects, and all kinds of other communication. Using semiotics may seem just like "common sense" except that most of the time, just using common sense doesn't offer as complete and sophisticated an analysis of topics of interest to us. Let me offer two quotations that help explain what semiotics does.

The first, by linguist Jonathan Culler (1976), makes an important point about social and cultural phenomena:

> The notion that linguistics might be useful in studying other cultural phenomena is based on two fundamental insights: first, that social and cultural phenomena are not simply material objects or events but objects or events with meaning and hence signs; and second, that they do not have essences but are defined by a network of relations. (p. 4)

We must learn to see all kinds of things as signs, and when we do, we must think about relations among these phenomena to understand their meaning. Meaning is based on relationships, to recall Saussure's notion that concepts are defined differentially.

Maya Pines (1982) made a similar point about humans as sign-creating and sign-generating creatures:

> Everything we do sends messages about us in a variety of codes, semiologists contend. We are also on the receiving end of innumerable messages encoded in music, gestures, foods, rituals, books, movies, or advertisements. Yet we seldom realize that we have received such messages, and would have trouble explaining the rules under which they operate. (p. G1)

Thus, semiotics helps us understand how to decipher the messages we are sent and better understand the messages we send about ourselves to others. We are often unaware of the messages we're sending and how others are interpreting them.

Pointy teeth are conventionally recognized signifiers of vampires.

I can offer an interesting example here. In a seminar I taught on semiotics, I asked students to bring in some object that "reflected" them somehow. They were to bring these objects in brown paper bags so nobody in the class would know who brought each one. And they were to list, on a piece of paper, what they thought the object reflected about them and put their list in the bag, as well. One woman brought a large seashell. She listed the attributes of the shell that she thought reflected her: beautiful, delicate, natural, and simple. The other members of the seminar found different attributes in the shell when I showed it to them: empty, sterile, brittle, and vacuous. The point is that we often make mistakes about the messages we think we're sending to others.

Vladimir Propp

❖ SYNTAGMATIC ANALYSIS OF TEXTS

We can look at stories, narratives, or tales (that is, texts) as being similar to sentences, except they are stretched out and made more complicated. Semioticians use the term **syntagmatic analysis** to refer to interpretation that looks at the sequence of events that give texts meaning—in the same way that the sequence of words we use in a sentence generates meaning. (The term *syntagm* means "chain.")

One of the outstanding figures in analyzing narratives was Russian folklorist Vladimir Propp, author of *Morphology of the Folktale* (1928/1968), a pioneering study of the way narratives generate meaning. The term *morphology* means the study of forms or structures and how the components of something relate to each other and to the whole, of which they are all parts. Propp's book argues that narratives are best understood in terms of the functions of their main characters. He studied a group of Russian fairy tales and tried to make sense of how these tales worked and what they added up to. As he wrote,

> We are undertaking a comparison of the themes of these tales. For the sake of comparison we shall separate the component parts of fairy tales by special methods; and then, we shall make a comparison of the tales according to their components. The result will be a morphology (that is, a description of the tale according to its component parts and the relationship of these components to each other and to the whole). (p. 19)

Propp decided to use a morphological approach because other approaches—looking at the tales in terms of styles or kinds of heroes and other classification approaches—didn't work.

Propp suggested that the basic or minimal unit in narratives is what he called a function, which he defined as "an act of a character, defined from the point of view of its significance for the course of action." He added several other important points:

- Functions of characters serve as stable, constant elements in a tale, independent of how and by whom they are fulfilled. They constitute the fundamental components of a tale.

- The number of functions known to the fairy tale is limited.

- The sequence of functions is always identical.

- All fairy tales are of one type in regard to their structure.

In each fairy tale, Propp argued, there are 31 functions and an initial situation (in which the hero or heroine and the members of his or her family are introduced). Each function also includes many sub-categories, representing different ways the function can be realized. Propp's ideas can be adapted to analyze contemporary texts and his functions modernized. A list of his functions is shown in Table 3.1 along with his list of principal characters in these Russian fairy tales.

It's quite remarkable how many television programs, films, and other narratives can be seen as fairy tales and analyzed using updated and modernized versions of Propp's functions, as long as you don't worry about his rule that the sequence of functions is always identical. For example, you can apply Propp's functions to the James Bond stories quite easily. Bond is always sent on a mission by M, who has Q give Bond "secret weapons" (what Propp called "magic agents"). Bond is often pursued and captured by a villain, whom he eventually outwits and destroys. And usually he gets to have sex—or so we are led to believe—with some beautiful woman he has rescued from the villain (the equivalent of "the hero is married and ascends the throne").

Another important method of analyzing narrative texts needs to be explained—paradigmatic analysis, a search for the oppositions found in texts that help give them meaning.

❖ PARADIGMATIC ANALYSIS OF TEXTS

Another important method of analyzing narrative texts needs to be explained: paradigmatic analysis, a search for the oppositions found in

Table 3.1 Propp's Functions

α	*Initial situation*	Members of family introduced or hero introduced.
β	*Absentation*	One of the members of the family absents self from home.
γ	*Interdiction*	An interdiction addressed to hero.
δ	*Violation*	An interdiction is violated.
E	*Reconnaissance*	The villain makes attempt at reconnaissance.
ζ	*Delivery*	The villain receives information about his victim.
η	*Trickery*	The villain attempts to deceive his victim.
θ	*Complicity*	The victim submits to deception, unwittingly helps the enemy.
A	*Villainy*	The villain causes harm or injury to a member of a family.
a	*Lack*	One member of a family lacks something or wants something.
B	*Mediation*	Misfortune is made known, hero is dispatched.
C	*Counteraction*	Seekers agree to decide on counteraction.
↑	*Departure*	The hero leaves home.
D	*First function of donor*	Hero tested, receives magical agent or helper.
E	*Hero's reaction*	Hero reacts to actions of the future donor.
F	*Receipt of magic agent*	Hero acquires the use of a magical agent.
G	*Spatial transference*	Hero led to object of search.
H	*Struggle*	Hero and villain join in direct combat.
I	*Victory*	Villain is defeated.
K	*Liquidation*	Initial misfortune or lack is liquidated.
↓	*Return*	Return
Pr	*Pursuit*	A chase: the hero is pursued.

(Continued)

(Continued)

Rs	Rescue	Rescue of hero from pursuit.
O	Unrecognized arrival	The hero, unrecognized, arrives home or in another country.
L	Unfounded claims	A false hero presents unfounded claim.
M	Difficult task	A difficult task is proposed to the hero.
N	Solution	The task is resolved.
Q	Recognition	The hero is recognized.
Ex	Exposure	The false hero or villain is exposed.
T	Transfiguration	The hero is given a new appearance.
U	Punishment	The villain is punished.
W	Wedding	The hero is married and ascends the throne.
There are seven dramatis personae in Propp's scheme		
1	Villain	Fights with hero.
2	Donor	Provides hero with magical agent.
3	Helper	Aids hero in solving difficult tasks.
4	Princess and her father	Sought-for person. Assigns difficult tasks.
5	Dispatcher	Sends hero on his mission.
6	Hero	Searches for something or fights with villain.
7	False hero	Claims to be hero but is unmasked.

texts that help give them meaning. While syntagmatic analysis focuses on the sequence of events in a text and how the order of events generates meaning, **paradigmatic analysis** concerns itself with how oppositions hidden in the text generate meaning. It stems from the work of French anthropologist Claude Lévi-Strauss and his analysis of myths. As folklorist Alan Dundes (1928/1968) wrote in his introduction to Propp's *Morphology of the Folktale*:

> Paradigmatic analysis seeks to describe the pattern (usually based on an a priori binary principle of opposition) which allegedly underlies the folkloristic text. This pattern is not the same as the sequential structure at all. Rather, the elements are taken out of the "given" order and are regrouped in one or more analytic schema. (p. xi)

We are back now to Saussure's notion that concepts have meaning differentially. Roman Jakobson, a famous linguist, made the same point—that binary oppositions are the fundamental way the human mind produces meaning (Culler, 1986). In every text, the human mind searches not only for concepts but also for oppositions that enable it to make sense of things. We do this because that is how language works; concepts are always defined differentially.

Skyfall: A Paradigmatic Analysis

Let me offer a paradigmatic analysis of a James Bond film, *Skyfall*. The oppositions we find in this text are either stated or implied and provide those who view the film with an understanding of what it means. *Skyfall*, the 23rd James Bond film, was released in 2012. It made more than $1 billion and is the seventh-highest-grossing film ever made. It stars Daniel Craig as Bond and Javier Bardem as Raoul Silva, a former MI6 agent who felt he was betrayed by M (Judi Dench) and plots revenge against her and the agency she runs. The film contains many battles between Bond and various villains and culminates in a battle scene in which Silva and a large group of his men, in a helicopter, attack Bond and M, who have lured Silva to Skyfall, Bond's childhood home and family estate in Scotland. M is wounded during the attack. Bond blows up Skyfall, destroying the helicopter and killing many of Silva's men. Silva survives, tracks down M, holds a gun to her head and puts his head next to hers, and asks her to pull the trigger. Bond has followed Silva and throws a knife into Silva's back, killing him. M, who was wounded, dies.

Hero	Villain
James Bond (Daniel Craig)	Raoul Silva (Javier Bardem)
Works for MI6	Worked for MI6
Defends MI6 and M	Attacks MI6
Blows up Skyfall	Blows up MI6 headquarters
Motive: Patriotism	Motive: Revenge (for being left to die by M)
Captures Silva on island near Macau	Wants to be captured, brought to London, escapes
Chases Silva through London Underground	Evades Bond
Lures Silva to Skyfall	Attacks Skyfall with helicopter and many killers

With allies, kills many attackers	With attackers, wounds M (who eventually dies from wound)
Kills Silva: Throws knife into his back	Is killed by Bond while holding gun to M's head

When people see this film, these polar oppositions give it meaning. This is true even if people aren't consciously making these distinctions, because it is through binary oppositions that we make sense of concepts and texts. Some critics argue that paradigmatic analysis does not discover structures in texts but "reads them in" or invents them ("hocus-pocus"); others claim that it finds structures (sets of oppositions) that are really there, hidden in the text ("God's truth") and that our minds recognize them, even if we don't always bring these oppositions to consciousness.

Remember that there is a difference between negations and oppositions. Oppositions use two different terms (for example, *happy* and *sad*), while negations use the same term.

Oppositions	Happy versus sad
Negation	Happy versus unhappy

With each pair of opposites, there is always a concept or notion that links the two. In the case of *happy* and *sad*, it would be something like "mental state." Every text generates meaning two ways, then—first, by the order in which events happen (the syntagmatic structure) and second, by the hidden oppositions found in the text (the paradigmatic structure).

❖ APPLICATIONS OF SEMIOTIC THEORY

Let's consider how semiotic theory can be applied. I will discuss some "signs" that are part of our everyday lives: eyeglasses and teeth. They also have significance in television shows and movies, where they can be used to suggest things about characters. And that is because we all try to "read" faces for clues to personality, character, status, and other things. This is, of course, a semiotic enterprise—even for those who have never heard of semiotics. Many articles in newspapers and magazines are semiotic in that they attempt to make sense of objects and phenomena semioticians would call "signs." (A person may never have heard the term *schizophrenic*, but that doesn't prevent him or her from being one!)

I will start with eyeglasses. In 1991, Henry Allen, a reporter for the *Washington Post*, wrote an article titled "Everything You Wanted to Know About Specs" that was really an exercise in applied semiotics. The article began as follows: "Eyeglasses are not only optical instruments, but they are also costume, manifesto, clothing for the face, and societal fetish." Allen pointed out that eyeglasses were a $12 billion-a-year industry in America and that about 60% of Americans at the time owned glasses. He continued, discussing men's glasses from a semiotic perspective:

> Men's glasses got sexy in their own right in the '50s, when intellect, alienation, and flaws became sexy in men. The tortured James Dean was seen in glasses. Buddy Holly wore black plastic rims that said, I wear glasses, I don't care if you think I'm handsome or not.

Allen (1991) then offered interpretations of the meaning of various styles of glasses, which I present as a chart:

Signifier	Signified
KIND OF GLASSES	MEANING
Small glasses	Earnest intensity
Small glasses in wire	Industry and fierce modesty
Big glasses	Not embarrassed to wear glasses
Round glasses	Tradition, authenticity, intellect
Squared off glasses	Technology, can-do, engineering
Aviator (teardrop)	Masculine adventure
Eye high in frame	Introspection
Eye low in frame	Optimism, action
Silver wire	Mechanical practicality
Black wire	Solid state electronics, minimalist art
Heavy plastic frames	Big ego, big bucks
Colored rims	Playful, creative, eccentric
Rimless	Cool, modest, denying one has glasses
Tinted	Mysterious

These interpretations are semiotic, and Allen was aware of the science, for he concluded his article with a discussion of World War II general Douglas MacArthur, seen as a great strategist by some and a great self-promoter by others:

> At the heart of the aesthetics of glasses, from deliberate contradiction to preempting of stereotype, is coyness.
>
> Contradiction: General Douglas MacArthur decorated his face with aviator sunglasses, symbol of technological daring, and a corncob pipe, symbol of primitive wisdom—one of the semiotic masterstrokes of the century. (Allen, 1991)

Thus, we can see that eyeglasses are used for many purposes—not only to allow us to see more clearly.

Teeth would seem an unlikely candidate for semiotic analysis, but according to a dentist, they are important signs and may have a great deal to do with our love lives and success in the business world. We all know, of course, what a couple of sharp and pointy teeth sticking out of the mouth of a pale and tired-looking man mean—he's a vampire. We've learned this convention from films. But teeth have other meanings as well. A San Francisco cosmetic dentist named Jeff Morley caught the attention of the *Wall Street Journal* (Chase, 1982) a number of years ago by arguing that people unconsciously "read" teeth. Because of this, Morley argued, people have to make sure their teeth convey the right messages and make sure their teeth are perfect.

An advertisement by Morley and an associate tells the story:

> Your smile says a lot about you. The alignment, shape, color, and condition of your teeth are powerful communicators to friends, family, and business associates. They may also have a lot to do with your self-esteem.

As Morley explained, in an interview with the *Wall Street Journal*:

> "What it comes down to is this: buck teeth imply people are dumb. Large canines imply aggressiveness. Weak chins imply passivity, while strong chins imply a macho, studly personality—I don't know who made these up, but the fact is, they're cultural standards." (Chase, 1982, p. 1)

Thus, our eyeglasses and teeth function as signs that people interpret to gain information about us. We are always sending messages, even if we don't say a word—and it is the task of semiotics to help us determine how to "read" the messages others are sending us and make sure that the messages we are sending are the ones we want to send.

❖ PAUL EKMAN ON FACIAL EXPRESSION

Paul Ekman, probably the foremost authority on **facial expression,** did extensive research and found that there are seven universal facial expressions and one "neutral" state that doesn't show any emotion (Ekman & Sejnowski, 1992). They are as follows, in alphabetical order:

Anger	Neutral (no particular emotion)
Determination	Pouting
Disgust	Sadness
Fear	Surprise

In a classroom exercise, I showed photographs of Ekman demonstrating these emotions to my students and found they could not correctly identify most of the emotions.

Ekman developed a facial action coding system, which states that there are 43 muscles in the human face that in different combinations show our emotions. Sometimes an emotion lasts for just a fragment of a second on our faces (what Ekman calls "microexpressions") and we aren't aware of having shown it. In a report to the National Science

Figure 3.1   Five Facial Expression Images

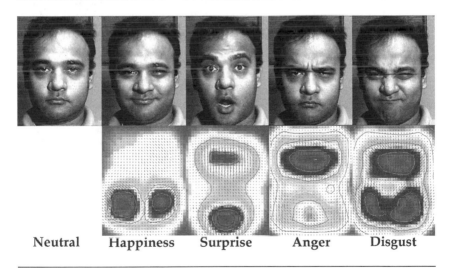

Neutral   Happiness   Surprise   Anger   Disgust

These images reflect five emotions reflected in facial expressions. The images below them show the energy expended for each facial expression going from neutral to the expression. ©Irfan Essa.

Foundation, *Facial Expression Understanding* (1992), cowritten with Terrence J. Sejnowski, we find the following information about facial expressions:

- They provide information about our emotions and our moods.

- They reflect cognitive activity like perplexity, concentration, and boredom.

- They reveal truthfulness and lying.

- They offer diagnostic information about depression, mania, and schizophrenia and about our responses to treatment for these afflictions.

The report adds that "the technological means are now in hand to develop automated systems for monitoring facial expressions and animating artificial models. . . . Face technology . . . could revolutionize fields as diverse as medicine, law, communications, and education" (§ I-A). So faces can reveal a great deal to the trained observer.

❖ SEMIOTICS: APPLICATIONS AND EXERCISES

1. Find an advertisement that has both metaphor and metonymy and explain how they function to sell the product. Study the facial expressions of the people in the advertisement. What do you think they reveal? On what basis do you come to your conclusions?

2. Find articles that use semiotics to analyze hairstyles and hair color for women, men, or both. What insights did they offer? How convincing are the articles?

3. Write a 1,000-word semiotic analysis of *Avatar* or some other film or television program chosen by your instructor. Start your paper with an applications chart (see Table 3.2) on a separate page. To make the chart, list semiotic concepts on the left-hand side of the page and applications of the concepts to events and dialogue in the film on the right-hand side of the page. In your paper, amplify and explain your applications.

   Note: Use applications charts for all your analyses of texts.

4. Using semiotic methods, write a 1,000-word analysis of "The Schizoid Man" episode of *The Prisoner* (available free on the Internet). Use the applications chart format described in Exercise 3.

Note: Free videos of *The Prisoner* can be found at http://www .amctv.com/.

5. Record and review a television commercial and discuss the signs and other aspects of the commercial that you found interesting. Use an applications chart to list the semiotic terms you used in your analysis and to show how you have applied them. Make a syntagmatic (Propp) and paradigmatic (Lévi-Strauss) analysis of the text.

Table 3.2   Sample Applications Chart

Sample Concepts/Applications Chart for *The Prisoner*, "Arrival"		
Semiotic Concepts	**Applications to "Arrival"**	
1. Signifier/ Signified	Filing Cabinets The Village Numbers Blonde housekeeper	Bureaucracy Small Town Prisoners Innocence
2. Syntagmatic analysis	See chart in essay.	
3. Paradigmatic analysis	See chart in essay.	
4. Metaphor	One important metaphor in this text is that the village is a prison.	
5. Synecdoche	Rover stands for the authority of Number Two and the administration.	
6. Icons	Some of the more important icons are the photographs of Number Six and the statues found in the village.	
7. Indexes	The smoke that pours into the agent's room while he is packing is a gas that knocks him out and enables people to bring him to the village.	
8. Symbols	The helicopter is a symbol for escape and the pawns on the chessboard symbolizes the villagers.	
9. Intertextuality	*The Prisoner* is related to a program that McGoohan was on earlier, *Danger Man*, and to spy and science fiction genres in general.	
10. Codes	One important code is the smaller the number, the greater the power. Another is duplicity: Nobody can be trusted. Another is lack of privacy: Number Six and others are always being monitored.	

❖ CONCLUSIONS

Semiotics, then, is a valuable tool for understanding how people find meaning in life—in objects, in rituals, in texts of all kinds. When you see the world as "perfused with signs, if not made up entirely of them," and know something about how signs communicate, you have an extremely useful research tool to analyze texts found in the mass media as well as communication in everyday life.

❖ FURTHER READING

Barthes, R. (1973). *Mythologies* (A. Lavers, Trans.). New York, NY: Hill & Wang.

Berger, A. A. (1984). *Signs in contemporary culture: An introduction to semiotics* (2nd ed.). Salem, WI: Sheffield.

Berger, A. A. (1992). *Reading matter: Multidisciplinary perspectives on material culture.* New Brunswick, NJ: Transaction Books.

Berger, A. A. (1997). *Bloom's morning: Coffee, comforters, and the secret meaning of everyday life.* Boulder, CO: Westview/HarperCollins.

Berger, A. A. (2009). *What objects mean: An introduction to material culture.* Walnut Creek, CA: Left Coast Press.

Berger, A. A. (2010). *The objects of our affection: Semiotics and consumer culture.* New York, NY: Palgrave Macmillan.

Berger, A. A. (2012). *Understanding American icons: An introduction to semiotics.* Walnut Creek, CA: Left Coast Press.

Berger, A. A. (2015). *Ads, fads and consumer culture: Advertising's impact on American character and society.* Lanham, MD: Rowman and Littlefield.

Bignell, Jonathan. (2002). *Media semiotics: An introduction* (2nd ed.). Manchester, UK: Manchester University Press.

Blonsky, M. (1992). *American mythologies.* New York, NY: Oxford University Press.

Chandler, D. (2002). *Semiotics: The basics.* London, UK: Routledge.

Danesi, M. (1995). *Interpreting advertisements: A semiotic guide.* Toronto, Canada: Legas.

Danesi, M. (2002). *Understanding media semiotics.* London, UK: Arnold.

Eco, U. (1984). *The role of the reader: Explorations in the semiotics of texts.* Bloomington: Indiana University Press.

Eco, U. (1991). *The limits of interpretation.* Bloomington: Indiana University Press.

Gottdiener, M. (1995). *Postmodern semiotics: Material culture and the forms of postmodern life.* Cambridge, MA: Blackwell.

Gottdiener, M. (1997). *The theming of America: Dreams, visions, and commercial spaces.* Boulder, CO: Westview Press.

Kress, G. (2009). Multimodality: A social semiotic approach to contemporary communication. New York, NY: Routledge.

Leeds-Hurwitz, W. (1993). *Semiotics and communication: Signs, codes, cultures.* Mahwah, NJ: Lawrence Erlbaum.

Rapaille, C. (2006). *The culture code.* New York, NY: Broadway Books.

Solomon, J. (1990). *The signs of our time: The secret meanings of everyday life.* New York, NY: Harper & Row.

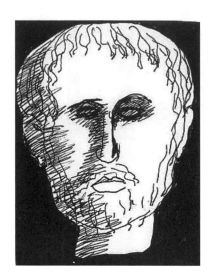

Aristotle

Rhetoric may be defined as the faculty of observing in any given case the available means of persuasion. This is not a function of any other art. Every other art can instruct or per-suade about its own particular subject-matter; for instance, medicine about what is healthy and unhealthy, geometry about the properties of magnitudes, arithmetic about num-bers, and the same is true of the other arts and sciences. But rhetoric we look upon as the power of observing the means of persuasion on almost any subject presented to us; and that is why we say that, in its technical character, it is not con-cerned with any special or definite class of subjects.

—Aristotle (cited in McKeon, 1941, p. 1,329)

4

Rhetorical Analysis

CHAPTER 4 FOCUS QUESTIONS

- How does Aristotle define rhetoric? What are its three branches?
- How is rhetoric useful in analyzing the mass media?
- What's the difference between the Jakobson and Lasswell models of the media?
- How does Robert L. Root Jr. apply rhetorical concepts?
- What does Certeau say about the "subversions" of texts by readers and viewers?
- What was said about using rhetoric to analyze visual images and images in narratives?
- What rhetorical concepts were used in the analysis of the Crème de la Mer advertisement?

Rhetorical analysis used to be confined to speech and written materials, but with the explosive development of the mass media, rhetorical theory is now also being used to interpret works found on radio, television, and film—that is, what we now call mass-mediated culture.

Wayne Booth, a well-known critic from the University of Chicago, was one of the first to point out the need for rhetoricians to pay attention to the mass media. And his call has been heeded, for now rhetoricians have become increasingly interested in the mass media. As he wrote in "The Scope of Rhetoric Today" in *The Prospect of Rhetoric*,

> If all good art has no rhetorical dimension, as so many have argued, then the "rhetoric" is left to those who will use it for the devil's purposes. . . . How much better it would be if we could develop a way of understanding how great literature and drama does in fact work rhetorically to build and strengthen communities. Reading *War and Peace* or seeing *King Lear* does change the mind, just as reading *Justine* or taking a daily dose of TV fare changes minds. A movie like *The Graduate* both depends on commonplaces shared much more widely than our slogans of fragmentation and alienation would allow for, and strengthens the sharing of those commonplaces; like *Midnight Cowboy* or *Easy Rider*, it can be said to make a public as well as finding one already made. All of them work very hard to appear nonrhetorical; there are no speeches by anyone defending the graduate's or the cowboy's values against the "adult" world that both movies reject so vigorously. But the selection from all possible worlds is such that only the most hard-bitten or critical-minded viewer under forty is likely to resist sympathy for the outcasts and total contempt for the hypocritical aging knaves and fools that surround them. If sheer quantity and strength of pressure on our lives is the measure, the rhetoric of such works, though less obvious, is more in need of study than the open aggressive rhetoric of groups like The Living Theatre. (cited in Medhurst & Benson, 1984, p. 102)

Booth mentions several important films as worthy of rhetorical analysis. Even though they don't have speeches or oratory in them, that doesn't mean they don't have an impact on viewers. We have to broaden our understanding of rhetoric from the way it has been defined from Aristotle's day until the relatively recent past.

❖ ARISTOTLE ON RHETORIC

Aristotle's *Rhetoric* was the most influential rhetorical text for thousands of years, and he was endlessly cited as the authority on matters rhetorical. He divided **rhetoric** into two general areas—public speaking and logical discussion—and explained that although every field of thought has its own means of persuasion, *rhetoric* is the term for means of persuasion useful in all fields. He suggested three modes of persuasion in rhetoric: what he called ethos, pathos, and logos.

He wrote in *Rhetoric* Book 1, Chapter 2,

> Of the modes of persuasion furnished by the spoken word there are three kinds. The first kind depends on the personal character of the speaker; the second on putting the audience into a certain frame of mind; the third on the proof, or apparent proof, provided by the words of the speech itself. (cited in McKeon, 1941, p. 1329)

Aristotle wrote about speeches and the spoken word, but we can expand rhetorical analysis to include all kinds of texts, especially commercials. And when it comes to commercials, it is good to keep in mind Aristotle's distinction between proofs and apparent proofs.

Mode of Persuasion	Persuasion Based Upon
Ethos	Personal character of speaker (credibility)
Pathos	Speaker stirring emotions in listeners
Logos	Logical arguments in speech

We can see all three of Aristotle's modes of persuasion in medical television commercials in which a physician praises a particular medicine and suggests how it will help people. A doctor speaking about medicine has credibility, he stirs emotions in viewers about the seriousness of the disease, and he suggests that the medicine will help people (though it may have many negative side effects).

Aristotle wrote another book, *Poetics*, about tragedy and comedy, the nature of plots, and related matters, but for our purposes, we can think of poetics as a part of rhetoric (although some scholars would not agree with this). Our focus is not limited to argumentation, per se (as in speeches and debates) but is on persuasion in a broader sense—that is, on how creators of all kinds of texts achieve their ends. That involves topics such as how advertising agencies "convince" us to buy the products and try the services they advertise, how novelists "move" us, and how filmmakers and playwrights create characters with whom we empathize.

This point, about broadening our understanding of rhetorical analysis, was made by Barry Brummett in his book *Rhetoric and Popular Culture* (2011):

During all the centuries in which rhetoric was defined primarily in terms of traditional texts, people still experienced signs, artifacts, and texts that were not in that traditional form. Informal conversation, architecture, clothing styles, common entertainments, food—in short, the whole range of cultural artifacts other than traditional rhetorical texts—were experienced by people as influential and moving, while rhetorical theorists continued to call only traditional texts rhetoric. . . .

That shift in understanding raises the question of what changed rhetorically between the eighteenth century and the present. Are people being influenced by signs in different ways now, such that we must call the texts of everyday experience rhetorical but did not need to call them that two hundred years ago? Have rhetorical theorists awakened to truths that were always there but went unrecognized until recently? In other words, does a change in thinking about what rhetoric is follow from a change in the world or a change in theory? (p. 53)

Brummett concluded that both the world and notions of what constitutes rhetoric have changed. His book deals with the way rhetorical theory can be applied to popular culture and by extension, I would say, the mass media.

❖ RHETORIC AND THE MASS MEDIA

In the preface to Martin J. Medhurst and Thomas W. Benson's *Rhetorical Dimensions in Media: A Critical Casebook* (1984), we find a rationale for applying rhetoric to the mass media. Medhurst and Benson pointed out that the Greeks and Romans considered rhetoric a very important subject because it played a role in enabling individuals to live together in society:

With rhetoric—*the attempt by one person or a group to influence another through strategically selected and stylized speech*—a society could perpetuate itself, debate its internal problems, and decide which norms and values it would follow without resorting to violence. (p. vii)

In the present day, as they noted, human speech is still the basic means we have of influencing one another:

The study of how people choose *what to say* in a given situation, *how to arrange or order* their thoughts, *select the specific terminology* to employ, and decide precisely *how they are going to deliver their message* is the central focus of rhetorical studies. (p. vii)

A SHORT THEATRICAL PIECE ON RHETORIC

Grand Inquisitor:	*What are the ways?*
Arthur:	When I was in the army (yes, it's true—I'm a *trained* killer) I was told that there were three ways: the right way, the wrong way, and the army way.
Grand Inquisitor:	*Are there any other ways?*
Arthur:	Yes! For media students, there's the segue.
Grand Inquisitor:	*Is that the last way?*
Arthur:	Not at all. Now that we live in a multicultural world, there's also the Zimbabwe! And the Amway!
Grand Inquisitor:	*Did anyone ever tell you that you're "far out"?*
Arthur:	No, I'm not far out. Your problem is that you're "far in"!
Grand Inquisitor:	*Is that what being a foreigner means?*
Arthur:	I'm supposed to be the one making the puns!

What is important to recognize, the authors add, is that platform oratory—the delivery of formal speeches—is no longer the crucial element in exchanging communication. We live in an age of mass media, and we can use rhetoric to analyze this mass-mediated communication. Medhurst and Benson (1984) mentioned two important rhetoricians, Kenneth Burke and Wayne Booth, who suggested that all symbolic communication is inherently rhetorical because it is intended to communicate, and rhetorical criticism is concerned with how symbols communicate.

I should mention, in passing, that some of the terms found in semiotic thought are also found in rhetorical thought and analysis. Ferdinand de Saussure, one of the founders of semiotics, was a professor of linguistics, we must remember. However, which discipline lays claim to these terms is not particularly important for our concerns.

In their preface to *Rhetorical Dimensions in Media* (1984), Medhurst and Benson listed a number of understandings of the term *rhetoric* as it applies to media. Here is an adaptation of their list:

1. Intentional persuasion

2. Social values and effects of symbolic forms found in texts (whether intentionally placed or not)

3. Techniques by which the arts communicate to audiences

4. Persuasion techniques used by characters in dramatic or narrative works

5. Study of **genres** or types of texts

6. Implicit theories about human symbolic interaction implied by authors of symbolic works

7. An ideal for the conduct of communication among humans

8. Study of what makes form in texts effective (known as pragmatics)

Medhurst and Benson offered this list as a guide for readers wondering what the authors of the articles in the book were doing. We can also use the items on this list when we make our own rhetorical analyses of texts such as print advertisements, radio and television commercials, television shows, films, and other forms of mass-mediated entertainment.

The term *entertainment* deserves a bit of explanation. Many people assume that entertainments are trivial and have no significance. We now recognize that our entertainments—television programs, films, commercials, music videos, songs, and video games—play an important role in shaping our consciousness, as the quote from Booth early in this chapter suggests.

❖ A BRIEF NOTE ON THE COMMUNICATION PROCESS

At this point, it is useful to clarify who is communicating what to whom. I will use a well-known model for the communication process by linguist Roman Jakobson, discuss an equally well-known model by Harold Lasswell, and tie these to one I have developed on the five **focal points** in communication: the **artist** (creator), the work of **art**, the **audience,** the **medium** used by the artist, and **America** (or any society). Jakobson's model (see McQuail & Windahl, 1993) is shown here:

Context
Message

Sender --- Receiver

Contact (medium)
Code

Jakobson offered this model in an essay titled "Linguistics and Poetics":

> Language must be investigated in all the variety of its functions. . . . An outline of these functions demands a concise survey of the constituitive factors in any speech event, in any act of verbal communication. The ADDRESSER sends a MESSAGE to the ADDRESSEE. To be operative, the message requires a CONTEXT . . . seizable by the addressee, and either verbal or capable of being verbalized; a CODE fully, or at least partially common to the addresser and addressee (or in other words to the encoder and decoder of the message); and finally, a CONTACT, a physical channel and psychological connection between the addresser and addressee, enabling both of them to enter and stay in communication. (cited in Lodge, 1988, pp. 34–35)

Whatever kind of communication we are dealing with, Jakobson suggested, involves a message that someone (the sender) sends to someone else (the receiver). The message is delivered through a contact (medium), is given in a code (such as the English language), and is affected by the context in which it is given. Thus, the message "pass the syringe" means one thing in a dark alley and another in a hospital, so context plays an important role in the communication process. What complicates things is that even if people get a message, they may not understand its meaning the way the sender thought they would, a matter I will discuss shortly.

Jakobson suggested that messages can have a number of functions:

1. The **referential function,** involving the surroundings in which senders find themselves

2. The **emotive function,** involving the emotions expressed by senders

3. The **poetic function,** involving the use of literary devices such as metaphor and metonymy by senders

Harold Lasswell (cited in McQuail & Windahl, 1993), a political scientist, offered perhaps the most famous phrase in communication research when he said communication researchers should ask the following:

Who?

Says what?

In which channel?

To whom?

With what effect?

Table 4.1   Theories of Communication

Lasswell	Berger	Jakobson
Who?	Artist	Sender
Says what?	Artwork (Text)	Message
In which channel?	Medium	Contact
To whom?	Audience	Receiver
With what effect?	America (society)	Meaning

I have dealt with more or less the same concerns with my five focal points—although when I elaborated them I didn't realize that they corresponded with Lasswell's famous question or dictum.

We can see this if we line up the Lasswell formulation with my focal points and with Jakobson's model as shown in Table 4.1. In essence, all of these **models** contain the same fundamental elements, and communication researchers tend to focus on some relationship among these elements when doing their research.

There are problems in communication at all levels arising from things such as the differences between the way senders encode their messages and the way receivers decode these messages. That is why Umberto Eco (1976), the distinguished Italian semiotician, suggested that when dealing with the mass media, we often find **aberrant decoding** as audiences decode messages (that is, interpret dialogue and events in television programs, for instance) differently from the way the writers expect them to. But the same thing often happens in personal conversations. We say something, and the person we are talking to takes it "the wrong way," by which we mean he or she didn't interpret what we said the way we meant it. This matter of aberrant decoding is also discussed by French media theorist Michel de Certeau, who suggested that audiences often "aberrantly" decode messages from the mass media on purpose, to suit their particular needs.

Michel de Certeau

❖ CERTEAU ON SUBVERSIONS BY READERS AND VIEWERS

In his book *The Practice of Everyday Life* (1984), Certeau suggested that we must pay more attention to the uses people make of media; media audiences put their own interpretations on what they see and hear, and their responses are not always the ones the senders of messages expect. Discussing the impact of the media, he wrote,

> To a rationalized, expansionist and at the same time centralized, clamorous, and spectacular production [of media] corresponds *another* production, called "consumption." The latter is devious, it is dispersed, but it insinuates itself everywhere, silently and almost invisibly, because it does not manifest itself through its own products, but rather though its *ways of using* the products imposed by a dominant economic order. (pp. xii, xiii)

He offered an example of the way Indians reacted to their Spanish conquerors. The Indians, he said, seemed to be submissive and consenting, but they subverted the various rituals and laws imposed on them in various ways for their own purposes. Certeau suggested that audiences of modern mass media do the same thing and, using various tactics, subvert the messages imposed on them by dominant elites in contemporary societies. Certeau's point was that we cannot assume that everyone is affected the same way by the messages to which they are exposed in the media and that people reinterpret the texts to which they are exposed in ways that suit their needs.

❖ APPLIED RHETORICAL ANALYSIS

Rhetoricians traditionally were interested in one element of the communication process, the matter of persuasion (covered in the models about media in rather general ways by terms such as *effects* or *impact on society*). This stems, in part, from Aristotle's definition of rhetoric as being the art of persuasion. Thus, in his book *The Rhetorics of Popular Culture: Advertising, Advocacy, and Entertainment*, Robert L. Root Jr. (1987) offered a description of how he planned to conduct his analyses:

> In every case I will attempt to apply rhetorical analysis to a specific aspect of popular culture and repeatedly ask the same questions about them: What is the mode of presentation? How does the mode affect the presentation? What is the purpose of the discourse? Who is the audience for the discourse? How is the discourse directed at that audience? What person is created, how is it created, and why is it created? What is the argument of the discourse? How is it arranged? Upon what is it based? Generally these are questions of rhetoric which can be asked of any discourse. (p. 21)

Root, drawing on Aristotle, suggested that there are certain universal elements of rhetorical analysis: ethos, pathos, and logos, which I discussed earlier. To this list he added list aim—the purpose of the discourse—and mode—the medium used. These were Root's concerns, which he suggested rhetorical critics should share, regardless of what kind of communication they are researching.

When analyzing advertising and commercials, you might also consider some of the specific rhetorical devices or means that copywriters use, such as alliteration, rhyme, rhythm, definition, metaphor and metonymy (discussed in detail in Chapter 3 on semiotics), comparison, exemplification, and irony. Dictionaries and handbooks list hundreds of technical terms, generally with Latin names, used by rhetoricians. The following are some of the more common rhetorical devices you can use in analyzing popular culture and mass-mediated texts.

❖ A MINIGLOSSARY OF COMMON RHETORICAL DEVICES

Allegory. Allegories are narratives in which abstract ethical and philosophical beliefs are represented by characters and events—that is, made concrete. One of the most famous television allegories is the Kafkaesque British cult series *The Prisoner*, starring Patrick McGoohan,

broadcast in the late 1960s. (Reruns of it are shown constantly, and there are numerous books about it, as well.) Allegories can be seen as extended metaphors in which the meanings of events in a text lie outside of the text itself, and the characters can be seen as personifications of abstract ideas.

Alliteration. Generally, using a number of words in a passage that start with the same letter or that repeat some vowel. Let me offer an example:

"Magazines Move Millions. One Mind at a Time."

(This was the headline of a newspaper advertisement by Magazine Publishers of America.) Alliteration has a certain playfulness to it and also helps people remember messages better. I used alliteration in my model of the focal points of communication: artist, artwork, audience, America (or society), and medium.

Ambiguity. This refers to statements whose meaning can be several different things. It can be intended or inadvertent, but in both cases it can lead to misunderstandings.

Antithesis. Using oppositions or conjoining contrasting ideas.

Comparison. As I explained earlier when quoting Saussure (1966), meaning arises out of comparisons. "Comparisons are odious," it has been said. We can see, then, that speakers and writers use comparisons to reinforce the arguments they are making. For example, in the 1970s, my book *The TV-Guided American* was reviewed in the *New York Times Book Review.* The reviewer concluded his review with the following statement: "Berger is to the study of television what Idi Amin is to tourism in Uganda."

Definition. There are many kinds of definitions. There are *lexical* or dictionary definitions, which refer to the way words are conventionally used. There are also *stipulative* definitions, which refer to a definition given for the purpose of argument. And there are *operational* definitions, which do not rely on words but offer a list of operations to perform that will lead to an understanding of what is being defined.

Encomium. An encomium praises a thing (or a person) by dealing with its inherent qualities. This is a widely used technique in advertising. The advertising slogan "tastes great, less filling" is an encomium.

Exemplification. We often use examples to support our position in some argument. We must be careful, of course, that we don't allow selective perception to blind us to examples that would cast doubt on our argument or overgeneralize from examples. For example, I once mentioned in a class that smoking is bad for people, and one of my students told me about an uncle of his who smoked two packs of cigarettes a day and was 85. My student's uncle, I would suggest, is not representative of the American **public.**

Irony. Verbal irony involves using words to convey the opposite of what they literally mean. One problem with irony is that many people do not recognize a statement as ironic and take it at face value. This can lead to all kinds of misunderstandings. An example of verbal irony in humor is illustrated by the following joke:

> A man named Katzman decided to change his name to a French name so people wouldn't be able to recognize that he was Jewish. He went to a judge for help. "French, you say," said the judge. "Well, the French word for cat is 'chat,' and the French word for man is 'l'homme,' so we'll change your name to Chat-l'homme."

The irony in this joke is that *Chat-l'homme* is pronounced "shalom," the Hebrew word for "hello," so the man ended up with a more Jewish name than his original name. There are other kinds of irony: *dramatic irony*, in which the fates lead to a resolution that is the opposite of what a character intended, and *Socratic irony*, which involves pretending to be ignorant. A stronger and more insulting form of irony is sarcasm, which means, literally, "tearing the flesh."

Metaphor. Metaphor uses analogy to generate meaning. Metaphor means equivalence, as in "My love *is* a red rose."

Metonymy. Metonymy uses association to generate meaning. Advertisers who want to inform their readers or viewers that someone is very wealthy can use mansions and Rolls-Royce automobiles to convey this information. Metonymy is one of the most commonly used techniques by advertisers because it builds on information that audiences already have and thus is very economical.

Rhyme. The repetitive use of words with similar terminal sounds is a commonly used device to attract people's attention and help them remember things. It is found in much poetry, as in the spoof of the poem "Trees,"

> I think that I shall never see
>
> A billboard lovely as a flea . . .

but also in other forms of communication, such as advertising. Let me offer a classic example of a rhymed jingle from my younger days:

Pepsi-Cola hits the spot

Twelve full ounces, that's a lot

Twice as much for your money, too . . .

Pepsi-Cola is the drink for you.

Rhyme has the power to stick in our minds, which explains why it is often used in advertising jingles.

Rhythm. Rhythm refers to patterned and recurring alternations, at various intervals, of sound or speech elements. Another term for rhythm is *beat*. If you look at the lyrics of rock and roll songs, they often look idiotic, but that's because the printed versions of the lyrics don't convey the beat at which they are sung or the melody of the song.

Simile. A weaker form of metaphor, using *like* or *as*. Metaphor is based on equivalence, but simile is based on similarity: "My love is *like* a red rose."

Synecdoche. A weaker form of metonymy in which part is used to stand for the whole or vice versa. For example, we use *the Pentagon* to stand for the entire American military establishment or *the White House* to stand for the American presidency.

❖ OTHER CONSIDERATIONS WHEN MAKING RHETORICAL ANALYSES

In addition to the spoken language, there are other considerations when doing rhetorical analysis of texts in the mass media. In film and television, we might consider matters such as the use of sound effects, the way actors and actresses speak and use body language and facial expressions, the use of music, the way these texts are edited, and the use of keyed-in written material. Analyzing a television commercial or MTV video from a rhetorical perspective can be an extremely complicated matter.

❖ A SAMPLE RHETORICAL ANALYSIS: A CRÈME DE LA MER ADVERTISEMENT

We can use rhetorical concepts to analyze advertisements—in this case, the Crème de la Mer advertisement shown below. I have numbered each sentence to make it easier to follow my analysis.

La Mer advertisement

1. SEA TO SKIN

2. *A daily transformation*

3. Crème de la Mer™

4. LA MER jar

5. Moisturizing Cream on jar's label

6. *Crème régénération intense* on jar's label

7. Born from the healing powers of the sea, Crème de la Mer is infused with potent, cell-renewing Miracle Broth.™

8. Carefully crafted from nutrient-rich sea kelp, it immerses the skin in moisture and energy.

9. Radiance is restored, fine-lines fade, skin looks softer, firmer, virtually ageless.

10. Even the driest complexions are healed.

11. LaMer.com

12. Bloomingdale's—Nordstrom

Allegory. Line 7 suggests this advertisement is an allegory, presenting a product "born from the healing powers of the sea" (or nature) with magical powers—to restore radiance in women's faces. Crème de la Mer, we read, contains a "Miracle Broth," which suggests there is something almost religious about it. It vaguely resembles something from Greek mythology—a product that has the power to restore youth and make a person look "virtually ageless." It can be seen as a modern version of the search for the fountain of youth that will allow us to live forever. Line 9 deals with women's anxiety that as they age they "dry up" and lose their radiance and will not be loved the way they were when they were young. In an ad for another moisturizer I analyzed a number of years ago, the copywriter suggested you use the brand of moisturizer being advertised so you don't change from looking like a peach (smooth skin, juicy) to looking like a prune (dried up).

Alliteration. We find a number of examples of alliteration. The first is the title of the advertisement—Sea to Skin. The next examples are at the beginning of line 8, where "carefully crafted" and then "kelp" all have a *k* sound. We also find alliteration in line 8 with "radiance is restored" and "fine lines fade." The use of alliteration intensifies the ideas and attitudes expressed in texts and helps us remember them better.

Allusion. This is a device that refers to something not in the text but of significance to it.

The term *Crème de la Mer* is French and is meant to suggest commonly held notions about the French being sophisticated and having excellent perfumes and other beauty products. The sea is also generally seen as something beautiful, endlessly fascinating, and a source of life. Line 8, which talks about "immersing the skin," may even suggest baptism, in which one is cleansed of sin—and, in this case, "fine lines." The term "potency" is meant to deal with the power of La Mer to make the skin softer and firmer, but it also suggests sexuality.

Comparison. In line 4, La Mer promises a "daily transformation," from what we were—someone with "fine lines" or facial creases—to what we will be: a more radiant, smooth-skinned and younger-looking woman who is "virtually ageless." We move, in our mind's eye, from "driest complexions," a kind of illness, to being "healed." La Mer can deal with the "driest complexions," a superlative but not one desired by women, because it has, as line 7 states, "potent, cell-renewing Miracle Broth."

Definition. There is a subtle or indirect use of definition here. The sea is defined as something which has healing powers. Also, the opposite of healing is getting sick, which means dry skin is implicitly defined as a kind of illness that can be healed by using La Mer.

Encomium. An encomium praises something's inherent qualities and this advertisement can be seen as an encomium for La Mer. There are many terms that are positive such as "healing," "nutrient-rich," and "potent cell-renewing."

Euphemism. The ad uses the term "fine lines" instead of "creases" or "wrinkles," as a way of avoiding their negative connotations. We use euphemisms to avoid using words that might be upsetting and disturbing. Thus, instead of saying a person died, we use the euphemism "passed on."

Metonymy. There is an association made between the sea, which allegedly has magical healing powers and is ageless, and La Mer cream, which promises to make a woman "virtually ageless." La Mer does this by using its potent, cell-renewing cream, made from sea kelp.

The Image. The advertisement is all in different shades of green, with the type in white against a green background. Green suggests nature and has positive connotations. The fronds of the kelp shown in the advertisement play a role beyond simply showing people what kelp looks like. The frond on the left leads the viewer's eye to the bottle of La Mer, and the frond on the right leads the viewer's eye to the text. The text is flush right and ragged left, an inversion of the more common ways of presenting text. This product sells for $285 for 2 ounces, so it is very expensive. But what's $285 if you can hold off the ravages of time?

❖ RHETORICAL ANALYSIS OF THE VISUAL IMAGE

It has been estimated that the average person in the United States spends around 8 hours a day looking at screens, and while many of those screens have the written word on them, many also have images or a combination of both. We watch around 4 hours of television each day and spend time looking through magazines; watching videos on YouTube; and checking Facebook, Pinterest, and other social media sites in a typical day. In all of these activities, we are exposed to visual images. So it makes sense to extend our use of rhetorical methods of analyzing written texts to visual images. Defining a visual image isn't easy, but let me suggest that images found, for example, in photographs, paintings, drawings, television shows, films, and advertisements have the following attributes:

They are composed of visual signs (signifiers and signifieds, symbols, icons, indexes).

They represent something real or imagined.

They generally contain objects and people in various places and sometimes also words.

They generate meaning in those who see them.

They have a denotational and connotational significance.

They often generate emotional responses.

There are many definitions of the term *image*, but it is the aspects of images just described that I consider in this analysis.

Pates Panzani advertisement

Roland Barthes, the French semiologist/semiotician, made one of the most famous analyses of images in his chapter "Rhetoric of the Image," found in his book *Image, Music, Text* (1977). He wrote,

> There are those who think the image is felt to be weak in respect of meaning: there are those who think that the image is an extremely rudimentary system in comparison with language and those who think that signification cannot exhaust the image's ineffable richness. . . . How does meaning get into the image? Where does it end? And if it ends, what is there *beyond?* We will start by making it considerably easier for ourselves: we will only study the advertising image. Why? Because in advertising the signification of the image is undoubtedly intentional; the signifieds of the advertising are formed

a priori by certain attributes of the product and these signified have to be transmitted as clearly as possible. If the image contains signs, we can be sure that in advertising these signs are full, formed with a view to the optimum reading: the advertising image is *frank,* or at least emphatic. (pp. 32–33)

In the chapter, Barthes discussed an advertisement for Panzani pasta and dealt with the linguistic message in the advertisement and signs of what he calls "Italianicity" generated by the image of "some packets of pasta, a tin, a sachet, some tomatoes, onions, pepper, a mushroom, all emerging from a half-open string bag, in yellows and greens on a red background" (p. 33). What Barthes does is "skim off" the messages the advertisement contains: its linguistic message and the message contained in the image.

When we interpret an image, let me suggest we keep in mind some ideas, taken from the writings of semioticians, important to the analysis of visual images. Here are four of them:

1. Yuri Lotman (1977) wrote that nothing is accidental in a work of art and texts have incredible richness and many meanings.

2. Ferdinand de Saussure (1966) explained that concepts are purely differential and take their meaning from oppositions.

3. Charles S. Peirce (1977) emphasized the role of interpreters in finding meaning in signs.

4. Umberto Eco (1976) discussed lying with signs and said if signs can tell the truth, they can also lie.

What follows is a list of things to consider in analyzing images, with a focus on print advertisements, which are complicated texts that generally make use of language and images in making their appeals to us.

What is the general ambience of the image or advertisement?

What is the image about? What is the subject of the image?

What signifiers, signifieds, and symbols do you find in the image?

What use is made of metaphors and metonymies in the image?

What is the primary message of the image? Are there secondary messages?

What is the denotated message of the image?

What is the connotated message of the image?

What feelings and connotations are created by the image?

What intertextual references can be found (if there are any)?

What is the spatiality of the image like? Is there a great deal of "white" (empty) space?

What role does lighting play in the image?

What colors are found in the image? How is the color used?

What are the people in the image like? What are they wearing? What objects do they have?

What facial expressions are found on people in the image? What do their faces convey?

What cultural codes are found in the image?

What is the significance of the arrangement of elements in the image?

What kind of balance is found in the image? Axial balance? Asymmetrical balance?

What is emphasized in the image?

What is the tone in the image? How is the subject presented?

What kind of camera shots are found in the image? Close-ups? Extreme close ups?

What product is being sold in the image (for advertisements)?

What do you think is the target audience for the image (especially in advertisements)?

What typefaces are found in the image? Why were those typefaces chosen?

What visual persuasive techniques are found in the images? In the copy (for advertisements)?

What do you find in the image that the creators may not have realized or intended?

This list gives you a number of topics to think about when you interrogate an image. As you can see, there are many things to consider when making a rhetorical analysis of an image. You can write endlessly about an image and describe it in great detail, but nothing you write can make your readers "see" the image or get as much information about it as showing them the image. For example, many years ago I had someone take a photograph of me holding paintbrushes. I had short hair, was wearing a bow tie, and wore an expression of seriousness. I could add more to this description, yet you still wouldn't know what I look like. Here is the image:

Portrait of the young man as an artist

❖ IMAGES IN NARRATIVE TEXTS

"1984" commercial still

In narratives like films and television commercials, an analysis of an image or shot from the commercial or film has to also consider the images that went before it. Consider, for example, the image above taken from the famous Macintosh "1984" commercial. There are a number of levels of analysis we can consider in dealing with this image:

The literal level. A blonde woman with a sledgehammer runs into a large auditorium.

The textual level. This image is part of the "1984" commercial, and the meaning of the image is connected to the events in the commercial.

The intertextual level. The commercial calls to mind George Orwell's dystopian novel, 1984.

The mythic level. The story of David and Goliath in the Bible.

We see, here, that the meaning of an image is dependent both on its place within the text, which I call the "textual" level, and connections the image has to information the interpreter of the image brings from a knowledge of literature, the "intertextual" and "mythic" levels. So context and knowledge help establish the meaning of this text in the same way that the context of words in a sentence helps establish their meaning.

In recent years interest in visual images and their role in the communication process has given us many books on visual culture and related concerns. Since we spend so much time looking at images, it only makes sense that we start thinking about what effect these images may be having on us, as individuals, and on our culture and society.

❖ RHETORICAL ANALYSIS: APPLICATIONS AND EXERCISES

1. Using the terms in the miniglossary of common rhetorical devices and the analysis of the Sea to Skin advertisement as a model, make a 1,000-word rhetorical analysis of an advertisement that has a large number of words and many rhetorical devices in it. Use the applications chart format to list the concepts and their applications to the advertisement on the first page. Turn in the advertisement with your paper.

2. Make a rhetorical analysis of the passage from Musil's *The Man Without Qualities* found on page xviii. Use as many terms from the miniglossary as you can and use the applications chart format. List rhetorical concepts on the left-hand side of the chart and their applications to the passage from Musil on the right-hand side of the chart.

3. How would you characterize Musil's style of writing? Do you like his style? Explain your answer.

4. Make a rhetorical analysis of the lyrics of a popular song. Use an applications chart in your analysis.

5. Examine a political advertisement from a semiotic point of view. What techniques of persuasion are the creators of this text using? What images are in the text? What role do they play?

❖ CONCLUSIONS

The more you know, the more you see and understand. It is our conceptual knowledge that enables us to move beyond simple descriptions and make sense of what we are seeing. Thus, in media and communication research, rhetoric plays an important role because it gives us a large number of concepts that enable us to understand how a text generates meaning and helps shape people's emotions and their behavior.

❖ FURTHER READING

Barthes, R. (1977). *Image, music, text* (S. Heath, Trans.). New York, NY: Hill & Wang.

Berger, A. A. (1997). *Narratives in popular culture, media, and everyday life*. Thousand Oaks, CA: SAGE.

Berger, A. A. (2012). *Seeing is believing: An introduction to visual communication*. New York, NY: McGraw Hill.

Berger, A. A. (2014). *Media analysis techniques* (5th ed.). Thousand Oaks, CA: SAGE.

Berger, A. A. (2015). *Ads, fads, and consumer culture: Advertising's impact on American character and society* (5th ed.). Lanham, MD: Rowman & Littlefield.

Booth, W. (1961). *The rhetoric of fiction*. Chicago, IL: University of Chicago Press.

Brooke, C. G. (2009). *Lingua franca: Toward a rhetoric of new media*. Creskill, NJ: Hampton Press.

Esslin, M. (1982). *The age of television*. San Francisco, CA: W. H. Freeman.

Evans, J., & Hall, S. (Eds.). (1999). *Visual culture: The reader*. London, UK: SAGE.

Foss, S. K. (2008). *Rhetorical criticism*. Long Grove, IL: Waveland Press.

Gries, L. (2015). *Still life with rhetoric: A new materialist approach for visual rhetoric*. Logan: Utah State University Press.

Lakoff, G., & Johnson, M. (1980). *Metaphors we live by*. Chicago, IL: University of Chicago Press.

Lanham, R. A. (1991). *A handlist of rhetorical terms* (2nd ed.). Berkeley: University of California Press.

Mitchell, C. (2011). *Doing visual research*. Thousand Oaks, CA: SAGE.

Mitzoeff, N. (1999). *An introduction to visual culture*. New York, NY: Routledge.

Olson, L. C., Finnegan, C. A., & Hope, D. S. (Eds.). (2008). *Visual rhetoric: A reader in communication and American culture*. Thousand Oaks, CA: SAGE.

Rice, J. (2007). *The rhetoric of cool: Composition studies and new media*. Carbondale: Southern Illinois University Press.

Ridolfo, J., & Hart-Davidson, W. (Eds.). (2015). Rhetoric and the digital humanities. Chicago, IL: University of Chicago Press.

Root, R. L., Jr. (1987). *The rhetorics of popular culture: Advertising, advocacy, and entertainment*. New York, NY: Greenwood.

Smith, M. (2008). *Visual culture studies: Interviews with key thinkers*. Thousand Oaks, CA: SAGE.

Karl Marx

We begin with real, active men, and from their real life-process show the development of the ideological reflexes and echoes of this life-process. The phantoms of the human brain are also necessary sublimates of men's material life-process, which can be empirically established and which is bound to material preconditions. Morality, religion, metaphysics and other ideologies, and their corresponding forms of consciousness, no longer retain therefore their appearance of an autonomous existence. They have no history, no development; it is men, who, in developing their material production and their material intercourse, change, along with this their real existence, their thinking and the products of their thinking. Life is not determined by consciousness, but consciousness by life.

—Karl Marx, *Selected Writings in Sociology and Social Philosophy* (1964, p. 75)

5

Ideological Criticism

- What does Mannheim say in the passage from his *Ideology and Utopia*?
- How is ideology defined by the authors quoted?
- What points does Roland Barthes make in his *Mythologies* about the media and about wrestling?
- What is "hegemony"? Why is it a problem for Marxist critics?
- What points were made in the Marxist interpretation of the Fidji "Snake" advertisement?
- What does John Berger say about glamour and the way advertising uses it?
- What are the basic issues raised by feminist critics of the media?
- What does Mannheim discuss in his analysis of the "social conception of knowledge"?
- What is grid-group theory? How does it get its four political cultures or lifestyles?
- How are our pop culture and media references tied to the four political cultures or lifestyles?

What is ideological criticism, and why is it important? The matter is complicated by the fact that **ideology** is a difficult and complex concept. By ideological criticism, I refer to any kind of criticism that bases its evaluation of texts or other phenomena on issues, generally political or socioeconomic, of consuming interest to a particular group. Traditionally, the term *ideology* refers to a systematic and all-inclusive sociopolitical explanation of what goes on in a society. In this chapter, I deal mostly with Marxist criticism, but I also consider feminist criticism and the work of political scientist Aaron Wildavsky (1982) on political cultures. His work suggests that all democratic societies have four **political cultures** that compete for **power.** One of these cultures, which he calls *egalitarians*, has values similar to **Marxism.**

❖ MANNHEIM'S *IDEOLOGY AND UTOPIA*

In one of the classic studies of ideological thinking, Karl Mannheim's *Ideology and Utopia* (1936), Mannheim writes,

> The concept "ideology" reflects the one discovery which has emerged from political conflict, namely, that ruling groups can in their thinking become so intensively interest-bound to a situation that they are simply no longer able to see certain facts which would undermine their sense of domination. There is implicit in the word "ideology" the insight that in certain situations the collective unconscious of certain groups obscures the real condition of society both to itself and to others and thereby stabilizes it. (p. 40)

In opposition to the ideologists, Mannheim argues, are utopians, who come from repressed subcultures and other groups and see only the negative aspects of the societies in which they find themselves. Mannheim's ideologists see no evil in their societies, and his utopians see no good; both, of course, are deluded.

❖ DEFINING IDEOLOGY

One of the most useful explanations of ideology is found in the introduction to Meenakshi Gigi Durham and Douglas M. Kellner's *Media and Cultural Studies: Key Works* (2001):

> The concept of *ideology* forces readers to perceive that all cultural texts have the distinct biases, interests, and embedded values, reproducing the point of view of their producers and often the values of the dominant social groups. Karl Marx and Friedrich Engels coined the term

"ideology" in the 1840s to describe the dominant ideas and representations in a given social order. . . . During the capitalist era, values of individualism, profit, competition, and the market became dominant, articulating the ideology of the new bourgeois class which was consolidating its class power. Today, in our high-tech and global capitalism, ideas that promote globalization, new technologies, and an unrestrained market economy are becoming the prevailing ideas—conceptions that further the interests of the new governing elites in the global economy. . . . Ideologies appear natural, they seem to be common sense, and thus are often invisible and elude criticism. Marx and Engels began a critique of ideology, attempting to show how ruling ideas reproduce dominant social interests trying to naturalize, idealize, and legitimate the existing society and its institutions and values. (p. 6)

Ideological analysis argues that the media and other forms of communication are used in capitalist nations, dominated by a bourgeois ruling **class**, to generate false consciousness in the masses or, in Marxist terms, the proletariat. Just because people are not aware they hold ideological beliefs does not mean they don't hold them. They may not have brought their ideological beliefs to consciousness and may not be able to articulate them, but from a Marxist perspective, everyone has ideological beliefs.

A SHORT THEATRICAL PIECE ON IDEOLOGICAL CRITICISM

Grand Inquisitor:	*Are you a Marxist?*
Arthur:	I'm a double Marxist! The two philosophers who have shaped my thinking most are Karl Marx and Groucho Marx!
Grand Inquisitor:	*Karl Marx wrote about alienation and the heartlessness of bourgeois (boo-jwah) capitalist consumer societies. He argued that we needed a revolution to liberate the proletarian from oppression. How was Groucho Marx political?*
Arthur:	Groucho was a poet of anarchy. With his brothers, he waged war on WASPish snobbishness as personified by the long-suffering

(Continued)

(Continued)

	Margaret Dumont, who starred in many of his films. His famous line, "Either you're dead or my watch has stopped," is, when you think about it, as devastating an attack on the bourgeoisie (boo-jwah-zee) as anything Karl Marx wrote.
Grand Inquisitor:	*I don't know why I pay any attention to you. Sometimes I think I'm my own worst enemy.*
Arthur:	Not as long as I'm alive! (Stolen from Groucho Marx)

❖ MARXIST CRITICISM

It is the task of Marxist critics (and all ideological critics, of whatever persuasion) to point out the hidden ideological messages in mediated and other forms of communication. These hidden messages, the argument goes, shape the consciousness of those who receive them. Even more insidious, Marxist critics argue, many people—in the media, for example—do not recognize the extent to which the texts they create (situation comedies, comic strips, video games, novels, films, and so on) contain ideological content.

Marx argued that society shapes our consciousness. As he wrote in *Selected Writings in Sociology and Social Philosophy* (1964),

> In the social production which men carry on they enter into definite relations that are indispensable and independent of their will; these relations of production correspond to a definite state of development of their material powers of production. The totality of these relations of production constitutes the economic structure of society—the real foundation, on which legal and political superstructures arise and to which definite forms of social consciousness correspond. The mode of production of material life determines the general character of the social, political and spiritual processes of life. It is not the consciousness of men that determines their being, but, on the contrary, their social being determines their consciousness. (p. 51)

It is the mode of production in society that ultimately shapes our thinking, though the relationship between our thoughts and society is complicated. Marxist thought is materialistic, arguing that economic relations and our "social being" are fundamental in shaping consciousness.

Donald Lazere (1977), a Marxist critic, explains how Marxists interpret cultural messages of all kinds:

> Applied to any aspect of culture, Marxist method seems to explicate the manifest and latent or coded reflections of modes of material production, ideological value, class relations and structures of social power racial or sexual as well as politico economic or the state of consciousness of people in a precise historical or socio-economic situation. . . . The Marxist method, recently in varying degrees of combination with structuralism and semiology, has provided an incisive analytic tool for studying the political signification in every facet of contemporary culture, including popular entertainment in TV and films, music, mass circulation books, newspaper and magazine features, comics, fashion, tourism, sports and games, as well as such acculturating institutions as education, religion, the family and child rearing, social and sexual relations between men and women, all the patterns of work, play, and other customs of everyday life. . . . The most frequent theme in Marxist cultural criticism is the way the prevalent mode of production and ideology of the ruling class in any society dominate every phase of culture, and at present, the way capitalist production and ideology dominate American culture, along with that of the rest of the world that American business and culture have colonized. (pp. 755–756)

If Lazere is correct, for Marxists there is political significance to everything in culture. And it is the job of Marxist critics to point out the ideological content "latent" or hidden in mass-mediated texts, artifacts, or forms of collective behavior such as fashion.

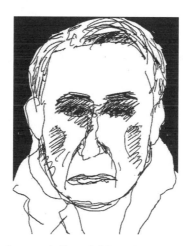

Roland Barthes, an influential French Marxist semiotician

❖ ROLAND BARTHES ON *MYTHOLOGIES*

French Marxist semiotician Roland Barthes was one of the most important critics of media, **popular culture,** and everyday life. His book *Mythologies,* published in France in 1957 and translated into English in 1972, is one of the most influential semiotically informed Marxist analyses of media and popular culture. In the preface to his book, Barthes wrote,

> This book has a double theoretical framework: on the one hand, an ideological critique bearing on the language of so-called mass-culture; on the other, a first attempt to analyze semiologically the mechanics of this language. I had just read Saussure and as a result acquired the conviction that by treating "collective representations" as sign-systems, one might hope to go further than the pious show of unmasking them and account in detail for the mystification which transforms petit-bourgeois culture into a universal nature. (p. 9)

The book has two parts. The first part of the book consists of 28 short essays in which Barthes deals with topics such as "The World of Wrestling," "The Romans in Films," "Soap-Powders and Detergents," "Operation Margarine," "The Face of Garbo," "Striptease," "The New Citroën," "Photography and Electoral Appeal," and "Plastic." The second part of the book, "Myth Today," deals with Barthes's theories about myth and its relationship to bourgeois culture and society.

"The World of Wrestling," the first essay in the section on "Mythologies" and the longest one as well, is a good example of Barthes's writing. In it, he offered a number of insights about wrestling as "theater," such as the following:

The quality of light in wrestling generates extreme emotions.

Wrestling is not a sport but a spectacle.

Wrestling is "an excessive portrayal of suffering."

Wrestling is full of excessive gestures.

Each sign in wrestling is "endowed with absolute clarity."

The bodies of wrestlers are signs about the way they wrestle.

Wrestling provides the image of passion, not passion itself.

In America, "wrestling represents a sort of mythological fight between Good and Evil."

At only 158 pages, *Mythologies* is a slender volume. But it has had enormous impact and is commonly held as one of the seminal books for semioticians, Marxists, and cultural theorists interested in media and communication analysis.

Antonio Gramsci

❖ THE PROBLEM OF HEGEMONY

The term *hegemony*, made popular by Italian Marxist thinker Antonio Gramsci (1891–1937), refers to the notion that ideological domination is invisible because it is all-pervasive. Since, according to Marxists, there is an ideological content to everything, it becomes impossible to see this domination because we have nothing to compare it to, no way of isolating it. The situation is made worse because, Marxists argue, the forces contending against this domination, if any exist at all, are relatively weak and powerless.

In essence, the media are used to manipulating the masses into accepting the status quo economically and in many other areas as well, although many Marxists argue that the term *manipulation* is too simplistic and even old-fashioned. Manipulation suggests that the people who do the manipulating, the petit bourgeois types who run the newspapers and television stations and make the films, actually recognize what they are doing. But this is not the case, say the Marxists, because the petite bourgeoisie believes the ideology it is peddling and therefore does not recognize it as ideology.

❖ THE BASE AND THE SUPERSTRUCTURE, FALSE CONSCIOUSNESS, AND THE "SELF-MADE MAN AND WOMAN"

There have been many developments in Marxist thought since Marx, of course, but the essence of his argument is still generally accepted—namely, that the base, the economic relations in a society, shape (but do not determine) the cultural institutions in that society and in turn shape the consciousness of people brought up in that society. (The notion that the base determines the superstructure is known as "vulgar Marxism" and hasn't been in vogue for many years.) This process of ideological indoctrination is subtle and invisible; people do not recognize the extent to which their consciousness has been shaped by external forces. People are full of illusions about themselves and their possibilities.

As Marx (1964) explained in his discussion of false consciousness and the way the ruling class shapes our thinking,

> The ideas of the ruling class are, in every age, the ruling ideas: i.e., the class which is the dominant *material* force in society is at the same time its dominant *intellectual* force. The class which has the means of material production at its disposal has control at the same time over the means of mental production, so that in consequence the ideas of those who lack the means of mental production are, in general, subject to it. The dominant ideas are nothing more than the ideal expression of the dominant material relationships, the dominant material relationships grasped as ideas, and thus of the relationships which make one class the ruling one; they are consequently the ideas of its dominance. The individuals composing the ruling class possess among other things consciousness, and therefore think. Insofar, therefore, as they rule as a class and determine the whole extent of an epoch, it is self-evident that they do this in their whole range and thus, among other things, rule also as thinkers, as producers of ideas, and regulate the production and distribution of the ideas of their age. Consequently their ideas are the ruling ideas of their age. (p. 78)

In the United States, for example, people embrace the notion of the "self-made man and woman." This means we downgrade the importance of social, economic, and political matters and place too much importance on individual psychology and personality, the will to succeed, personal resolution, and the ability to "market" oneself. We are, one could argue, "prisoners of psychology" in that we don't see society as important; only we, our willpower, and our personality are important. Like Margaret Thatcher, former prime minister of England, we believe that only persons exist; society is just an abstraction. If only people count, psychology is the master science!

This notion of being self-made is of great use, Marxists argue, to the bourgeoisie, that element in society—or more to the point, that class—that owns and controls the mode of production. Anyone who does not "make it" (whatever that means) has only himself or herself to blame and has failed, logic tells us, because of some deficiency in willpower, resolution, or character. Success is purely personal, and so is failure. The Marxist attacks this notion as an ideology that justifies the status quo, and the status quo is just what the ruling class desires. The concept of the self-made man or woman puts the blame for failure or poverty, or what Marxists would describe as a social ill, on those who suffer from it and turns everyone's attention away from the ruling classes and socioeconomic matters. In recent years, I should point out, Americans are beginning to recognize that classes are important and that the top 1% of the population here dominates the economy and plays an important role in politics, since the members of this 1% can contribute enormous amounts of money to political parties they like, to political campaigns they favor, and, in some cases, to certain politicians. Income inequality is now a topic of interest to both political parties and to the American public.

❖ POST-SOVIET MARXIST CRITICISM

The downfall of Soviet communism has led Marxist critics to pull in their horns, but many Marxist critics didn't approve (to put it mildly) of what was going on in Russia and didn't regret, by any means, seeing the totalitarian government there disappear. In countries such as the United States, Marxist critics focus their attention now on the following:

- Inequality in the United States and all problems that stem from it

- The way the wealthy are able to dominate the political agenda

- The extent to which the media are becoming more and more centralized and function as tools of the ruling classes

The wealthy own the media and thus, Marxist critics argue, are able to use them to maintain their dominance. "He who pays the piper calls the tune," as the saying goes. Further, Marxist critics suggest that the forces of globalization are now spreading bourgeois capitalist ideology all over the world. This is because the media are increasingly controlled by gigantic multinational corporations in the United States (and other first-world nations) whose films and television programs and other kinds of media are now seen all over the world.

The media spread consumer lust, a desire for goods instilled in people by films, television programs, newspapers, and other forms of **mass communication,** especially advertising. Bourgeois societies are consumer cultures and need to be, Marxists argue, because bourgeois societies generate alienation, a sense of estrangement from oneself and others, and use consumer lust to assuage the pangs of alienation. Marxists argue that everyone in bourgeois societies is alienated—the wealthy as well as the poor. The capitalist classes use ideological persuasion when able and when necessary, force.

❖ BASIC IDEAS IN MARXIST CRITICISM

Let me summarize the points I have made about Marxist ideological criticism:

- In all countries, the base, or mode of economic relations, shapes the superstructure—institutions such as art, religion, and education that shape people's consciousness.

- There are different classes in bourgeois societies. The bourgeoisie are the ruling class; the proletariat is the working class. The petite bourgeoisie run the factories, make the television shows, and do other tasks for the bourgeoisie. For Marxists, class conflict is a basic force in history.

- The bourgeoisie maintains its dominance over the proletarian class by generating in it a **false consciousness** manifest in the ideas that the relationships in society are natural, that success is a function of willpower (and those who are successful deserve their success), and that those who fail have only themselves to blame. When necessary, the ruling classes use force.

- Bourgeois societies generate alienation, which is assuaged by consumer lust or commodity fetishism but only partially and temporarily. All classes in bourgeois societies suffer from alienation, which means, literally, the absence of connections or ties with others.

- Consumer cultures reinforce privatism and the sense that community and social classes are not important. The focus is on personal expenditures instead of social expenditures (for things like schools, public health, the infrastructure, etc.).

- The globalization of the media and economic institutions allows the ruling classes to spread their bourgeois ideology and export problems to the third world. Marxists call this phenomenon "cultural imperialism."

This is a very brief, highly schematic picture of Marxist ideological thought, although "classical Marxist thought" may be more accurate. Just like any group, entity, or party, there are different kinds of Marxism, each of which emphasizes different things in Marxist thought.

Now that I've explained some of the basic elements of Marxist theory, let's apply some of its concepts to an advertisement for Fidji perfume, shown in Photo 5.4.

❖ A MARXIST INTERPRETATION OF THE FIDJI "SNAKE" ADVERTISEMENT

One point a Marxist critic would make about this advertisement is that it reflects, in graphic manner, the exploitation of people of the third world, the world of people of color, by people in the first world. This

Fidji Perfume "Snake" advertisement

Source: Fidji Perfume "Snake" Advertisement.

exploitation is done by first-world bourgeois capitalist societies—the kind full of corporations such as Guy Laroche. According to Marxist theory, capitalism has survived by exporting its problems, and thus the Fidji advertisement is really not only for perfume but also a reflection of capitalist cultural imperialism.

The woman is alone, and we don't even see all of her face. She's one more anonymous figure in the third world, who has nothing but her first-world fantasy, as represented by the bottle of Fidji perfume she holds in her hands. We, in the first world, are invited to her world to have our fantasy of uninhibited sex with an innocent and "natural" woman like her. But is she a natural woman? In some respects, yes. But although the flower in her hair and the snake suggest some kind of Edenic, primitive innocence, that bottle of perfume she holds in such a curious way suggests that she has been captured by a fantasy manufactured by our bourgeois capitalist system of indoctrination. What city, after all, is more "civilized" and more bourgeois than Paris?

The Fidji advertisement is also a classic example, Marxist critics would argue, of the excesses of bourgeois consumer culture, which has come to dominate every aspect of our lives, especially our sexuality. Our sexuality can be used "against us" by the ruling classes to encourage us to ever greater wasteful expenditures in the name of a spurious value, glamour.

Advertising is, then, one of the central institutions of contemporary bourgeois cultures and is not to be thought of as merely a form of product entertainment. The price we pay for our so-called free media is much higher than we can possibly imagine. Advertising exists to sell products, but it also has a political mission—distracting us from the breakdown of our civic cultures and focusing our attention on private expenditures and personal fantasies. We revel in our personal luxuries, Marxists argue, as our society disintegrates around us into chaos, and we take refuge in gated and guarded communities to escape from the dangers of the social disorganization and pathology our **lifestyles** have generated.

What advertisements such as this one for Fidji perfume demonstrate is that alienation is very **functional,** by which I mean useful, for those who own the means of production. We attempt to assuage our alienation by creating consumer cultures and continually purchasing things, which creates greater and greater profits for those who own the instruments of production and distribution. That is, alienation generates consumption. And because bourgeois capitalist societies have even "sexualized" the act of consumption, the inducements for people to participate in consumer cultures are even stronger.

The bottle of Fidji perfume the maiden holds so lovingly might be construed to represent, symbolically, the domination of bourgeois capitalist cultures over second- and third-world cultures. That is, this advertisement might be seen as a reflection of the **cultural imperialism** we find in contemporary society. Because the cost of making media texts is so high, third-world countries import most of their television programs and films. The "cultural imperialism" argument made by Marxists and others is that these first-world media are destroying the native cultures of the third world, leading to an eventual homogenization of culture. This culture will, of course, be dominated by capitalist bourgeois values hidden in the texts that third-world cultures import and will work so perniciously on people who watch first-world television programs and films, listen to first-world music, and play first-world video games.

One problem with a Marxist analysis of this advertisement—and other advertising and consumer cultures—is that it is so doctrinaire, so predetermined. The "party line" covers advertising and just about every other aspect of capitalist societies and knows what it is going to find before it looks at any text. In addition, Marxism, politically speaking, has imploded, and former Soviet-dominated societies are now feverishly obsessed with consuming, trying, it would seem, to make up for lost time. It has even been suggested that the consumer culture caused Marxist regimes in Eastern Europe and Russia to lose power.

And although the critique Marxists offer of bourgeois societies may be logical and even correct in some respects, we face many problems when looking at communist societies. Studies have shown that Communist Party members and members of the political elite in previously communist societies exploited people terribly and consumed enormous amounts of food and goods in proportion to their numbers. Communism has failed as a form of government, but Marxism is alive and well as a means of critiquing the failures in contemporary societies.

Thus, Marxist criticism faces many problems. Although it often reveals inequities and other troubling aspects of capitalist societies, it tends to turn a blind eye to similar problems in communist societies. Furthermore, there are few communist societies around anymore, as Marxism and communism have been discredited in some countries and abandoned in others. It has been suggested that a large percentage of the Marxist critics you find nowadays are teaching in American universities. There's a certain amount of truth to this notion.

Neiman Marcus advertisement

This advertisement is a good example of the way
photography can glamorize people. Her pose, her facial expression, and the
spatiality of the advertisement all suggest refinement and "class."

❖ JOHN BERGER ON GLAMOUR

British Marxist writer John Berger has offered some interesting insights
into the nature of glamour. In his book *Ways of Seeing* (1972), he dealt
with the role of advertising (he used the term *publicity* to stand for
advertising) in creating a sense of glamour:

> Publicity is usually explained and justified as a competitive medium
> which ultimately benefits the public (the consumer) and the most
> efficient manufacturers—and thus the national economy. It is closely
> related to certain ideas about freedom: freedom of choice for the
> purchaser: freedom of enterprise for the manufacturer. . . .
>
> It is true that in publicity one brand of manufacture, one firm,
> competes with another; but it is also true that every publicity image
> confirms and enhances every other. Publicity is not merely an
> assembly of competing messages: it is a language itself which is
> always being used to make the same general proposal. . . .
>
> It proposes to each of us that we transform ourselves, or our lives,
> by buying something more. . . .
>
> Publicity persuades us of such a transformation by showing
> people who have apparently been transformed and are, as a

result, enviable. The state of being envied is what constitutes glamour. And publicity is the process of manufacturing glamour. (pp. 130–131)

Advertising or publicity works, he added, because it feeds on our natural desire for pleasure. Advertising, in the final analysis, is about pleasure and not the products it tries to sell us.

John Berger (1972) wrote that advertising works by offering us an image of ourselves made glamorous by using the products it sells us, which means that advertising is really about social relations and the promise of happiness and not about the things we purchase. Advertising uses the power of envy to motivate us—the envy we have of ourselves and that others have of us after we've been transformed by purchasing this or that product. This envy by others justifies our loving ourselves. Publicity images work, he asserted, by stealing our love of ourselves as we are and offering it back to us for the price of whatever it is we purchase.

French literary scholar René Girard had a theory that is relevant here. In his book *A Theater of Envy: William Shakespeare* (1991) he argued that Shakespeare's characters and people in general are all motivated by what he called **mimetic desire.** *Mimesis* means imitation, and Girard believed that imitation plays a major role in social relationships. As he explained,

> When we think of those phenomena in which mimicry is likely to play a role, we enumerate such things as dress, mannerisms, facial expressions, speech, stage acting, artistic creation, and so forth, but we never think of desire. Consequently, we see imitation in social life as a force for gregariousness and bland conformity through the mass reproduction of a few social models.

> If imitation also plays a role in desire, it contaminates our urge to acquire and possess; this conventional view, while not entirely false, misses the main point. Imitation does not merely draw people together, it pulls them apart. Paradoxically, it can do these two things simultaneously. Individuals who desire the same thing are united by something so powerful that, as long as they can share in whatever they desire, they remain the best of friends; as soon as they cannot, they become the worst of enemies. (p. 3)

When we purchase goods and services, Girard explained, we imitate the desire of celebrities and others we see in advertisements using various products. In essence, our envy leads us to imitate the desire of those we see in advertisements and, in some cases, our everyday lives.

❖ IDENTITY POLITICS

Even though Marxist thought and political philosophy is not wide-spread in the United States, Marxists' coherent ideological critique of American culture and society has been influential. One consequence is the spread of so-called identity politics, the all-consuming passion groups have about their situations, problems, and needs. This kind of thinking is very close to what Mannheim called utopian thought.

Some groups focus mostly on their particular desires and their ideological critique of American culture and society, and others do the same thing but are also concerned with social justice. Thus, we have movements such as queer (now lesbian, gay, bisexual, and transgender) theory, as well as politics based on racial and ethnic groups, many of which are absorbed in their own particular concerns but others of which argue that the solution to their difficulties lies in creating a more just society.

There is a famous joke that points to this phenomenon:

> Mordecai Goldberg, a little Jewish boy, comes running in one day to his grandfather and says, "Grandpa, Babe Ruth just hit his 60th home run!" "Very interesting," says the old man, who doesn't know who Babe Ruth is or perhaps even what a home run is. "But tell me, this home run . . . is it good for the Jews?"

To paint with a rather broad brush, in identity politics, different groups react to any news about social, economic, or political matters by asking a similar question: "Is it good for women?" "Is it good for

Judith Butler

lesbians, gays, bisexuals, and transgender people?" "Is it good for African Americans?" "Is it good for Italian Americans?" "For Polish Americans?" (You can substitute any racial, religious, or ethnic group here.) "Is it good for children or the elderly?" Some groups, however, argue these questions but look outward as well. They argue that major changes are necessary in society for their goals to be met. This applies to feminist media and communication theory.

❖ FEMINIST CRITICISM OF MEDIA AND COMMUNICATION

One area of conflict in **feminist criticism** involves the social construction of gender, which explains the title of Judith Butler's book, *Gender Trouble: Feminism and the Subversion of Identity* (1999). She began her book with a discussion of certain assumptions found in mainstream feminist theory:

> In 1989 I was most concerned to criticize a pervasive heterosexual assumption of feminist literary theory. I sought to counter those views that made presumptions about the limits and propriety of gender and restricted the meaning of gender to received notions of masculinity and femininity. (p. vii)

Butler (1999) raised issues about the nature of gender and critiqued the way it has been dealt with by many feminist thinkers. We will see, shortly, that this issue and others have led to conflicts within feminist criticism about politics and the media, but most feminist theory shares concerns about the following:

- The roles women are given in texts, the business world, and everyday life

- The exploitation (some would say "sexploitation") of women in the media and everyday life as sexual objects—objects of male desire and lust

- The exploitation of women in the workplace and the domination of women in life, including sexual relationships, which legitimate male supremacy

- The need for women to develop consciousness of their situation and to do something about it politically

In speaking of feminists, it is important to note that, as within any group, be it a family, a church, or a baseball team, not every group member thinks exactly the same way as every other member. In an article titled "Class and Gender in Prime-Time Television Entertainment: Observations From a Socialist Feminist Perspective," by H. Leslie Steeves and Marilyn Crafton Smith (1987), we find a distinction between liberal and socialist or Marxist feminists:

> In contrast to liberal feminists, socialist feminists, as Marxists, assume that the class system under capitalism is fundamentally responsible for women's oppression. At the same time they agree with radical feminists that "patriarchy" (gender oppression) is fundamental in its own right and certainly existed long before capitalism. Thus, most socialist feminists argue that patriarchy and capitalism must be simultaneously addressed, largely via the eradication of divided labor by both gender and class. . . . Also, in contrast to liberal feminists' focus on how media affects individual attitudes and behaviors, socialist feminists emphasize the centrality of media (and other communication processes, such as language, education and art) in actually constructing ideology, including the ideology of women's secondary status. (pp. 43–44)

The authors, writing as Marxists, argued that capitalism is the core of the problem and has to be dealt with along with the specific problems women face. And Marxist feminists are concerned with how the media portray or represent women and how the media and communication affect society as a whole rather than this or that woman.

I'm not sure this is a fair characterization of what the authors describe as "radical" feminism, because many radical feminists concern themselves with the way the media affect culture and society in the United States. For example, in the same issue of the journal in which the Steeves and Smith article appears, an issue devoted to feminism and communication, we find Kathryn Cirksena (1987) offering her understanding of feminist criticism:

> Three facets of a radical feminist critique that I consider pertinent to communication processes include: the social construction of knowledge and information, especially those assumptions concerning gender; the role of language in supporting gender-based inequities; and conceptions of "difference" as they challenge masculinist philosophers' assertions about the universality of the human condition and related methodological and political positions. (p. 20)

Tanqueray advertisement

Notice how by using untanned portions of her body,
this woman's body is turned into an advertisement for Tanqueray.

Cabana advertisement

What is it that makes this photograph of a woman's legs so erotic? Note the way
the untanned portion of the woman's body leads our eyes toward her vulva.

There is a considerable difference, let me point out, between the socialist conception that capitalism is at the root of women's subordination (and every other group's problems, as well) and the social conception of knowledge.

❖ THE SOCIAL CONCEPTION OF KNOWLEDGE

The social conception of knowledge recognizes that education, the media, our families, and other parts of society play a major role in giving people the ideas they hold. The idea, for example, that only individuals are important and that society is irrelevant is, ironically, socially transmitted—learned by people from reading, talking with others, exposure to the media, and so on. One of the classic statements about the social origin of knowledge is found in Karl Mannheim's book *Ideology and Utopia* (1936):

> Strictly speaking it is incorrect to say that the single individual thinks. Rather it is more correct to insist that he participates in thinking further what other men have thought before him. He finds himself in an inherited situation with patterns of thought which are appropriate to this situation and attempts to elaborate further in inherited modes of response or to substitute others for them in order to deal more adequately with the new challenges which have arisen out of shifts and changes in his situation. Every individual is therefore in a two-fold sense predetermined by the fact of growing up in a society: on the one hand he finds a ready-made situation and on the other he finds in that situation preformed patterns of thought and conduct. (p. 3)

There is a problem with this analysis; namely, it becomes difficult to see how new ideas come into being. One solution to this is to suggest that new ideas (and even the possibility of a critique of existing society) are the result of what might be described as the imperfect **socialization** of people and also arise from **subcultures** that reject many of the basic norms of the societies in which they find themselves. Mannheim's "utopians" reject much of what they find in their societies. Feminists, from this perspective, can be understood as utopians. We turn now to another aspect of feminist thought, the notion that male power is phallocentric.

Washington Monument

❖ PHALLOCENTRIC THEORY: THE PHYSICAL BASIS OF MALE DOMINATION

Some feminists locate the source of male domination not in the class system and capitalism but in the bodies of men, specifically in their genitals, and talk about patriarchal "phallocentric" domination. According to **phallocentric theory,** men assume that the power relationships they find in society (in which men are dominant) are natural and are unable to recognize the fact that women are subordinated, treated unfairly, and so on. The institutions found in societies, the roles played by men in these societies, and the representations of women in the arts and media are all shaped, ultimately, by male sexuality and, in particular, the symbolic power of the phallus. Men, of course, do not recognize this and react with shock and often laughter and ridicule (reflecting their sense of power and dominance) when feminists make this argument.

Feminists also talk about phenomena such as the "male gaze," in which men look at women as sexual objects and this perspective is normalized. Women, of course, are frequently portrayed in mass-mediated texts as sexual objects or objects of desire, and what is worse, many women in real life, taking their cues from the media, present themselves as sexual objects. The reason we have such varied critical approaches to mediated texts is that these texts are so complicated and contain so much information that they are susceptible to many kinds of analysis. Some would argue they require a multidisciplinary form of analysis, one that considers, for example, political, economic, social, psychological, and other matters.

I have taken feminism, one of the more important ideological approaches to media and communication, as a case study representing other oppressed groups. And, of course, it is possible to have combinations of oppressed groups such as Islamic feminists or gay and lesbian African Americans. Let me suggest another approach to understanding the political aspects of media and communication that offers valuable insights and puts things in perspective, an approach that deals with political cultures in American society.

❖ POLITICAL CULTURES, THE MEDIA, AND COMMUNICATION

This analysis draws on the work of Mary Douglas, an English social anthropologist, and Aaron Wildavsky, an American political scientist. Douglas developed what she called **grid-group theory.** Her theory is described in Michael Thompson, Richard Ellis, and Aaron Wildavsky's *Cultural Theory* (1990):

> [Douglas] argues that the variability of an individual's involvement in social life can be adequately captured by two dimensions of sociality: group and grid. Group refers to the extent to which an individual is incorporated into bounded units. The greater the incorporation, the more individual choice is subject to group determination. Grid denotes the degree to which an individual's life is circumscribed by externally imposed prescriptions. The more binding and extensive the scope of prescriptions, the less of life is open to individual negotiation. (p. 5)

Wildavsky argued that focusing on interest groups in politics was not useful because these groups can't determine where their interests lie. He suggested that the best way to understand politics is to recognize the importance of political cultures, which are tied to people's values and shape a great deal of the decision making and voting by people who often know little about the issues they vote on.

As Wildavsky wrote in *Conditions for a Pluralist Democracy, or Cultural Pluralism Means More Than One Political Culture in a Country* (1982):

> What matters to people is how they should live with other people. The great questions of social life are "Who am I?" (To what kind of a group

do I belong?) and "What should I do?" (Are there many or few prescriptions I am expected to obey?). Groups are strong or weak according to whether they have boundaries separating them from others. Decisions are taken either for the group as a whole (strong boundaries) or for individuals or families (weak boundaries). Prescriptions are few or many, indicating the individual internalizes a large or a small number of behavioral norms to which he or she is bound. By combining boundaries with prescriptions . . . the most general answers to the questions of social life can be combined to form four different political cultures. (p. 7)

The following figure shows how these four political cultures are related to one another.

		Group Boundaries	
		Weak	*Strong*
Rules &	*Numerous*	Fatalists	Elitists
Prescriptions	*Few*	Individualists	Egalitarians

Wildavsky's Four Political Cultures

Wildavsky slightly changed the names he used for these four political cultures over the years. I will use the terms that offer the easiest understanding. The four political cultures form on the basis of group boundaries (weak or strong) and prescriptions (few or numerous):

1. *Fatalists:*   Group boundaries weak, prescriptions numerous

2. *Individualists:*   Group boundaries weak, prescriptions few

3. *Elitists:*   Group boundaries strong, prescriptions numerous

4. *Egalitarians:*   Group boundaries strong, prescriptions few

Wildavsky described these four political cultures as follows:

Strong groups with numerous prescriptions that vary with social roles combine to form hierarchical collectivism. Strong groups whose members follow few prescriptions form an egalitarian culture, a shared life of voluntary consent, without coercion or inequality. Competitive individualism joins few prescriptions with weak boundaries, thereby encouraging ever new combinations. When groups are weak and prescriptions strong, so that decisions are made for them by people on the outside, the controlled culture is fatalistic. (cited in A. A. Berger, 1990, p. 6)

These four cultures, found in all democratic societies, can be described in terms of some basic beliefs.

Individualists believe in free competition and as little government involvement as possible; government should maintain a level playing field and protect private property. Elitists believe that stratification and hierarchy are necessary and correct, but they have a sense of obligation toward those beneath them. Egalitarians focus their attention on the fact that everyone has certain needs to be looked after (thus, they try to raise up the fatalists) and criticize elitists and individualists. Egalitarians tend to be in opposition to mainstream American political thought. Fatalists believe they are victims of bad luck and tend to be apolitical. The combination of elitists and individualists represents the dominant belief system in America and in democratic societies, but you need all four for democracy to flourish. All the groups need one another, and none is viable without the others.

One of the values of Wildavsky's analysis of political cultures is that it shows how each of them responds to certain problems, such as how to deal with envy and leadership, who to blame when things go wrong, what to do about risk, and related matters. The responses of each culture to these and other matters are dealt with in Table 5.1, which shows the attributes of the four political cultures. In later years, Wildavsky changed some of his terms, and thus we find him writing about hierarchical elitists instead of hierarchical collectivists, for example. We see from Table 5.1 that the four political cultures deal with matters such as equality, ostentation, scarcity, and control in different ways. (Wildavsky spelled out these matters in considerable detail in his writings.)

I should add that people (except for fatalists, that is) can move from one political culture to another if they are not getting what they consider to be "payoff" from the political culture they identify with. Let me offer an example. A neighbor of mine who was a pilot for a major airline was what Wildavsky would describe as a competitive individualist. But in the late 1980s, when the airline started doing things that my neighbor considered to be unfair, such as cutting his salary and assigning him tasks that he considered beneath him, he switched his allegiances and became very pro-union (and thus much more of an egalitarian).

❖ POP CULTURAL AND MEDIA PREFERENCES OF THE FOUR POLITICAL CULTURES

These four political cultures relate to popular culture and the mass media. Let us assume two things:

1. People wish to reinforce their beliefs and thus tend to choose films, television programs, songs, books, and other similar materials that are congruent with their beliefs and support their values.

2. People wish to avoid cognitive dissonance and thus tend to avoid films, television shows, and other forms of mass-mediated culture that challenge their belief systems.

Table 5.1 Attributes of Wildavsky's Four Political Cultures

	Individualist	**Elitist**	**Egalitarian**	**Fatalist**
Leadership	Each own leader	Authority valid	Rejects	Led by others
Envy	Differences okay	Not a problem	Big problem	No envy
Blame	Personal	Deviants	System blame	Fate
Fairness	Chance to compete	Treat all according to station	Treat all equally	Life not fair
Wealth	Create more, keep more	Collective sacrifice	Equality of condition basic	Luck
Risk	Opportunity to create new wealth	Short-run dangers	System inequality basic	Luck
Control	By results	Process basic	Consensual decisions	Avoidance
Ostentation	Okay due to need to build networks	Public events only	Little display of	Hide
Equality	Equal chance to compete	Before law	Equality of result basic	Inequality inevitable
Scarcity	Use resources while valuable	Bureaucratic control to allocate	System exploits nature	Natural

If people desire reinforcement of their beliefs and to avoid challenges to their beliefs and values (**cognitive dissonance**), it suggests that there are, in reality, four audiences—or taste and value publics—in the United States (and any other democracy), each one of the four political cultures Wildavsky discussed. What this means, then, is that we can look at specific television programs, songs, films, books, sports, and so on in terms of which of these four political cultures or taste publics it would most likely appeal to. Most of the decisions people make about which television shows to watch, books to read, and films to see are not consciously made on the basis of the political culture one belongs to. In part, that's because most people do not recognize that they are, in fact, members of one of Wildavsky's political cultures. But they are.

Being a member of a political culture enables people to make decisions about politics (who to vote for, what party to join, and so on) with relatively little information. All one has to know is "he's one of us" or "this issue is one we believe in." As Wildavsky put it, "Culture is the India rubber man of politics, for it permits preferences to be formed from the slimmest clue" (cited in A. A. Berger, 1989, p. 40). It is conceivable, then, that the fundamental values and beliefs connected to one's political culture may be at work, secretly, in our decision making about what television shows to watch.

If you ask people why they watch television, they say they want to be entertained. But why is it that one person watches televised wrestling and another watches a situation comedy and a third watches a nature documentary? In Table 5.2, I offer a number of examples of specific songs, films, television programs, and other forms of popular culture according to the degree to which they reflect a given political culture. This table stems from classroom discussions in my media criticism courses many years ago and reflects the consensus of my students. Many new films, books, television programs, and so on could be substituted for the ones mentioned in the table.

If people were consistent, their choices would all (or mostly) fall under one of the four political cultures; of course, we know that they aren't. In the same light, one could simply list all of the films and television shows, books, magazines, and other media or texts found in the table and ask people which of them they like. If they formed a pattern, one could argue that these people, whether they recognized it or not, belonged to one of the four political cultures. If they were strongly ideological, there would be a distinctive pattern found of texts that were egalitarian, elitist, individualist, or fatalist.

One thing that Wildavsky's work on the four political cultures offers us, as researchers, is a means of gaining information about people's politics indirectly, by studying their taste in media and popular culture. We can use survey research about people's preferences for

Table 5.2   Political Cultures and Popular Culture

Topic Analyzed	Elitist	Individualist	Egalitarian	Fatalist
Songs	"God Save the Queen"	"I Did It My Way"	"We Are the World"	"Anarchy in the UK"
TV Shows	*PBS News Hour*	*Dynasty*	*The Equalizer*	*A-Team*
Films	*Top Gun*	*Color of Money*	*Woodstock*	*Rambo*
Magazines	*Architectural Digest*	*Money*	*Mother Jones*	*Soldier of Fortune*
Books	*The Prince*	*Looking Out for Number One*	*I'm Okay, You're Okay*	*1984*
Heroes	Reagan	Iacocca	Gandhi	Jim Jones
Heroines	Queen Elizabeth	Ayn Rand	Mother Teresa	Madonna
Games	Chess	Monopoly	New games	Russian roulette
Sports	Polo	Tennis	Frisbee	Roller derby
Fashion	Uniforms	Three-piece suit	Jeans	Thrift store

particular texts in media and popular culture to find out which political culture they belong to, and this may lead to insights into their past or future behavior.

It is risky, but we may also be able to generalize from individuals to societies as a whole by looking at bestsellers, successful television programs, and films that attract huge audiences. We can study the basic values found in such texts to see which of the four political cultures they belong to, and if we find that the same values and beliefs of one particular political culture seem to be growing stronger or weakening, we can infer that there may be significant changes going on in that society. What we discover should be used in conjunction with other ways of studying society to see whether our research about mediated texts and political cultures agrees with findings in other studies.

❖ MARXIST PERSPECTIVES ON SOCIAL MEDIA

Marxists have interesting things to say about social media. While some communication scholars are very positive about social media, emphasizing their role in our so-called "participatory culture," Marxist scholars focus on the exploitative aspects of social media and their role in helping maintain capitalism. For example, Christian Fuchs wrote in *Social Media: A Critical Introduction* (2014) that the social media should be seen as a means of exploiting people:

> I have stressed throughout this book the double logic of commodification and ideology that shapes corporate social media. Capital accumulation on corporate social media is based on Internet prosumer [a term combining producer and consumer] commodification, the unpaid labour of Internet users, targeted advertising and economic surveillance. Google is the dominant player in Internet prosumer commodification. It has developed a sophisticated targeted advertising system that collects a multitude of data about users' interests and activities (demographic, technological, economic, political, cultural, ecological information), **communications**, networks, and collaborations. Facebook is the dominant social networking site. It has developed a prosumer commodification system that is especially based on commodifying networks, contacts, user profiles and user-generated content that are created by unpaid user labour. (p. 255)

Fuchs argued that we should see Facebook and other social media as helping maintain the unequal power relationships and class divisions that exist in capitalist societies; in essence, social media are tools of the ruling classes who make huge amounts of money exploiting user-generated content on various sites and information about users which is of use to marketers and advertisers. The people who post messages on social media are, according to Marxist critics, unaware of the degree to which they are being exploited, since they have what Marx described as "false consciousness."

❖ A PREVIEW OF CRITICAL DISCOURSE ANALYSIS

In Chapter 7, I deal with various kinds of discourse analysis. We will find that one branch of discourse analysis, Critical Discourse Analysis (CDA), has been influenced by Marxist thought and focuses attention on the hidden ideological content of discourse. In a textbook on *How to Do Critical Discourse Analysis* (2012), the authors David Machin and Andrea Mayr explained,

> CDA assumes that power relations are discursive. In other words, power is transmitted and practiced through discourse. Therefore we can study "how power relations are exercised and negotiated in discourse" (Fairclough and Wodak, 1997: 242). . . . Fairclough (1989: 5) sums up the idea of "critical" language study as the processes of analyzing linguistic elements in order to reveal connections between language, power and ideology that are hidden from people. (pp. 4–5)

Generally speaking, when you see the term "critical" attached to studies of communication, it indicates a concern with power and ideology and is Marxist in nature—though often Marxism combined with feminism or other social, political and cultural matters. So we will return to the study of ideology and power in the new chapter I've written on discourse analysis.

❖ IDEOLOGICAL CRITICISM: APPLICATIONS AND EXERCISES

1. You are appointed media critic for the Marxist journal *Arts/Comrade*. Using the most important concepts from Marxist theory, write a 1,000-word Marxist interpretation of the film *The Hunger Games* or one that your instructor assigns. Use the applications chart format described earlier. Which of the four political cultures does *The Hunger Games* or the film you review appeal to most? Explain your answer.

2. Using Marxist concepts, write a 1,000-word analysis for *Arts/Comrade* of "The General" episode of *The Prisoner*. You can find this episode on the Internet and see it at no cost. Use the applications chart format. Is a psychoanalytic or semiotic analysis of this episode a better approach?

3. Write a Marxist analysis of the role social media are playing in American culture and society. How have social media affected (1) relations between parents and their children, (2) politics, (3) sexual relationships?

❖ CONCLUSIONS

One of the things we look at when we examine media and popular culture is the ideological content of particular films, television shows, songs, and advertisements. People with different ideological positions see different things in a given text, which is why qualitative media research is often so complicated. That is because works of art are enormously complex and rich and often are susceptible to many modes of analysis and interpretation. As Russian critic Yuri Lotman explained in his book *The Structure of the Artistic Text* (1977),

> Since it can concentrate a tremendous amount of information into the "area" of a very small text (cf. the length of a short story by Chekhov or a psychology textbook) an artistic text manifests yet another feature: it transmits different information to different readers in proportion to each one's comprehension: it provides the reader with a language in which each successive portion of information may be assimilated with repeated readings. It behaves as a kind of living organism which has a feedback channel to the reader and thereby instructs him [or her]. (p. 23)

Lotman also argued that everything in an artistic text is meaningful, which makes interpreting them even more complicated. The works carried by the media may not be great works of art, from an aesthetic point of view, but their influence and significance is, if Marxist and other ideological critics are correct, of great importance.

❖ FURTHER READING

Artz, L., & Macek, S. (2006). *Marxism and communication studies: The point is to change it.* Berne, Switzerland: Peter Lang.

Barthes, R. (1972). *Mythologies* (A. Lavers, Trans.). New York, NY: Hill & Wang.

Berger, A. A. (1990). *Agitpop: Political culture and communication theory.* New Brunswick, NJ: Transaction Books.

Berger, A. A. (2011). *Ads, fads, and consumer culture: Advertising's impact on American character and culture* (4th ed.). Lanham, MD: Rowman & Littlefield.

Berger, J. (1972). *Ways of seeing.* London, UK: British Broadcasting System and Penguin Books.

Butler, J. (1999). *Gender trouble: Feminism and the subversion of identity.* New York, NY: Routledge.

Dorfman, A. (1983). *The empire's old clothes: What the Lone Ranger, Babar, and other innocent heroes do to our minds.* New York, NY: Pantheon.

Durham, M. G., & Kellner, D. (2001). *Media and cultural studies: Key works.* Malden, MA: Blackwell.

Fuchs, C. (2014). *Social media: A critical introduction.* Thousand Oaks, CA: Sage.

Fuchs, C. (2015). *Culture and economy in the age of social media.* New York, NY: Routledge.

Gramsci, A. (1971). *Selections from the prison notebooks* (Q. Hoare & G. N. Smith, Eds. & Trans.). New York, NY: International Publishers.

Hammer, R., & Kellner, D. (Eds.). (2009). *Media/cultural studies: Critical approaches.* New York, NY: Peter Lang.

Haug, W. F. (1986). *Critique of commodity aesthetics: Appearance, sexuality, and advertising in capitalist society.* Minneapolis: University of Minnesota Press.

Jameson, F. (1991). *Postmodernism, or, The cultural logic of late capitalism.* Durham, NC: Duke University Press.

Kellner, D. (2003). *Media spectacle.* London, UK: Routledge.

Kendall, D. (2011). *Framing class: Media representations of wealth and poverty in America* (2nd ed.). Lanham, MD: Rowman & Littlefield.

Lefebvre, H. (1984). *Everyday life in the modern world.* New Brunswick, NJ: Transaction Books.

Lotman, J. M. (1977). *The structure of the artistic text.* Ann Arbor: Michigan Slavic Contributions.

McGuigan, J. (2010). *Cultural analysis.* Thousand Oaks, CA: Sage.

Tomlinson, J. (1991). *Cultural imperialism: A critical introduction.* Baltimore, MD: Johns Hopkins University Press.

Wayne, M. (2003). *Marxism and media studies: Key concepts and contemporary trends.* London, UK: Pluto Press.

It was a triumph for the interpretive art of psychoanalysis when it succeeded in demonstrating that certain common mental acts of normal people, for which no one had hitherto attempted to put forward a psychological explanation, were to be regarded in the same light as the symptoms of neurotics: that is to say, they had a meaning, which was unknown to the subject but which could easily be discovered by analytic means. The phenomena in question were such events as the temporary forgetting of familiar words and names, forgetting to carry out prescribed tasks, everyday slips of the tongue or pen, misreadings, losses and mislaying of objects, certain mistakes, instances of apparently accidental self-injury, and finally habitual movements carried out seemingly without intention or in play, tunes hummed "thoughtlessly," and so on. All of these were shorn of their physiological explanation, if any such had ever been attempted, and were shown to be strictly determined and were revealed as an expression of the subject's suppressed intentions or as a result of a clash between two intentions one of which was permanently or temporarily unconscious. . . .

Finally, a class of material was brought to light which is calculated better than any others to stimulate a belief in the existence of unconscious mental acts even in people to whom the hypothesis of something at once mental and unconscious seems strange and even absurd.

—Sigmund Freud, *Character and Culture*
(1910/1963b, pp. 235–236)

6

Psychoanalytic Criticism

- What did Freud write about the unconscious? How is the psyche like an iceberg?
- What are the four stages we go through in our sexual development?
- What is the Oedipus complex? How does it shape texts such as *King Kong* and the Bond novels?
- Define the id, ego, and superego.
- How is the id, ego, and superego typology applied to media and society?
- What are the most important "defense mechanisms"?
- What does psychoanalyst Martin Grotjahn say about horror films and mysteries?
- What did Freud say about masculine and feminine symbols?
- How are the theories of Erik Erikson applied to smartphone use?
- What did Jung and Jungians say about archetypes, the collective unconscious, and the "myth of the hero"?
- What was said about the anima and the animus?
- What did Jung write about the shadow element in the psyche?

On the cover of *Time* magazine's issue dealing with the century's greatest minds (March 29, 1999), who should we find but Sigmund Freud (listening to Albert Einstein, who is lying on a couch, talking about his mother, no doubt). In the article, we find Freud's impact characterized as follows:

> For good or ill, Sigmund Freud, more than any other explorer of the psyche, has shaped the mind of the 20th century. The very fierceness and persistence of his detractors are a wry tribute to the staying power of Freud's ideas. (p. 66)

Freud's ideas have always been controversial, and he is continually being relegated to the ash heap of history. But it seems every time you turn around, you see Freud's theories, and those of his followers, being used to help people deal with their problems (psychotherapy) and to help make sense of people's behavior, in real life and in the arts (psychoanalytic theory).

Freud was born in 1856 and died in 1939. He earned a medical degree in 1881 and published his masterpiece, *The Interpretation of Dreams*, in 1900, when he was 43 years old. His ideas have been with us for more than 100 years, and they are still both controversial and influential.

Psychoanalytic theory applies the insights of Sigmund Freud and other thinkers, such as Carl Jung, to texts of all kinds—works of serious literature as well as mass-mediated texts. The focus here is on Freud's ideas, but I also discuss some important concepts from Carl Jung, whose ideas are also very useful for psychoanalytic criticism. Both had theories about how the human mind functions that can be used to interpret matters such as the creative process and the motivations of characters in stories.

Sigmund Freud, the father of modern psychoanalytic theory

❖ FREUD'S CONTRIBUTION

The Unconscious

Psychoanalytic theory tells us that the human psyche is divided into three spheres: the conscious, the preconscious, and the unconscious. Although Freud might not have discovered the unconscious, it is fair to say that he was aware of its significance and used it in his work to an unprecedented degree. He offered a classic description of the unconscious in his essay "One of the Difficulties of Psychoanalysis" (1910/1963b):

> You believe that you are informed of all that goes on in your mind if it is of any importance at all, because your consciousness then gives news of it. And if you have heard nothing of any particular thing in your mind you confidently assume that it does not exist there. Indeed, you go so far as to regard "the mind" as coextensive with "consciousness," that is, with what is known to you. . . . Come, let yourself be taught something on this one point. What is in your mind is not identified with what you are conscious of; whether something is going on in your mind and whether you hear of it, are two different things. (pp. 188–189)

It was then, and still is, difficult for many people to recognize that there can be contents of their minds of which they are unaware.

Conscious

Preconscious

Unconscious

The three levels of the psyche (Freud's topographic hypothesis) can be represented by an iceberg. The tip of the iceberg, which we can all see, is consciousness. The part of the iceberg five or six feet below the waterline, which we can dimly make out, is the preconscious. And the part of the iceberg below that line, which cannot be seen, is the unconscious. It makes up most of the iceberg and, it is important to recognize, the human psyche.

Gerald Zaltman, a professor of marketing at the Harvard Business School made this point in his book *How Customers Think: Essential Insights Into the Mind of the Market* (2003). He suggested that there is a 95%–5% split in our minds. He argued that only 5% of our cognition is found in "high-order" consciousness and 95% is in our unconscious, in what he called "the shadows of the mind," below the level of our awareness. He added that unconscious memories also play an important role in shaping our conscious experience. It is these unconscious aspects of our psyches that were of interest to Zaltman as a marketing scholar, since they play a major role in our purchasing decisions—but one unrecognized by us.

According to Freud, all of our experiences are stored in the unconscious and have an effect on our minds and behavior. Psychoanalytic criticism suggests that works of art resonate with this unconscious material in our minds. It is likely, psychoanalytic critics suggest, that works of art send messages, in hidden and rather mysterious ways, from the unconscious of creative artists to the unconscious of the audience for their works.

The Oedipus Complex

If people found the idea of an unconscious difficult, they found Freud's notion of the Oedipus complex outrageous. And it's still very controversial, as scholars argue about whether it exists or was just a fantastic notion of Freud's. He believed that we all experience, when we are young children (around the age of 3), Oedipal strivings. That is, we all desire to have the undivided attention and love of our parent of the opposite sex. Freud called this phenomenon the Oedipus complex because it resembled in important ways the myth of Oedipus, the Greek hero who unwittingly killed his father and married his mother.

Most people, Freud suggested, resolve these Oedipal strivings, which are always unconscious, so they do not cause trouble. But some people do not resolve them, and Oedipal strivings have a major impact on their lives. These hidden Oedipal strivings, Freud suggested, explain why people are so moved when they see Sophocles's play *Oedipus Rex*, which is based on the Oedipus myth. The same applies to other works where the connection is not as obvious, such as Shakespeare's *Hamlet*.

On October 15, 1897, Freud wrote a famous letter to his friend Wilhelm Fleiss:

> The Greek myth seizes on a compulsion which everyone recognizes because he has felt traces of it in himself. Every member of the audience was once a budding Oedipus in fantasy, and the dream-fulfillment played out in reality causes everyone to recoil in horror, with the full measure of repression which separates his infantile from his present state. The idea has passed through my head that the same thing may lie at the root of *Hamlet*. I am not thinking of Shakespeare's conscious intentions, but supposing rather that he was impelled to write by a real event because his own unconscious understood that of his hero. (cited in Grotjahn, 1957, pp. 84–85)

Although this theory is very controversial, it is useful in dealing with works of art. The Oedipus complex has been used by critics to interpret everything from *King Kong* to the James Bond stories and films.

Let me offer an example. In his article "The Fascinating King Named Kong," Mark Rubinstein wrote,

> It should be clearer now, at least to those who have seen the movie of 1933, why the story of King Kong has the power to move us the way it does. It not only retells certain basic myths of human society and

religion, but it also recounts stories of our childhood passions and development. (cited in A. A. Berger, 1991, p. 189)

He referred to King Kong as a "father" figure and the battle between him and an ordinary-sized human being (symbolically a "child" figure) as a struggle to possess a woman (symbolically the "mother" figure). We might also think of the relationship between Luke Skywalker and his father Darth Vader in *Star Wars*. James Bond, the hero of numerous books and films, deals with villains who are usually fixated on controlling the world; they tend to be older and very powerful men who capture Bond and torture him but are ultimately defeated by Bond, who then makes love to a beautiful woman. The Oedipal aspects of these relationships are obvious.

Human Sexuality

Freud used the term *libido* for the "force by which the sexual instinct is represented in the mind." He suggested that all human beings pass through four stages in their sexual development. These stages—the oral, the anal, the phallic, and the genital—are described in *The Encyclopedia of Psychoanalysis* (Eidelberg, 1968) in the following manner:

> The mouth represents an erotogenic zone for the infant. Sucking and later eating represent the gratification of oral needs. The fact that the infant often sucks a pacifier indicates that he is not only concerned with the incorporation of calories. When the infant begins to have teeth, the need to bite expresses his sadistic desires. The second stage of development is usually referred to as the sadistic-anal, and is characterized by the infant's interest in excreting or retaining his stools. Finally, the third stage is referred to as the phallic, in which the boy is interested in his penis and the girl in her clitoris. The boy's interest in his penis appears to be responsible for his positive Oedipus complex, which is finally dissolved by the fear of castration. The girl reacts with penis envy, if she considers her clitoris to be an inferior organ to the penis.
>
> Freud pointed out that the stages are not clear-cut, and that the fourth stage, the genital phase, is achieved only with puberty. (pp. 210–211)

Thus, according to Freud, our sexual life during infancy is rich, but it is unfocused and not directed at others. That happens only with puberty.

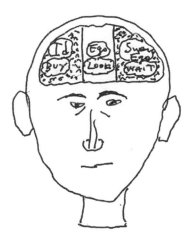

The Id, Ego, and Superego

Freud developed a second theory about the psyche as his thought evolved. This theory, known as Freud's "structural" hypothesis, suggests that the psyche has three parts: the id, the ego, and the superego. Freud suggested that an unconscious conflict goes on in all people between the id and superego aspects of their personalities. Freud described the **id** as "chaos, a cauldron of seething excitement" and said it is characterized by impulse and the desire for gratification. When we think of the id, we should focus on matters such as sexual desire, lust, passion, and desire. Opposed to the id we find the **superego,** which represents parental influence, conscience, and restraint. According to Brenner's *An Elementary Textbook of Psychoanalysis* (1974), the superego can be characterized as follows:

> 1. the approval or disapproval of actions and wishes on the grounds of rectitude, 2. critical self-observation, 3. self-punishment, 4. the demand for reparation or repentance of wrong-doing, 5. self-praise or self-love as a reward for virtuous or desirable thoughts and actions. Contrary to the ordinary meaning of "conscience," however, we understand the functions of the superego are often largely or completely unconscious. (pp. 111–112)

The id says, "I want it all and I want it now," and the superego says, "Don't do it or you'll be sorry." The id provides energy and is necessary, but if it is not restrained, we cannot accomplish anything. The superego provides restraint, but if not controlled would overwhelm us all with guilt. These forces operate, generally speaking, at the unconscious level.

The **ego** mediates between the id and superego. It is that agency in the human psyche that Freud said "stands for reason and good sense." The ego is charged with helping us relate to the environment and helping us preserve ourselves. If the ego can maintain a decent balance between id and superego forces, all is well, and we are able to avoid becoming neurotic. However, if either the id or superego becomes dominant, all kinds of problems follow.

We can use these three components of the psyche in criticism by finding characters in texts who tend to be essentially (that is, not always purely) "id" or "ego" or "superego" characters. For example, in *Star Trek*, it is possible to see the three main characters as follows:

Id	Ego	Superego
McCoy	Spock	Kirk
Emotion	Rationality	Command

I'm not suggesting that the creators of the television series or films consciously intended to create characters that represent components of the psyche. We must remember that what we are conscious of represents but a small portion of our psyches, and that applies to creative artists, too. It is interesting to note that *Kirk* means "church" in German, which gives added support to my suggestion that he is a superego figure.

We can use the id/ego/superego **typology,** roughly speaking, to understand other texts, as the following chart shows.

Topic	Id	Ego	Superego
Books	Romances, vampire novels	Textbooks	Bible, Koran.
Magazines	*Playboy*	*National Geographic*	Religious publications
Films	*Twilight*	*Agora*	*The Girl Who Played With Fire*
Television shows	Dance shows, romantic comedies	Nature shows	Religious shows
Cities	Las Vegas	Boston area (Harvard)	Rome
Heroes (fictional)	Don Juan	Sherlock Holmes, Mr. Spock	Superman, Batman, Spider-Man

Cities are important because they give people ideas about what kind of actions to expect in films and other texts. People are not aware of the id, ego, or superego aspects of the characters they follow in mass-mediated texts, but there are strong elements from the typology in all media. Certain genres can be analyzed in terms of Freud's structural hypothesis. Thus, news programs are ego texts; cop shows and religious programs are superego texts; and soap operas, pornographic films, and many music videos are id texts.

A SHORT THEATRICAL PIECE ON PSYCHOANALYTIC CRITICISM

Grand Inquisitor:	*Psychoanalytic thought is mostly nonsense! Don't you agree?*
Arthur:	You mean you don't believe in repression, condensation, displacement, regression, or symbolization? In the id, the ego, and the superego? In the Oedipus complex? In the unconscious?
Grand Inquisitor:	*I like the superego best of all. I'm big on guilt! There's nothing personal in it, mind you. We must control the id! Where there is id, let there be superego.*
Arthur:	Don't you sometimes deal with unconscious heretics—people who think they are believers but, without recognizing what they are doing, hold heretical beliefs?
Grand Inquisitor:	*Of course I do. They're a major problem. "Sometimes a cigar is only a cigar," and sometimes a person who thinks he's a true believer is really a heretic. These unconscious heretics . . . they really burn me up!*
Arthur:	That's odd. I thought it was you who burned them up!

Defense Mechanisms

Freud suggested that the ego uses a number of **defense mechanisms** to help people ward off anxieties and maintain psychological equilibrium. The following are a number of the more important defense mechanisms:

Ambivalence: A simultaneous feeling of opposite emotions, such as love and hate, toward the same person or object.

Avoidance: Refusing to deal with subjects that distress or perturb us because they are connected to our unconscious aggressive or sexual impulses.

Denial: Unwillingness to recognize the reality of subjects that distress and generate anxiety in us by blocking them from consciousness or becoming involved in a wish-fulfilling fantasy.

Fixation: An obsessive attachment or preoccupation with something or someone, usually as the result of a traumatic experience.

Identification: The strong desire to be like someone or something in some aspect of thought or behavior.

Projection: Denying some negative or hostile feelings by attributing them to someone else.

Rationalization: Offering seemingly rational reasons or excuses for behavior generated by unconscious and irrational forces. (The term **rationalization** was introduced to psychoanalytic theory by Ernest Jones [1908].)

Reaction formation: Suppressing one element of an ambivalent attitude (and keeping it in our unconscious) and maximizing and overemphasizing the other (its opposite).

Regression: Returning to an earlier stage of development when confronted by an anxiety-producing or stressful situation or event.

Repression: Unconsciously barring instinctual desires from consciousness; generally considered the most basic defense mechanism.

Suppression: Consciously deciding to put something out of mind. This is the second most basic defense mechanism, after repression. Because suppression is voluntary, suppressed material can be brought back to consciousness without too much difficulty. That is not the case with repression, which unconsciously bars material from consciousness.

It is useful for critics to know these defense mechanisms in order to identify them in characters when making a psychoanalytic interpretation of a text. When we recognize them, we are able to understand better the motives of the characters and gain some insight into why these texts are so important to their readers and viewers.

Martin Grotjahn on Horror

In *The Voice of the Symbol* (1971), psychiatrist Martin Grotjahn offered a fascinating discussion of horror television shows that explained how defense mechanisms play an important role, at the unconscious level, in our attraction to this genre. He wrote,

> The fascination of horror shows for so many people can be explained only when we consider the dynamic of the child's attraction to and fear of them. Horror is experienced when an old and long-repressed childhood fear seems to come true. The child fears ghosts or dead people returning. He fears that thoughts may come true; or that magic-mystic beliefs may prove to be effective. Fantasies may no longer be restricted to the unconscious but may become true events before our eyes on the television screen. We all are full of dangerous, bad wishes and thoughts which suddenly may emerge from repression and seem to become real and true; we can actually see them happening on the screen. The projection of repressed trends into symbols on the television screen would offer rare opportunity for working through of unconscious conflicts. Television could develop new means of art expression and an entirely new field of communication could be opened. (p. 9)

Unfortunately, Grotjahn lamented, television focuses its energy on entertaining us, in contrast to the theater, which makes us confront our conscious and unconscious conflicts.

In his analysis of horror television shows, we find an understanding of why horror appeals to so many people and of the way horror relates to defense mechanisms such as repression and projection. In returning to our childhood fears, there is an element of regression. At the unconscious level, we attempt to conquer our childhood fears and may also derive some pleasure from a regression to a period when life was simpler, when we may have experienced unconditional love and admiration from our parents and others, and when we didn't have to struggle with problems of gaining independence and attaining an identity and the responsibilities of maturity.

Symbols

A symbol is anything that can be used to stand for something else. In *The Voice of the Symbol*, Grotjahn (1971) also wrote that a symbol is a "message from our unconscious which communicates truth, beauty and goodness" (p. xi). He added,

> A book on the symbol is therefore a book about life and its mastery. It is also a book about death, which we must master in order to progress from maturity to wisdom. Insight into one's own unconscious or that of our fellow man is insight communicated by the symbol. Insight is inner vision and therefore closely related to art and intuition, to tact and empathy. (p. xii)

Symbols, then, play an important role in our understanding of life and of art. It was Freud, Grotjahn explained, who discovered a method to understand the symbol and the role it plays in our unconscious life and in art and media. For Grotjahn, television shows were like collective dreams that we all dream at the same time—while we are watching a show, that is.

Perhaps no aspect of Freudian thought seems more far-fetched and absurd than his writings on symbolization. Symbols play a very important role in psychoanalytic thought. They were defined by Hinsie and Campbell in their *Psychiatric Dictionary* (1970) as follows:

> The act or process of representing an order or idea by a substitute object, sign, or signal. In psychiatry, symbolism is of particular importance since it can serve as a defense mechanism of the ego, as where unconscious (or forbidden) aggressive or sexual impulses come to expression through symbolic expression and thus are able to avoid censorship. (p. 734)

Symbols enable us to mask or disguise unconscious aggressive or sexual desires and thus avoid the feeling of guilt that would be generated by the superego if it recognized what we were doing.

Freud (1953) explained that in our dreams the id uses symbols to trick the superego and obtain desired gratification:

> The male genital organ is symbolically represented in dreams in many different ways. . . . Its more conspicuous and, to both sexes, more interesting part, the penis, is symbolized primarily by objects which resemble it in form, being long and upstanding, such as *sticks, umbrellas, poles, trees,* and the like; also by objects which, like the thing symbolized, have the property of penetration, and consequently of injuring the body—that is to say pointed weapons of all sorts: *knives, daggers, lances, sabres;* firearms are similarly used: *guns, pistols, and revolvers.* (pp. 161–162)

Freud added other items that also function as phallic symbols—objects from which water flows and objects that can raise themselves up, mirroring erections in males. All of these symbols, Freud explained, are tied to wish fulfillment and the desire of men to be with women.

If men are symbolized by penetrating objects and those that resemble the penis functionally, women are represented by incorporative objects:

> The female genitals are symbolically represented by all such objects as share with them the property of enclosing a space or are capable of acting as receptacles: such as *pits, hollows, and caves,* and also *jars and bottles,* and *boxes* of all sorts and sizes, *chests, coffers, pockets,* and so forth. *Ships,* too, come into this category. Many symbols refer rather to the uterus than to the other genital organs: thus *cupboards, stoves,* and above all, *rooms.* Room symbolism here links up with that of houses, whilst *doors and gates* represent the genital opening. (Freud, 1953, pp. 163–164)

To this list, Freud added other phenomena such as woods and thickets (symbols of pubic hair) and jewel cases.

Freud's theory of symbolization actually is close in many respects to semiotic theory. He was, from a semiotic perspective, talking about icons when he discussed phallic symbols being long and thin, like sticks, snakes, or cigars, which resemble the penis. Freud realized, of course, that it was possible to take his theory of symbols and push it to extremes. He is reported to have said "Sometimes a cigar is just a cigar." This has been used by his critics to attack his theory, for even Freud recognized that a cigar is not always a phallic symbol. But we must recall that if "sometimes a cigar is just a cigar," it means that sometimes a cigar isn't just a cigar!

Source: © H. Lundgaard.

❖ SMARTPHONES AND THE PSYCHE: APPLYING THE THEORIES OF ERIK ERIKSON

Cell phones—specifically, smartphones, which can be seen as portable computers—play an increasingly important role in our everyday lives and different roles in our lives as we grow older. I have adapted psychoanalyst Erik Erikson's model of developmental crises, presented in the form of polar oppositions, and connected these crises to our cell phone usage. According to Erikson, human beings all face certain developmental crises at different stages of their lives. I suggest, here, the role smartphones play in each of these crises. Keep in mind that children as young as 9 years now have cell phones or smartphones.

I have adapted a chapter—"The Eight Ages of Man"—from Erikson's book *Childhood and Society* (1963), leaving out infancy, when the first two stages take place.

Stage	Crisis	Telephone Functions
Childhood	Initiative/guilt	Family integration, play
School	Industry/inferiority	Socialization, schoolwork, skills
Adolescence	Identity/role confusion	Peer group bonding, schoolwork, romance
Young adult	Intimacy/isolation	Love, career, initiation
Adult	Generativity/stagnation	Career, community
Maturity	Ego integrity/despair	Contact, community

Erikson developed his analysis of the crises we face as a series of oppositions we must confront and resolve. His discussion of the crises that adolescents face—identity/role confusion—is particularly interesting in light of statistics indicating that many adolescents send as many as 100 text messages a day to friends. At this stage, Erikson (1963) explained, young people are disturbed by their inability to settle on an occupation and "temporarily over-identify, to the point of an apparent complete loss of identity, with the heroes of cliques and crowds" (p. 261). He offered an insightful analysis of "young love":

> To a considerable extent adolescent love is an attempt to arrive at a definition of one's identity by projecting one's diffused ego image on another and by seeing it thus reflected and gradually clarified. This is why so much of young love is conversation. (p. 261)

From Erikson's perspective, we all must deal with developmental crises at different stages in our lives. The countless text messages young people send one another have a deeper and more significant meaning than we might imagine, for they are attempts at self-definition, among other things.

❖ NEUROPSYCHOANALYSIS: FREUD AND NEUROSCIENCE

In Kat McGowan's "The Second Coming of Sigmund Freud (which appeared in the April 2014 issue of *Discover*), we find that, to their surprise, many neuroscientists have found Freud's insights useful. McGowan suggested that though a number of Freud's theories are incorrect or flawed, many of his major ideas have been found to be correct—in particular, Freud's theories about the importance of unconscious thought. Unfortunately, brain scientists ignored the role of unconscious mental processing for almost a hundred years. It was only around 1980 that researchers started taking the unconscious seriously. McGowan wrote,

> In a study that is now legend, cognitive scientist Benjamin Libet asked people to press a button whenever they felt like it while he monitored the electrical activity in their brains. He could see that movement-controlling brain regions become active about a quarter of a second before subjects said they'd consciously decided to push the button. Some unconscious part of the brain decided well before the conscious mind did.

Since then, thousands of studies have proven that people process most information, especially social data like other people's behavior, unconsciously. We also make many decisions without much input from conscious thought. If anything, Freud underestimated the power and sophistication of unconscious thought, says social psychologist Timothy Wilson of the University of Virginia. The nature of unconscious thought that emerges from contemporary experiments is radically different from what Freud posited so many years ago. ("Freud's Ideas Endure")

Contemporary neuroscientists, McGowan suggested, see the unconscious as a mechanism for processing data rather than an area controlled by impulses, but believe that Freud was correct in stressing the importance of the unconscious.

This 2014 article points out that many of Freud's most important theories are valid, though he might have been incorrect about certain details. If Freud was correct about the importance of the unconscious and about inner conflicts, as neuroscientists now claim, there is reason to suggest that Freud's contribution to our understanding of human beings remains relevant and valuable. Freud's ideas endure and have led to a new field, **neuropsychoanalysis**, which exists in the overlap between psychoanalysis and neuroscience.

Carl Jung

❖ JUNGIAN THEORY

After Freud, Carl Jung (1875–1961) is probably the most important psychoanalytic theorist for our purposes—criticism of texts in the media and popular culture. Jung was originally associated with Freud, who thought Jung might be his disciple. They met for the first time in 1907 in Vienna. But Jung broke away from Freud in 1913 and created his own school of "analytic psychology." Jung developed a number of concepts and theories that led to different methods of helping people. His theories also are of great help to us in analyzing societies and interpreting texts. I will list and briefly discuss some of his most widely known concepts.

Archetypes

According to Jung, there are universal themes found in dreams, myths, religions, and works of art. These universal themes, which he called **archetypes,** exist independent of the personal unconscious of individuals. The archetypes are connected, Jung suggested, to past history and to what Jung asserted was a collective unconscious found in all people. These archetypes are unconscious, Jungians argue. We become aware of them only as the result of works of art, images that come to us in our dreams, or everyday emotional experiences that connect us to these archetypes in ways that, suddenly, somehow, we recognize.

As Jung (1968) explained,

> What we properly call instincts are physiological urges, and are perceived by the senses. But at the same time, they also manifest themselves in fantasies and often reveal their presence only by symbolic images. These manifestations are what I call archetypes. They are without known origin; and they reproduce themselves in any time or in any part of the world—even where transmission by direct descent or "cross fertilization" through migration must be ruled out. (p. 58)

Jung suggested that "the hero figure is an archetype, which has existed from time immemorial," as does the myth of paradise or of a past golden age, where people lived in peace and abundance. Heroes and heroines, of course, play a major role in mass-mediated texts. Whether the archetypes are "hardwired" in people is a matter of considerable debate.

The Collective Unconscious

These archetypes are found, Jung said, in what he described as the collective unconscious. Jung (1968) made an analogy with instincts in explaining the collective unconscious:

> We do not assume that each new-born animal creates its own instincts as an individual acquisition, and we must not suppose that human individuals invent their specific human ways with every new birth. Like the instincts, the collective thought patterns of the human mind are innate and are inherited. They function, when the occasion arises, in more or less the same way in all of us. (p. 64)

Jungians argue that myths' instinct-like origin explains why they are universal. This also explains why certain themes and motifs are, so Jungians assert, found in works of art all through history and everywhere in the world. I should add that Jung's notions about archetypes, the collective unconscious, and the universality of myths are extremely controversial, and many psychologists and other social scientists take issue with them. There is no way to demonstrate, for instance, that the Jungian collective unconscious actually exists.

The Myth of the Hero

Heroes, according to Jung, are the most important kind of archetypes and are manifestations of the collective unconscious. As such, they play a crucial role in Jungian thought. Joseph L. Henderson, a Jungian, wrote,

> The myth of the hero is the most common and the best known myth in the world. We find it in the classical mythology of Greece and Rome, in the Middle Ages, in the Far East, and among contemporary primitive tribes. It also appears in our dreams. . . .
>
> These hero myths vary enormously in detail, but the more closely one examines them the more one sees that structurally they are very similar. They have, that is to say, a universal pattern, even though they were developed by groups or individuals without any direct cultural contact with each other. . . . Over and over again one hears a tale describing a hero's miraculous but humble birth, his early proof of superhuman strength, his rapid rise to prominence or power, his triumphant struggle with the forces of evil, his fallibility to the sin of pride (*hybris*), and his fall through betrayal or heroic sacrifice that ends in his death. (cited in Jung, 1968, p. 101)

Henderson's description deals with tragic heroes. Most heroes, especially those found in today's mass media, generally don't succumb to the sin of pride. Instead, they survive to fight new villains, in endless succession, who keep appearing with incredible regularity.

According to Henderson, the myth of the hero has an important role—it helps people develop their ego consciousness. This enables them to deal with the many trials and problems they will face as they grow older. Heroes help people with one of the biggest problems they face—separation and individuation from their parents and other tutelary figures. That explains why heroes are found all through history and why they are so important.

The Anima and the Animus

In Jungian thought, the anima represents the female element found in all males, and the animus represents the male element found in all females. This duality, according to Jungians, is symbolized in hermaphrodites (people with sexual organs from both sexes) and in witches, priestesses, medicine men, and shamans. Jungian theorist Marie-Louise von Franz (cited in Jung, 1968) discussed the impact of the anima and animus on personality, the arts, and related phenomena:

> The most frequent manifestations of the anima take the form of erotic fantasy. Men may be driven to nurse their fantasies by looking at films and strip-tease shows, or by day-dreaming over pornographic material. This is a crude, primitive aspect of the anima, which becomes compulsive only when a man does not sufficiently cultivate his feeling relationships—when his feeling attitude toward his life has remained infantile. (p. 191)

Franz pointed out that the anima also has a positive side; it enables us to do things such as find the right marriage partner and explore our inner **values,** leading to deeper and more profound insights into our psyches. The animus, according to Franz, functions in much the same way for women. The animus is formed, she suggested, essentially by a woman's father and can have positive and negative influences. On the one hand, it can lead to coldness, obstinacy, and hypercritical behavior. However, on the other hand, the anima can help women develop an enterprising approach to life, realize inner strength, and learn how to relate to men in positive ways.

The Shadow Element in the Psyche

The **shadow,** for Jungians, refers to the dark side of the human psyche—the side we generally keep hidden from our consciousness.

But we must recognize and deal with our shadow if we are to escape neurosis. Henderson explained Jung's concept of the shadow:

> Dr. Jung has pointed out that the shadow cast by the conscious mind on the individual contains the hidden, repressed and unfavorable (or nefarious) aspects of the personality. But this darkness is not just the simple converse of the conscious ego. Just as the ego contains unfavorable and destructive attitudes, so the shadow has good qualities— normal instincts and creative impulses. Ego and shadow, indeed, although separate, are inextricably linked together in much the same way that thought and feeling are related to one another. (cited in Jung, 1968, p. 110)

According to Jungians, a battle for deliverance occurs in the psyche between the shadow and the ego. Heroes provide the means by which the ego symbolically "liberates the mature man from a regressive longing to return to a blissful state of infancy in a world dominated by his mother" (p. 111).

Freudians do not have the shadow concept, but it is easy to see that the battle between the shadow and the ego that Jungians talk about is vaguely analogous to what Freudians describe as going on in the psyche. The struggle for dominance between the shadow and the ego is similar to the battle that Freudians assert goes on between the id and the superego—a battle that the ego tries to mediate. Although Jung's shadow seems to be more negative than Freud's id, both the shadow and the id are, it turns out, the source of creative activity.

As an overview of Jung's theories and contributions, I offer the following from Ellis Cashmore and Chris Rojek's *Dictionary of Cultural Theorists* (1999):

> For Jung, as for Freud, a basic part of his analytical process was based upon dream analysis, and he published extensively on this topic. Jung also considered and defined the process of individuation as the path to individual self-knowledge. According to Jung, everyone has an innate desire to achieve this self-realization, and the prevention of this from external influences (from other people in close contact with the individual or from societal pressures) is the root cause of an individual's dysfunctional behavior. According to Jung, a person's personality can be described in terms of the persona and shadow: the persona representing the mask which mediates between a person and the world and the shadow representing that part of the personality which the individual will not allow himself or herself to express. An individual also has both a masculine and feminine side, labeled animus and anima. For a man the masculine side (animus) is resident

in the conscious mind with the anima being present in the unconscious, while for a woman, the reverse is the case. In his later career, Jung became extremely interested in and knowledgeable concerning the religions, myths and rituals of primitive societies and, as a result, after his break with Freud, he became more concerned with the interpretation of society rather than individual psychology. . . . Much of his later work has a mystical aspect to it and this aspect of his work has led to a resurgence in popularity in Jungian psychology in recent years among alternative communities. Indeed, the psychology of Jung provides much of the foundations of "New Age" psychology and spirituality. (p. 262)

Jung book cover

Source: Jacket Cover copyright © 1968 by Dell, a division of Random House, Inc., from *Man and His Symbols* by C. G. Jung. Used by permission of Dell, a division of Random House, Inc.

In the course of his long career, Jung published many books. Perhaps his most accessible is *Man and His Symbols* (1968), in which many of the quotations used in this chapter can be found.

❖ PSYCHOANALYTIC CRITICISM: APPLICATIONS AND EXERCISES

1. You are appointed media critic of *Psyche* magazine. Write a psychoanalytic interpretation of *The Hunger Games* (or some other film or television episode chosen by your instructor). Use an applications chart to make your analysis. (For a reminder of how to make an applications chart, consult Table 3.2 in Chapter 3.)

2. Write a 1,000-word psychoanalytic interpretation for *Psyche* magazine of the "A, B, and C" episode of *The Prisoner*. Use an applications chart for the first page of your paper.

3. Find an advertisement that uses sexuality to sell a product. Offer a 1,000- to 1,500-word psychoanalytic interpretation of the symbolism, language, and other matters for *Psyche* magazine. Use an applications chart for the first page of your analysis. Turn in the advertisement with your paper.

4. Using scholarly journals, investigate psychoanalytic studies of horror as a genre and of a particular horror film, television show, or video. What does the recent popularity of horror texts in all media say about American culture? Why were *Buffy, the Vampire Slayer* and *Twilight* such big hits? Why are vampires so interesting to audiences? Do women relate differently from men to vampire stories?

5. Investigate articles and books by psychologists and psychoanalysts on cell phone use. Apply Erikson's work on the "Eight Ages of Man" to some television shows and films. Does his theory provide any insights?

6. Investigate the field of neuropsychoanalysis. What research is being done in this field? What insights does this field provide to us about the human psyche?

❖ CONCLUSIONS

As might be expected, there have been many developments in psychoanalytic theory. Stephen A. Mitchell and Margaret J. Black covered some of these developments in their book *Freud and Beyond: A History of Modern Psychoanalytic Thought* (1996):

Very little of the way Freud understood and practiced psychoanalysis has remained simply intact. The major pillars of his theorizing— instinctual drives, the centrality of the Oedipus complex, the motivational primacy of sex and aggression—have all been challenged and fundamentally transformed in contemporary psychoanalytic thought. And Freud's basic technical principles—analytic neutrality, the systematic frustration of the patient's wishes, a regression of an infantile neurosis—have likewise been reconceptualized, revised, and transformed by current clinicians. (p. xvii)

Despite many reconceptualizations and transformations in psychoanalytic theory, Freud's ideas and discoveries still remain at the heart of the enterprise.

Psychoanalytic criticism rests on the assumption that we are not always aware of all that is in our minds and that often we are governed by forces and motivations beyond our consciousness. Freud's goal was a noble one; he wished to rescue people from being dominated by their unconscious id forces, which often function in destructive ways. Freud summed this up in his famous statement, "Where Id was, there Ego shall be." Freud's one-time collaborator, Jung, also made many important contributions. His theories have been of interest to sociologists, historians, anthropologists, and critics of both "elite" literature and the mass media.

❖ FURTHER READING

Bettelheim, B. (1977). *The uses of enchantment: The meaning and importance of fairy tales.* New York, NY: Vintage.

Brenner, C. (1974). *An elementary textbook of psychoanalysis.* Garden City, NY: Doubleday.

The century's greatest minds. (1999, March 29). *Time, 153*(12). Retrieved from http://content.time.com/time/magazine/0,9263,7601990329,00.html

Erikson, E. H. (1963). *Childhood and society.* New York, NY: W. W. Norton.

Freud, S. (1963). *Character and culture: Vol. 9. The collected works* (P. Rieff, Ed.). New York, NY: Collier. (Original work published 1910)

Freud, S. (1965). *The interpretation of dreams.* New York, NY: Avon. (Original work published 1900)

Fromm, E. (1951). *The forgotten language: An introduction to the understanding of dreams, fairy tales, and myths.* New York, NY: Grove.

Grotjahn, M. (1971). *The voice of the symbol.* New York, NY: Delta.

Jung, C. G. (with von Franz, M-L., Henderson, J. L., Jacobi, J., & Jaffe, A.). (1968). *Man and his symbols.* Garden City, NY: Doubleday.

Jung, C. G. (2009). *The red book.* New York, NY: W. W. Norton.

Mitchell, S. A., & Black, M. J. (1996). *Freud and beyond: A history of modern psychoanalytic thought.* New York, NY: Basic Books.

Northoff, G. (2011). *Neuropsychoanalysis in practice: Brain, self, objects.* New York, NY: Oxford University Press.

Rutherford, P. (2007). *World made sexy: Freud to Madonna.* Toronto, Canada: University of Toronto Press.

Schwartz, C. (2015). *In the mind fields: A personal exploration of neuropsychoanalysis.* New York, NY: Pantheon.

Zaltman, G. (2003). *How customers think: Essential insights into the mind of the market.* Cambridge, MA: Harvard University Business School Press.

Discourse analysis shares the concerns of all qualitative approaches with the meaningfulness of social life, . . . but it attempts to provide a more profound interrogation of the precarious status of meaning. Traditional qualitative approaches often assume a social world and then seek to understand the meaning of this world for participants. Discourse analysis, on the other hand, tries to explore how the socially produced ideas and objects that populate the world were created in the first place and how they are maintained and held in place over time. Whereas other qualitative methodologies work to understand or interpret social reality as it exists, discourse analysis endeavors to uncover the way in which it is produced. This is the most important contribution of discourse analysis: it examines how language constructs phenomena, not how it reflects and reveals it. In other words, discourse analysis views discourse as constitutive of the social world—not a route to it—and assumes the world cannot be known separately from discourse.

—Nelson Phillips and Cynthia Hardy,
*Discourse Analysis: Investigating
Processes of Social Construction* (2002, p. 6)

7

Discourse Analysis

- What is discourse analysis?
- What are the two kinds of discourse analysis?
- What are the three most important themes in discourse analysis?
- What are the three dimensions of the field according to Teun A. Van Dijk?
- What is style? How do discourse analysts deal with style?
- How does critical discourse analysis (CDA) define ideology?
- What is multimodal critical discourse analysis? How does it differ from CDA?

This chapter is about discourse analysis. Most of us know what analysis is—looking at the components of something and investigating their relationships—but what is discourse? Defining *discourse* is, it turns out, rather difficult. Dictionary definitions generally state that discourse has to do with talk and with texts about some subject. *Merriam-Webster's Collegiate Dictionary* (11th edition) defines *discourse* as follows:

1 *Archaic:* the capacity of orderly thought or procedure: RATIONALITY **2** : verbal interchange of ideas; *esp.* CONVERSATION **3 a:** formal and orderly and usu. extended expression of thought on a subject **b** : connected speech or writing **c** : a linguistic unit (as a conversation or a story) larger than a sentence.

The dictionary also provides a definition of *discourse analysis*: "*n* (1952): the study of linguistic relations and structures in discourse."

In their book *Working With Written Discourse* (2014), Deborah Cameron and Ivan Panović suggested that discourse has three basic themes:

1. Discourse is language "above the sentence."

2. Discourse is "language in use."

3. Discourse is a form of social practice in which language plays a central role. (p. 3)

Cameron and Panović described discourse analysis as being "above the sentence" to differentiate it from traditional linguistics, which tends to focus on parts of sentences or at the sentence level. In contrast, **discourse analysis** is interested in texts (spoken or written, and including visual images), their relation to other texts, the contexts in which written language is used, and the role these texts play in society.

Humpty Dumpty says, "When I use a word,
it means just what I choose it to mean."

❖ DEFINING DISCOURSE ANALYSIS

The *Webster's Collegiate* definition is helpful in that it focuses our attention on discourse analysis's interest in talk (which can have many different manifestations) and texts and informs us that discourse analysis has been around since the 1950s. But discourse analysis is much more complicated than that. I googled "discourse analysis" on March 27, 2015, and found, to my surprise, that 6,390,000 sites mention it and more than 43,000 books on Amazon.com deal with it. So there is a great deal of interest in the subject, even though many people have never heard of it.

In their book, *Discourse Analysis: Investigating Processes of Social Construction* (2002), Nelson Phillips and Cynthia Hardy helped us understand a bit more about discourse analysis:

> We need to differentiate between discourse analysis and other qualitative methods that explain the meaning of social phenomena. . . . We also describe its status as a methodology rather than just a method, that is, an epistemology that explains how we know the social world, as well as a set of methods for studying it. In this way we differentiate discourse analysis from other qualitative research methods, such as ethnography . . . ethnomethodology . . . conversation analysis . . . and narrative analysis. . . . Social reality is produced and made real through discourses, and social interactions cannot be fully understood without references to the discourses that give them meaning. (p. 3)

From this quotation we learn several things. First, discourse analysis is a qualitative methodology. Second, discourse analysis helps us understand social interactions and how social reality is produced, which is through our discourses or, more specifically, through talk, texts, and images. Third, it is broader and more comprehensive than its main components, namely conversation analysis (which is about talk) and narrative analysis (which is about written texts).

Teun A. van Dijk

❖ TEUN A. VAN DIJK ON DISCOURSE ANALYSIS

Teun A. van Dijk, one of the preeminent scholars in the field, offers other insights into discourse analysis. A book he edited, *Discourse as Structure and Process,* the first of two volumes of *Discourse Studies: A Multidisciplinary Introduction,* includes a chapter titled "The Study of Discourse." This chapter describes his sense of what discourse analysis is about and discusses the three main dimensions of the field:

> (a) *language use,* (b) the *communication of beliefs* (cognition), and (c) *interaction* in social situations. Given these three dimensions, it is not surprising to find that several disciplines are involved in the study of discourse such as linguistics (for the specific study of language and language use), psychology (for the study of beliefs and how they are communicated), and the social sciences (for the analysis of interactions in social situations).
>
> It is typically the task of discourse studies to provide *integrated* descriptions of these three main dimensions of discourse: how does language use influence beliefs and interaction, or vice versa, how do aspects of interactions influence how people speak, or how do beliefs control language use and interaction? Moreover, besides giving systematic descriptions, we may expect discourse studies to formulate *theories* that *explain* such relationships between language use, beliefs and interaction. (1997, p. 2)

Van Dijk added that while discourse analysis focuses a great deal of attention on talk and oral communication, it also studies written language and written texts. From his discussion of discourse analysis, we can see that it is interested in all kinds of human communication, with a focus on language use and the interactions among people who are talking and communicating with one another or writing texts of one kind or another.

To see the range of interests of researchers in discourse analysis, it is useful to list some of the chapters in his book:

Discourse Semantics	Narrative
Discourse and Grammar	Argumentation
Discourse Style	Genres and Registers of Discourse
Rhetoric	Discourse Semiotics

In the second volume of the series, *Discourse as Social Interaction*, some of the chapters discuss the following topics:

Gender in Discourse	Discourse, Ethnicity, Culture, and Racism
Organizational Discourse	Discourse on Politics
Discourse and Culture	Applied Discourse Analysis

We can recognize from these lists of chapters that discourse analysis covers a lot of territory, though it tends to focus on oral discourse (talk, conversation) and written discourse of all kinds, (including texts with visual components and computer-mediated texts).

❖ SPOKEN AND WRITTEN DISCOURSE

Deborah Cameron, a professor of language and communication at Oxford University, has written books on both approaches: *Working with Spoken Discourse* (2001) and, with Ivan Panović, *Working With Written Discourse* (2014). In the introduction to her book on written discourse, she explained that discourse analysis is of use to scholars in a variety of fields such as cultural studies, law, literature, philosophy, media studies, sociology, and social psychology. She added that she and her colleague wrote the book on written discourse because most discourse analysts, while they recognize the importance of written discourse, tend to focus their analyses on spoken discourse.

The authors added that many researchers in a variety of fields study the way people use language, but generally they do so to gain information about people's attitudes, beliefs, and behavior. They do this by having people fill out questionnaires; by interviewing people; and by making content analyses of what they watch on television or read or, lately, how people interact with researchers who use social media. Discourse analysis, on the other hand, focuses attention not only on the content of written material but on the style that writers use, the language they use to express themselves, and the strategies they adopt to get their ideas across. The focus, we may say, is on the "how" not the "what."

❖ STYLES AND WRITTEN DISCOURSE

Every word that writers use represents a choice they make and each word is used to create a deliberate impression. It is not too much of a stretch to say that writing is a form of impression management. As a writer, I know how difficult it can be to choose the right word—what the French call *le mot juste*. Many times, when I'm writing something, I think about what word I can use to express my ideas as clearly as possible and the way I want to express them. Each word choice generates a slightly different meaning. This applies, especially, to adjectives, adverbs, and verbs. For example, there is a big difference between describing people as "tight," "careful with their money," "thrifty," or "cheap." Descriptions play an important role in the way writers portray people and their behavior, and these descriptions play a role in the

way we react to conversations about other people (or ourselves), writings by scholars, portrayals of characters in novels, drawings of heroes and villains in comic books, and all kinds of other modes of communication that encompass spoken, written, and pictorial forms.

My discussion of language choice suggests a larger theme of styles of speaking and writing (and images and forms of pictorial representation), a topic of considerable importance to discourse analysis. A remarkable book, *Exercises in Style* by French writer Raymond Queneau (1947/1958), shows how a short passage about a young man with a long neck who is riding a bus in Paris can be written in more than 60 different styles. Here are some examples:

Biblical	Archaic language, *thees* and *thous* and *thys*
Bureaucratic	Formal and impersonal
Using Dialects	Phrases from French, German, Italian, and other languages
Discursive	Always going off on tangents
Intellectual	Jargon and a high level of abstraction
Poetic	Lyrical and metaphoric
Primer	Short sentence with few connectives
Paradoxical	Full of contradictions
Psychotic	Delusional, offers evidence of madness
Rap	Rhyming verse with a strong beat
Telegraphic	Skips words to get ideas across

Let me offer portions of two examples from Queneau's book.

Bureaucratic/Official Style

I beg to advise you of the following facts of which I happened to be the equally impartial and horrified witness. Today, at roughly twelve noon, I was present on the platform of a bus that was providing up the rue de Courcelles . . .

Dreamy

I had the impression that everything was misty and nacreous around me with multifarious and indistinct apparitions, among whom however was one figure that stood out fairly clearly which was of a young man whose too long neck . . .

We learn from Queneau that of the many styles we can use in our various oral and written communications, the style we adopt in many cases depends on to whom our communication is addressed: a dean at a university, a judge, a friend, a lover—we adopt different styles for each of these addressees.

In the conclusion to their chapter on "Discourse Styles" (found in van Dijk's *Discourse as Structure and Process*, Volume 1), Barbara Sandig and Margaret Selting wrote,

> Styles are socially interpreted and socially meaningful ways of using language variation as a resource in written and spoken interaction. It is language variation, typically in conventionalized co-occurring structures, which is interpreted in relation to speakers, text types, communication tasks, activity types, contexts, settings, etc. (1992, p. 153)

The styles we adopt, then, are shaped by our intended audiences, the kind of texts we are writing, the situations in which we find ourselves, and various other social factors that play a role in our interactions with others.

❖ POLITICAL IDEOLOGIES AND DISCOURSE ANALYSIS

Ideologies can be defined as systematic beliefs about politics held by members of some groups or members of political parties. If we look carefully, we can find ideologies in cultural texts that express values, biases, and belief systems. As Meenakshi Gigi Durham and Douglas M. Kellner wrote in *Media and Cultural Studies: Key Works*, quoted in Chapter 5, ideologies seem to be natural and the result of common sense. If people think something is natural, they believe it cannot be changed; it is only when they see political arrangements as social and cultural that they recognize that they can change things.

Generally speaking, when social scientists investigate ideologies, they focus their attention on the ideological content of texts. Discourse analysis, on the other hand, is concerned with the linguistic content of ideologies and how the ideologies are expressed. Teun A. van Dijk discussed this in his essay "A Linguistic Study of Ideology"):

> Ideologies are usually studied in the social sciences, and in linguistics. And yet, in his contribution, I would briefly like to make a case for a

linguistic approach to ideology. The most obvious argument for such an approach is the fact that ideologies often are expressed and reproduced by langue, that is, by language use or discourse. Communism, liberalism, feminism, racism or anti-racism are unthinkable as powerful ideologies, with their ideas being formulated and reformulated in the daily utterances of their leaders and followers.... It is this fundamentally discursive nature of the reproduction of ideologies that also takes a linguistic approach indispensable in a broad, multidisciplinary study of ideology (van Dijk, 1998). Although ideologies are not only expressed in and reproduced by language use, but also by other social practices (such as those of discrimination and exclusion), we may boldly claim that ideology is inconceivable without language. (2001, p. 26)

Van Dijk added that although some work has been done by discourse analysis scholars on language and ideology, it is a field that demands much more attention. In the 1970s, a new kind of discourse analysis developed for those who were not satisfied with the then dominant descriptive form of discourse analysis—critical discourse analysis.

❖ CRITICAL DISCOURSE ANALYSIS

Practitioners of this new form called it **critical discourse analysis** (CDA) and focused attention on the use of language by powerful groups in societies to dominate others and on the strategies of resistance by subjugated groups. Unfortunately, van Dijk added, much of the work by critical discourse analysis researchers was not very sophisticated. Even worse, he suggested, these researchers did not develop a theory about the ways in which ideological language functions and how ideological groups maintain their power. We must recognize that

A SHORT THEATRICAL PIECE ON DISCOURSE ANALYSIS

Grand Inquisitor: *I don't want people to analyze my discourse. Just listen to what I say and believe it. Don't analyze it. Don't think too much about it. And if someone's discourse is not to my liking, a bit of torture is helpful.*

(Continued)

(Continued)

Arthur:	But in order to understand discourse, you have to analyze it. Otherwise, you are just listening to words and don't know what they mean.
Grand Inquisitor:	*People have listened to words without knowing what they mean for thousands of years. My definition of faith is believing what I say without knowing what my words mean. That's why I liked Latin so much.*
Arthur:	It seems to me you believe in the power of sounds, not words.
Grand Inquisitor:	*What's a word? Air, a trim reckoning. I'll have none of it.*
Arthur:	I have a suggestion. Keep away from critical discourse analysts. They wouldn't understand you.
Grand Inquisitor:	*I keep away from anyone who is critical. It's a good policy for peace of mind. I just want to be loved!*

van Dijk was writing this critique in 2001. Since then, it is reasonable to suggest that critical discourse analysis has become more refined and has developed theories to use in analyzing discourse.

❖ ADVERTISING AND CRITICAL DISCOURSE ANALYSIS

Advertising is an industry that has attracted the attention of scholars in many fields, from communications, rhetoric, and marketing to political science, semiotics, psychoanalytic theory, and, of course, critical discourse analysis. During election years in the United States, enormous amounts of money are spent on political advertising by the Republican and Democratic parties and by individual and groups supporting a variety of ideological beliefs. Print advertisements often combine language and images (including different typefaces, each of which conveys a message), and television commercials have dialogue, actors, sound effects, and music, making them extremely complex texts for analysis.

There are considerable differences between the kind of analysis that a social linguist makes and the kind that a critical discourse analyst makes. Social linguists focus on *style*, structural patterns found in genres such as news stories or editorials. Critical discourse analysis includes these concerns but also considers how stories are framed, how readers are positioned relative to the texts they consume, and how the use of language leads readers to make certain interpretations of the text. (For more about this, see Cameron and Panović's discussion of the work of Colleen Cotter [2014].)

In *Written With Written Discourse,* Cameron and Panović (2014) offered a chapter on critical discourse analysis. It began,

> Critical discourse analysis (CDA) is an approach that highlights the social, ideological and political dimension of discourse. Its practitioners regard discourse in the same way as critical social theorists like Foucault . . . as something that does not just describe a pre-existing reality, but actively shapes our understand of reality. (p. 66)

Shortly after this passage, they moved on to a discussion of advertisements, which they argued are interesting not only for what they say about the products being advertised but what they say about consumers. It follows, then, that the goal of advertising and consumer capitalism is not only to sell products but to create consumers. Consumption becomes a form of self-expression, and our purchases, in the form of brands we favor, reflect our sense of ourselves.

When making a critical discourse analysis of an advertisement, Cameron and Panović (2014) suggested, we should do several things:

> If we are going to apply CDA to advertising texts, one question we might ask is how the linguistic choices made in these texts do the work of constructing and addressing the various categories or types of consumer identified by advertisers. A related "critical" question is to what extent these textual constructions depend on and recycle dominant ideologies, so that in identifying with the positions on offer, consumer are also "buying into" certain kinds of power and inequality. (p. 76)

Cameron and Panović offered us both insights into how advertising works and a guide to analyzing advertisements and commercials. We might say that they suggested we pay attention to the power of language and the language of power.

❖ MULTIMODAL DISCOURSE ANALYSIS

The home discipline for discourse analysis is linguistics. As I have pointed out earlier, discourse analysis represents an attempt by some linguists to move beyond the sentence and deal with not only talk but also written texts and, as imagery has become increasingly important, visual images. It has been estimated that visual images (including photographs, cartoons, and videos) make up more than 70% of Facebook. I have a page on Facebook, "Arthur Asa Berger and the Literary Life," and almost every time I post something on this page, on which I write about my literary activities, I also generally include a visual image: a cover of one of my books, a drawing I've made, a photograph I've taken, and so on.

Discourse analysts use the term **multimodal discourse analysis** to deal with the way discourse analysts work on texts with both written material and visual images in them. The basic methodology that multimodal discourse analysts use in working with images is semiotics, which I dealt with in Chapter 3 of this book. There is a debate in the field about how to analyze the different elements in a text with written material. Should each part of these texts be analyzed separately, or should discourse analysts find ways to integrate the different approaches, such as by using semiotics for the images and linguistic analysis for the language? I assume that generally speaking, there is a relationship between written material and visual images in a text and so deal with everything that I find without considering disciplinary boundaries.

❖ MULTIMODAL CRITICAL DISCOURSE ANALYSIS

Multimodal critical discourse analysis, as differentiated from multimodal discourse analysis, involves dealing with complex texts (such as those found on Facebook, in advertisements, and in various audio-visual-mediated texts) in a critical manner—that is, looking for what we might describe as their hidden ideological content. Critical discourse analysis suggests that ordinary discourse analysis tends to be descriptive and doesn't deal with ideological aspects of discourse. The ideology in texts is generally not recognized by people exposed to this discourse, even though this ideology often shapes their thinking. As David Machin and Andrea Mayr explained in *How to Do Critical Discourse Analysis* (2012),

> A linguist might, for example, be able to provide a thorough and revealing analysis of the language used in an advertisement. But much of the meaning in this advertisement might be communicated by visual features. The same would apply to a news text that was accompanied by a photograph or a textbook where an exercise was part linguistic and part visual. (p. 6)

It is because so much modern communication involves images—on Facebook, Pinterest, and other social media sites—that a multimodal approach is necessary. Here, everything from the typefaces used in texts, the facial expressions on models in advertisements and actors in commercials and television shows, the lighting, the use of color, and so on plays a role in generating meaning in texts. In Chapter 5, I quoted Yuri Lotman to the effect that everything in a text helps generate meaning. Discourse analysists would agree.

Machin and Mayr (2012) then added the critical component to multimodal discourse analysis by explaining its focus on power:

> The question of power has been at the core of the CDA project. Basically, power comes from privileged access to social resources such as education, knowledge and wealth, which provide authority, status and influence to those who gain this access and enables them to dominate, coerce and control subordinate groups. The aim in CDA has been to reveal what kinds of social relations of power are present in texts both explicitly and implicitly. . . . Since language can (re)produce social life, what kind of world is being created by texts and what kinds of inequalities and interests might this seek to perpetuate, generate or legitimate? Here language is not simply a vehicle of communication or persuasion, but a means of social construction and domination. (p. 24)

It is discourse, in all its forms and complexities, that helps give people a sense of what the world is like and how to make sense of it. The problem, Machin and Mayr argued, is that discourse is often used as a tool of domination by elites of one kind or another.

❖ A MULTIMODAL CRITICAL DISCOURSE ANALYSIS OF AN ADVERTISEMENT

With this discussion of discourse analysis, critical discourse analysis, and multimodal critical discourse analysis in mind, let me offer an example of multimodal critical discourse analysis that incorporates semiotics, ideological analysis, and rhetorical theory in an examination of a very interesting advertisement that first appeared in 2014.

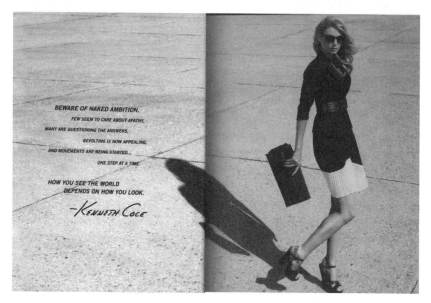

BEWARE OF NAKED AMBITION.
FEW SEEM TO CARE ABOUT APATHY,
MANY ARE QUESTIONING THE ANSWERS,
REVOLTING IS NOW APPEALING;
AND MOVEMENTS ARE BEING STARTED...
ONE STEP AT A TIME.

HOW YOU SEE THE WORLD
DEPENDS ON HOW YOU LOOK.

—Kenneth Cole

Kenneth Cole advertisement

We see a slender model, carrying a long handbag, who is walking on a concrete surface in what seems to be a plaza of some kind. The text is enigmatic and doesn't seem to be about fashion. Cole is known to support progressive causes, which may help explain something about this advertisement.

I have numbered each line of text in order to make it easier to follow my analysis.

1. Beware of naked ambition

The word *beware* serves as a warning, a kind of reverse encomium. The phrase is a curious one. We can understand being warned about being too ambitious, but why "naked ambition"? It could be an allusion to a 2009 film about the pornography industry or to a number of other works that use that phrase, which can be found with Google. Literally speaking, it suggests that people who are too obviously ambitious should be avoided. Ambition might be acceptable. It is only when it is "naked" that it is problematical. The term *naked* in fashion ads might generate fantasies in the minds of people who look at the advertisement and see the model, in their mind's eye, as naked.

2. Few seem to care about apathy

Here we have an example of a kind of definition, for "few seem to care" would itself be a good example of apathy. Apathy involves not caring about certain things, yet the model in the advertisement is walking briskly into the sun, casting a shadow that leads to the textual material in the advertisement. *Apathy* means, generally speaking, free of emotions and passions.

Apathy might also be construed to characterize the American voting public, in which small percentages of Americans vote except during presidential elections—and even then, we do not see large number of voters.

3. Many are questioning the answers

This relies on the same techniques as the phrase above, but it is slightly different. There is a bit of play between *questions* and *answers*, but in this case we have "many" who are engaged in this activity. This has ideological implications if the "answers" involve politics and society. We have an example of reversal here, with "many questioning" and "answers" opposed to one another. If large numbers of people are "questioning" the "answers," that is, the ideological suppositions they have held, then one can infer that society is not particularly stable.

4. Revolting is now appealing

Here we have another opposition, of *revolting* and *appealing*. The term *revolting* might be applied to something that is ugly and unappealing, but it also is ambiguous and can also be tied to political revolution, which is found to be appealing. It is the ambiguity that gives this phrase its power. *Revolting* can be construed several ways here. The ruling class may see the masses as revolting, and the masses may have adopted a strategy of revolting relative to the ruling classes in society.

5. And movements are being started

Literally speaking, we see a young woman, dressed in Kenneth Cole clothes, who is walking—or, perhaps, starting to walk. But the movement that is implied in the ad, given its ethos, is political—a movement, perhaps even some kind of revolution, that we must surmise will support Cole's progressive beliefs.

6. One step at a time

This statement also has a double meaning. On the overt level, it refers to the model who is taking a step across the concrete plaza in which she finds herself. But it also can refer to a political agenda and the notion that political and social movements grow gradually and must be nurtured, one step at a time, rather than enacted through revolution. This is an appeal for gradualism.

7. How you see the world depends on how you look

This phrase also contains a double message. Literally speaking, it says that the way we "see" or interpret the world is a function of the way we look at it, but in a fashion advertisement, it also references the model's "look," including her clothes, sunglasses, and handbag. She is very slender, and her hair seems to be blowing in the wind since it doesn't fall by her face. How we look, of course, is a function of the clothes we buy and the "look" we adopt by selecting various brands to shape our identities. I have suggested in an essay on brands, that our selves are now constructed to a considerable degree out of our brand choices (Berger, 2011).

8. Kenneth Cole

Cole's printed signature informs us that the statements in this advertisement are congruent with his perspective on politics and society and, he believes, are accurate. The signature is not written but printed, and in large letters. The *e*'s in *Kenneth* are different from the *e* in *Cole*. This would suggest an element of indecision on Cole's part about how to sign his name.

9. Kenneth Cole   Facebook   Twitter

This line (not shown) signifies that Cole is "hip" and has a presence on social media—in particular, Facebook and Twitter, two of the most important social media sites.

The graphic aspects of the advertisement are worth discussing. The advertisement is full of blank space and is extremely simple: The copy is on the left-hand side of a two-page spread, and the image of the model is on the right-hand side of the advertisement. Empty space in advertisements is a sign of "upscale" products. The wide spaces between the lines of the text also suggest "upscale."

The model's shadow leads our eyes to the copy, which is all in capital letters, with two phrases—BEWARE OF NAKED AMBITION and HOW YOU SEE THE WORLD DEPENDS ON HOW YOU LOOK in large capital letters. She is wearing sunglasses and is expressionless.

We must recognize that magazine advertising plays an important role in the construction of gender. From this advertisement, we see that it is important to be slender, to be pretty, to be guarded (she is wearing sunglasses to help her maintain distance from others), and to wear beautiful clothes—such as the kind manufactured by Kenneth Cole.

Unlike many fashion advertisements in women's magazines, this advertisement doesn't focus on the sexploitation of women's bodies, with revealing shots of their breasts, cleavage, or whatever, but it does have the model with a bent knee and a skirt that reveals her legs. Like women in many fashion advertisements, she is alone and the focus of attention as readers turn pages and glance, for a moment, at this advertisement and other advertisements like it.

The copywriter for this advertisement has cleverly used ambiguous and seemingly self-contradictory statements to play with readers. On the literal level, it is a somewhat confusing advertisement that concludes that the way we feel about the world depends on how we look at it (and look), but the copy also can be seen as a socially conscious appeal for joining in movements that are societally conscious—which means we look at the world not in terms of what we are wearing but our demands for social justice.

❖ DISCOURSE ANALYSIS: APPLICATIONS AND EXERCISES

1. Using the discussion of the Kenneth Cole advertisement as a model, make a critical discourse analysis of a print advertisement that has images and text you find intriguing.

2. Make a critical, multimodal analysis of a popular music video on YouTube. Discuss the language used in the song and the nature of the dancing. What problems did you face in making your analysis?

3. Write a narrative of three or four sentences and then rewrite it in six different styles. What did you learn from this exercise?

❖ CONCLUSIONS

Discourse analysis, with its focus on language, language use, and the role language plays in interactions among people, offers us a multi-disciplinary approach to research that combines other kinds of research into language, language use, and the texts in which language plays an important role. We always face, of course, the problem of what Umberto Eco calls "aberrant decoding," which means that people who look at advertisements don't always take away the messages in the text that the copywriter thought the ad would convey. That is because the codes of the copywriters and advertising people are different from the codes of the people who look at the advertisements. Nevertheless, in making us turn our attention to language and the way language has the power and capacity to shape our actions (in the case of advertising, buy what is advertised) and beliefs (in the case of politics, be persuaded by the arguments made by a group or political party), discourse analysis has taught us how to look more carefully at the role language (and in some cases images) plays in speech, conversation, and written texts.

❖ FURTHER READING

Cameron, D. (2001). *Working with spoken discourse.* London, UK: Sage.

Cameron, D., & Panović, I. (2014). *Working with written discourse.* London, UK: SAGE.

Machin, D., & Mayr, A. (2012). *How to do critical discourse analysis.* London, UK: SAGE.

Oukhvanova-Shmgova, I. F. (Ed.). (2001). *Perspectives and methods of political discourse and text research: Vol. 2.* Minsk: Belarusian State University Minsk Media Group.

Phillips, N., & Hardy, C. (2002). *Discourse analysis: Investigating processes of social construction.* Thousand Oaks, CA: SAGE.

van Dijk, T. (Ed.). (1997). *Discourse as structure and process.* London, UK: SAGE.

van Dijk, T. (Ed.). (1997). *Discourse as social interaction.* London, UK: SAGE.

Part III

Qualitative Research Methods

An investigator sits with pages of tape-recorded stories, snips away at the flow of talk to make it fit between the covers of a book, and tries to create sense and dramatic tension. There are decisions about form, ordering, style of presentation, and how the fragments of lives that have been given in interviews will be housed. The anticipated response to the work inevitably shapes what gets included and excluded. In the end, the analyst creates a metastory about what happened by telling what the interview narratives signify, editing and reshaping what was told, and turning it into a hybrid story—values, politics, and theoretical commitments enter once again. Although a kind of betrayal . . . it is also necessary and productive; no matter how talented the original storyteller was, a life story told in conversation certainly does not come ready-made as a book . . . an article, or a dissertation. The stop-and-start of oral stories of personal experience gets pasted together into something different.

—Catherine Kohler Riessman,
Narrative Analysis (1993, pp. 13–14)

8

Interviews

CHAPTER 8 FOCUS QUESTIONS

- What did the Prisoner want to know when he interviewed Number Two?
- What are the four kinds of research interviews?
- What problems do we face when using focus groups?
- What considerations should we keep in mind when interviewing people?
- What questions do investigative reporters typically ask?
- What is the typical structure of a conversation?
- What steps should be taken when coding interviews?
- What problems do researchers face with interview material?

❖ THE PRISONER INTERVIEWS NUMBER TWO

The Prisoner was an existential British spy/science fiction series broadcast from September 1967 to February 1968. It was a "cult" series, and some critics consider it one of the most important television series ever made. Most of the episodes start with the repetition of the opening sequences from the first episode. In this episode, Patrick McGoohan, the hero of the series, resigns from his job as a spy, drives to his apartment, and starts packing his suitcase. He is gassed and loses consciousness. When he awakens, he is in a mysterious place called the Village. He goes to the administrative center of the Village and confronts someone with a badge signifying he or she is Number Two. This leads to the following dialogue, which we can consider an interview by the Prisoner:

Prisoner: Where am I? (orientation request)

Number Two: In the Village. (answer)

Prisoner: What do you want? (information request)

Number Two: Information. (answer)

Prisoner: Which side are you on? (allegiance question)

Number Two: That would be telling. We want information, information, information . . . (answer)

Prisoner: You won't get it. (refusal to comply answer)

Number Two: By hook or by crook we will. (answer showing determination)

Prisoner: Who are you? (identity request)

Number Two: The new Number Two. (answer)

Prisoner: Who is Number One? (information question)

Number Two: You are . . . Number Six. (answer)

Prisoner: I am not a number! I am a free man. (identity affirmation)

Number Two: (Laughing hysterically) Ha, ha, ha, ha . . . (belittling reply)

In this interview, notice how the Prisoner takes on the role of researcher. He asks questions so he can gain information about what happened to him and follows up on replies by Number Two. Number Two is played by different actors throughout the series. The Prisoner wants to find out where he is, what Number Two wants from him, who Number Two is, which side Number Two is on, and who Number One is. Number Two wants information and will obtain it "by hook or by crook." Number Two is fixated on one question—why the Prisoner resigned. The Prisoner turns out to be a bad informant as far as Number Two is concerned—he won't reveal why he resigned—and it takes 17 episodes to resolve the conflict between the Prisoner and the various Number Two figures who run things in the Village under the control of Number One.

The Prisoner

❖ WHAT IS AN INTERVIEW?

Interviews are one of the most widely used and most fundamental research techniques—and for very good reason. They enable researchers to obtain information they cannot gain by observation alone. Perhaps the simplest way to describe an interview is as a conversation between a *researcher* (someone who wishes to gain information about a subject) and an *informant* (someone who presumably has information of interest on the subject).

We most commonly think of interviews as part of the process of obtaining a job, and most of us have, at one time or another, been interviewed for a job by one or more members of a company where we wanted to work. The goal of these interviews is similar to the goal of interviews conducted by all researchers—to obtain information. The term *interview* is related to the French term *entrevue*, which means "to see one another or meet." This points out an important element of interviewing—usually there is a face-to-face relationship. But not always. Some interviews are conducted by telephone or other electronic means, such as the Internet.

When conducting a face-to-face interview, be especially mindful of nonverbal communication between you and your informant. Facial expression plays an important role in interviews, and you must find a way to establish a friendly relationship—such as smiling when you meet your informant—and avoid nonverbal reflections of disapproval or any other kind of judgmental response. You must learn how to maintain eye contact to show interest and to manage and control the interview. In their book *Nonverbal Communication: Science and Applications* (2013), David Matsumoto and Hyi Sung Hwang discussed the role that facial expression plays in face-to-face interactions:

> The face is arguably the most prominent nonverbal channel, and for good reason. Of all the channels of nonverbal behavior, the face is the most intricate. It is the most complex signaling system in our body. . . .
>
> One of the most important signals the face displays is emotion. Being able to read the emotional states of the person you are talking to is an incredible skill that can help anyone whose profession requires face-to-face interaction. Being able to read others' emotion can give you insights not only to their emotional states but their intentions, motivations, personalities, trustworthiness, and credibility. Emotions can inform us of malicious intent, hidden information, or downright deception. (p. 15)

When interviewing people, we must be mindful of their emotional states and use our insights into facial expression to get a sense of how honest they are and whether there may be some "hidden information" to search for.

❖ FOUR KINDS OF RESEARCH INTERVIEWS

There are four kinds of interviews found in scholarly research.

> *Informal interviews.* There are few controls in these interviews; they just take place, are not organized or focused, and are generally used to introduce researchers to their informants. Informal interviews are, in essence, conversations to help the researcher gain the confidence of his or her informant. Interviewers hope that their informants will provide important information.

Unstructured interviews. In these interviews, the researcher is focused and is trying to gain information, but he or she exercises relatively little control over the responses of the informant.

Semistructured interviews. Here, the interviewer usually has a written list of questions to ask the informant but tries, to the extent possible, to maintain the casual quality found in unstructured interviews. **Focus groups,** which are widely used in market research, are considered semistructured interviews.

A NOTE ON PROBLEMS WITH FOCUS GROUPS

Focus groups are free-form discussions by a group of people, usually from 6 to 12 individuals, led by a moderator and designed to obtain information about some topic. Focus groups are commonly used by advertising agencies and other organizations to get an idea of how people feel about some product or service—or, during elections, some politician or campaign issue.

Gerald Zaltman, a professor at the Harvard Business School, discussed the weaknesses of focus groups in his book *How Customers Think: Essential Insights Into the Mind of the Market* (2003). He argued that focus groups are overrated and that one-on-one interviews are much more efficient and reliable. He wrote,

> Focus groups are easy and affordable to implement. Like every research method, focus groups do have a place in the research toolbox. For example, they can provide feedback on the attractiveness of an existing product design and ease of product use. Contrary to conventional wisdom, they are not effective when developing or evaluating new product ideas, testing ads, or evaluating brand images. Nor do they get at deeper thoughts and feelings among consumers. In fact, focus groups fail an important test for any method: Is the method based on well-founded insights from the biological and social sciences and the humanities? (p. 122)

Zaltman pointed out that if focus group leaders have 5 or 10 topics and eight people, the focus group leaders only can devote a couple of minutes to each topic with each person. Focus groups

(Continued)

(Continued)

also can be skewed by matters like social dominance (some people in the group doing most of the talking), some group members' eagerness to please, anxiety about privacy, and so on. The best way to get information, Zaltman argued, is to use one-on-one interviews, which get beyond superficial opinions and at the deeper meanings people hold, generally below their level of awareness, about things.

Structured interviews. Here the researcher uses an interview schedule—a specific set of instructions that guide those who ask respondents questions. For example, the instructions might tell what follow-up questions to ask if a question is answered in a certain way. Self-administered questionnaires are also classified as structured interviews. (Interviewing techniques are also an important element of survey research, a methodology discussed in Chapter 13.)

❖ WHY WE USE INTERVIEWS

As mentioned earlier, there are a number of ways of getting information about people: first, observing what they do; second, asking them about what they are doing; and third, analyzing texts and artifacts they produce, which is done when we make content analyses (discussed in Chapter 12). Unless we have the chance to observe people for a long period of time, we cannot know much about their past activities—their history. But we can discover this information by asking them about it.

We also can find out about people's ideas, thoughts, opinions, **attitudes,** and what motivates them by talking to them and asking the right questions. Let me suggest some basic differences between observation and interviewing in the following chart.

Observation	Interviewing
Present	Past and present
Actions	Attitudes
Context	Motivations
Seeing	Hearing and probing

In many cases, we use the two approaches together, but this is not always practical. Observation does give us a sense of context, which often helps explain what people do. But it doesn't help us get inside people to understand why they do things, what motivates them, and what problems and anxieties they have. One advantage of interviews is that one can generally record and transcribe them and thus have a written record that can be analyzed in detail. In some cases, it is possible to videotape interviews to capture visual information, but this is much more difficult.

This chapter focuses on unstructured interviews. Interviews, as suggested earlier, are widely used in research because they provide information that cannot be obtained any other way. You can observe people (for example, if you are doing participant observation research in a gymnasium or video game arcade or bar), but you can't know what the people you are observing are thinking or what they know from just observing them. In some respects, an interview (and remember, I will be talking about unstructured interviews when I use the term *interview* in this chapter) is like a psychoanalytic consultation. The interviewer is probing for information that the informant presumably has but may not be aware of or consider important.

❖ HOW TO INTERVIEW PEOPLE

There's an art to interviewing people, and it takes time for researchers to become good interviewers. Let me offer a list of some important considerations to keep in mind when interviewing people. At the beginning of the interview, you should obtain, if possible, the following information from your informants:

Surname and given name

Date and place of birth

Gender

Race

Religion

Ethnicity

Occupation

Information on siblings, family life, occupation of parents

Guarantee anonymity. Explain to your informants or respondents that what they tell you will be kept anonymous and that nobody (except you) will know who provided the information you obtain. Generally speaking, a distinction is made between *informants* (people you've gotten to know and will have a chance to interview a number of times) and *respondents* (people who will be interviewed only once).

Make sure you're accurate. You can record your interviews to ensure that you have complete information. If this is not possible, you'll have to jot down notes as you proceed with the interview. If it is not possible to take notes, write down what you remember immediately after the interview. Make certain you always obtain the following:

The date of the interview

Where it took place

Name of person interviewed

If you don't have a dedicated recording device, such as a digital recorder, find some other way to record the interview, such as with a video camera or smartphone. In any event, make sure your device is fully charged and that you have extra batteries if applicable. A memory card or flash drive will ensure you have enough space to store the recording file. Finally, make sure you know how the technology works before you try using it—read the instructions and practice with it ahead of time.

Avoid leading questions. Don't offer leading questions, which more or less push your respondent toward an answer. For example, let's imagine you are interviewing a student about a class she's taking, and she says her teacher is unfair. You can respond to this statement several ways:

Leading question: "Is that because your teacher favors men over women?"

Asking for definitions: "What do you mean by *unfair*?"

This suggests our next point.

Have your informants define terms. If your informants use terms you are unfamiliar with or that you think need some attention, ask them to define what they mean by the terms. Make them give their own definition of a term; don't ask them whether your understanding of a term is correct.

Stay focused. Once your informants have started talking, make sure your questions don't get off-track; focus on getting more details about what your informants are saying. In conversations, there is often a tendency to wander about on all kinds of side issues. You must resist this and stay on target.

Make sure your questions are clear. If you ask unclear questions, you'll get ambiguous and relatively useless answers. Your respondents may be trying to answer your questions as accurately as possible, but if they don't understand your questions or your questions are "fuzzy," informants won't be able to supply the information you are seeking.

Ask for amplifications and examples. When talking with your informants, keep in mind some ways of getting more details about the subject being discussed. Here are some useful responses to a statement by an informant about something that happened:

1. "And then what happened?"

2. "Who was involved?"

3. "When did it happen?"

4. "Why did it happen?"

5. "Where did it happen?"

6. "What was the result?"

7. "How do you feel about it?"

You can also ask informants for examples—anything to get more information and details, as long as it is related to the subject being investigated and does not lead you off on a tangent.

❖ QUESTIONS INVESTIGATIVE REPORTERS ASK

We can learn something from the questions investigative reporters, generally experts in conducting research, ask. Let's consider a situation in which an investigative reporter is asked to do a story about a trial in which the defendant is accused of running a Ponzi scheme and defrauding stockholders. Here are some questions the reporter might want to ask:

WHO: Who is involved in the case? Who has been accused of running the Ponzi scheme, and who are the victims? Who is the judge? Who are the suspect's lawyers? Who discovered what was going on?

WHAT: What is a Ponzi scheme? What are the facts about the case? What are law enforcement officials doing? What does the suspect's lawyer have to say?

WHEN: When did the accused start running the Ponzi scheme? When was it discovered?

WHERE: Where was the accused located? Where were the victims located?

WHY: If the alleged Ponzi schemer engaged in illegal activities, why did he or she do so?

HOW: How did the Ponzi scheme go on for as long as it did? How was the scheme eventually discovered?

These types of questions are at the heart of all inquiries researchers make. They require investigators to offer descriptions, explanations, narratives, and interpretations.

Sometimes, instead of just asking a general question such as "Where?" you can ask for more detail and say something like, "Could you tell me some places where that happened?" to obtain more information from the informant. "Where?" suggests one place while "some places where" asks for more information.

Prepare some questions before the interviews. Even though you don't use a prepared list of questions in unstructured interviews, you should do some thinking about your topic and do what you can to stay focused and avoid going off on tangents. Some researchers suggest that a research protocol be developed to guarantee uniformity and accuracy. A typical interview protocol contains material such as the following:

A title or heading for the interview

Instructions for the interviewer to follow

A list of key questions to be asked

Follow-up questions (or probes) once the key questions have been asked

Comments and notes by the interviewer relative to the interview

Be nonjudgmental. This is absolutely imperative. You should never suggest by the questions you ask, the tone of your voice, your facial expression, or your body language how you feel about the information you are given by your informant. If you show any signs of judgment, either positive or negative, they will have a profound impact on your informant and will color the information you are given.

Use "Uh-huh" and other phatic communications. In some cases, just saying "Uh-huh" or "I see" is sufficient to continue the interview. This phatic communication (*phatic* means speech made for social or emotional purposes rather than to communicate information) is a commonly recognized cue to the informant to keep talking. It is a form of acknowledgment that means, in effect, "I hear what you are saying . . . please continue."

Take notes about other matters. Take notes while conducting the interview about matters that strike your attention. For example, you might note whether the informant was nervous or relaxed, there were interruptions, there were distracting noises or music, and so on.

Be a good listener. Don't interrupt your informants or complete their sentences. Make sure your mind doesn't wander when you are listening and look for questions you can ask to obtain more information from your informant. Watch Charlie Rose on television and notice how he picks up on things his guests say and asks for more information or details.

❖ THE STRUCTURE OF CONVERSATIONS AND INTERVIEWS

Conversations (extremely informal interviews) and interviews (conversations with a defined purpose) share a common structure. This structure is shown as follows:

Q&A **Q&A** Q&A **Q&A** Q&A **Q&A** Q&A

That is, typically a conversation involves questions and answers and turn taking between those talking. (The turn taking is represented by the regular and boldface type in the example shown.) Conversations seldom take the form of simple declarative statements by themselves. Frequently, questions are used as transitional devices to keep a conversation going. In an ordinary conversation, the answers are usually considerably longer than the questions.

It might be useful to think of trial interrogations by district attorneys as a metaphor for interviewing, except that in interviewing, the questions are not asked with hostility—with the aim of convicting someone of something. But the goal is the same—to gain detailed information, to obtain "the truth, the whole truth, and nothing but the truth."

A SHORT THEATRICAL PIECE ON INTERVIEWS

Grand Inquisitor:	*Being a Grand Inquisitor is very hard! I seem to have lost my touch in recent years.*
Arthur:	What do you mean by "touch"?
Grand Inquisitor:	*I used to put people on the rack with a certain amount of flair. I wielded a wicked knout and was renowned for my skill in pouring hot lead down the throats of heretics.*
Arthur:	When did all this happen?
Grand Inquisitor:	*About a thousand years ago, give or take a few centuries.*
Arthur:	Why did the Inquisition occur?
Grand Inquisitor:	*We had so many heretics that we had to do something. The worst cases were the people who thought they were believers but were really unconscious heretics.*
Arthur:	Sounds vaguely Freudian. Fortunately, there's no more Inquisition and no torturing to speak of nowadays.
Grand Inquisitor:	*Ha! Ever hear of adolescents? And adolescence? Or freshman composition?*

One thing we learn from seeing films about trials and television coverage of trials (think of the O. J. Simpson trial or President Clinton's impeachment hearings) is that witnesses sometimes contradict themselves and sometimes lie and that different witnesses frequently offer different accounts of the same event. (The classic movie about different accounts of the same event is the Japanese masterpiece *Rashomon*.) But the fact remains that in interviewing informants and respondents—as in trials—every word is potentially important.

The reason the O. J. Simpson trial was so fascinating is that it became a narrative—a story with dramatic qualities, which means, according to Aristotle, a story with a beginning, a middle, and an end. Viewers and listeners kept asking themselves questions as the trial progressed: Who is telling the truth? Who is lying? What do the jurors believe? What will the verdict be?

Researchers who study how people construct conversations, such as W. Labov and J. Waletzky (cited in Riessman, 1993), have suggested that conversations or "personal narratives" about some event of significance have the properties found in the following table.

Symbol	Property	Function
A	An abstract	Summary of the narrative's content
O	Orientation	Time, place, situation, those involved
CA	Complicating action	Sequence of events
E	Evaluation	Significance and meaning of the action
R	Resolution	How things turned out
C	Coda	Returns the discussion to the present

Source: Adapted from Catherine Kohler Riessman, *Narrative Analysis*, 1993.

Labov and Waletzky suggested that when informants discuss things with interviewers, researchers can generally find one or more of these functions in a given segment of conversation. Interviewers must be especially mindful of judgments, criticisms, and evaluations made by the informants, for they point to important attitudes and beliefs. In principle, almost every interview segment can be classified as having a particular function and can be labeled by one of the symbols. This helps researchers interpret what was said by informants because it shows what the function of a particular statement was.

❖ TRANSCRIBING RECORDED INTERVIEWS

The recordings you've made of your interviews have to be transcribed. With audiotapes, this was done with a transcription machine, which cost a few hundred dollars. Today, most digital recorders have variable-speed playback functionality to help with transcription, and you can upload the audio file to your computer or the cloud for safekeeping. It may also be possible to use word recognition software to do transcriptions. (It is also possible to bring a laptop with voice recognition software and have the interview directly recorded and transcribed by the program, but that is risky, because the voice recognition program may misinterpret some words.) Some of these software programs claim 95% accuracy, and that may be enough to enable interviewers to avoid the time-consuming process of transcribing tapes.

Because it takes something like 7 or 8 hours to transcribe an hour of tape, using software programs may save you an enormous amount of time—if you can get them to work. But even with these programs, you'll have to go over the material and fix errors, so the process will consume a considerable amount of time whatever method you use. If you are worried about missing important material when recording directly to a voice recognition program, you can also use an audio recorder to record the interview at the same time.

❖ MAKING SENSE OF TRANSCRIBED INTERVIEWS

When you have the interviews transcribed and have checked them for accuracy, the next step is to make sense of it as best you can. One thing you must do is look for information that will be useful to you. What "facts" did you learn? What information about people, practices, ideas, beliefs, and so on did you get? (And how reliable is it?)

You also must classify and categorize the material in the transcripts. I have already suggested one way of classifying this material—using the functions in the Labov and Waletzky chart and determining whether a given passage functions as an abstract, an orientation, a sequence of action, an evaluation, or a resolution. But there are other procedures to consider. For example, we should see how our informant categorizes things. How are *old* and *young* and *good* and *bad* defined by the informant? What kinds of groups are mentioned? How does the respondent categorize people—by age, membership in a group, **gender,** occupation, status?

I sometimes ask students in my classes to talk about their high schools (this is, in effect, a group interview), and generally, I get lists of groups or subcultures found in their high schools: preppies, greasers, skaters, surfers, white punks on dope, jocks, cheerleaders, nerds, geeks, creeps, and so on. That is, when young people are asked about high schools, they often respond by categorizing their fellow students into various interest groupings. This offers an insight into how they think about their high school experiences.

The purpose of looking for classifications and categories in interviews with informants is to get a sense of how their minds work, how they make sense of the world. We assume that these usages are culturally conditioned, so finding out how informants think offers important clues about their culture, subculture, or group. This process of determining categories and classification systems is done by coding.

❖ CODING

When you have transcriptions of the interviews you've conducted, you have to find ways of making sense of the material. This is done, as suggested earlier, by looking for patterns, classifications, themes, and categories in this material. Researchers use coding to help identify common themes and topics that may emerge from the interview transcripts; these common themes will help researchers see what is important to informants and what is secondary.

There are no absolute rules about how coding is done; a great deal depends on the nature of the material being coded. The list that follows is a general guide to the process of coding drawn from John W. Creswell's *Research Design: Qualitative and Quantitative Approaches* (1994).

1. Read over the material as a whole and get an overview of it.

2. Pick one transcript and examine it carefully, looking for topics covered.

3. Do this for several transcripts and make a list of all the topics that were covered.

4. Make abbreviations for each topic and go through the transcripts, putting down the appropriate abbreviation beside each example of a given topic. If your topics list doesn't cover all the material, see if you can think up new topics that will help you do the job.

5. Turn your topics into categories. Make sure that the categories cover all your transcripts and don't duplicate one another.

6. Decide on a final set of abbreviations for your categories and alphabetize them. You now have an alphabetical list of codes in the transcripts.

7. Assemble all the material found under each category in one place and analyze it to see what you find.

8. See whether you can refine your coding and get fewer and more descriptive categories.

Creswell drew on the ideas of R. C. Bogdan and S. K. Biklen (1992, pp. 167–172), who suggested using abstract coding categories as topics. They proposed that researchers look for the following kinds of codes:

Setting and context codes

Perspectives held by subjects

Subjects' ways of thinking about people and objects

Process codes

Activity codes

Strategy codes

Relationship and social structure codes

Preassigned coding schemes

There are also software programs that help researchers find ways of coding their transcripts and catch coding errors.

A number of years ago, I did some research on humor. I was looking specifically for techniques that humorists used in creating humor. I examined a wide range of materials, including joke books, folklore books, comic books, books on humor, humorous plays, humorous short stories, and comic novels. From this research, I elicited 45 techniques that, I believe, are the building blocks of all humor and are used, in various permutations and combinations, by all humorists. When I got my list, I started examining it and discovered that each of the techniques fit into one of four mutually exclusive categories—humor of logic, humor of identity, linguistic humor, and visual or action humor (see Table 8.1).

Any example of humor contains, my argument goes, one or more of these techniques. It took a considerable amount of thinking and speculation before I became aware of the categories "hidden" in the 45 techniques. My point is that finding categories is not always an easy task.

Table 8.1   Techniques of Humor According to Category

Language	Logic	Identity	Action
Allusion	Absurdity	Before/after	Chase
Bombast	Accident	Burlesque	Slapstick
Definition	Analogy	Caricature	Speed
Exaggeration	Catalogue	Eccentricity	
Facetiousness	Coincidence	Embarrassment	
Infantilism	Comparison	Exposure	
Insults	Disappointment	Grotesque	
Irony	Ignorance	Imitation	
Misunderstanding	Mistakes	Impersonation	
Overliteralness	Repetition	Mimicry	
Puns/wordplay	Reversal	Parody	
Repartee	Rigidity	Scale	
Ridicule	Theme and variation	Stereotype	
Sarcasm	Unmasking		
Satire	Variation		

❖ PROBLEMS WITH INTERVIEW MATERIAL

One debate is whether interviewers are looking for data, information, and facts or whether the way informants speak and organize their information that is most important. That is, should researchers focus on what people are doing and have done or on the way they express themselves about what they've done and are doing? Which is most important and yields the most interesting information: *what* informants say or *how* they say it?

There is a link between the two, or maybe it is best to suggest that the two are connected (two sides of a coin) because the analysis of expression is also the analysis of thought and thinking. It is useful to keep in mind what E. W. Said (1978) wrote in *Orientalism*,

> [The] real issue is whether indeed there can be a true representation of anything, or whether any and all representations, because they are representations, are embedded first in the language and then in the culture, institutions, and political ambiance of the representator. If the latter alternative is the correct one (as I believe it is), then we must be prepared to accept the fact that a representation is *eo ipso* implicated, embedded, interwoven with a great many other things besides the "truth," which is itself a representation. (pp. 272–273)

Said's point was that we must consider the extent to which a culture shapes the way people talk and give information (that is, give a "representation"), so we must always be cautious about accepting what people tell us as the truth. Is the information respondents give *the* truth or *their* truths?

Just because a person agrees to be an informant and tell you something about some group or entity doesn't mean that you'll be getting "the truth, the whole truth, and nothing but the truth." Let me suggest some of the problems researchers face in dealing with informants and respondents (which apply to all other forms of research, such as focus groups, questionnaires, and surveys).

1. *People don't always tell the truth.* People want to put their best foot forward—they want to appear nobler and better than they actually are— so they often lie or distort things. Sometimes they actually have convinced themselves that their accounts are not lies but are the truth.

2. *People don't always remember things accurately.* Even if people want to tell the truth, sometimes their memory lets them down, and without recognizing what they are doing, they fabricate the truth—that is, they make up things.

3. *People don't always have useful information.* They may think they do and may feel important because they are being interviewed, but in reality, they have little to say of interest.

4. *People sometimes tell you what they think you want to hear.* In some cases, informants tailor their responses to questions to their perceptions of what will best satisfy the interviewer. They do

this because they like you and want to give you helpful material, they are bored and want to get through the interview as soon as they can, or they want to impress you.

5. *People use language in different ways.* The problem is one of communicating and interpreting meaning. The intended meaning may not be the communicated or articulated meaning, and, most important, the meaning received or gained by the interviewer may be different from the meaning intended by the interviewee. Thus, it is important to be an efficient and active listener who seeks clarifications and uses feedback techniques to ascertain that the meaning received is the meaning intended.

When possible, ask several informants about the same thing to see whether there's any consistency. You can also see, sometimes, whether there's a difference between what people say and what they do. You want to get accounts from your informants and respondents that are true, reliable, and complete. You must remember that your respondent's point of view is not a reliable explanation of behavior. Some of the reasons for this have already been given and are due to the way we represent ourselves to others and to the illusions we all have about ourselves. People tend to justify their actions to themselves and others, so you have to be careful about accepting anyone's point of view as being accurate, correct, and unbiased.

The material gained in interviews can be understood in terms of the figure/ground metaphor. An informant's interview should be seen as a figure against a ground of everything from the interview itself to some event in or aspect of the culture or subculture the informant is providing information about. The background has an effect on the figure; context makes a great deal of difference.

❖ INTERVIEWS: APPLICATIONS AND EXERCISES

1. An alien arrives from Mars in a spaceship. You are a reporter for a major television news show. Prepare a list of key interview questions to ask the Martian and a list of follow-up questions. Explain your rationale for asking each question. What problems did you face in making your list of interview questions? How do your questions solve these problems? You can practice interviewing this Martian with someone in your class to get a sense of the difficulties one faces in conducting an interview.

2. The president of the United States grants you an interview but says you can only ask 10 questions. What questions would you ask him or her? How did you decide on your questions? Compare your list of questions with those asked by other members of your class. Are there any questions that everyone asked? Any surprising questions? Any important questions that should have been asked?

3. Tape a television interview and analyze the questions the interviewer asked, questions that should have been asked, and other topics dealt with in this chapter. Observe things such as facial expressions, body language, the tone of the interview, and the relationship between the interviewer and person being interviewed.

❖ CONCLUSIONS

Interviews are one of the most fundamental techniques researchers use to get information. But interviews are difficult to do and involve a great deal of work (recording them, transcribing them, coding them), and the information gained is always suspect. So one must proceed with caution when generalizing from interviews, but they are unique in allowing researchers to get inside the minds of people and to gain access to material of considerable importance. Like many high-risk activities, they also offer high gains.

❖ FURTHER READING

Atkinson, R. G. (1998). *The life story interview.* Thousand Oaks, CA: SAGE.

Fetterman, D. M. (2010). *Ethnography: Step-by-step* (3rd ed.). Thousand Oaks, CA: SAGE.

Flick, U. (2009). *Introducing research methodology: A beginner's guide to doing a research project.* Thousand Oaks, CA: SAGE.

Gilham, B. (2005). *Research interviewing: The range of techniques.* London, UK: Open University Press.

Kvale, S. (2009). *Interviews: An introduction to qualitative research interviewing* (2nd ed.). Thousand Oaks, CA: SAGE.

Kvale, S., & Brinkman, S. (2009). *InterViews: Learning the craft of qualitative research interviewing* (2nd ed.). Thousand Oaks, CA: SAGE.

Laver, J., & Hutcheson, S. (1972). *Communication in face to face interaction: Selected readings.* Baltimore, MD: Penguin.

Matsumoto, D., Frank, M. G., & Hwang, H. S. (Eds.). (2013). *Nonverbal communication: Science and applications.* Thousand Oaks, CA: SAGE.

Psathas, G. (1994). *Conversation analysis: The study of talk-in-interaction.* Thousand Oaks, CA: SAGE.

Rubin, H. J., & Rubin, I. S. (2012). *Qualitative interviewing: The art of hearing data* (3rd ed.). Thousand Oaks, CA: SAGE.

Rubin, R. B., Palmgreen, P., & Sypher, H. E. (2009). *Communication research methods: A sourcebook.* New York, NY: Routledge.

Seidman, I. (2006). *Interviewing as qualitative research: A guide for researchers in education and the social sciences* (3rd ed.). New York, NY: Teachers College Press.

Stewart, C. I., & Cash, W. B. (2013). *Interviewing: Principles and practices* (14th ed.). New York, NY: McGraw-Hill.

Wengraf, T. (2001). *Qualitative research interviewing: Semistructured, biographical, and narrative methods.* London, UK: SAGE.

Zaltman, G. (2003). *How customers think: Essential insights into the mind of the market.* Cambridge, MA: Harvard University Business School Press.

The coexistence of the upper and lower levels forces upon the historian an illuminating dialectic. How can one understand the towns without understanding the countryside, money without barter, the varieties of poverty without the varieties of luxury, the white bread of the rich without the black bread of the poor?

It remains for me to justify one last choice: that of introducing everyday life, no more no less, into the domain of history. Was this useful? Or necessary? Everyday life consists of the little things one hardly notices in time and space. The more we reduce our vision, the more likely we are to find ourselves in the environment of material life: the broad sweep usually corresponds to History with a capital letter, to distant trade routes, and the networks of national or urban economies. If we reduce the length of time observed, we either have the event or the everyday happening. The event is, or is taken to be, unique; the everyday happening is repeated, and the more often it is repeated, the more likely it is to become a generality or rather a structure. It pervades society at all levels, and characterizes ways of being and behaving which are perpetuated through endless ages. . . . Through little details, travellers' notes, a society stands revealed. The ways people eat, dress, or lodge, at the different levels of that society, are never a matter of indifference. And these snapshots can also point out contrasts and disparities between one society and another which are not all superficial.

—Fernand Braudel, *The Structures of Everyday Life:
Civilization and Capitalism, 15th–18th Century* (1981, p. 29)

9

Historical Analysis

CHAPTER 9 FOCUS QUESTIONS

- What is history? What important points were made in the quotes on history by Berkhofer and Stearns?
- Is history objective, subjective, or a combination of the two?
- What are the different kinds of historical research?
- What was said about the use of primary and secondary sources in writing history?
- How does postmodernism relate to the study of history?
- What questions were raised for those doing historical research to consider?
- What is history, and what should historians do? Who should write what? Who can do research and write historical studies with authority?

❖ WHAT IS HISTORY?

This is not an easy question to answer, but let me deal with some of the more common understandings of the term. First, when we think of history, we think of studies of the past, and in that respect, history is about the past. That means we have to rely on documents and other materials. If we are dealing with the recent past, we can interview people and get firsthand information that way. If we are dealing with the distant past, we have to confine ourselves to the materials that historians typically use to make sense of the past: books, articles, records of one sort or another, works of art, objects, and whatever else can be used to gain information.

A problem arises here. From the immense amount of material available to historians, they have to select relevant and important sources. How do they do this? The answer is that historians always have some concept or **theory** that guides them. As Robert F. Berkhofer Jr. (1969) explained in his book *A Behavioral Approach to Historical Analysis,*

> Historians do not recapture or reconstruct the past when they analyze history; they interpret it according to surviving evidence and conceptual frameworks. All of past reality can never be known to them because not all evidence remains. Furthermore, historians do not choose to deal even with all the facts derivable from the available evidence. They confine their interest to man's past, but not even all of that concerns them, for they further select from these data those parts that can be organized according to some interpretation or theory. Thus an historical synthesis is a highly selective account of a postulated past reality. Theory in the most general sense is crucial to every phase of historiography. (p. 23)

That is, all historians have some theory or conceptual framework that guides them and helps them select materials to use in writing history.

Berkhofer (1969) then explained that because views of and theories about people and society keep changing, historical interpretations of any given subject also keep changing:

> It should now be evident why history must be and is rewritten constantly in terms of the historians' own times. Every step of producing history presumes theoretical models of man and society, which in turn seem to change in terms of the shifting conceptions of man and society occurring in the historian's own society. (p. 24)

For example, were Berkhofer writing today, he quite likely would have added the words *and women's* to his sentence "They confine their interest to man's past," and ended up with the following sentence: "They confine their interest to men *and women's* past." And that is because of the influence of feminist thought on contemporary historians and other scholars. Other factors are historians' training and background.

Peter N. Stearns (1998) discussed what historians do and the skills they develop. He suggested that historians need to have the following:

The ability to assess evidence. The study of history builds experience in assessing evidence—the sort of evidence historians use in shaping the most accurate pictures of the past. . . . Learning how to combine different kinds of evidence—public statements, private records, numerical data, visual materials—develops the ability to make coherent arguments.

The ability to assess conflicting interpretations. Learning history means gaining some skill in sorting through diverse, often conflicting interpretations. Understanding how societies work—the central goal of historical study—is inherently imprecise, and the same certainly holds true for understanding what is going on in the present day. Learning how to identify and evaluate conflicting interpretations is an essential citizenship skill for which history, as an often-contested laboratory of human experience, provides training.

Experience in assessing past examples of change. Experience in assessing past examples of change is vital to understanding change in society today—it's an essential skill in what we are regularly told is our "ever-changing world." Analysis of change means developing some capacity for determining the magnitude and significance of change, for some changes are more fundamental than others. Comparing particular changes to relevant examples from the past helps students of history develop this capacity. The ability to identify the continuities that always accompany even the most dramatic changes also comes from studying history, as does the skill to determine probable causes of change. ("What Skills Does a Student of History Develop?")

A SHORT THEATRICAL PIECE ON HISTORICAL ANALYSIS

Grand Inquisitor: *Things are going to hell. I've not tortured anyone or put anyone on the rack for a thousand years! I particularly liked burning witches!*

Arthur: You miss the good old days, eh?

(Continued)

(Continued)

Grand Inquisitor:	*We did wonderful research during the Inquisition. We discovered a lot of people who didn't recognize that they were heretics. Research is so important.*
Arthur:	With you and your colleagues one could say, "Heretic today, gone tomorrow!"
Grand Inquisitor:	*Are you mocking me? Dostoevsky never treated me like this. In* The Brothers Karamazov *I had, at least, a certain amount of gravitas.*
Arthur:	A thousand pardons to someone who I imagine gave none. But you were doing your work, you must keep in mind, before Newton discovered the law of gravitas.

❖ HISTORY AS METADISCIPLINE OR SPECIALIZED SUBJECT

Can historians study anything they want? Is history, like rhetoric, an overarching metadiscipline that studies the past and change over time and is applicable to all subjects? Or is history tied to specific subjects? If the latter is the case, it would mean the history of philosophy should be written by philosophers, the history of science should be written by scientists, the history of **political theory** should be written by political theorists, and so on.

A different way to put this dilemma is to ask the following question about training historians: Do we teach students who wish to be historians a certain methodology and let them specialize in whatever they wish, or do we take specialists and teach them historical methods? This is a problem because our understanding of what history is has changed over the years, and history now is much broader than the way it once was defined, as "the study of past politics." The corollary to that definition was the definition of politics as "present-day history."

Metadiscipline	Specialized Discipline
Trained in history	Trained in a subject area
Can deal with all areas	Deals only with own subject
May lack knowledge	May lack technique

You can see from this chart that there are problems with both approaches. In many cases, we now find people with areas of specialized knowledge who study history and apply what they learn in their particular areas, merging the two oppositions, so to speak.

❖ IS HISTORY OBJECTIVE, SUBJECTIVE, OR A COMBINATION OF THE TWO?

Many people think that history is objective, based only on facts. This perspective suggests that historians tell us what happened in the past and how things changed over time. It's as simple as that: a fact-based chronology.

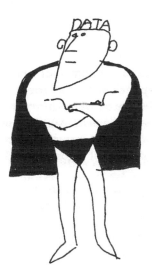

Now it is true, no doubt, that historians base their writings on facts or on what they think are facts. After all, historians are not supposed to be writing fiction. But even if all historians were to write their histories based only on factual material, it is obvious that they cannot include all the facts involved. They have to select those facts—those events—they consider to be most significant and most revealing from all the material they have.

Thus, there is an element of interpretation involved in history based on the selection process. That explains why historians often differ with one another when they write about the same topic. In the passage quoted earlier, Berkhofer (1969) mentioned that historians change their interpretations over the years, as new concepts and theories are developed. The work of French historian Fernand Braudel, quoted at the beginning of this chapter, played an important role in suggesting that historians consider the importance of everyday life or ordinary men and women in writing history (more about his theories shortly).

At any given moment, different kinds of historians, with different theories, methodologies, and beliefs about what is important and what is unimportant, clash over how to write about a given subject. Marxist historians focus their attention on topics such as the economic system, the class system, imperialism, the control of the media by the ruling class, alienation, and other concepts derived from Marx and similarly inclined thinkers. Psychoanalytically inclined historians, who write psychohistories of important figures, are concerned with the families of their subjects, their personalities, and similar topics. Nixon, for example, was the subject of any number of psychohistories that attempted to explain his career in terms of his psychological makeup and problems.

Historians used to focus their attention mostly on important military and political figures and pay little attention to "ordinary people," to everyday life, to cultural matters and artistic works and other seemingly unimportant matters. Now, in recent years, with the development of the Annales school of history, championed by historians such as Fernand Braudel, many historians are also looking at things like the growth of certain crops by farmers, the consumption of bread, and similar topics. These topics, which seem mundane and trivial, provide valuable information about the past and may explain more about what caused things to happen, such as great migrations of people, than events in the lives of kings and queens and the decisions made by parliaments.

❖ KINDS OF HISTORICAL RESEARCH

G. Phifer (1961) in his article "The Historical Approach" (in *An Introduction to Graduate Study in Speech and Theatre*, edited by C. W. Dow), suggested seven types of historical studies. They are listed here in slightly modified form:

1. *Biographical studies,* focusing on the lives and psyches of important persons

2. *Movement or idea studies,* tracing the development of political, social, or economic ideas and movements

3. *Regional studies,* focusing on particular cities, states, nations, and regions

4. *Institutional studies,* concentrating on specific organizations

5. *Case histories,* focusing on social settings of a single event

6. *Selected studies,* identifying and paying close attention to a special element in some complex process

7. *Editorial studies,* dealing with the translating or processing of documents

There are also different kinds of historians. Thus, intellectual historians are basically interested in how ideas have affected history and focus their attention on the concepts and theories of important thinkers, writers, artists, and political figures and the way the beliefs of these persons have affected ordinary people. Biographical historians focus on the lives of important figures. For example, many historians have written about FBI director J. Edgar Hoover, an enigmatic and psychologically complicated figure. Quantitative historians, on the other hand, use statistics and other numerical data to make their arguments.

Consider an analogy with medicine. We find (especially as we grow older) many kinds of medical specialists who sometimes disagree about what a symptom means and how best to treat a medical problem. Often even specialists of the same kind (for example, neurologists or urologists) disagree about how a specific medical problem should be dealt with. That is why in medicine the rule is to "get a second opinion." In history, if you don't like a particular interpretation, the rule is to "get a second historian." I might add that researchers in all fields disagree about many things; as I've pointed out elsewhere, even economists with the same statistical data often disagree about how to interpret them.

❖ THE PROBLEM OF WRITING HISTORY

We find another complicating factor to the historical approach, and that is connected with the way historians write. Generally speaking, they take the material they have gathered—from primary sources such as newspaper articles; records from diaries and journals; and data from governmental agencies and from secondary sources such as statements by persons of consequence; material from scholarly books and articles; autobiographies and biographies; and ideas from philosophers, artists, and others—and weave a narrative (that is, tell a story).

Primary Sources	Secondary Sources
Newspaper articles	Articles by other historians
Records from diaries	Articles and books by scholars
Data from agencies	Ideas from philosophers and other thinkers
Speeches	Editorials
Interviews	Commentaries
Autobiographies	Biographies
Videos about oneself	Popular culture and mass media

Now, all of this material historians use must be considered suspect—including data, because researchers often make mistakes in gathering them. People have biases or lie about things when answering questionnaires. Newspaper articles are sometimes full of errors, and so are books and articles from the scholarly and general press. People who write autobiographies tend to focus on the positive aspects of their careers and downplay the negative ones. Wherever one looks, there are problems in finding and interpreting historical data.

The need historians have to tell stories, to write narratives, also poses problems, for the narrative form imposes some limits on writers. Historians want their books to be interesting, coherent, and stylishly written, as well as factually correct. Historians also want to give their books an element of drama and suspense. So putting materials into a narrative may lead to simplifications, exaggerations, or other deviations from reality. Historians writing narratives do not recognize, I would suggest, the degree to which the requirements of historical writing shape their perceptions. If they are legitimate historians, who are trying to be fair and objective, they do not consciously distort things. Of course, some historians are so ideological that they twist the story around to make history fit their ideological preconceptions.

Nor do historians recognize that they often are reductionist— taking complicated matters and simplifying them excessively. A common tendency in research is to use overly strict limitations on the kinds of concepts and variables to be considered as causes in explaining behaviors or processes. Reductionism tends to suggest that certain elements used in the analysis may be more relevant than others, based on the researcher's preconceptions and scientific orientation.

❖ THE PROBLEM OF MEANING

Historians have to find patterns to make human behavior meaningful. A random collection of facts about some topic doesn't tell us anything. Neither does a simple chronology. The question is whether historians impose a pattern on the material they are dealing with (because of their theories about how to interpret historical data and other material) or whether they elicit from this material—or, to be more precise, discover in this material—a pattern. Are historians ingenious thinkers who impose their conceptual theories on past events to explain what happened, or are they gifted analysts who find in past events the pattern that helps explain them?

This question is analogous to the debate over structuralist critics who interpret literary works, films, television shows, videos, and other kinds of texts. There are two views about what structuralists do. One says it is all "hocus-pocus," and the structuralist critic imposes on the text some ingenious structure of his or her own making. The other says it is "God's truth," and structuralist critics are astute at finding structures hidden in these works. These differences are shown in the chart that follows, which is applied to history.

God's Truth	Hocus-pocus
Discover what's in text	Impose structures on texts
Elicit patterns from history	Impose patterns on history
Theory helps discover pattern	Theory creates patterns

History helps us find meaning in the events of the past, and to do this, historians have to find patterns to help organize the data they work with. Whether the patterns historians write about are discovered or imposed is always something to keep in mind when we read works by historians. Another way of stating the problem is to point out that facts don't speak for themselves. Someone has to interpret the facts and put them into perspective. This process of establishing perspective requires some theory that explains how society works.

❖ HISTORICAL PERIODS

Dividing the past into periods is another method historians use to make sense of things. Thus, history departments have courses on ancient history, medieval history, modern history, contemporary history, and so on. In addition to these very broad categories, historians often use much narrower ones, such as centuries or, in the case of US history, decades. They make distinctions among American culture, political thought, and social practices in different decades, such as the Gay Nineties or the Roaring Twenties, as the following chart shows:

Decade	Typical Characterization
1920s	Era of the robber barons
1930s	The Depression years
1940s	World War II and postwar period
1950s	Eisenhower stability
1960s	Post-Vietnam: Flower children and hippies
1970s	The Quiet Decade
1980s	Reagan years, Me Decade
1990s	Generation Xers
2000s	Generation Z: Internet generation
2010s	Aught generation?

Each of these decades is different from the others, some historians argue, and each can be characterized by dominant ideas, social practices, economic conditions, art styles, fashions, and so on.

These ideas have filtered into society, in general, and now newspapers often write about social trends, such as "returning to the '50s" or the impact of the 1960s on contemporary American culture. Of course, historians often disagree about how to characterize the decades, but I've offered some generally held descriptions of each. It is also worth noting that these decades didn't necessarily all start on January 1 and end on December 31 of the decade; often, there was considerable overlap.

It is natural to use our knowledge of the past to try to understand the present because we believe the past has influenced the present. That is one of the things history teaches us. How the past has influenced the present and what impact the past may have on the future is a different matter. To the extent that future developments in social thought shape the consciousness of historians, we can also argue that the future influences the past as we learn to interpret and understand it.

Fredric Jameson, an important theorist of postmodernism

❖ BAUDRILLARD AND JAMESON ON POSTMODERNISM

Postmodernism is based on the notion of periods as well—the term *postmodernism* suggests "after" **modernism** and "different from" modernism. This topic is discussed in the glossary, but it is useful to say something about postmodernism and media here. There are many definitions and understandings of postmodernism, but most postmodern theorists suggest that it is connected to the rise of mass media and what Jean Baudrillard, a prominent French theorist of the subject, described as simulations and "hyperreality." For Baudrillard, media and simulated models have replaced manufacturing as the basic way of organizing societies.

As Steven Best and Douglas Kellner explained in *Postmodern Theory: Critical Interrogations* (1991),

> For Baudrillard the models of the United States in Disneyland are more real than their instantiations in the social world, as the USA becomes more and more like Disneyland. . . . The hyperreal for Baudrillard is a condition whereby models replace the real, as exemplified in such phenomena as the ideal home in women's or lifestyle magazines, ideal sex as portrayed in sex manuals. (p. 119)

Fredric Jameson, another important theorist of postmodernism, dealt with the impact of postmodernism on media and culture in *Postmodernism, or, The Cultural Logic of Late Capitalism* (1991). He discussed some characteristics of postmodern culture:

> this whole "degraded" landscape of schlock and kitsch, of TV series and *Reader's Digest* culture, of advertising and motels, of the late show

and grade-B Hollywood film, of so-called paraliterature, with its air-
port paperback categories of the gothic and the romance, the popular
biography, the murder mystery, and even the science fiction or fantasy
novel. (pp. 2–3)

Jameson argued that postmodernism is just a name for a new form
of capitalism and is connected, in direct ways, to the development of
consumer cultures.

❖ POSTMODERNISM AND HISTORIOGRAPHY

Postmodernist thought is relevant to our interest in the way history is
written. For some postmodernists, history has come to an end since we
no longer accept the "metadisciplines" that history needs to make sense.
In Ingeborg Hoesterey's *Zeitgeist in Babel: The Postmodernist Controversy*
(1991), a chapter by Gianni Vattimo titled "The End of (Hi)story" deals
with this matter. Discussing postmodernist theory, Vattimo explained,

> If this notion has a meaning at all, it has to be described in terms of
> the end of history. What is finished is not simply a certain view (or a
> set of views) of history but history itself. If the *metarécits* [metadisci-
> plines] that made it possible for us to think about history as a unitary
> course have been confuted, as Lyotard assumes, history itself has
> become impossible. To imagine that history, as a course of events,
> keeps going on no matter what we feel about the *metarécits* we used
> to believe in would amount to assuming that the specific *metarécit* that
> conceives of history as an objective course of events has not been dis-
> solved; or, in other words, that the course of history as a unitary and
> continuous course of events, is not "simply" a *metarécit* but the true
> description of the very reality of history. Now, this is exactly what the
> *metarécit* used to claim and exactly what postmodern consciousness
> does not believe anymore. This, by the way, is not only an extravagant
> idea of postmodernist theorists like Lyotard; recent theory of histori-
> ography (e.g., the "metahistorical" research of H. White) has clearly
> pointed out the "rhetorical" character of the schemes by means of
> which we reconstruct the past. (p. 134)

What Vattimo is doing is showing how postmodernism (keeping in
mind Lyotard's description of it as involving "incredulity toward metanarratives") logically implies that historical writing, which is based on
the metanarrative that history is a study of order and continuity, no
longer makes sense. Life goes on, but the notion that history tells us

what happened in an objective manner cannot be supported. We have to look upon history's claim to validity in a different manner now.

❖ THE HISTORICAL AND THE COMPARATIVE APPROACH

I'm making a somewhat simplified argument here to clarify the differences between historical and comparative research methods. In reality, the two are not necessarily antithetical. History, for our purposes, deals with the past and with changes over time. Comparative analysis, on the other hand, deals with changes over space—with the difference, say, between the US Constitution and the constitution of some other country, such as the Japanese constitution, or between the American Revolution and the French Revolution. A historical approach to Disneyland would deal with its evolution over the years, and a comparative approach would deal with Disneyland in the United States and in France or Japan (or both).

Let me suggest the differences between these two approaches in the following chart:

Historical Research	Comparative Research
Change over time	Differences over space
Before and after	Here and there
Early articles on Disneyland and later ones	Articles on Disneyland in the United States, France, and Japan

Because, as Saussure argued, we make sense of concepts differentially, we can choose either the time axis or the space axis for our research. But there is nothing to prevent historians from doing both—looking at changes over time and differences in space—when they do their research. Fernand Braudel, the great French historian whom I quoted at the beginning of the chapter, uses both a historical and a comparative approach, which greatly enriches his book.

❖ HISTORY IS AN ART, NOT A SCIENCE

Many scholars regard history as an art, not a science. At first, history was written by amateurs—that is, people not trained in universities to be historians but involved, in some cases, in events of consequence or interested in writing about these events. History is now much more professionalized, and most historians are based at universities where they do their research and teach history courses and, in some cases, historiography—the art of being a historian. Some historians now use quantitative methods and adapt scientific approaches to their research; they see history as a social science, not as an area in the humanities or as an art. There is, therefore, considerable disagreement among historians about how they should do historical research and write history.

❖ DOING HISTORICAL RESEARCH

So what does this mean for you? If you keep in mind the following questions, they will guide you as you proceed with your research.

Can you narrow your focus? Have you narrowed your topic of research so you can deal with it in the amount of time at your disposal and the length of paper that is required of you? That is, you can't do a history of television news in 15 pages that is not superficial, but you can write about the history of a news program such as *60 Minutes* that need not be superficial.

Can you find primary and secondary sources? You may be interested in some very focused subject but may not be able to obtain information about it—even through the Internet. So you have to be careful that you choose a topic for your research that has available primary sources (records, data, interviews, statistics) and secondary sources (articles and books by scholars and others).

Are your sources reliable? All historians face the problem of how reliable their sources are. We know that people interviewed—primary sources—sometimes lie about their opinions (for a variety of reasons). In the same light, people who write articles about themselves and their activities may put a spin on what actually happened, or they may give a biased and only partially true account to newspaper reporters or others who interview them. You always have to consider the reliability of your sources. One way to get around this is to find a few other sources and see whether there's agreement about the topic you are investigating.

Are the authorities you are citing reliable? As I mentioned earlier, historians often disagree with one another. So if you are citing historians, can you be sure they are correct? And if you are citing written materials from primary sources—those involved in an event—can you be sure they are telling the truth? It is a good idea to find primary sources—that is, people who can give you detailed firsthand information (but remember to be suspicious)—as well as secondary sources, such as writings by historians, that can give you perspective and background. Also, if you can find a few primary sources written about a given event, then you see whether they agree with one another. For example, consider Watergate. There's an almost endless number of books and articles by people who were in the White House with Nixon—by Nixon, by reporters, and by historians who have studied the matter. By balancing primary and secondary sources, you may find that a consistent story will emerge.

What concepts or theory of history are you using? You may not recognize that you are using concepts or a theory of history, but when you write history, you have to have an organizing principle that tells you what material is good and what isn't, what you should focus on and what you shouldn't. What concepts or theory of history do you hold?

History is the record of progress.

History is the study of class conflict.

History is bunk!

History is the story of great figures.

History is the study of everyday life.

What does anything mean? Let us suppose that you are researching the way the 1999 World Series was televised (to give ourselves a good media research topic) and have found material about the series in newspapers, sports magazines, scholarly journals, and books by sociologists and psychologists. You also have statements from athletes involved in the series, television executives, media critics, and other sources directly or indirectly involved in the games. You might also have video recordings of the series.

As a historian, your task is not only to describe the televised version of the 1999 World Series (and the controversies about how it was televised) but to say something about how the series and the way it was televised reflect society and culture in the United States. You not only have to describe and interpret the televised version of the series, but you also have to speculate about its economic, social, and cultural significance—that is, say what you think the event means. When speculating, however, be sure to use appropriate language to make clear that you are offering hypotheses or interpretations or opinions; do not offer your speculations as "facts." A good historian may offer an interpretation of what an event means, but she or he always makes clear the difference between facts and interpretation of facts.

What's the impact? In addition to speculating about the meaning of the event you are dealing with, and let's assume, once again, that you are writing about the televised version of the 1999 World Series, you should concern yourself with what impact the series might have had on baseball, attitudes toward professional athletes, team owners, television networks, society and culture in the United States, and people in other cultures—to name a few of the topics you might consider. You do this because one of the tasks of the historian is to assess the impact that events might have on our lives and on the societies in which we live.

❖ HISTORICAL ANALYSIS: APPLICATIONS AND EXERCISES

1. Investigate reviews of the writings of historian Arnold Toynbee. Compare reviews in newspapers and popular magazines with reviews in scholarly journals. What differences of opinion do you find in the two kinds of publications about Toynbee's status as a historian?

2. Do a research project on new trends in historical analysis. What new approaches have historians come up with in recent years? Why have they developed these approaches?

3. How has postmodernism affected historical research? Find scholarly articles and books on the subject and report on what you learned. Attach copies of the first page of the articles that you found.

4. Do a historical content analysis of a newspaper comic strip to see how it has changed over time. Take a strip from the 1940s such as *Dick Tracy*, *Li'l Abner*, *Batman*, or *Superman* or a more contemporary comic hero such as Spider-Man. What do the changes found in these comics reflect about American culture and society?

❖ CONCLUSIONS

Most research has a historical dimension, as the researchers describe and explain what they did and what they found. In a sense, when we write about things in the past, whether we are writing about the remote past (kings and wars) or the recent past (experiments we conducted), there is no escaping history. We can learn from historians important things, such as being accurate, organized, logical, and honest. As Jacques Barzun and Henry F. Graff (1957) wrote in an old but excellent book, *The Modern Researcher,*

> It is from historical scholarship—originating with the antiquarian— that the world has copied the apparatus of footnotes, references, bibliography, and so on, which have become commonplace devices, not to say household words. It is from the historical study of texts by philologists and historians that writers at large have learned to sift evidence, balance testimony, and demand verified assertions. . . . Whatever its purpose, a report is invariably and necessarily historical. Insofar as it reports facts it gives an account of the past. (p. 5)

Historians have provided researchers with some fundamental ways of searching for facts and recording them. One other important thing we've learned from first-rate historians is to be mindful of style when writing up our findings. The new research methodologies we have created do not displace the historical perspective but build on it. If you think about it, when we write up our reports, we are writing what can be described as short-term microhistories of our activities and findings and using this material to speculate about the present or the future (or both). There is no escaping the historical dimension, whether it is establishing a sense of context to give your research grounding or talking about other research similar to the research you will be conducting.

❖ FURTHER READING

Appleby, J. (with Jacob, M.). (1994). *Telling the truth about history.* New York, NY: Norton.

Barzun, J., & Graff, H. F. (1992). *The modern researcher* (5th ed.). New York, NY: Thomson Learning.

Benjamin, J. R. (1998). *A student's guide to history* (7th ed.). Boston, MA: Bedford.

Berkhofer, R. F., Jr. (1969). *A behavioral approach to historical analysis.* New York, NY: Free Press.

Breisach, E. (1995). *Historiography: Ancient, medieval and modern* (2nd ed.). Chicago, IL: University of Chicago Press.

Foucault, M. (1973). *Madness and civilization: A history of insanity in the age of reason* (R. Howard, Trans.). New York, NY: Vintage.

Gilderhus, M. T. (2009). *History and historians: A historiographical introduction* (7th ed.). Upper Saddle River, NJ: Prentice-Hall.

Godfrey, D. G. (2005). *Methods of historical analysis in electronic media.* London, UK: Routledge.

Hoesterey, I. (1991). *Zeitgeist in Babel: The postmodernist controversy.* Bloomington: Indiana University Press.

Howell, M. C., & Prevenier, W. (2001). *From reliable sources: An introduction to historical method.* Ithaca, NY: Cornell University Press.

Iggers, G. G. (1997). *Historiography in the twentieth century: From scientific objectivity to the postmodern challenge.* Middletown, CT: Wesleyan University Press.

Noble, D. (1965). *Historians against history.* Minneapolis: University of Minnesota Press.

Phifer, G. (1961). The historical approach. In C. W. Dow (Ed.), *An introduction to graduate study in speech and theatre.* East Lansing: Michigan State University Press.

Startt, D. (2003). *Historical methods in mass communication.* San Ramon, CA: Vision Press.

The ethnomethodological emphasis on cultural studies ... stresses that the researchers should not try to suggest interpretations of people's worlds of meaning, to try to move into their minds. The interpretation of meaning is regarded as an activity that is characteristic of everyday situations of interaction: we look at what other people do, and infer on that basis what they "mean" or "think," and then respond on the basis of the interpretation we have made. It is one of the key tenets of ethnomethodology that the researcher should not compete with laypeople over such interpretations of meaning; the researcher should not try to offer the ultimate interpretation of what things "really" mean. Rather, the ethnomethodologist is concerned to study the methods or the rules of interpretation that people follow in their everyday lives. Ethnomethodology, as the name implies, is concerned with studying the "ethno-methods" of popular interpretation. Its object of study consists of observable, concrete, incarnated social activities through which actors produce everyday situations and practices and are capable of acting in those situations.

—Pertti Alasuutari, *Researching Culture: Qualitative Method and Cultural Studies* (1995, p. 36)

10

Ethnomethodological Research

CHAPTER 10 FOCUS QUESTIONS

- How is ethnomethodology defined?
- What did you learn about ethnomethodology from the discussion by Dirk vom Lehn?
- What experiments did Garfinkel have his students conduct?
- How can ethnomethodology be used to conduct media and communication research?
- How do metaphors reflect our psyches?
- What are the implications of the metaphor "Love is a game"?
- In the joke about the minister, what codes were violated?
- Which of the 45 humor techniques were found in the joke about the minister?
- How can ethnomethodology be used to study communication?

Ethnomethodological research is one of the most fascinating and also one of the most troublesome kinds of research there is. One reason for this is that ethnomethodology tends to resist being easily defined. It's not much of an overstatement to say that nobody is really sure what ethnomethodology is. Another problem is that some scholars consider its findings interesting but not terribly significant, because it seems to deal with trivial matters.

❖ DEFINING ETHNOMETHODOLOGY

The term **ethnomethodology** was thought up by distinguished sociologist Harold Garfinkel. In an article titled "The Origins of the Term 'Ethnomethodology'" (based on a transcript of a symposium on the subject), Garfinkel explained how he thought up the name:

> "Ethno" seemed to refer, somehow or other, to the availability to a member of common-sense knowledge of his society as common-sense knowledge of the "whatever." If it were ethno-botany, then it had to do somehow or other with his knowledge of and his grasp of what were for members adequate methods for dealing with botanical matters. Someone from another society, like an anthropologist in this case, would recognize the matters as botanical matters. The member would employ ethnobotany as adequate grounds of inference and action in the conduct of his own affairs in the company of others like him. It was that plain, and the notion of "ethnomethodology" or the term "ethnomethodology" was taken in this sense. (cited in Turner, 1974, pp. 16–17)

Garfinkel made a number of important points about ethnomethodology in this passage (and I will add others taken from his writings and those of other ethnomethodologists):

- The focus of ethnomethodology is on people's "commonsense" knowledge of society.

- There is an interest among ethnomethodologists in people's "adequate grounds of inference."

- There is a concern among ethnomethodologists for actions people undertake in the company of others like themselves.

- Ethnomethodologists are interested in studying everyday life, which is generally neglected by sociologists.

- The ethnomethodologist's concern with people's understanding of things suggests that ethnomethodologists do not offer their interpretations of the meanings of people's activities but search for the way *they* make sense of things and find meaning in things—especially conversations people have and things people do.

Thus, ethnomethodology is interested in how people think and act in everyday-life situations, in contrast to, for example, laboratory experiments or focus groups or other situations in which people recognize that they are, one way or another, being studied. "Common sense" becomes a subject of inquiry, not just a "given" neglected for other concerns.

These interests of ethnomethodologists have implications for advertising, in that advertisers want to know how people make sense of the world and how they react to "commonsense" appeals. Advertisers want to be able to "reach" targeted segments of the population and to influence them, which means they want to understand people's "grounds for inference." Thus, ethnomethodology has important applications when it comes to creating commercials and print advertisements.

Ethnomethodologists assume that people have common understandings—which they don't always articulate—and this leads them to examine how people reason and what's behind their everyday activities. It isn't easy to find these common understandings or to determine how people reason.

Garfinkel offers several other definitions of ethnomethodology in his book *Studies in Ethnomethodology,* a collection of his papers published in 1967. Let me offer a sampling.

> The following studies seek to treat practical activities, practical circumstances, and practical sociological reasoning as topics of empirical study, and by paying to the most commonplace activities of daily life the attention usually accorded extraordinary events to learn about them as phenomena in their own right. (p. 1)

In Garfinkel's (1967) essay "Studies of the Routine Grounds of Everyday Activities," he makes the same point in slightly different terms:

> Although sociologists take socially structured scenes of everyday life as a point of departure they rarely see, as a task of sociological inquiry in its own right, the general question of how any such common sense world is possible. . . . As a topic and methodological ground for sociological inquiries, the definition of the common sense world of everyday life, though it is appropriately a project of sociological inquiry, has been neglected. My purposes in this paper are to

demonstrate the essential relevance to sociological inquiries, of a concern for common sense activities as a topic of inquiry in its own right and, by reporting a series of studies, to urge its "rediscovery." (p. 36)

These quotations point, then, to the subject of ethnomethodological research—whose most important tasks are the following:

- To define the common sense world of everyday life

- To show the relevance of everyday activities to sociological theory

- To rediscover the significance of the common sense world of people

The researcher does not try to interpret the meaning of everyday activities but, rather, to find the rules or codes by which people interpret statements made to them by others, through which they make sense of the world.

Thus, ethnomethodology focuses on speech and conversation. It is described in David Deacon, Michael Pickering, Peter Golding, and Graham Murdock's *Researching Communications: A Practical Guide to Methods in Media and Cultural Analysis* (1999) as follows:

Conversation analysis was pioneered in the 1960s in the work of Harvey Sacks and his colleagues, and is closely aligned with the microsociological analysis known as ethnomethodology. . . . It is in view of this alignment that conversation analysis can be said most generally to be concerned with meaningful conduct in routine social settings. More specifically, its focus is on how talk operates to enable interactions between people. (p. 305)

It is the codes and belief systems found in conversation that are of particular interest to ethnomethodologists.

A SHORT THEATRICAL PIECE ON ETHNOMETHODOLOGICAL ANALYSIS

Grand Inquisitor:	*29–35–25–29–2*
Arthur:	(Laughing) I never heard that joke before. It's very funny!
Grand Inquisitor:	*How about 29–35–18–19–1?*

Arthur:	(Laughing) I love that joke about the rabbi and the minister's wife.
Grand Inquisitor:	*Don't you think it is quite absurd to reduce jokes to formulas?*
Arthur:	Not at all. Let me tell you a joke. The comedians have a conference every year. Since they know all the jokes in the world, they've reduced them all to numbers to save time when they tell them. A comedian gets up in the hall where they are all meeting and yells "24–16–3–44!" Nobody laughs. One comedian in the back of the hall leans over to his friend and says, "He never could tell a joke."
Grand Inquisitor:	*I give up.*

❖ GARFINKEL'S INGENIOUS AND MISCHIEVOUS RESEARCH

In his chapter on the routine grounds of everyday activities, Garfinkel (1967) stated that he likes to take familiar scenes in people's everyday lives and "ask what can be done to make trouble" (p. 37). He asked his students to do things in their everyday lives (talking with friends, having dinner at home) that "produce and sustain bewilderment, consternation, and confusion; to produce the social structured affects of anxiety, shame, guilt and indignation; and to produce disorganized interaction" (pp. 37–38). How did he do this? Rather easily, it turns out. Why did he do this? Because his little "experiments" enable ethnomethodologists to discover important and interesting things about the way people relate to one another.

What these case studies show is that important segments of everyday life escape our attention and are really fertile ground for understanding how people live and make sense of things. Our common understandings and background expectancies are so routinized and strong that it doesn't take much, as the experiments of Garfinkel's students showed, to cause all kinds of problems and difficulties when these expectancies are not met.

Let me offer some examples.

Clarifying comments. In one experiment (a term that is, perhaps, somewhat loosely used here), he asked students to take everything anyone said to them literally and to ask people to clarify their remarks. Thus, when a person was telling one of his students that he had a flat tire, the student asked him what he meant by flat tire. That led to the friend's getting flustered. In another example from the same experiment, a friend of one of his students asked him how his girlfriend was feeling. The student asked whether his friend meant physically or mentally. The person asking the question looked peeved and went on to a different subject.

Acting like boarders while at home. In this experiment, Garfinkel asked 49 of his students to spend from 15 minutes to an hour at home acting like boarders. That is, they were to be very circumspect and polite, were to avoid getting personal, were to use formal address, and were to speak only when spoken to.

In something like 80% of the cases, the families of the students were "stupefied" and "astonished" and tried to make sense of the strange actions of the students. Some thought the students had been working too hard, were ill, had broken up with boyfriends or girl-friends, and so on. A number of family members got angry.

The reason for this reaction by the families was that the normal behavior of the students (and people, in general, in family situations)—taking snacks when they feel like it, grabbing food, taking larger portions for themselves than others take at the dinner table, interrupting others while they are speaking—was no longer going on, and the students' family members felt confused.

What the experiment revealed is that we take certain kinds of actions for granted, and when someone acts out of character one way or another, we get disturbed. A member of a family acting like a boarder, even though other family members might not recognize the behavior for what it is, disturbs the equilibrium and violates everyone's expectations. We can describe this in terms of figure and ground: When the figure suddenly changes, it stands out against the ground of expectations and becomes problematic.

Describing a household as if one were a boarder. In this experiment, students were asked to spend from 15 minutes to an hour in their household assuming they were boarders (but not to act as if they were boarders). They were to describe what they saw as if they knew nothing of the people involved. They were only to describe what they observed, as objectively as possible, and not make any assumptions about the motives of those involved or the propriety of people's behavior.

What the students learned, to their surprise, was the personal degree to which family members treated each other. Garfinkel (1967) wrote,

> Displays of conduct and feeling occurred without apparent concern for the management of impressions. Table manners were bad, and family members showed each other little politeness. . . . Many [students] became uncomfortably aware of how habitual movements were being made; of *how* one was handling the silverware, or *how* one opened the door or greeted another member. Many reported that the attitude was difficult to sustain because with it quarreling, bickering, and hostile motivations became discomfitingly visible. (pp. 45–46)

Many of the students argued that their descriptions of their families were not *true* and that their families really got along together well and were happy.

WHAT IS ETHNOMETHODOLOGY?

Dirk vom Lehn

Harold Garfinkel (1917–2011) developed ethnomethodology in the 1950s when he studied for a PhD with the well-known sociologist Talcott Parsons at Harvard. At the time, Parsons was working to develop a "grand theory" of sociology (i.e., a theory that could be used to explain all social phenomena). With this project Parsons hoped to align sociology with the methods and procedures used in the other sciences. While studying at Harvard, Garfinkel frequently met in New York with Alfred Schutz, with whom he discussed a phenomenological perspective on the social world. Schutz's phenomenological analyses were concerned with understanding people's immediate experience of the world. He proposed that social scientists not analyze the social world by filtering their data through abstract concepts and models but instead conduct studies that allow for an unmediated understanding of participants' experience of the social world. The goal of Schutz's endeavor was to develop a social science that can reveal universal structures of how people experience the world (Schutz & Luckmann, 1974).

In his doctoral dissertation, Garfinkel compared and contrasted the social scientific perspectives of Parsons and Schutz and used

(Continued)

(Continued)

them to develop his own "sociological attitude" (Garfinkel, 2006), which in later years became known as ethnomethodology. The term *ethnomethodology*—a sociological attitude that examines the *methods* people use to go about their everyday life—came to prominence only after the publication of Garfinkel's (1967) now classic book *Studies in Ethnomethodology*. In this book, we find a collection of articles, some of which were published previously in academic journals without gaining much resonance, that discuss how ethnomethodology differs from traditional sociology and illustrate studies conducted with Garfinkel's sociological attitude (vom Lehn, 2014).

Although ethnomethodology has changed since its inception in the 1950s, most of its characteristics have remained unchanged and still differentiate ethnomethodological studies from other, "traditional" kinds of sociology. Garfinkel's study of the work of jury deliberations published in his *Studies* illustrates the change in perspective implied by ethnomethodology. Together with a colleague, Saul Mendlovitz, Garfinkel was asked to provide an analysis of jury deliberations. Garfinkel and Mendlovitz used audio recordings of the deliberations as their data. While traditional sociologists would have used an analytic scheme or theory to examine the data, Garfinkel and Mendlovitz decided to start with the data and study the organization of the activities of the participants in the recordings. In particular, they became interested in the forms of argumentation used and the knowledge and theories the participants deployed so that the recorded situation became recognizable as the deliberations of a jury rather than as conversations of a small group. In their presentation at the annual conference of the American Sociological Association in 1954, Garfinkel and Mendlovitz used the term *ethnomethods* to describe the organization of activities through which the jury deliberations were accomplished (vom Lehn, 2014).

A focus on the methods that participants use to recognizably produce "familiar scenes," such as jury deliberations, lectures at university, waiting in queues, news interviews, traffic jams, dance lessons, museum visits, medical consultations, and many others has become the key characteristic of ethnomethodological studies. These familiar scenes themselves have properties that cannot be understood when applying abstract social scientific theories, but their analysis requires a sociological attitude that aligns itself with the perspective of the participants in the situation. Some ethnomethodologists therefore have acquired the knowledge and competencies of participants in particular situations in order to produce ethnomethodological studies that are relevant not only for the academic community that reads journal publications but also the professional community of those subject to the study. Thus, David Sudnow (1979) analyzed the temporal organization of piano playing, Eric Livingston (1986) studied the work of mathematicians, and Ken Liberman (2007) examined the practices of Tibetan dialecticians. Many other ethnomethodologists acquired the skills, knowledge, and competency of particular professions when investigating the organization of the practices that differentiate these professions from others.

Many other ethnomethodologists took a very different approach and in a way continued the work that Garfinkel and Mendlovitz had begun with their investigation of the jury deliberations in the 1950s. They used audio and later video recordings of talk and interaction as their principal data. The starting point for this kind of analysis is Harvey Sacks's examination of conversations. Sacks closely collaborated with Garfinkel in the 1950s and 1960s. In the course of his short career—sadly, Sacks died in a car accident in 1975—he revealed the "sequential" organization of talk. His analysis shows that the meaning of utterances is not made clear to others by a particular utterance itself but by the sequential context of its production. *Sequential context* thereby refers to the relationship between actions; the researcher examines how an action is produced in response to an immediately prior action and how the action provides the basis for a next action (Heritage, 1984).

Over the past decades, "conversation analysis," as Sacks's analyses are called today, has developed as a distinct social scientific endeavor (Sacks, 1992; Schegloff, 2007). Since the 1980s, however, scholars, some of whom have a background in conversation analysis, have turned to audio and video recordings as the principal data for the analysis of interactions. Their studies often begin with the examination of participants' talk before an interaction (including their bodily action) as well as their interaction with the material and visual environment. In this way, bodily, visual, and material actions are treated like utterances in their relevance to the organization of a situation. The researcher therefore unpacks short sequences of action

(Continued)

(Continued)

to reveal how, even if only for a short moment, participants in interactions reach a common understanding of an action or the meaning of an object.

Ethnomethodology, conversation analysis, and video-based studies of interaction are now key elements used to train sociology students at universities around the world. In addition to their importance in academic sociology, ethnomethodological studies have also had an important influence on research and practice in the technical sciences and the development of new systems and devices in the research labs of major technology companies, including Xerox, PARC, Microsoft, and Yahoo!. Ethnomethodological analysis is also of great relevance to media studies in which scholars explore how meaning is produced through "texts" and how audiences—as they encounter media presentations in theaters and museums, in newspapers and on television, as well as on their mobile devices—make sense of these "texts" when they view, read, or listen to them.

❖ USING ETHNOMETHODOLOGY IN MEDIA AND COMMUNICATION RESEARCH

How can we use ethnomethodology in our research in communication and media analysis? Let me suggest a few options. What ethnomethodology provides us, we must remember, is a way of studying the codes and unconscious belief systems that lie behind our utterances and everyday actions. We can adapt ethnomethodological approaches to the media by asking the same questions ethnomethodologists ask—not about conversations but about dialogue in films and television shows, lyrics in songs, and similar phenomena.

The analysis of dialogue in media and the analyses ethnomethodologists make of real-world conversations differ in that dialogue in mass-mediated texts is created by writers. In a sense, therefore, when we do research on dialogue in a film or other mass-mediated text, we are dealing with a writer's perception of the world. Nonetheless, because writers create texts for large numbers of people, who presumably share their perceptions and beliefs, we can assume that analyzing dialogue in mediated texts is not that different from analyzing dialogue in everyday situations.

We can still look for the unconscious, nonarticulated background understandings that people share, except that they are reflected in dialogue, actions, and typical behavior expressed by actors and created by writers or, in many cases, teams of writers. A situation comedy such as *Modern Family* has a dozen writers thinking up the ideas for stories and writing the scripts, but we must assume that these writers share a common perception of the world with the people who watch the show.

Let me suggest the difference between what might be described as pure ethnomethodological research as practiced by sociologists (and other researchers, such as linguists and psychologists), which focuses on everyday life routines, and the adapted or applied form of this research, which uses films, television programs, songs, and other mediated texts.

Pure Research	Applied/Adapted Research
Everyday life	Mass-mediated texts
Ordinary people	Actors, singers
Routine interactions	Scripted interactions
Search for codes	Search for codes

Although there are differences, the goals of both are the same: discovering the background expectations and codes that lie behind everyday behavior. Mass-mediated texts may have scripted interactions, but these interactions reflect the codes held by the scriptwriters that are similar to the codes held by people in everyday interactions.

❖ METAPHORS AND MOTIVATION

I dealt with metaphors in Chapter 3, in my discussion of semiotics. Let me return to the topic now with a discussion of how metaphors reflect unconscious beliefs and attitudes and the role they play in our thinking. Gerald Zaltman, a professor of marketing at the Harvard Business School, discusses the way marketers use metaphors to discover what motivates people. He wrote (2003),

Researchers from various disciplines have developed numerous devices for mining the unconscious and using those revelations to create real value for consumers. One particularly intriguing device involves metaphors. By inviting consumers to use metaphors as they talk about a product or service, researchers bring consumers' unconscious thoughts and feelings to a level or awareness where both parties can explore them more openly together. . . . Because metaphors can reveal cognitive processes beyond those shown in more literal language, they can also surface important thoughts that literal language may underrepresent or miss completely. (p. 76)

By examining metaphors people use, or are asked to use by researchers, we can gain valuable information about the values and beliefs they hold. Sometimes, I must add, people are unaware of these values and don't recognize the role they play in their lives. That is because, Zaltman (2003) explained, "Ninety percent of thinking takes place in our unconscious minds—that wonderful, if messy, stew of memories, emotions, thoughts, and other cognitive processes we're not aware of or that we can't articulate" (p. 9). Metaphors, we shall see, have logical implications that can guide our thinking and behavior. To see how they do this, let's investigate romantic love.

❖ LOVE IS A GAME

Many years ago, in the 1940s and 1950s, before rock 'n' roll and before rap, romantic ballads were popular. These ballads were sung by crooners and told stories, usually about romantic love. (Many radio stations play these "golden oldies" for people who grew up in those years, so these songs are still being listened to, but not by young people as a rule.) One song I found particularly interesting was a ballad called "It's All in the Game," which states that love is a wonderful game. In my classes, I often ask my students what the metaphor "Love is a game" implies about love. They supply the following notions, which we might describe as logical imperatives or common sense beliefs found in this metaphor.

1. *Someone wins and someone loses.* Games generally have winners and losers, and so we can expect winners and losers in the wonderful game called love. But what does it mean to "win" at love? Or to "lose" at love?

2. *Sometimes you are winning, and other times you might be losing.* In other words, like most games, we're never sure whether we'll win or lose at the end. That helps make it exciting.

3. *Love is not serious.* Games aren't really serious, so if love is a game, it isn't serious either. We play games to amuse ourselves, but when we grow bored with these games, we stop playing. Or we find another way to amuse ourselves or another person with whom to play the game.

4. *There are rules to follow in games.* Games are rule bound, and you must follow rules in the game of love. You can't make up the rules to suit yourself as you proceed. Or you shouldn't, that is.

5. *You have to watch out for cheating.* Some people cheat at games, and so you have to be careful that you are not victimized. Cheating in the game of love suggests things such as lying about how you really feel or, perhaps, playing the game of love with more than one person at a time.

6. *Games end after a while.* Eventually someone wins a game or the players get bored and stop playing. The high rate of divorce in the United States (and in other countries as well) suggests that many people, without being aware of what they think about love, see it as a game.

We can see, then, that describing love as a game means adopting certain understandings about what love is and how to "play" the game of love. Certain logical implications and expectations—not found in other notions about love—are contained in the notion that love is a game. Metaphors ("love is a game") and similes ("love is like a game") play an important role in the way we think; they are not just literary devices used by poets and writers. Recognizing that people see love as a game and tracing out the implications of this metaphor is a form of applied ethnomethodological research.

❖ HUMORISTS AS CODE VIOLATORS

Another form of applied ethnomethodological research is the study of humor. Humor is a subject that has perplexed philosophers, psychologists, sociologists, linguists, communication theorists, and many other kinds of scholars and thinkers for thousands of years. One way to look at humorists that is relevant to our interest in applying ethnomethodological theory is as code violators. If we are interested in codes, schemas, and scripts (whatever you want to call our background understandings learned from growing up in a given culture and subculture), then humor is useful, if in fact, as I have suggested, it is connected to code violations.

Consider **jokes,** which are generally defined as having the following characteristics:

- They are short narratives.

- They are meant to amuse people and generate mirthful laughter.

- They have punch lines.

A joke can be diagrammed as follows:

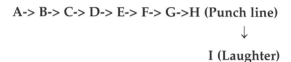

A-> B-> C-> D-> E-> F-> G->H (Punch line)

↓

I (Laughter)

The punch line represents an unexpected resolution of the narrative being told, one that surprises and amuses us and, if the joke is good, causes laughter. We tend to use the term *joke* loosely for things such as riddles, which take the form of questions and answers, and witticisms and puns, which involve wordplay. But technically speaking, a joke is a funny story with a punch line. Let me offer an example. I will use a letter to characterize each part of the joke.

A. A minister comes home early and finds his wife lying in bed naked. There is a strong smell of cigar smoke in the apartment.

B. He looks out the window and sees a priest, smoking a big cigar, leaving the apartment building.

C. With superhuman strength fueled by his rage, the minister lifts up the refrigerator in his apartment, and just as the priest crosses beneath the window, the minister drops the refrigerator on the priest, killing him.

D. Then, consumed by conscience, the minister jumps out the window.

E. A few seconds later, the priest, the minister, and a rabbi appear before St. Peter in heaven.

F. "How did you get here?" St. Peter asks the priest. "I don't know," replies the priest. "I had been visiting a parishioner who was ill, and a refrigerator dropped on me, killing me."

G. "And how did you get here?" St. Peter asks the minister. "I dropped the refrigerator on the priest," replies the minister. "And then, I felt so guilty about what I'd done, I jumped out the window and killed myself."

H. "And how did you get here?" St. Peter asks the rabbi. "I don't know," replies the rabbi. *"I was minding my own business, sitting in a refrigerator and smoking a cigar . . ."* (punch line)

I. Laughter (response to punch line)

I have put the punch line in italics here. If this joke is told by a good joke teller, it generally elicits laughter. We have to learn how to tell jokes successfully and to listen to jokes correctly, which means we must respond, on cue, when told a joke. The cue is the punch line. We have to pay attention to the joke teller so we laugh at the correct time, not letting too much time pass between the punch line and our laughter.

Several codes are violated in this joke. First, we have the matter of logical thinking. Priests are celibate . . . or at least they are supposed to be celibate. The minister jumps to conclusions about the priest because he is smoking a cigar. Second, the minister violates the code "Thou shalt not kill." Third, the minister drops a refrigerator on the priest, an act that is quite impossible. And fourth, the rabbi violates the code of common sense. One does not sit in refrigerators smoking cigars. Of course, we know why the rabbi was sitting in the refrigerator. He was "minding his own business."

It is worth looking at jokes to see what kinds of behavior codes are assumed and then violated by the punch lines. You can also look at comedians' monologues to see how they deal with, and in many cases violate, our ideas of normalcy and common sense. Humor involves some kind of a play frame that states "this is not for real" or "I don't really mean this," and that helps jokes—many of which are insulting to women, ethnic groups, racial groups, professional groups, and others—take on a veneer of acceptability so that people are willing to tell these jokes to one another. As Freud pointed out, humor is connected to masked aggression, and one of the joys of listening to jokes is participating, guilt-free, in aggression. But humor can have very negative psychological consequences, which is why the media try to censor humor that is too insulting.

Character	Code Violated
Priest	Celibacy (assumed violation)
Minister	Thou shalt not kill
Minister	Physical capacity of human beings
Rabbi	Thou shalt not commit adultery
Rabbi	Humans sitting in refrigerators

❖ TECHNIQUES OF HUMOR

As I mentioned earlier, I've made a content analysis of humor (from jokes, plays, comic books, literature) and elicited from the material I examined 45 techniques that, in various permutations and combinations, are used to generate humor. In Chapter 8, I listed these techniques by their categories. In Table 10.1, I list these techniques

Table 10.1   Techniques of Humor in Alphabetical Order

1. Absurdity	16. Embarrassment	31. Parody
2. Accident	17. Exaggeration	32. Puns
3. Allusion	18. Exposure	33. Repartee
4. Analogy	19. Facetiousness	34. Repetition
5. Before/after	20. Grotesque	35. Reversal
6. Bombast	21. Ignorance	36. Ridicule
7. Burlesque	22. Imitation	37. Rigidity
8. Caricature	23. Impersonation	38. Sarcasm
9. Catalogue	24. Infantilism	39. Satire
10. Chase scene	25. Insults	40. Scale, size
11. Coincidence	26. Irony	41. Slapstick
12. Comparison	27. Literalness	42. Speed
13. Definition	28. Mimicry	43. Stereotypes
14. Disappointment	29. Mistakes	44. Theme and variation
15. Eccentricity	30. Misunderstanding	45. Unmasking

alphabetically. These techniques enable us to examine any example of humor and determine the techniques found in the work that generate laughter.

If we apply this chart to the joke about the priest, minister, and rabbi, we find the following techniques at work:

- *Mistakes (29):* The minister smells cigar smoke and thinks it comes from the priest's cigar.

- *Reversal (35):* The minister attempts to get revenge against the priest.

- *Exposure (18):* The rabbi reveals that he's the source of the cigar smoke.

- *Facetiousness (19):* The rabbi says he was innocently sitting in a refrigerator.

- *Absurdity (1):* The rabbi was smoking in a refrigerator.

This analysis suggests, then, that jokes can be extremely complex texts, with all kinds of techniques that generate humor and laughter. It is possible to use this typology of humor techniques to study jokes and other forms of humor to see whether certain techniques are being used or whether the humor is based on language, logic, identity, or visual phenomena and action.

❖ ETHNOMETHODOLOGY AND THE COMMUNICATION PROCESS

In addition to being used to analyze phenomena such as routine conversations, dialogue in narratives, song lyrics, and jokes, ethnomethodology has other uses. For example, the study of intercultural communication looks for national codes used by members of each culture to determine why there may be problems when people from different cultures and countries try to communicate.

The same process can be used to examine the communication practices of subcultures in a given culture and, in particular, marginalized subcultures such as drug abusers, prostitutes, and criminals. We can make ethnomethodological studies of the communication practices of certain movements, such as feminist and gay liberation movements. The communication practices of certain occupations and organizations also lend themselves to ethnomethodological research. How does an organization decide on record keeping? What codes tell people in organizations "record this" or "don't record that"? In short, many areas of communication can be analyzed using ethnomethodological research techniques.

❖ ETHNOMETHODOLOGICAL RESEARCH: APPLICATIONS AND EXERCISES

1. Using Garfinkel's method, in which you pretend you are a boarder, write a detailed description of a meal with your family or some friends. Describe what happened as carefully as you can, assuming you don't know the people and without making any assumptions about their motives.

2. Find a transcript for a situation comedy such as *Modern Family* or *The Big Bang Theory* and analyze the conversation from an ethnomethodological perspective. What assumptions do the characters have about one another and about life? Are there any behavioral codes that inform the dialogue?

3. Make an ethnomethodological analysis of song lyrics with interesting metaphors or metonymies. Use the "love is a game" analysis as a model.

4. Using the techniques of humor chart, analyze a joke or other comic text. I offer the following texts for you to practice this kind of analysis:

A person calls Radio Erevan and asks, "Is it true that comrade Gorshinko won 5,000 rubles at the lottery?" "Yes," replies Radio Erevan. "But it was not comrade Gorshinko but comrade Kataev, and it was not 5,000 rubles but 10,000 rubles, and he didn't win it at the lottery but lost it gambling."

A person calls Radio Erevan and asks, "Is it true that one can use a glass of water for birth control?"

"Yes," replies Radio Erevan.

"Before or after?" asks the caller.

"Instead of," replies Radio Erevan.

Jack eating rotten cheese did say,

Like Samson I my thousands slay;

I vow, quoth Roger, so you do.

And with the self-same weapon, too.

—Benjamin Franklin

Why did the moron bring a ladder to the party?

He heard the drinks were on the house!

A man goes to Miami for a vacation. After four days, he notices he has a tan all over his body, except for his penis. So the next day he goes to a deserted area of the beach early in the morning, takes his clothes off, and lies down. He sprinkles sand over himself until all that remains in the sun is his penis. Two little old ladies walk by on the boardwalk and one notices the penis. "When I was 20," she says, "I was scared to death of them. When I was 40, I couldn't get enough of them. When I was 60, I couldn't get one to come near me . . . *and now they're growing wild on the beach."*

❖ CONCLUSIONS

We can take the concerns and methods of ethnomethodologists—for the codes that shape and inform our everyday behavior (what we say, do, and think)—and apply them to mass-mediated texts. These mediated expressions are not "pure" like the ones found in everyday life, but they still must make sense to the millions of people who watch films and television programs, listen to music, read books, and tell jokes to one another. Thus, these mediated expressions of everyday life offer us fertile ground for ethnomethodological research.

❖ FURTHER READING

Alasuutari, P. (1995). *Researching culture: Qualitative method and cultural studies.* Thousand Oaks, CA: SAGE.

Button, G. (Ed.). (1991). *Ethnomethodology and the human sciences.* Cambridge, UK: Cambridge University Press.

Francis, D., & Hester. S. (2004). *An invitation to ethnomethodology: Language, society and interaction.* London, UK: SAGE.

Garfinkel, H. (1967). *Studies in ethnomethodology.* Englewood Cliffs, NJ: Prentice Hall.

Have, P. ten (2004). *Understanding qualitative research and ethnomethodology.* Thousand Oaks, CA: SAGE.

Heritage, J. (1985). *Garfinkel and ethnomethodology.* Oxford, UK: Blackwell.

Kessler, S., & McKenna, W. (1985). *Gender: An ethnomethodological approach.* Cambridge, UK: Cambridge University Press.

Jacobsen, M. H., & Kristiansen, S. (2015). *The social thought of Erving Goffman.* Thousand Oaks, CA: SAGE.

Lynch, M. (1993). *Scientific practice and ordinary action: Ethnomethodology and social studies of science.* Cambridge, UK: Cambridge University Press.

Rawls, A. (Ed.). (2006). *Seeing sociologically: The routine grounds of social action.* Boulder, CO: Paradigm.

Lynch, M., & Sharrock, W. (2011). *Ethnomethodology* (Vols. 1–4). Thousand Oaks, CA: SAGE.

Turner, R. (Ed.). (1974). *Ethnomethodology: Selected readings.* Baltimore, MD: Penguin.

vom Lehn, D. (2014). *The creation and development of ethnomethodology.* Walnut Creek, CA: Left Coast Press.

Zaltman, G. (2003). *How customers think: Essential insights into the mind of the market.* Boston, MA: Harvard Business School Press.

There is a series of phenomena of great importance which cannot possibly be recorded by questioning or computing documents, but have to be observed in their full actuality. Let us call them the imponderabilia of actual life. Here belong such things as the routine of a man's working day, the details of his care of the body, of the manner of taking food and preparing it; the tone of conversational and social life around the village fires, the existence of strong friendships or hostilities, and of passing sympathies and dislikes between people; the subtle yet unmistakable manner in which personal vanities and ambitions are reflected in the behaviour of the individual and in the emotional reactions of those who surround him. All these facts can and ought to be scientifically formulated and recorded, but it is necessary that this be done, not by a superficial registration of details, as is usually done by untrained observers, but with an effort at penetrating the mental attitude expressed in them.

—Bronislaw Malinowski, *Argonauts of the Western Pacific* (1961, pp. 18–19)

11

Participant Observation

- How do we define participant observation?
- What do we hope to discover when doing participant observation?
- What considerations must we keep in mind when doing participant observation?
- What did Janice Radway discover about readers of romance novels?
- What problems do we face when doing participant observation?
- What are the benefits of participant observation studies?
- How do we make sense of our findings when doing participant observation?
- What ethical dilemmas do we face when doing participant observation?

We learn a great deal about the world from reading about people and events, from listening to the radio and watching television, from talking with people, and from observing others. Reading, listening to the radio, and watching television give us information about people and events, but this information is mediated. That is, it is filtered through someone else's consciousness and shaped by someone else's decision about what to point a camera at or what questions to ask.

❖ DEFINING PARTICIPANT OBSERVATION

Much research provides knowledge about people, but this knowledge is often somewhat abstract and gained by studying people in experiments and other controlled situations. **Participant observation** is different; it is a **qualitative research** technique that provides the opportunity to study people in real-life situations. It is a form of field research in which observations are carried out in real settings and where there is a lack of the kind of control and structure you have in experiments, for example. In participant observation, as the name suggests, researchers become involved in the group, organization, or entity they are studying. Researchers have to balance two roles: that of being participants and that of being observers. Researchers also have to avoid "going native," which means becoming so identified with the group that they lose their objectivity.

There are, then, several decisions you must make about your participant observation research. First, you have to decide whether to conceal your observations from the group you are studying, which raises ethical questions. If you tell the group that you are studying them, that information may affect their behavior. Second, you have to decide whether to just observe the group or to participate in the group's activities and, if you participate, to what degree—keeping in mind that you want to avoid going native.

Participant observation is typically carried out by a researcher in one of the two following roles:

(a.) *Participant as observer,* where the researcher participates with the group being observed and is a functioning part of the group. As such, the person is an "insider" enjoying a close understanding of the context and the process while performing the added role of an observer and recorder.

(b.) *Observer as participant,* in which the observer is a neutral outsider who has been given the privilege of participating for the purpose of making observations and recording them.

Both methods are legitimate, and each has advantages and draw-backs. Basically, the researcher faces a trade-off between familiarity on the one hand and neutrality on the other.

There is a difference between everyday observation and partici-pant observation. In our everyday lives, we are always observing people and events and trying to make sense of things. We are con-cerned about matters such as what people say to one another, relation-ships, or how people use body language. But our speculations are random and fugitive—that is, quickly moving on to other matters. Scientific observation is different. It is focused—on what the observer wants to find out—objective, and systematic.

Here are some of the things we hope to discover through par-ticipant observation of what people do and say to one another. This is an adaptation of the "Who?" "What?" "Where?" questions I discussed in Chapter 8. I am taking liberties here with a song from my youth that included the following line: "How come you do me like you do, do, do?" Our focus here is on group members being observed:

Where do people do what they do?

What common ideas and background knowledge do people have?

What do people do?

Who does what to whom?

Who originates actions, who reacts, and how do they react?

Why do they do what they do?

When (and how often) do they do what they do?

How do they do what they do?

How long do they do what they do?

You, as a researcher, must always keep in mind the following ques-tions about your participant observation: What do you want to find out about the people involved in this group? Is there some question that you want to answer? Is there some problem you hope to solve? Why are you doing this particular participant observation and dealing with this specific group?

A SHORT THEATRICAL PIECE ON PARTICIPANT OBSERVATION

Grand Inquisitor: *Where are we?*

Arthur: In a gym where people are working out.

Grand Inquisitor: *The machines here sort of remind me of some of our torture devices.*

Arthur: There are certain similarities.

Grand Inquisitor: *I notice there are men and women here of all ages. Don't they work? How do they have time to come here? Why are they here?*

Arthur: You've asked some interesting questions.

Grand Inquisitor: *The outfits of the women are curious: Many of them wear spandex clothes that cover them completely but are very revealing. I don't think I should be here, where I can be tempted, though I'd like to try some of the torture machines.*

Arthur: Notice that people don't talk to one another very much . . . and that men often wear shirts that reveal their muscles and that the gym is full of mirrors so people can look at themselves—at their big arms or small butts.

Grand Inquisitor: *I rather like the ambience of suffering and pain that I see all about me. But these people are torturing themselves—we never thought of that during the Inquisition.*

❖ SIGNIFICANT CONSIDERATIONS WHEN DOING PARTICIPANT OBSERVATION

Here are some important matters to focus on when doing a participant observation of your group.

1. *The setting.* Where are you doing your observation, and what impact does the setting have on the behavior of the people

being observed? Does the setting facilitate certain kinds of behavior and retard other kinds of behavior? For example, at a bar, you'd expect some flirting might go on and wouldn't expect people to be praying.

2. *The participants.* Who are you observing? How many people are involved? How are they related to one another? What is their function in the group being studied? What is the nature of the group being studied? Record pertinent demographic data, if you can obtain this information, about each of the participants:

Age	Socioeconomic class
Gender	Race and/or ethnic group
Occupation	Education

3. *The nature and purpose of the group.* You should describe the group and explain what kind of group it is. What is it that brings the people in the group together? Is the group tightly organized, or can people enter and leave it in a casual manner? Is the group ongoing, or is it based on chance events and only occasionally comes together? Does the group have many rules that members observe, or are there few (or no) rules?

4. *The behavior of people in the group.* What do members of the group do? How do they do it? Why do they do it? Who gives the group its direction? How do people in the group interact with one another? What do they say to each other? Who is involved with decision making in the group? Who says what to whom with what effects? We are basically interested in what people say to one another, what they do, and the relationship between what people say and do.

5. *The frequencies and durations of behavior.* As an observer, you want to record whether certain behaviors occur frequently or just take place occasionally and how long the people you are observing spend doing certain things. Are the behaviors typical or unique? When do they tend to take place? Is there something that tends to provoke or lead to certain behaviors?

6. *Record what you see.* Record what you see in as much detail as possible. If you have access to informants, you should make an audio recording of your interviews with them (if you can do so) so you have an accurate record of what they said. You should keep written records that are as detailed and complete

as possible and should concern yourself with what people actually say and do and not with your impressions of things. Now, with inexpensive video cameras and cell phones with video capabilities, it is easier to record videos.

Pertti Alasuutari suggested, in his book *Researching Culture: Qualitative Method and Cultural Studies* (1995), that we should take careful notes when doing participant observation research:

> Participant observation is the classic type of research where field notes are a self-evident part of the study. . . . Usually researchers write down something at the site of participant observation, for instance, direct quotations of what was said, or just some key words that will help to remember events. After returning home from, say, an evening of participant observation, one then types a report of the night, using the notepad markings as an *aide-memoire*. To put it briefly, keeping a field diary means that one scrupulously reports on events and impressions. One has to bear in mind that they can be used in the published study as direct quotations. After reporting on an event, and on one's feelings associated with it, one can write a separate section about the hypotheses and interpretations that come to mind at the time. (pp. 178–179)

The purpose of participant observation, we must remember, is to obtain information about people to formulate some kind of hypothesis that helps explain what is being studied.

7. *Self photographs and videos by group members.* Have group members take photographs or make videos connected to the topic you are investigating and discuss what their photographs and videos reveal. These photographs and videos will reveal what those who make them consider to be important and provide additional insights into the group. You can also ask the people taking photos and making videos to keep journals to document their activities. You might ask them to take "selfies" with their colleagues, from time to time, to document their activities.

Some participant observers develop tally sheets that enable them to keep track of aspects of behavior they are observing. For example, if you were doing a participant observation of young children playing in a sandbox, you might make a tally sheet to record when and how often specific children talked to one another or took one another's toys. You might have to redesign your tally sheet a number of times as you do your participant observation because you will discover that certain behaviors you hadn't planned on recording are important. If you have detailed data on a tally sheet, you can develop tables and charts showing your findings. In this way, there can be a quantitative aspect to participant observation, although many participant observers are not concerned with quantitative matters.

What I've been discussing to this point is rather abstract. Let me move down the ladder of abstraction and deal with some of the problems participant observers face when conducting field research. We must keep in mind that participant observation is a kind of fieldwork; the methods used in participant observation derive, in part, from those of anthropologists who studied preliterate tribes and cultures.

❖ A CASE STUDY OF PARTICIPANT OBSERVATION: READERS OF ROMANCE NOVELS

Janice Radway's 1991 book *Reading the Romance: Women, Patriarchy, and Popular Literature* is an exemplary case study in participant observation. Radway was interested in what the people who read romance novels are like and why they read these works. Originally, she wanted to find out how romance readers interpreted the novels they read, but when she became involved with a group of readers (the Smithton, New York, romance readers), she discovered the more important question was the way they used the novels and integrated them into their lives. As she explained,

> What the book gradually became, then, was less an account of the way romances as texts were interpreted than of the way romance reading as a form of behavior operated as a complex intervention in the ongoing social lives of actual subjects, women who saw themselves first as wives and mothers. (p. 7)

Radway's notion that she would use these readers to see how they interpreted romance novels gave way to something more important—the way the Smithton romance readers used these novels in their everyday lives. Radway asked the women in the group to fill out questionnaires to help her understand them better and lived, for a short while, with the leader of the group. She also tape-recorded her sessions with the group.

Her conclusions about the importance of spending time with actual romance novel readers are important:

> The nature of the group's operation suggests that it is unsatisfactory for an analyst to select a sample of romances currently issued by American publishers, draw conclusions about the meaning of the form by analyzing the plots of the books in the sample, and then make general statements about the cultural significance of the "romance." (1991, p. 49)

Her point is that even if we take a representative sample of romance novels and analyze their plots and other features, we cannot assume, from the texts alone, that we understand what they reflect about American culture or know how readers of these novels are affected by them. We learn from Radway's book that sometimes while conducting a participant observation study, we have to switch our focus when we discover something more important than our original notion of what we wanted to investigate.

❖ PROBLEMS WITH PARTICIPANT OBSERVATION

In theory, participant observation is easy. You find a group you are interested in studying, become connected with it (or find some way to participate in it), observe the group, record your observations as unobtrusively as possible, and write up what you've found. In practice, participant observation is much more complicated.

The Problem of Focus

When you do participant observation, you have to be looking for something. You don't just observe everything that everyone does in the group you are studying. Thus, if you are a student and studying the behavior of your classmates in class (and here, taking notes is not a problem), you have to find a focus or topic narrow enough to examine given the amount of time at your disposal. Are you interested in the relationships between your professor and certain students or the relationships between some students?

Sometimes, you will find that you started looking for information on one topic but discovered something more important, so you have to be ready to shift focus.

The Problem of Observers Affecting Behavior

Observers affecting (by their presence) what goes on in a group is known as **reactivity.** Does your presence, as a participant observer, change the way people normally relate to one another? If you are studying a very small, cohesive group, your presence—as a stranger— may have some impact on the way the group normally operates. Over time, this reactivity may subside, as people get to know you and accept your presence. In larger groups, or groups not as tightly organized, this is not such a problem.

The Problem of Unrecognized Selectivity

There is a problem of maintaining your objectivity in choosing where to focus your attention, what to record in your notes, and what to omit. At times, without recognizing it, participant observers neglect certain important behavior because they think a different behavior, which is actually relatively trivial, is more interesting. It's quite difficult to maintain your objectivity while doing participant observation and develop the facility to determine what is important and what is of secondary interest.

The Problem of Mind Reading

Mind reading, as I use the term, involves observers going beyond recording *what* people do and assuming they can read people's minds and figure out *why* people are doing something. As researchers, we are always looking for meaning, but we must be careful that we don't assume that our interpretations of some person's behavior is what the person meant by that behavior. One way to avoid mind reading is to ask people why they did or said something and to observe whether there is a connection between what people say and what they do. Of course, we must remember what we learned in Chapter 8 on interviews—people don't always know why they do things, and sometimes they don't tell interviewers the truth when answering their questions.

The Problem of Validity

Here you must consider how representative the activities you observed were and whether the reactivity effect might have shaped the behavior of the group in certain ways. Participant observation is high-risk research. It may yield important insights, but your findings can also be questionable.

❖ BENEFITS OF PARTICIPANT OBSERVATION STUDIES

Let me suggest some benefits that come from doing participant observation research. First, it helps you understand what's going on in a setting you are studying. If you spend time with a group of people, you start seeing things that were not apparent or evident when you first started studying them. Our minds search continually for meaning, and one way we find meaning is by finding relationships and patterns. Systematic observation of groups helps us discover these patterns and relationships.

Second, participant observation helps you determine which questions to ask informants. Participant observers frequently make themselves known to the members of the group they are studying and thus are free to ask people questions. It only makes sense to use these opportunities to ask your informants questions that will be useful to you and provide insights about the group and people in it.

Third, participant observation is, relatively speaking, an unobtrusive way of getting information about groups and their behavior. A great deal depends on the skill of the researcher and the setting. In certain cases, it is possible to take notes and record interviews with informants; in other cases, researchers have to try to remember what they can and then record their notes later. But in optimal situations, the observer becomes "taken for granted," and members of the group behave the way they usually do.

❖ MAKING SENSE OF YOUR FINDINGS

Once you have done your observation and recorded what you saw, you have to make sense of your research. That is, you have to interpret it. As I mentioned earlier, facts don't mean anything by themselves; they have to be put into context and explained.

Dealing With Actions

By *actions* I mean what certain people in the group you were observing did and said. You have to consider such matters as the following:

Who originates actions?

Who responds to these actions?

How do they respond?

Participant observation, we must remember, focuses on what people do with one another, do to one another, and say to one another. We observe behavior; we cannot observe what people think, and it is dangerous to assume that we can know what they are thinking on the basis of their actions. We focus on process and then on the events of the group—on sequences of actions and behaviors that, we hope, will reveal information of value.

Dealing With What People Think

We cannot observe what people think, but we can ask people about their thoughts and, if possible, record their answers. As I mentioned earlier, one of the things that participation observation does is help us determine what questions to ask informants.

Using Concepts to Interpret Your Findings

One thing we do when we look at the material we have gathered from our participant observations is to try to find concepts that will help us understand the behavior we've observed. We make sense of the world by applying concepts that offer explanations of things we observe. Let me offer an example. Suppose we observe someone who washes his hands 200 times a day. We have a concept that explains that behavior: We say that person is obsessive-compulsive. And that concept is part of a broad field known as psychoanalytic theory. We can see the relationships in the following chart:

Theory	Psychoanalytic theory
Concept	Obsessive-compulsive behavior
Behavior	Washing hands 200 times a day

A person who never heard of the concept "obsessive-compulsive" would not be able to explain this behavior except in relatively vague and useless everyday terms—*freaky, weird, strange,* and so on—that could be applied to many behaviors. Concepts function in between abstract theories and specific behavior. We use the concepts we know to interpret or explain the behavior we observe. Naturally, the more concepts we know, the more we can understand what we see. So, to a degree, your conceptual knowledge plays a very important role in enabling you to make sense of the behavior you observed and the interviews you made from your participant observation. Our conceptual knowledge is used in all our research, of course; we need concepts to understand what we can learn about people from interviewing them and observing their behavior.

❖ WRITING UP A PARTICIPANT OBSERVATION STUDY

Here are some suggestions for writing a report of a participant observation study.

1. Provide an introduction that gives your reader a sense of where you made your study, what you were trying to find, and any books and articles you consulted to gain information on participant observation methods or the topic you were investigating.

2. Tell your reader what interesting information you discovered from doing your participant observation and any conclusions you reached from your research.

3. Make sure you define and explain any concepts you used in your research.

4. Discuss any latent—that is, hidden and unrecognized—functions to the behaviors you observed.

Social scientists make a distinction between manifest functions, which are intended, and latent functions, which are unrecognized but are often of great importance. For example, college students may join a political organization because of their interest in politics (manifest function), but they also may be interested in meeting potential sexual partners (latent function).

5. Describe any problems you faced in making your participant observation and difficulties you faced in drawing conclusions about your research.

6. Discuss any differences in age, race, gender, ethnicity, or socioeconomic class among the people you studied and the role these differences (if any important differences existed) played in the group you studied.

When writing your report, it will be helpful to provide diagrams, charts, or tables that enable your readers to see important relationships. Your report should take the form of a narrative in which you cover the suggestions discussed above.

❖ AN ETHICAL DILEMMA

An ethical dilemma participant that observers face is whether to pretend to join the group they are observing in order to associate with the people in it or to tell people in the group they are doing research on them. Personally speaking, I think the ethical thing to do is to tell people you are observing them and not pretend you aren't. If you don't tell people what you are doing, you are, in a sense, using them, and you are also lying to them about your interest in the group. In addition, you will make things more difficult for yourself because you won't be able to record interviews or take notes as easily as you can if people know you are conducting research on them. I don't believe that people will change their behavior that much—at least not over the long run—if they know they are being observed. A great deal depends on your ability to "fade into the woodwork," to keep to the background, to keep your presence muted.

❖ ETHICS AND RESEARCH INVOLVING HUMANS

When your research involves humans, you have a responsibility to deal with those you are studying in an ethical manner. Let me suggest some ethical rules to keep in mind.

1. *You shouldn't deceive people.* This means that when conducting participant observation, you should tell the group you are studying what you are doing.

2. *You should not use people as a means toward other ends, even if you think those ends are positive.* Ethicists often make this point—you shouldn't use people for your own purposes, even if you think your findings will be important.

3. *You should not do anything that will have negative effects on those you study.* As the result of a famous study by Stanley Milgram about obedience, in which those who participated in the study ended up with many psychological problems, research involving humans in universities now has to be accepted by boards that deal with ethical considerations.

4. *You must be honest in designing your research and reporting your findings about those you study.* You have to avoid letting an outcome you may (perhaps unconsciously) desire shape your research and your findings.

❖ PARTICIPANT OBSERVATION: APPLICATIONS AND EXERCISES

1. Taking the role of participant observer, observe the behavior of people at a restaurant or cafeteria. Answer questions listed in the book about things we hope to learn from making a participant observation and use the list of significant considerations as well. What problems did you face in making your analysis? How did you solve these problems?

2. Take a series of photographs from your typical day, from the time you get up in the morning until you go to bed. When you look at these photographs, do you find anything that reveals some aspect of your life you were unaware of? When you compare your photographs with those your classmates have made of their typical days, do you discover anything the images have in common? Do you find any surprising differences between them?

3. Watch several episodes of a situation comedy and use techniques you've learned about participant observation to observe the behavior of the characters in it. Base your analysis upon at least 3 hours (six episodes) of viewing the show.

❖ CONCLUSIONS

Participant observation is one of the more widely used and interesting forms of research. It is also one of the most difficult because humans are so difficult to fathom and interpersonal and individual–group communication and relationships are so complicated. But participant observation is one of the few ways we can do research in natural (nonlaboratory) settings and obtain information about what people actually do in contrast to what they say they do. We also can use participant observation methods in analyzing mass-mediated texts. If we watch a television series, such as a soap opera, medical drama, or science fiction show, one way to interpret the show is to think of it as similar to a group one is observing and use participant observation techniques to analyze a selected set of episodes. This is an unconventional way of conducting participant observation, but it might yield interesting results.

❖ FURTHER READING

Burawoy, M. (1991). *Ethnography unbound: Resistance in the modern metropolis.* Berkeley: University of California Press.

DeWalt, K. M., & DeWalt, B. R. (2010). *Participant observation: A guide to fieldwork* (2nd ed.). Lanham, MD: AltaMira Press.

Emerson, R. M., & Fretz, R. I. (2011). *Writing ethnographic field notes* (2nd ed.). Chicago, IL: University of Chicago Press.

Heron, J. (1996). *Co-operative inquiry: Research into the human condition.* Thousand Oaks, CA: SAGE.

Hume, L., & Mulcock, J. (2005). *Anthropologists in the field: Cases in participant observation.* New York, NY: Columbia University Press.

McIntyre, A. (2008). *Participatory action research.* Thousand Oaks, CA: SAGE.

Reason, P. (Ed.). (1994). *Participation in human inquiry.* Thousand Oaks, CA: SAGE.

Smith, C. D., & Kornblum, W. (Eds.). (1996). *In the field: Readings on the field research experience.* New York, NY: Praeger.

Spradley, J. P. (1980). *Participant observation.* New York, NY: Holt, Rinehart, & Winston.

Part IV

Quantitative
Research Methods

As an experiment in content analysis, a year's publication of the Saturday Evening Post *(SEP) and of* Collier's *for the period from April 1940 to March 1941 was covered. It is regrettable that a complete investigation could not be made for the most recent material, but samples taken at random showed that no basic change in the selection or content structure has occurred since this country's entry into the war. . . . We put the subjects of the biographies into three groups: the spheres of political life, of business and the professions, and of entertainment (the latter in the broadest sense of the word). Looking at our table we find for the time before World War I very high interest in political figures and an almost equal distribution of business and professional men, on the one hand, and of entertainers on the other. The picture changes completely after the war. The figures from political life have been cut by 40 per cent; the business and professional men have lost 30 per cent of their personnel while the entertainers have gained 50 per cent. This numerical relation seems to be rather constant from 1922 up to the present day. . . . We called the heroes of the past "idols of production"; we feel entitled to call the present day magazine heroes "idols of consumption." Indeed, almost every one of them is directly, or indirectly, related to the sphere of leisure time: either he does not belong to vocations which serve society's basic needs (e.g., the heroes of the world of entertainment and sport), or he amounts, more or less, to a caricature of a socially productive agent.*

—Leo Lowenthal, "Biographies in
Popular Magazines" (1944, pp. 508, 510, 516)

12

Content Analysis

- How is content analysis defined?
- Why do we use content analysis?
- What methodological questions do we face when making content analyses?
- What problems do we face in defining violence in content analysis?
- What are the advantages and difficulties involved in doing content analysis?
- What steps do we take when making a content analysis of media?

Content analysis is one of the most commonly used research method-ologies among scholars dealing with media and communication. This is because it can measure human behavior, assuming, that is, that ver-bal behavior is a form of human behavior. In contrast to opinion polls, which measure what people say they did (or will do) but do not show us what people have actually done, content analysis deals with actual behavior—such as people talking with one another; characters acting certain ways in comic strips, video games, films, and television programs; or writers describing "heroes" in magazine biographies.

❖ DEFINING CONTENT ANALYSIS

The term *content analysis* tells us, broadly, what the methodology does: It analyzes the content of something. But there's much more to content analysis than that. Let me offer an excellent definition of the term found in Charles R. Wright's (1986) *Mass Communication: A Sociological Perspective:*

> Content analysis is a research technique for the systematic classification and description of communication content according to certain usually predetermined categories. It may involve quantitative or qualitative analysis, or both. Technical objectivity requires that the categories of classification and analysis be clearly and operationally defined so that other researchers can follow them reliably. For example, analysis of the social class memberships of television characters requires clear specification of the criteria by which class is identified and classified, so that independent coders are likely to agree on how to classify a character. . . . It is important to remember, however, that content analysis itself provides no direct data about the nature of the communicator, audience, or effects. Therefore, great caution must be exercised whenever this technique is used for any purpose other than the classification, description and analysis of the manifest content of the communication. (pp. 125–126)

A number of concepts mentioned in this passage require definition and clarification—*operational definition, coding,* and *manifest content*—which I explain in the following pages.

Let me offer a second definition that helps clarify content analysis. This comes from Donald Treadwell's *Introducing Communication Research: Paths of Inquiry* (2011). Treadwell started by quoting a famous definition by Bernard Berelson, an important media researcher from the 1950s:

> In the context of communication research, content analysis is a quantitative, systematic, and objective technique for describing the manifest content of communications. (p. 178)

Then Treadwell offered the following amplifications:

- *Quantitative* means that we count occurrences of whatever we are interested in.
- *Systematic* means that we count all relevant aspects of the sample. We cannot arbitrarily pick what aspects get analyzed.

- *Objective* means that we seek units for analysis and categorize them using clearly defined criteria.

- *Manifest* means that we count what is tangible and observable. For example, we cannot count patriotism in consumer advertising because patriotism is ultimately an abstract or latent (hidden) notion. What we can count is the frequency with which the word *patriotism* occurs, the frequency with which a national flag appears, or perhaps the number of minutes music defined as patriotic is played in the background.

We can apply content analysis to all forms of communication, from the personal to the mass mediated. Many scholars would add that content analysis cannot tell us the effects on audiences of the material being studied. Content analysis tells us what is in the material being studied, not how it affects people exposed to this material. On the other hand, if you find, for example, that children's television shows have a great deal of violence in them, whether it is comic or not, you cannot help but wonder about what impact this violence is having upon children. Fortunately, other research methods have explored this question in great detail.

Like many other research methodologies discussed in this book, most of us do a personalized form of content analysis all the time—of what people say to us, of what we read in papers and magazines. We are always searching for meaning and trying to figure out why people do things and what their actions signify. But content analysis is different from our attempts to make sense of communication in that it is much more systematic and objective. And it is quantitative; it measures and counts things of interest to us.

❖ WHY WE MAKE CONTENT ANALYSES

We use content analysis as a research method for a number of reasons. First, we want to get information about a topic and believe that content analysis, rather than other research methods, will help us get the information we're seeking. Thus, we might want to know how much violence there is on American television and whether there's more violence now than there was in earlier years. Content analysis is the methodology that helps us obtain the answers to these questions. We may also be interested in whether the amount of violence on American television differs from the amount of violence on British or French television (or some other country of interest to us) and use content analysis to find out.

A SHORT THEATRICAL PIECE ON CONTENT ANALYSIS

Grand Inquisitor:	*What is your name?*
Arthur:	Conrad. Actually, that's my pseudonym.
Grand Inquisitor:	*Where are you from?*
Arthur:	Connecticut.
Grand Inquisitor:	*What do you do?*
Arthur:	I'm a con artist.
Grand Inquisitor:	*What's your favorite food?*
Arthur:	Consommé with confiture.
Grand Inquisitor:	*What's your biggest personal problem?*
Arthur:	Too controlling.
Grand Inquisitor:	*What's your best attribute?*
Arthur:	Confidence!
Grand Inquisitor:	*Are you married?*
Arthur:	Yes. My wife's name is Constance.
Grand Inquisitor:	*What does she do?*
Arthur:	She's a concierge at the Continental Hotel.
Grand Inquisitor:	*Is there anything else that you want to tell me about yourself?*
Arthur:	You want me to continue? Don't you think I'm to be congratulated?
Grand Inquisitor:	*Au contraire!*

Also, we may have a **hypothesis** (essentially a guess) about some topic and want to see whether it is correct. For example, we may offer a hypothesis that with the rise of feminism, the way women are portrayed in fashion ads has changed and there is less "sexploitation" of women's bodies now than in earlier years. Or we may hypothesize that with the rise of feminism, the portrayal of women in the media has changed: We see them more often, and they are more often shown in professional roles. Frequently, researchers doing content analysis state the problem they want to investigate in the form of a hypothesis to give their research more focus. It's one thing to devise—based on existing theories or previous research—interesting topics to investigate or hypotheses to explore; it's another thing to actually *do* a content analysis. Here are some methodological considerations to keep in mind when planning a content analysis.

❖ METHODOLOGICAL ASPECTS OF CONTENT ANALYSIS

Factual information—what we sometimes term *factoids*—by itself doesn't tell us very much. If one were to say, "In 2015, there were approximately 30 acts of violence per hour on American television," we wouldn't know very much, because we wouldn't know what this datum, the "factoid," means. What we need is some perspective, something with which to compare the 2015 factoid. Here are some ways to make this comparison.

Determine your research question. Before you begin, you have to decide what you are going to measure and what you hope to find out. Conduct a library search on the subject of your proposed content research before beginning to see whether others have done work on the same topic that might be useful to you. Also, make sure that your research topic fits your time constraints. Generally speaking, the narrower the focus, the better—especially for student projects.

Use a historical approach when making a content analysis. Only if we use a historical approach and can say (and I'm making all these figures up for illustrative purposes), "In 1985, there were approximately 10 acts of violence per hour on television, and in 2015, we see approximately 30 acts of violence per hour on television," do we have information of value. Now we know that in 2015, there is 3 times as much violence, per hour, on American television as there was 30 years ago. The historical approach has given us some perspective. Lowenthal's 1944 study, cited at the beginning of this chapter, is an example of historical content analysis. He compared biographies in an earlier period with those he studied in magazines published 1940–1941.

Use a comparative approach when making a content analysis. If we also do a comparative study of television violence and discover that in Sweden, for example, there were three acts of violence per hour on television in 2008, we have information that helps us gain additional perspective on violence on American television. Assuming that the content analysis has been done correctly, we can say that American television contains 10 times more violence than Swedish television.

My point, then, is that content analyses are most valuable when they have either a historical or comparative perspective—or both. And having numbers is important. If a researcher says, "There's a lot of violence on American television," we should want to know what that researcher means by "a lot." What is "a lot" to a professor of communication may be "a little" to the manager of a television station.

Be careful about defining your terms operationally. There are several kinds of definitions. The definitions you find in dictionaries are known as *constitutive definitions*—they define words in terms of other words and concepts. They are quite general and abstract. The definitions used in content analyses are *operational definitions*, which use operations and indicators to define concepts.

An operational definition tells how you will measure something and forces you to explain how you understand or interpret a concept. Thus, if you are dealing with media violence, you will have to describe what kind of actions or behaviors constitute violence. Is threatening talk violence? Is comedic violence (the kind found in children's television cartoons) violence? Is there an important difference between comedic and serious violence? Offering an operational definition of your term is very difficult, and its absence is a weak point in many content analyses. If others don't accept your definition of violence, they will reject your findings as being irrelevant or unsound.

Categories must be mutually exclusive. You must not define your concept in a way that can be applied to more than one kind of behavior. If you define violence too broadly or too narrowly, there will be problems. If your definition is too broad, researchers will argue that your measurements aren't reliable or of any value because you deal with too many things. If your definition is too narrow, researchers will say you neglected important matters. For example, some scholars do not consider the smacking and banging about by characters in animated comics and cartoon strips to be examples of violence. They see violence as something serious. Others would disagree with this assessment.

In *Violence and Terror in the Mass Media: An Annotated Bibliography,* George Gerbner and Nancy Signorielli (1988), who compiled the bibliography, wrote, "Reliable observation and systematic analysis usually require limited and objective definitions. Most research studies have defined media violence as the depiction of overt physical action that hurts or kills or threatens to do so" (p. xi). The book lists and briefly describes 673 articles on media violence by psychologists, sociologists, and other scholars. But one problem with all these articles is that there is no agreement among them on how to define violence in the media. This is because violence is such a complicated phenomenon. According to the definition offered earlier, it is questionable whether the mayhem in animated cartoons and comics is really violence because the characters don't seem to be affected by what happens to them. In the same light, your concept must deal with all the behaviors that can be studied. If your operational definition leaves out certain kinds of violence (perhaps because they are difficult to measure and quantify), your results may be viewed as invalid. So it is very important that your operational definition be carefully worded and thought out.

Determine measurable scoring units. This means figuring out your basic or standard unit of measurement. If you are doing a content analysis of the comics page of a newspaper, you could take the comic strip frame as your basic unit. If you are doing a content analysis of magazine articles, you could take number of words. and if you are studying a newspaper article, you could take number of column inches as your basic unit. If you are doing television programs, you could take number of minutes as your basic unit. The important thing is that your basic unit has to be the same for all the examples you study.

Determine how to do your coding. Coding is a process by which we classify data obtained from material studied and give each item in a category a symbol or number. We code so that we can carry out cross-tabulations when interpreting our research. In dealing with television violence, for example, we may classify the kinds of violence we find on television into a number of categories and give each category some number or symbol. In the case of violence, there are many kinds we might observe: men against women, women against men, adults against children, children against adults, and so on. Because *violence* is so vague a term and because it is so hard to operationalize a definition of violence, the concept is difficult to code in such a way that anyone replicating your study would use the same codes. I will return to these considerations later.

Measure only the manifest content. When making content analyses, examine only the manifest content of texts—that is, what is explicitly stated—rather than the latent content, the "hidden" material behind or between the words. If a male character in a comic strip says, "I love you," to a female character, you have to take that statement at face value and use it in your content analysis. You must not assume, because of his previous actions in the story, that he's insincere and thus discount his statement.

❖ ASPECTS OF VIOLENCE

In the following chart, taken from my book *Essentials of Mass Communication Theory* (A. A. Berger, 1995), I offer a number of under-standings of the term *violence* to show how difficult this concept is. Keeping in mind Saussure's (1966) admonitions about concepts defined negatively, consider the possibilities when it comes to aspects of violence. I list 31 polar oppositions that reflect various kinds of violence and by doing so show how complicated an issue violence is.

1. Mediated violence	Violence we see directly
2. Real mediated violence (wars)	Fictive mediated violence
3. Comic violence	Serious violence
4. Intended violence	Actualized violence
5. Violence to individuals	Violence to groups
6. Inferred violence	Documented violence
7. Police violence (just)	Criminal violence
8. Verbal violence	Physical violence
9. "Fake" violence (wrestling)	"True" violence (bar brawl)
10. Violence against heroes	Violence against villains
11. Violence against women	Violence against men
12. Violence in the past	Violence in the future
13. Violence by human agents	Violence by mechanical agents
14. Defensive violence	Offensive violence

15. Violence by children	Violence by adults
16. Weak violence (insults)	Strong violence (murder)
17. Accidental violence	Intentional violence
18. Visual images of violence	Prose descriptions of violence
19. Violence by the insane	Violence by the sane
20. Violence as means to end	Violence as end in itself
21. Causes of violence	Effects of violence
22. Violence as action	Violence as reaction
23. Many minor acts of violence	One major act of violence
24. Violence as emotional response	Violence as rational decision
25. Violence against others	Violence against self
26. Violence ordered by others	Violence decided by self
27. Sign of depravity	Cry for help
28. Violence caused by fear	Violence caused by hatred
29. Institutional violence	Individual violence
30. Violence as instinctive	Violence as cultural
31. Violence integral (sports)	Violence extraordinary (murder)

We can see, then, that violence is extremely complex and difficult to define—especially from an operational point of view. Because of the complexity of the concept, many content analyses of violence in the media have been challenged by researchers who defined violence differently.

❖ ADVANTAGES OF CONTENT ANALYSIS AS A RESEARCH METHOD

The many advantages of content analysis explain why it is such a popular form of research:

- It is unobtrusive.
- It is relatively inexpensive.

- It can deal with current events and topics of present-day interest.

- It uses material that is relatively easy to obtain and work with.

- It yields data that can be quantified.

One of the main advantages of content analysis is that it is unobtrusive. Unlike with research methods such as interviewing and participant observation, the researcher does not "intrude" on what is being studied and thus does not affect the outcome of the research. In addition, unlike some other research methods, content analysis is relatively inexpensive. It doesn't cost very much to obtain material to be studied—to duplicate printed matter or record television programs. Of course, the scope of the content analysis is a factor. If you're going to make a large-scale analysis of television news programs, for example, and use hundreds of hours of program material, then coding this material can be very time-consuming and expensive. But for most content analyses, costs of obtaining the material to be analyzed are not great.

Content analyses can be made of topics of current interest. That is, you can deal with matters of concern of the moment—though, as I've suggested earlier, data by themselves don't mean very much. You need to be able to put your data in perspective, a task accomplished, generally speaking, by making historical or comparative content analyses. In addition, the material used to make content analyses is readily available. If you are doing a content analysis of printed material, you can often find such material at a good library. And many past television programs can be obtained at certain research libraries. Contemporary television programs can be recorded, of course. What is most important, however, as far as our interest in **quantitative research** methods is concerned, is that the data you collect from your content analysis can be expressed in numbers. These numbers provide detailed information that can be interpreted to gain insights into the mind-set of those who created the texts. Possibly—although this is debatable—they can be used to infer the way audiences of these texts might be affected by them.

❖ DIFFICULTIES IN MAKING CONTENT ANALYSES

As with any research method, researchers face certain problems when making content analyses. I dealt with some of these topics earlier in my overview of content analysis. Here are a few issues to add to the previous discussion:

- Finding a representative sample

- Determining measurable units

- Obtaining reliability in coding

- Defining terms operationally

- Ensuring validity and utility in your findings

The first problem is determining a representative sample of the text you are studying. If you are studying Saturday morning network children's television, you have to decide which programs are representative and how much of each program to analyze. If your sampling is not representative, your findings will not be convincing.

Sometimes this problem is dealt with by choosing a random sampling for analysis and assuming that it will provide you with a representative sampling or at least one for which observer bias cannot be argued. You also have to determine your measurable units. With printed text such as newspaper or magazine articles, this is usually done in column inches or square inches or number of words. You can also use television shows or magazine issues. However you do it, you must find a way to make sure your units are standard. If you are studying fashion advertisements in magazines, the individual advertisement, not the number of inches it takes up, would be the unit; it doesn't make much difference whether your ads are in a magazine the size of *Vogue* or in the Sunday magazine section of the *New York Times*. If you are dealing with comic strips, the frame could be the fundamental unit.

You do have to figure out how to code your material so that every coder will classify the elements in the texts being analyzed the same way. This matter of coder reliability is important because if different coders code a certain action in a text different ways, your results will not be useful. To obtain coder reliability, you must make operational definitions of activities in the text to be coded. Thus, you must classify all of the actions you want coded (for example, different kinds of violence) and then offer operational definitions for each of them. I have discussed the difficulties of making operational definitions earlier.

The simplest (but also quite effective) way of testing reliability ("intercoding reliability" in content analysis jargon) is to have several coders analyze identical content and then compare the results. The researcher looks for percentage of agreement, and, of course, the higher the agreement level, the greater the reliability. Typically, a reliability level of 90% or higher is considered acceptable. You also must be sure that your findings are valid and useful—namely, that you actually measured what you planned to measure and that your results will be of some interest. This means you must pay a good deal of attention to formulating your research question so you have a chance of finding interesting things and getting good results.

Going back to the television violence example, there is also the intensity of the violence to be considered. One television show may have many acts of relatively "weak" violence while another show, of the same length, may only have one act of violence, but one so powerful that its impact on viewers is strong and long lasting.

❖ CONTENT ANALYSIS STEP-BY-STEP

I've discussed the methodological problems connected with doing content analyses, some of the difficulties involved in this kind of research, and some of the benefits gained. What follows is a list that takes you step-by-step through the process.

1. Decide what you want to find out and offer a hypothesis—that is, an educated guess—about what you expect to find. (For example, it is reasonable to hypothesize that as a result of the growth of feminism and the increased power of women in government and other aspects of society, the number of words spoken by women in comic strips will increase as we study samples from 1960 to 2010. Whether that hypothesis is correct or not has to be tested by making a content analysis.)

2. Explain what you'll be investigating and tell why this research is worth doing.

3. Offer an operational definition of the topic you'll be studying. If you're studying violence, tell how you define it.

4. Explain your basis for selecting the sample you'll be analyzing. How did you determine which examples to investigate?

5. Explain your unit of analysis.

6. Describe your classification system or system of categories for coding your material. Remember that the categories must be mutually exclusive and that you must cover every example of what you're analyzing.

7. Determine your coding system.

8. Test for intercoding reliability and make any necessary adjustments, such as increased training and practice for the coders or an adjustment of the operational definition and code guides.

9. Using your coding system, analyze the sample you have selected.

10. Present your findings using quantified data you've obtained from your content analysis.

11. Interpret your results using your numerical data and other material relevant to your research.

This list describes the steps researchers commonly use in doing content analyses. Of course, there's a big difference between having a list of steps to follow and actually doing the analysis. The latter means wrestling with problems such as how to select a sample and how to classify and code the material in it. And there is also the matter of interpreting your findings, for interpretations invariably "go beyond" the data and thus are open to criticism.

❖ CONTENT ANALYSIS: APPLICATIONS AND EXERCISES

1. Using the list of oppositions in kinds of violence, make a content analysis of the kinds of violence found in an episode of a crime television show. Prepare a coding sheet for the analysis. Did you find anything surprising in your analysis? If you can find an episode of the show done a number of years earlier, you can see whether there have been any changes in the way violence is used.

2. Make a content analysis of the words spoken by males and females in a newspaper's comic strip page on one weekday in 1995 and one weekday in 2015. Base your analysis on the step-by-step content analysis list and coding sheet from this chapter. What problems did you face in making your content analysis? What were your findings? Did they surprise you in any way? You can also study other topics in the comics, such as the kinds of violence found in them, the number of male and female figures found in them, and so on.

3. Find three magazine articles about "idols of production" (e.g., political figures, businesspersons) and three about "idols of

SAMPLE CODING SHEET FOR COMPARATIVE NEWSPAPER COMIC STRIP PAGE ANALYSIS

1. Name of newspaper

2. Dates of publication:
   month, day, for years   2000   2010

3. Page numbers for each day   2000 page(s):   2010 page(s):

4. List of names of all comic strips
   on each page(s) for each date 2000:   2010:

   _____   _____

   _____   _____

   _____   _____

   _____   _____

   _____   _____

5. Number of male and female
   figures on each page for
   each date   2000:   2010:

6. Number of words spoken by
   all male characters on each
   page for each date   2000:   2010:

7. Number of words spoken by
   all female characters on
   each page for each date   2000:   2010:

Note: This content analysis only deals with the number of words spoken by male and female characters on the comic strip pages of a newspaper in 2000 and 2010 (or any dates chosen by your instructor). It does not deal with age, gender, race, or other topics that might be investigated.

1. Speech in regular balloons

2. Thoughts in scalloped balloons

3. Sound effects in zigzagged balloons

4. Facial expressions

5. Lines to indicate movement

6. Panel for continuity

7. Setting

8. Art styles—light and dark, composition, and so on

9. Language—meanings of words and punctuation

10. Clothes, objects, and other examples of material culture

Source: Arthur A. Berger, *Media Research Techniques* (1998a).

consumption" (e.g., movie stars, entertainers, celebrities). Duplicate the first pages of the articles and bring them to class. What problems did you face in finding your "idols"? What interesting things did you find in the articles? Where did you go looking for idols of production?

❖ CONCLUSIONS

As with other research methods, there's a big difference between know-ing something about the methodology of content analysis and actually doing the research. But there's no such thing as a perfect methodology— one that does not have weaknesses and limitations. Do not be surprised if you run into difficulties in doing a content analysis (or any other kind of research, for that matter), and don't be too hard on yourself, either. It takes a good deal of practice and experience to learn how to manage the difficulties that researchers face. The important thing is to think clearly and work carefully, and if you have the opportunity, share what you've learned. Leo Lowenthal's 1944 content analysis of the *Saturday Evening Post* and *Collier's,* quoted at the beginning of this chapter, led to impor-tant insights about the way (what he termed) "idols of production" had been eclipsed by "idols of consumption." Idols of consumption still dominate many of our magazines and have played a major role, over the years, in shaping America's consumer society.

❖ FURTHER READING

Adams, W., & Adams, F. S. (1978). *Television network news: Issues in content research.* Washington, DC: George Washington University.

Gottschalk, L. A. (1995). *Content analysis of verbal behavior: New findings and clinical applications.* Mahwah, NJ: Lawrence Erlbaum.

Krippendorff, K. H. (2013). *Content analysis: An introduction to its methodology* (3rd ed.). Thousand Oaks, CA: SAGE.

Krippendorff, K. H., & Bock, M. A. (Eds.). (2009). *The content analysis reader.* Thousand Oaks, CA: SAGE.

Neuendorf, K. A. (2002). *The content analysis guidebook.* Thousand Oaks, CA: SAGE.

Riffe, D., Lacy, S., & Fico, F. (2013). *Analyzing media messages: Using quantitative content analysis in research* (3rd ed.). Mahwah, NJ: Lawrence Erlbaum.

Roberts, C. W. (Ed.). (1997). *Text analysis for the social sciences: Methods of drawing statistical inferences from texts and transcripts.* Mahwah, NJ: Lawrence Erlbaum.

Treadwell, D. (2014). *Introducing communication research: Paths of inquiry* (2nd ed.). Thousand Oaks, CA: SAGE.

Weber, R. P. (1990). *Basic content analysis* (2nd ed.). Newbury Park, CA: SAGE.

There is no perfect data collection method. However, self-administered questionnaires are preferable to personal interviews when three conditions are met: (a) You are dealing with literate respondents; (b) you are confident of getting a high response rate (which I put at 70%, minimum); and (c) the nature of the questions you want to ask does not require a face-to-face interview and the use of visual aids such as cue cards, charts, and the like.

Under these circumstances, you get much more information for your time and money than from the other methods of questionnaire administration. If you are working in a highly industrialized country, and if a very high proportion (at least 80%) of the population you are studying has its own telephone, then consider doing a phone survey whenever a self-administered questionnaire would otherwise not be appropriate.

—H. Russell Bernard, *Research
Methods in Anthropology: Qualitative
and Quantitative Approaches* (1994, p. 264)

13

Surveys

- What are surveys, and what do they aim to find out?
- How do descriptive and analytic surveys differ?
- How do personal interviews and self-administered questionnaires differ?
- What are the advantages and disadvantages of conducting surveys?
- What's the difference between shares and ratings when studying television viewers?
- When should open-ended and closed-ended surveys be used?
- How do you write good survey questions?
- What was said about samples and surveys?
- What kinds of samples are there?
- How do you evaluate the accuracy of surveys?
- What was said about surveys and the 2012 presidential election?

Surveying is a research method used to get information about certain groups of people representative of some larger group of interest. For example, manufacturers of products want to know how people feel about their products (and those of their competitors) and use **surveys** to find out. We use surveys to answer the following:

- What do people know?

- What do people think?

- What do people own?

- What do people do?

- What have people done?

- What are people planning to do?

- What are people's attitudes?

- What are people's tastes?

- What are people's prejudices?

- What are people's beliefs?

- What are people's values?

Politicians frequently use surveys to find out what issues are of importance to people and, during election periods, whom they intend to vote for. Most surveying is done by interviewers, but one kind of survey—the questionnaire—does not use interviewers but is sent through the mail or distributed in publications (or through other means, such as on the Internet). Both terms—*surveys* and *questionnaires*—are often used loosely.

❖ DEFINING SURVEYS

In their book *Field Projects for Sociology Students,* Jacqueline P. Wiseman and Marcia S. Aron (1970) offered an excellent definition of surveys:

> Survey research is a method for collecting and analyzing social data via highly structured and often very detailed interviews or questionnaires in order to obtain information from large numbers of respondents presumed to be representative of a specific population. (p. 37)

A more recent definition can be found in Donald Treadwell's *Introducing Communication Research.* He defined surveys as follows (2011):

> A survey is a series of formatted questions delivered to a defined sample of people with the expectation that their responses will be returned somewhere between immediately and in a few days. The survey process starts with theoretically derived research questions or hypotheses and continues through question design and ordering, delivering questions to respondents, and obtaining their answers and analyzing them. A **questionnaire** is the specific set of questions that respondents answer.

These definitions call our attention to four key points about surveying:

1. It is done to collect and analyze social, economic, psychological, technical, cultural, and other types of data.

2. It is based on finding people (respondents) and asking them for information.

3. It is done with **representative samples** of a population being studied.

4. It is assumed that information obtained from the sample is valid for the population being studied.

❖ KINDS OF SURVEYS: DESCRIPTIVE AND ANALYTIC

There are two basic kinds of surveys: *descriptive* and *analytic* (or explanatory). The descriptive survey, as the name suggests, describes the population being studied. These surveys seek to obtain information about demographic factors such as age, gender, marital status, occupation, race or ethnicity, income, and religion and to relate this information to opinions, beliefs, values, and behaviors of some group of people. For example, broadcasters use surveys to find out how **popular** their programs are, and manufacturers use surveys to determine who uses their products. The focus of descriptive surveys is on present-day behavior.

The second kind of survey, the analytic survey, seeks to find out why people behave the way they do. Researchers often use data from descriptive surveys to develop hypotheses and use analytic surveys to test their hypotheses about what causes certain kinds of behavior.

Analytic surveys attempt to determine whether there are causal relationships between certain kinds of behavior and social and demographic characteristics of people.

As you might imagine, it's much easier to obtain descriptions of people's behavior than it is to find out why people behave the way they do. You have to consider biological, psychological, social, economic, and political factors (among other things) in dealing with human behavior. There are so many variables behind people's choices that it is hard to know why people act the way they do or what factors of many are of primary importance.

VALS cartoon

❖ THE VALS TYPOLOGY SURVEY

In 1983, Arnold Mitchell, director of the Stanford Research Institute's **Values and Lifestyles (VALS)** program, published *The Nine American Lifestyles: Who We Are and Where We Are Going.* In his preface, he made some interesting points:

> People's values and lifestyles say a good deal about where we are going, and they help explain such practical, diverse questions as: why we support some issues and oppose others; why some people are strong leaders and others weak; why some people are economically brilliant and others gifted artistically—and a few are both; why we trust some people and are suspicious of others; why some products attract us and others don't; why revolutions occur.

By the term "values" we mean the entire constellation of a person's attitudes, beliefs, opinions, hopes, fears, prejudices, needs, desires, and aspirations that, taken together, govern how one behaves. . . . We now have powerful evidence that the classification of an individual on the basis of a few dozen attitudes and demographics tells us a good deal about what to expect of that person in hundreds of other domains. Further, the approach often enables us to identify the decisive quality-of-life factor or factors in a person's life. (p. vii)

Mitchell developed what is known as the VALS typology based on a large survey he and his colleagues conducted in 1980. The typology argues that there are nine groups of people who share similar values that shape their behavior, especially as consumers. The advertising industry was extremely interested in the VALS typology because it thought this tool would help them target groups of interest to them.

The first VALS typology (a second was developed later) had nine groupings. The groups are classified according to whether they are need driven, outer directed, inner directed, or both outer and inner directed.

Name	Group Classification
Survivors	Need driven
Sustainers	Need driven
Belongers	Outer directed
Emulators	Outer directed
Achievers	Outer directed
I-Am-Me's	Inner directed
Experientials	Inner directed
Societally conscious	Inner directed
Integrated	Outer and inner directed

This typology grew out of a huge survey that Stanford Research (not connected with the university) conducted. Mitchell described the role of the survey in developing the typology as follows (1983):

The Values and Lifestyle (VALS) typology . . . rests upon data obtained in a major mail survey conducted by VALS in 1980. . . . The survey asked over 800 specific questions on a great range of topics. Sample size exceeded 1600. Respondents constituted a national probability sample of Americans aged eighteen or over living in the forty-eight

> contiguous states. Statistical analysis of survey results quantified and enriched the basic concepts of the VALS typology and enabled us to provide detailed quantitative and human portraits of the VALS types, together with their activities and consumption patterns. (pp. 3–4)

This survey had a significantly sized sample, suggesting a high degree of reliability. What is interesting, for our purposes, is that VALS developed a short form of the survey for the convenience of the Stanford Research Institute's clients and discovered that it achieved an overall level of agreement of 86%.

We learn two things from this study. First, it is possible—if done correctly—to obtain useful results from a relatively small survey. The short form of the VALS survey was almost as accurate as the long form. Second, after one obtains results from a survey, it is necessary to interpret the results. Usually this takes the form of creating a typology— of aggregating or classifying the people who completed the survey into groups. The fact that Stanford Research came up with a second VALS typology, quite different from the first, suggests that this aspect of survey research analysis is based on interpreting the data and finding ways to classify it and that some interpretations and classifications of data are better than others.

❖ METHODS OF DATA COLLECTION

Conventionally, surveys collect data through two methods:

1. Interviews (individual or group interviews; in-person or telephone interviews)

2. Self-administered questionnaires

   - Supervised administration: One-to-one or group administration
   - Unsupervised administration: The questionnaire is mailed (or emailed) to people or freely distributed via magazines, the Internet, and so on.

Survey interviews are quite different from depth interviews. Survey interviews have lists of questions people are asked to answer and do not allow interviewers to explore subjects that come up, by chance, as is possible in less structured depth interviews. Survey interviews are shorter than depth interviews and more structured so information can be obtained to make valid generalizations about the population being studied. Telephone interviews are comparatively less expensive and possibly less intimidating than in-person interviews, but because not everyone has phones, the sample may be biased or unrepresentative.

Questionnaires are conventionally understood to be lists of questions given or sent to people who are asked to answer the questions and return the questionnaires to the senders. That is, they are self-administered surveys. Questionnaires should always be accompanied by cover letters explaining the purpose of the questionnaire and pointing out how it is in the interest of the respondent to answer the questionnaire. They should also be attractively designed and easy to fill out and return. It's a good idea to provide a stamped, self-addressed envelope to respondents. The easier you make things for your respondents, the better chance you have of getting the questionnaire returned.

The advantages and disadvantages of these two methods of surveying are noted briefly in the following chart.

Personal Interviews

Advantages	Disadvantages
Interviewer can explain questions in detail	Can be intrusive (too personal)
Interviewer can use a variety of data collection methods	Time-consuming and expensive
Interviewer can spend a lot of time with respondents	Hard to find people in sample at times
You know who is answering questions	People are reluctant to answer some questions
A higher likelihood of achieving a desired response rate	Needs well-trained interviewers
Not intimidating	Interviewer and respondent may have a language barrier

Self-Administered Questionnaires

Advantages	Disadvantages
Inexpensive	People may misinterpret questions
No interviewer bias to worry about	Low response rates the norm
You can ask about very personal matters	You don't know who actually filled out the questionnaire
You can ask complex, detailed questions	Sampling errors frequent

You can see from this chart that there are advantages and disadvantages to each of the two ways of collecting information. The choice you make should be based on what you want to find out, how much time you have, and how much money you have.

❖ ADVANTAGES OF SURVEY RESEARCH

There are a number of advantages to conducting surveys, which explains why they are so widely used. They are also widely reported on in newspapers and magazines, in part because people are interested in what the surveys reveal—even though individuals are often reluctant to participate in them.

- Surveys are inexpensive.

- Surveys can obtain current information.

- Surveys enable you to obtain a great deal of information at one time.

- Surveys provide quantitative or numeric data.

- Surveys are very common, and some of the information you seek may have already been discovered in a survey.

Surveys are, relatively speaking, inexpensive, especially when you consider the amount of information they are able to obtain. And the information you obtain is current. Surveys enable researchers (who work for manufacturers, marketers, and political parties) to find out, for example, what products people own, what products they intend to purchase, what issues are important to them in elections, whom they might vote for in elections, and all kinds of other information of interest.

What is particularly important is that surveys obtain information that can be quantified and analyzed statistically and thus can reach a degree of precision about the group being studied that other forms of research cannot duplicate. These data can be summarized so that readers are able to see, rather quickly, what the data reveal about the population being studied. I use the phrase "population being studied" because many surveys are interested only in one segment of the population—for example, people planning to buy cars, voters in a given state, homemakers, or audiences of television shows. Survey information is so important in the television industry that programs live or die based on their popularity—which is determined by data about viewers obtained from surveys.

So many surveys are conducted that the information you are interested in obtaining may have already been found in another survey. So you should make sure that you aren't expending a great deal of time and energy to find information that is already available. The other side of this coin is that people have developed resistance to being surveyed and may not cooperate with you. The following note comes from an October 1997 online media report, *Media Professional,* citing findings from a September 1997 issue of *Business Marketing:*

Business Researchers
Struggle to Get Valid Response Levels

Business researchers are finding it harder and harder to get 50% response rates to the surveys. As the number of surveys has increased, buyers have become less likely to respond to an individual survey. In addition, companies are beginning to discourage employees from spending their time responding. 50% response is the generally accepted threshold for accuracy.

❖ PROBLEMS WITH SURVEYS

There are a number of general problems connected with using surveys and questionnaires (and interviewing of all kinds) that you, as a researcher, should keep in mind:

- People often don't tell the truth, especially about personal matters.
- People make mistakes about what they've done, even if they are trying to tell the truth.
- Obtaining representative samples is frequently quite difficult.
- People often refuse to participate in surveys.
- Relatively small percentages of people answer and return questionnaires.
- Writing good survey questions is difficult to do.

Sometimes people won't tell the truth. They may be afraid, for example, that if they tell you what programs they typically watch, you'll think they are stupid, or maybe they are afraid that you'll think they watch too much television.

People also make mistakes about their behavior. They may, for example, understate the amount of television they watch in a given day. In other cases, people give incorrect answers because the questions are unclear or ambiguous or, somehow, threatening. Frequently, people intend to answer questionnaires but mislay them or forget about them. That's why it is often necessary to send follow-up letters to remind people to fill out their questionnaires and mail them back to you. It is crucial that you get questionnaires back from people in your sample; otherwise, the sample will not be representative.

Many people refuse to participate in surveys. Personally speaking, I know that I get irritated when I'm called around dinnertime and asked whether I'll answer some questions for some marketing survey. Like many people, I dislike giving certain kinds of information about myself to others, especially if I believe they'll be profiting from the information I provide.

❖ SURVEYS AND THE 2012 PRESIDENTIAL ELECTION

Surveys played an important role in the 2012 presidential election and enabled several statisticians to predict the outcome of the election for the presidency and many other offices.

In "Obama Holds Lead in Florida and Ohio Polls," Neil King Jr. (2012) explained the methodology used in telephone polls conducted by the *Wall Street Journal*, NBC News, and Marist polls. The data were based on landline and cell phone interviews of adults 18 and older. The Marist polls contacted 1,973 registered voters and 1,545 likely voters in Florida and 1,253 registered voters and 971 likely voters in Ohio on October 31 and November 1, 2012. The telephone numbers were selected to ensure a random selection of landline and cell phone users. King (2012) explained the methodology:

> Cell phone interviews comprised 24% of registered voters in Florida and 22% of likely voters in Florida and 27% of registered voters and 25% of likely voters in Ohio. In Florida, 37% of likely voters identified themselves as Democrats, 35% as Republicans and 33% as independent or other. Results for registered voters are statistically significant with plus or minus 2.2 percentage points in Florida and 2.8 points in Ohio. For likely voters, results are statistically significant within plus or minus 2.5 percentage points in Florida and 3.1 points in Ohio. Sample tolerances for subgroups within each state are larger.

Nate Silver, a statistician who used to write the "FiveThirtyEight" column for the *New York Times*, dealt with errors in polls that did not contact enough cell phone users. In his article "Google or Gallup?

Changes in Voters' Habits Reshape Polling World" (2012), he looked at the results of polls conducted during the last 3 weeks of the presidential campaign. He noted that some polling firms overestimated support for the Republican candidate, Mitt Romney, by as much as 4 points, giving the Republicans an inaccurate view of the voting public and leading some Republicans to believe they would win the presidency in a landslide. The Gallup poll in particular had very inaccurate results. As Silver wrote, "Gallup has now had three poor elections in a row. In 2008, its polls overestimated Mr. Obama's performance, while in 2010 they overestimated how well Republicans would do." Silver found that companies that conducted their polls online and by telephone had some of the best results, off by only 2 points. On the other hand, robopolls were off by 5 points, and live telephone polls were off by 3.5 points. One reason that some of the polls were off by so much, Silver suggested, is that they didn't take cell phone users into account; in addition, they were using models developed many years ago that are no longer adequate. He concluded with this possibility: "Perhaps it will not be long before Google, not Gallup, is the most trusted name in polling." Silver's accurate predictions, based on choosing good polls, made him a media celebrity. He left the *New York Times* and now has his own company, FiveThirtyEight, and blogs on sporting events and politics, among other topics.

❖ A NOTE ON MEDIA USAGE SURVEYS: SHARES AND RATINGS

When doing surveys dealing with what television programs people are watching, researchers distinguish between audience **ratings** and audience **shares**. Barry L. Sherman (1995) explained in *Telecommunications Management: Broadcasting/Cable and the New Technologies,*

> *Rating* refers to the percentage of people or households in an area tuned to a specific station, program, or network. For example, if, in a Nielsen sample of 1000 homes, 250 households were tuned to the ABC network, the rating for ABC during that time period would be (250 divided by 1000), or 25%. For ease of reporting, the percentage sign is dropped in the ratings book. *Share* refers to the number of people or households tuned to a particular station program or network correlated with sets in use. Continuing the above example, if only 750 of the sampled households were actually watching television in the time period covered, ABC's share would be (250 divided by 750) = 33%. Since there are always more sets in a market than there are sets in use, the share figure is always higher than the rating. (p. 389)

Because radio stations, television stations, and networks make money by delivering audiences to advertisers, the size (and nature) of the audiences of these stations and shows is of crucial importance. The larger the audience (as long as the **demographics** are acceptable), the more a station or network can charge for running commercials.

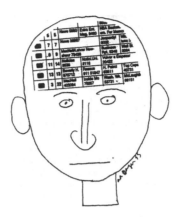

As you might imagine, the share is of particular interest because it tells station owners how well their station, as compared to other stations, is doing with the actual viewing or listening audience. And like much information gathered in research, relationships—generally stated in percentages—are crucial.

❖ OPEN-ENDED AND CLOSED-ENDED SURVEY QUESTIONS

One can use two kinds of survey questions: open-ended and closed-ended questions (or, in other terminology, constructed-response questions and selected-response questions). An open-ended question asks for an answer that the respondent should construct by himself or herself, writing it down in the space provided. Closed-ended questions ask respondents to select from lists of answers provided by the survey designer—lists such as multiple-choice questions or Likert scales. Examples of these two formats follow.

Multiple-choice questions. The two major criteria for generating good questions are that the answer choices are mutually exclusive (the respondent should be able to select one response only, unless multiple responses are requested) and that the answer choices are exhaustive (all possible choices should be mentioned, which is typically achieved by adding "other" as a choice). An example follows:

Which one of the following network television stations do you most regularly watch for national news?

(a.) NBC

(b.) CBS

(c.) ABC

(d.) Fox

(e.) Other

Likert scale questions. In *Research Methods in Anthropology,* H. Russell Bernard (1994) discussed **Likert scales:**

> Perhaps the most commonly used form of scaling is attributed to Rensis Likert (1932). Likert introduced the ever-popular 5-point scale. . . . The 5-point scale might become 3 points or 7 points, and the agree disagree scale might become approve disapprove, favor oppose, or excellent-bad, but the principle is the same. These are all Likert scales. . . . Likert's method was to take a long list of possible scaling items for a concept and find the subset that measured the various dimensions. If the concept were unidimensional, then one subset would do. If it were multi-dimensional, then several subsets would be needed. (pp. 297–298)

In the following Likert scale, a question is offered and people are asked to choose from among five positions: *strongly agree, agree, neutral, disagree, strongly disagree.*

The most important aspect of local news is accuracy.

1. Strongly agree

2. Agree

3. Neutral

4. Disagree

5. Strongly disagree

You can see that a Likert scale enables you to quantify opinions and beliefs and thus obtain more precise indications than with many other methodologies.

❖ WRITING SURVEY QUESTIONS

Donald Treadwell offered an important insight into the matter of writing survey questions. In his book *Introducing Communication Research: Paths of Inquiry* (2011), he wrote,

> Developing a successful survey—by which we mean one that captures what you want to capture from a maximum number of respondents—requires more than just sitting at a keyboard and typing questions. The question format, question wording, and question order can all influence respondents' answers and the results you get, so time developing and pretesting questions is well spent.
>
> Most surveys seek to find out four things about respondents. These are demographic data such as age, sex, religion, and marital status; knowledge; attitudes; and behavior. (pp. 125–126)

Writing good survey questions is an art. After you have decided what information you want, you have to write your survey questions. Good survey questions have the following characteristics:

- They are clear and not ambiguous.
- They are short.
- They use simple, easily understood language.
- They ask for only one piece of information per question.
- They avoid showing bias.
- They aren't "leading" or "loaded" questions.
- They don't embarrass respondents.
- They ask questions that the respondents can answer.
- The questions are logically grouped, with questions related to one another placed near one another.
- The scales for measurement of opinion are clear. (The Likert scale is highly recommended because it provides considerable detail—much more than "like/dislike" or "good/neutral/bad.")
- The order of the questions is worked out logically.

Expressing yourself clearly, so that people understand exactly what you want to know, is quite difficult. It's surprising how people can misunderstand, misinterpret, and become confused about questions you thought were simple to answer. You've got to be very careful about your choice of words and sentence structure.

One way to achieve clarity is to write sentences that are short and to the point. The shorter your sentences are, the less chance they will be misunderstood. Another matter to keep in mind is to ask for only one item or piece of information in a question and not write double-barreled questions. The following question is double-barreled and is an example of what to avoid. These questions usually have *and* in them:

Do you think this product tastes good and is nutritious?

This question should be separated into two questions: one about the taste and the other about the nutritional value:

Do you think this product tastes good?

Do you think this product is nutritious?

In writing questions, avoid showing bias that slants questions to reveal your beliefs and opinions. A similar problem involves writing leading questions, in which you ask your respondents, more or less, to agree with you about something or hint that they should answer a question in a certain way. Biased questions and leading questions both impose your ideas and perspectives on your respondents and defeat the purpose of surveys, which is to obtain information about how your respondents feel.

A SHORT THEATRICAL PIECE ON SURVEYS

Grand Inquisitor:	*During the Inquisition, we made a survey of our heretics.*
Arthur:	That's quite a surprise. What did you find?
Grand Inquisitor:	*We gave them one multiple-choice question: Which would you prefer?*

(Continued)

(Continued)

        A. To be boiled in oil

        B. To be stretched on the rack

        C. To be quartered by four horses after your joints were cut

        D. To be forced to die of old age

Arthur: What did you find?

Grand Inquisitor: *It was quite a surprise. It seems that 100% of those who answered their multiple-choice question checked D. They said they wanted to be forced to die of old age.*

Arthur: Did your findings have any effect on the Inquisition?

Grand Inquisitor: *No, because 100% of the inquisitors answered the multiple-choice question they were asked the same way; it turns out they wanted to save the heretics "the hard way"—namely, A, B, or C. I suspect that people often use surveys to suit their own purposes and do whatever they want, regardless of survey results.*

Of course, interest groups sometimes want to obtain certain results, so they word their questions to more or less guarantee that they'll get the answers they want. Consider the following yes-or-no questions on the same subject:

1. "Do you think innocent babies should be murdered before they are born?"

2. "Do you believe women have the right to reproductive freedom and control over their own bodies?"

Obviously, question 1, which is full of trigger words meant to evoke emotional responses, is not impartial and "leads" respondents to answer in certain ways. What really causes problems for researchers is when respondents answer yes to two questions like the pair above, thus agreeing with two contradictory positions.

❖ MAKING PILOT STUDIES TO PRETEST SURVEYS

Because people have a genius for misinterpreting and misunderstanding questions—even ones you think are simple and straightforward—you should make pilot studies. That is, you should test your surveys and questionnaires (the technical term for them, used by social scientists, is *instruments*) on a small group of people to see what problems arise. You should consider the following questions when assessing your **pilot study**:

- Can people easily understand all your questions?

- Do your questions enable you to obtain the information you want?

- Are there questions you didn't ask that you should ask?

- Are there questions you asked that you shouldn't ask?

- Does your pilot study suggest you should try a different method of data collection?

The advantage of doing a pilot study is that it frequently helps you discover problems in your questionnaire you couldn't have anticipated, which you then can solve before you undertake a larger study.

❖ CONDUCTING ONLINE SURVEYS

The Web is a convenient and inexpensive resource for conducting surveys. Students can take advantage of sites such as SurveyMonkey to conduct relatively simple surveys free of charge. In an article in the *Chronicle of Philanthropy*, Marilyn Dickey (2006) discussed some things to keep in mind when selecting a site to create a web survey. I offer an abbreviated version of the points she made:

- Is the site easy to use? Are the instructions clear?

- Does the site offer the question formats most suitable for your needs?

- Can the survey be conducted on the Web, or do people taking it have to print out questionnaires?

- Is there a limit on how many questions you can ask?

- Can the data you collected be downloaded to Excel or other statistical programs?

- Can you make good visual presentations (charts, graphs) with the program?

- Can the results be viewed on Windows and Macintosh computers?

Since you are students, you don't have to worry about many of these matters. If your instructor asks you to use SurveyMonkey or some other program, the software will provide you with any number of different kinds of questions you can ask and other help.

Whatever kind of survey you conduct, whether it is online or in person, you must ask yourself these questions:

- What do you want to find out?

- What questions should you ask to obtain this information?

- How do you avoid ambiguous or unclear questions?

- What kinds or types of questions will you use in the survey?

- What kind of answers are you looking for?

- Whom will you ask?

We make surveys to get answers to questions of interest and importance to us. Surveys can provide us with a great deal of information, but always keep in mind that when people answer survey questions, they don't always understand them and they don't always tell the truth.

❖ SAMPLES

The logic behind sampling is relatively simple. If you have a homogeneous population—that is, everyone is the same—a relatively small sample of this population will provide reliable information about the larger population you are studying. (We use the term *population* to cover all the members of a group.)

A reliable sample must be representative and adequate in size. I will demonstrate graphically how random selection works. Let us suppose we have a country with 1 million people in it and they all have the same genetic makeup, which can be symbolized as X'. Everyone in the population can be represented as X', with one X' representing 50,000 people.

General Population

X′ X′ X′ X′ X′   X′ X′ X′ X′ X′

X′ X′ X′ X′ X′   X′ X′ X′ X′ X′

Sample Needed

X′ (small fraction of)

Obviously, if you take even a very small sample of this particular population, you will obtain accurate information about their genetic makeup (X′) because everyone is the same. (Notice that in this case, it doesn't matter how you chose the sample.) Researchers can make a *simple random sample* and obtain reliable information. (Simple random samples can be made by numbering everyone in a population and using a table of random numbers to select certain members of the population to study. In the example just mentioned, any sample that is chosen will work.)

But suppose the population is heterogeneous, or mixed, as shown here:

General Population

X A B A B X A X B B X X

A X B B A A B B X X A A

Sample Needed

X A B

In the sample of this mixed, or heterogeneous, population, you would have to make sure you surveyed Xs, As, and Bs in the same proportion that they are found in the population. For these kinds of populations, it is often useful to take *stratified random samples*. To take a stratified random sample, you have to find representative groups and survey them randomly so you can have some confidence that you will get people from all groups.

You use stratified random samples when you wish to get some information about a characteristic in the population. Researchers select variables they are interested in and find respondents who have these characteristics so that each variable is represented in the sample in the same proportion that it is found in the larger population.

A third method of sampling, using *clustered samples,* is used to survey groups of people of interest to the researcher. For example, you might be interested in the newspaper-reading habits of people in a given city or area. This is based on the fact that people can be categorized as belonging to various groups based on their daily activities. The sampling unit is not individuals but naturally occurring groups of people—that is, already-formed groups. It is difficult to determine whom to choose from the clusters so as to get a representative sample. These three methods of sampling are explained below in more detail.

❖ OBTAINING RANDOM SAMPLES

Let's look at the three kinds of **random samples** just discussed:

1. Simple random samples

2. Stratified random samples

3. Clustered samples

There are many ways to obtain accurate samples, but—especially for students and others without great financial resources—random sampling is the most convenient method to obtain a representative sample of the population being studied.

Simple Random Samples

A simple random sample is one in which each member of a population being studied has an equal chance of being selected. The term *simple* is used because this kind of sampling involves only one step, using a table of random numbers (as shown in Table 13.1) to obtain a random sample.

You obtain a random sample by assigning sequential numbers to everyone in the population being studied and then using the table of random numbers to select your sample. Let's suppose you wish to choose a random sample of 10 students from a class of 100. You list all students in alphabetical order and assign a number, starting at 1 and going to 100, to each member of the class. Then you consult your table of random numbers and select your sample based on the random numbers. Computers can also generate such tables.

Table 13.1   A Table of Random Numbers

3941	1132	2271	6394	2438	1718	9548	5896	8618	0050
8915	2115	3784	4481	2866	1355	5590	6508	2495	5138
3962	6179	1507	3479	1272	7027	6268	8060	2718	1907
5449	4219	6262	2850	3516	6536	8036	8426	2901	4058
1342	2102	0902	5347	6769	3745	4938	0033	0902	7502
3594	1295	7766	0363	4732	6404	7003	4242	0000	5088
8876	7784	6445	0692	8029	5724	3604	6483	4323	1212
6445	0933	0887	9527	2189	8361	5930	4306	2759	9745
2167	3139	0986	2788	1920	5657	2932	5317	5960	8905
4581	7409	1191	1600	7184	6254	1835	4708	8613	6355
1849	3920	9947	3851	5875	6967	0823	0488	4030	0148
2408	6779	0796	7244	1625	8894	6075	8806	0273	1308
5688	4251	2068	2522	5905	8829	2734	0393	7240	4636
4518	4551	0008	9625	5584	1192	7829	7179	2902	1097
2590	6006	9961	1445	7221	3680	2901	6035	4834	1864
6752	1976	8687	5756	1527	0836	9931	2886	9392	0119
7967	7274	8498	0571	2632	3852	2433	3065	9471	5105
3511	9317	2022	6734	2506	2144	3194	4113	9709	7590
6637	9376	6538	5231	7599	6353	8136	0551	5810	5646
4815	7212	2329	8475	7429	2425	0271	8565	7581	9879
2253	4501	1808	3738	4078	3186	6108	9174	0207	6776
9288	8788	4298	4206	6595	1772	2838	0897	0881	0977
4954	4053	3599	8702	5157	1085	6589	0702	3249	8629
4096	6024	7876	9322	1771	2559	1251	1008	7846	9745
0903	1025	7333	9908	9048	3399	3003	9799	5244	1133

Note: Generated using PERL.

You then choose the first random number; if it is 13, you take student number 13 from your list of 100 students as the first person in your sample. If the next number is 26, you take student number 26 as the second person in your sample. And you continue doing this using the first 10 numbers in your list of random numbers to obtain your simple random sample.

Persons used in simple random samples usually are not used again; they are removed from later selections of random samples that might be needed to obtain other information. This is known as random sampling *without replacement.* (In more complicated kinds of sampling, they are replaced, but this is not the norm for inexpensive surveys.)

Stratified Random Samples

This technique enables us to obtain greater precision in our sampling by using other information we have about the population being studied to obtain representative samples. In doing stratified random sampling, you divide your population into subcategories relevant to the subject under investigation. These subcategories, technically known as *strata* (plural of the term *stratum*), should be mutually exclusive; that is, nobody can be a member of more than one stratum.

In creating a stratified random sampling, your random sample is selected from members of the population possessing a characteristic of interest to your study. For example, suppose you wish to study television news reporters in your city. You could study their sex, race, age, amount of experience, or college major. If you decide to study their college major or race, you then make your random sample based on these factors. You do simple random sampling within each stratum.

Clustered Samples

To create random samples, you need a list of all members of the population being studied—which, in many cases, is impractical. To get around this problem, researchers do clustered sampling, which involves sampling members of groups or categories. You divide your population into naturally occurring groups, such as people in particular ZIP codes or areas of a city or state, and sample from within each group. This technique is not as accurate as random sampling, but it saves a great deal of time and money.

❖ EVALUATING SURVEY ACCURACY

There are three considerations involved in evaluating surveys:

1. Sample size

2. Margin of error

3. Confidence level

The error of measurement strongly depends on the sample size. The margin of error decreases as your sample gets larger but in smaller increments, as can be seen in Figure 13.1. Technically speaking, the error of your measurement decreases with the square root of your sample size, which explains why samples don't provide a corresponding amount of accuracy as they get bigger. The law of diminishing returns is at work. Thus, a survey of 1,500 people gives you almost as much accuracy as a survey of 2,000 people.

Generally speaking, the larger the sample, the more confidence you can have that your findings will be accurate, but this works only up to a point. The most famous sampling error occurred in the 1936 presidential campaign between the Democratic candidate, Franklin Delano Roosevelt, and the Republican candidate, Alf Landon. The

Figure 13.1 Sample Size and Standard Error Relationship

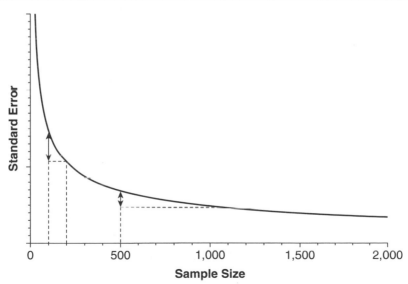

Literary Digest surveyed some 2.3 million people. This sample was based on responses to questionnaires sent to readers of the magazine and to some 10 million people who had telephones. This sample, however, was not representative of the entire voting population; it was composed, to a large degree, of the wealthier elements in American society, essentially wealthy Republicans, so the results were awry. The *Literary Digest* had, unknowingly, asked an essentially Republican (and very unrepresentative) sample of American society which candidate it would vote for and got a highly inaccurate picture of the American voting public.

So the size of the sample doesn't necessarily tell you very much. Of course, you could ask everyone in the population you wish to study and avoid sampling—this is called a *census*. But that is not practical. So you have to find a representative sample of the population you are studying. And the sampling error figure will provide you with an indication of the degree of accuracy of your research.

As its name suggests, the *confidence level* indicates how confident you can be that a particular result obtained in your survey sample reflects the corresponding parameter of the population. The confidence level is closely connected with the interval estimation. That is, the result is reported not as a single number (point estimation) but as a band (range), and one assumes, with a certain level of confidence, the parameter is within that range. The interval estimation is centered on the point estimation, and its width is proportional to its standard error (SE) and the level of confidence desired. The more confident we want to be, the broader the interval of estimation should be.

The most often used level of confidence is 95%, which corresponds to the interval with a lower limit of 2 standard errors to the left of the sample statistic and an upper limit of 2 standard errors to the right of the sample statistic. For example, if we found after a survey that 54% of the clients prefer Product A and that the standard error of this estimation is 3%, then we could conclude with 95% confidence that from 48% to 60% (54% − 6%; 54% + 6%) of the clients in the target population will prefer Product A. This means that if we repeated this survey 100 times, keeping the same sample size, in 95 cases, the preferences for Product A would be somewhere from 48% to 60%.

If we want a higher level of confidence—let's say 99%—then the corresponding interval will be broader, approximately 3 standard errors to the left and to the right of the sample statistic; for our example, it would mean preferences for Product A from 45% to 63%. In a case of lower confidence—for example 68%—the confidence interval will be smaller (1 SE), and the preferences for Product A will be from 51% to 57%.

A general rule of thumb is that the point estimation for a proportion in surveys of 1,500 people (assuming the surveys are carried out correctly) has a standard error of estimation of plus or minus 3%, and surveys of 350 people have a sampling error of plus or minus 5%. Many national political polls use samples of 1,000 to 1,200 people and obtain results accurate to plus or minus 3%. If the election is close and Candidate A is leading Candidate B by 51% to 49%, it means that either of the candidates can win because the error is larger than the difference between the two candidates; in other words, it would be possible for Candidate B to get 51% of the vote and for Candidate A to get only 49%. It could also be that Candidate A has 54% of the vote and Candidate B only 46%. All things being equal, Candidate A has a much better chance of winning than Candidate B.

❖ SURVEYS: APPLICATIONS AND EXERCISES

1. Using your classmates as your universe, prepare a questionnaire about the amount of television, radio, video games, and other media they use in a typical day. Also find out their cell phone and MP3 player usage during a typical day. Use the discussion of writing survey questions to create your survey. What are the most important things you want to find out? How can you avoid confusing questions, showing bias, obtaining incorrect information, or embarrassing those answering the questionnaire? Later, in class, compare the first five questions asked in each questionnaire.

2. Find a scholarly article that uses surveys and analyze the questions it asks. Do you find any problems with the questions? If so, explain. Could you have asked better questions? If so, write them down for classroom discussion. What problems did the writers of the survey face when designing it? How did they overcome them?

3. Using a web survey program such as SurveyMonkey, conduct a survey about a topic of interest to you or assigned by your instructor. Pay attention to the way you frame your questions to ensure you obtain valuable information.

❖ CONCLUSIONS

As you can see, using surveys and questionnaires is rather compli-cated. These instruments are used because they are relatively inexpen-sive and enable researchers to obtain a great deal of information. But great care must be taken in designing surveys and questionnaires and in obtaining sample populations to survey.

It's not a bad idea to think of surveys and questionnaires as a puzzle. How can I solve this puzzle? That is, how can I obtain reliable information about the population I wish to study given the difficulties involved in dealing with people and designing good instruments? You must consider which questions you will ask of members of your popu-lation or group being studied and how reliable the information you obtain will be. Despite the problems involved with this research method, surveys and questionnaires remain two of the most widely used means of obtaining reliable quantifiable data by researchers.

❖ FURTHER READING

Alreck, P. L., & Settle, R. B. (1994). *The survey research handbook*. New York, NY: Irwin Professional.

Babbie, E. R. (1990). *Survey research methods* (2nd ed.). Belmont, CA: Wadsworth.

Creswell, J. W. (2014). *Research design: Qualitative, quantitative, and mixed meth-ods approaches* (4th ed.). Thousand Oaks, CA: SAGE.

Fink, A. G. (2013). *How to conduct surveys: A step-by-step guide* (5th ed.). Thousand Oaks, CA: SAGE.

Fowler, F. J., Jr. (1995). *Improving survey questions: Design and evaluation.* Thousand Oaks, CA: SAGE.

Fowler, F. J., Jr. (2014). *Survey research methods* (5th ed.). Thousand Oaks, CA: SAGE.

Rea, L. M., & Parker, R. A. (2005). *Designing and conducting survey research: A comprehensive guide.* San Francisco, CA: Jossey-Bass.

Rubinstein, S. M. (1994). *Surveying public opinion*. Belmont, CA: Wadsworth.

Sapsford, R. (2007). *Survey research* (2nd ed.). Thousand Oaks, CA: SAGE.

Smith, J., & Christian, L. M. (2008). *Internet, mail, and mixed-mode surveys: The tailored design method.* Hoboken, NJ: Wiley.

Sue, V. M., & Ritter, L. A. (2012). *Conducting online surveys* (2nd ed.). Thousand Oaks, CA: SAGE.

Treadwell, D. F. (2014). *Introducing communication research: Paths of inquiry* (2nd ed.). Thousand Oaks, CA: SAGE.

Weisberg, H. F., Krosnick, J. A., & Bowen, B. D. (1996). *An introduction to survey research, polling, and data analysis* (3rd ed.). Thousand Oaks, CA: SAGE.

Experimentor

The major contribution of experimental method to communication research is its potential to identify variables that have a significant effect on other variables and to determine whether such variables have a causal relationship to others. . . . Experimentation means nothing more than manipulating one variable to see if another variable changes as a result. In the context of communication research that might mean exposing consumers to different versions of an advertisement to see which version is the most persuasive, asking Web users to use different Web sites to see which site is the most easily navigable, or asking groups to solve problems under different conditions of group size or leadership style to see which type of group performs most effectively.

In all such cases, the experimenters are doing something to see what happens rather than just asking people questions. The basic rationale for experimental design is summarized by Gilbert, Light, and Mosteller (1975): "We will not see how things will work in practice until we try them in practice. *(p. 46)"*

—Donald Treadwell, *Introducing Communication Research: Paths of Inquiry* (2011, pp. 142–143)

14

Experiments

- How do we define experiments?
- What is the typical structure of an experiment?
- What is the Hawthorne effect?
- What are the advantages and disadvantages of experiments?
- What was said about the "black rats" case and experimental fraud?
- What are the main points in the checklist on experimental design?
- Did Stanley Milgram conduct an experiment?
- What was the Facebook experiment? Was it a real experiment? Was it ethical?

Although we tend to think of the term *experiment* in connection with scientific work or the research of social scientists, most of us in our daily lives frequently do what might be described as unscientific experimentation.

❖ EVERYDAY EXPERIMENTATION

Suppose, for example, that you have a bad cold. You might try one remedy, and if it doesn't work, try another, and if that isn't effective, try something else—until you find something that will help you feel better.

What is important here is that you try one thing at a time. If you take aspirin and a cold remedy and have some hot chicken soup and your cold gets better, you don't know whether it was the aspirin or the cold remedy or the chicken soup or some combination of the three that was the important factor in helping you feel better. So the principle is to try one thing (or variable) at a time and see what happens. We do the same thing when we try different foods or kinds of dishwashing detergent. We give these things a try, and if we like the results, we keep purchasing them. If the "trial" (read "experiment") is unsuccessful, we try something else.

Experimentation, like the other methodologies discussed in this book, can be very complicated, and it is impossible to deal with all the different kinds of experiments and aspects of experimentation in detail. But I can offer a generalized overview of the nature of experimentation.

A SHORT THEATRICAL PIECE ON EXPERIMENTS

Grand Inquisitor:	*Tell me about your next experiment.*
Arthur:	I want to find out whether a person on a cruise ship who eats x amount eight times a day gains more weight than a person who eats 2x amount four times a day. You can eat eight meals a day on cruise ships.
Grand Inquisitor:	*So?*
Arthur:	I am applying for a $500,000 grant to cover the expenses I will incur in this research.
Grand Inquisitor:	*Will I be involved in this experiment?*
Arthur:	Yes. You have your choice. You can either be the person who eats x amount eight times a day or 2x amount four times a day.

Grand Inquisitor:	*I'll choose the eight-times-a-day regime. We developed big appetites in the Middle Ages. But why can't we just eat in restaurants? Why do we have to take cruises?*
Arthur:	The ocean is an important variable in this experiment. And I like cruises. But you make a good point. After the experiment on cruise ships, I'll replicate it at three-star restaurants in France.

❖ DEFINING EXPERIMENTS

For our purposes, we will understand an experiment to be a procedure or kind of test that

1. Demonstrates whether something is true,

2. Examines the validity of an hypothesis or theory, or

3. Attempts to discover new information.

In the first case, we try to show whether what is held to be true about something is actually true. This might involve, for example, replicating an experiment to see whether the findings in the first experiment are correct. In the second case, we test a hypothesis or theory to determine whether it is valid. We might think that there is a relationship between heavy television viewing and violent behavior in young people (having, of course, operationally defined *heavy* and *violent*). In the third case, we want to discover something we do not already know. We might try to find out how MTV affects the attitudes of male viewers of a particular age range about certain subjects, such as how to relate to women or what's stylish and so on.

❖ THE STRUCTURE OF AN EXPERIMENT

Let me offer an overview of the steps taken when conducting experiments—or what might be described as the "structure" of a typical experiment.

- Your experiment will involve two groups of people: the *experimental group* (also known as the *treatment group, intervention group,* or *stimulus group*) and the **control group.** Something will be done to the experimental group, but it will not be done to the control group.

- Persons must be randomly assigned to either the experimental group or the control group. How to do this is discussed in Chapter 13, on surveys and questionnaires, and involves the use of tables of random numbers (see Table 13.1).

- A *pretest* is done. There are two kinds of variables—*independent* and *dependent.* You measure the groups in terms of a dependent variable. (Independent variables are varied by researchers, whereas dependent variables are presumed to be affected by independent variables.)

- You perform the experiment and introduce one independent variable to the experimental group. Nothing is done with the control group.

- You conduct a *posttest* to see if there's a significant difference between the experimental group and the control group relative to the variable introduced.

An example of an experiment is to take 100 sophomore males and divide them randomly into two groups of 50 students. You then test the students on something specific, such as their attitudes toward women. Then you show the experimental group a certain number of violent MTV videos but don't have the control group see anything. Then, after showing the experimental group the MTV videos, you test the two groups again to see whether the exposure of the experimental group to the MTV videos has led to any changes in that group's attitudes toward women. (Note: This example describes one of several possible experimental designs—the classical pretest and posttest design. There are, of course, other designs or ways of structuring experiments.)

The logic of experiments is quite simple. We have two groups that are basically alike, and we expose one of the groups to X and don't expose the other group to X; then we see what effect X might have had on the group exposed to it. We can tell the effect by comparing the group exposed to X with the other group not exposed to X. It is assumed that the two groups are very similar to one another initially—a condition created through random assignment of subjects to groups (experimental or control). The underlying principle is that if the posttest shows differences between the two groups, the researcher can conclude that the experimental treatment had an effect because the treatment was the *only* variable distinguishing the two groups.

In this hypothetical experiment, we are, in effect, comparing the experimental group before and after the exposure to the MTV videos and contrasting them with the control group. This experiment is diagrammed in the following chart.

	Control Group	**Experimental Group**
1.	50 male sophomores	50 male sophomores
2.	Randomly selected	Randomly selected
3.	Pretested	Pretested
4.	*Not exposed to MTV*	*Exposed to MTV*
5.	Posttested	Posttested

The two groups are treated the same until step 4, when the independent variable (in this case exposure to a certain amount of MTV) is examined to see whether it had an effect on the experimental group.

This offers us a sense of the logic of experiments. We must be careful to introduce only one independent variable; if we introduce two or more variables, we cannot know which, if any, of the variables affected the experimental group. The technical term for introducing more than one independent variable is a *confound*. Confounds prevent researchers from determining what caused what in experiments.

Some experiments depart slightly from the classical form in that they don't use the control-experimental group model I've just described. In these experiments, the control group may be asked to perform certain tasks that resemble but are different from those given to the experimental group.

For example, an experiment conducted by Baba Shiv and Alexander Fedorikhin (1999) of Stanford University divided a group of students into two groups. The researchers asked the first group to remember a 2-digit number and the second group to remember a 7-digit number. The students were told to walk down the hall of a building, where they had a choice of snacks: a bowl of fruit salad or some chocolate cake. Shiv and Fedorikhin found that the students who were asked to remember 7 digits asked for the chocolate cake 2 times as often as those who had to remember 2 digits. The researchers concluded that the cognitive load of remembering seven digits overtaxed the prefrontal cortexes of those students. That part of the brain is involved with willpower. Thus, the overtaxed prefrontal cortexes of the students who had to remember 7 digits made them less able to resist the chocolate cake. This experiment helps explain why it is that when we are stressed, we tend to indulge in foods we know we shouldn't eat.

❖ THE HAWTHORNE EFFECT

From 1924 to 1932, a series of experiments was carried out on workers at the Hawthorne Works of the Western Electric Company in Cicero, Illinois. The purpose was to find out whether lighting had an impact on worker productivity at the plant and to discover what level of lighting was best for worker productivity. The researchers found, to their surprise, that worker productivity increased when the lighting was made brighter *and* when it was made dimmer. This finding led to another experiment by some Harvard professors to determine whether the measurements made during the Hawthorne experiment were reliable. They tested five young women and found that regardless of what changes were made, the productivity of the women increased.

It was concluded, then, that whenever people are being observed by researchers, they temporarily change their behavior—a phenomenon known as the **Hawthorne effect**. This means that we cannot be certain that the behavior we observe in experiments, when people know they are being studied, is their natural behavior. We also have to consider matters such as socioeconomic class, gender, race, and the groups to which people belong when we think about the way people being studied react in experiments. Further experiments suggested that workers are not solely motivated by economic matters—which had been a dominant theory of human motivation—and that informal groups to which they belong have an impact on their productivity.

A lecture by Mike Hart (2006–2007) about the Hawthorne effect—posted online—yields this insight:

> The preliminary findings were that behavior is not merely physiological but also psychological. This was a break with the Scientific Management school that saw work productivity as "mechanical," and led to the decision to learn more about worker behavior. George Pennock, Western Electric's superintendent of inspection, suggested that the reason for increased worker productivity was simply that the researchers interacted with the female employees; and this was first

time anyone had shown an interest in the workers. Basically, the workers were trying to please the researchers by continuing to increase their output and report satisfaction in the study, no matter what the intervention was. Later, the phenomenon of a researcher corrupting an experiment simply by his presence would be termed the "Hawthorne effect." (para. 3)

So the experiment had important implications for management and labor relations. Even though we might describe it as having been "corrupted" and not yielding the expected results, it did contribute to our knowledge. This suggests that experiments involving people are worthwhile, even if we always have to consider that the Hawthorne effect may impact our findings.

❖ ADVANTAGES OF EXPERIMENTS

Experiments, if carried out carefully and correctly, provide very strong evidence that a given independent variable (such as the exposure of the experimental group to mediated violence in MTV videos) actually has the effect discovered. Also, experiments give strong evidence that the discovered effect was not the result of some unrecognized phenomenon. We can, then, make all kinds of new discoveries by conducting experiments. And because experiments can be replicated, it makes it possible for other researchers to conduct the same experiment to confirm its validity.

Susanna Hornig Priest offered some insights into the advantages of experiments. In her book, *Doing Media Research: An Introduction* (2010), she wrote,

> Whenever a researcher is dealing with reasonably well-understood and readily observable or otherwise measurable phenomena and is interested in fairly clear-cut cause-and-effect relationships, experimental methods are a good choice. They can help determine, for example, whether male or female news anchors are more credible, whether viewing violent films results in short-term physiological or behavioral changes, which of several messages about an issue is the most persuasive, or whether one computer interface takes longer to master than another.
>
> Used creatively and cautiously, experimental methods can provide valuable answers to these and many other questions. The trick is to remember their origins and limitations. They will not provide answers to questions about long-term effects, nor can they reveal what effects might occur outside of laboratory conditions. These effects do not always carry over well into real life. (p. 22)

I deal with other limitations of experiments in the following section.

❖ DISADVANTAGES OF EXPERIMENTS

Probably the biggest problem with experiments is that they are artificial, conducted—generally speaking—in laboratories or in "nonnatural" situations. When people know that they are involved in an experiment, this information often affects their behavior.

There is also reason to believe that the design of experiments tends to overemphasize cause-and-effect relationships between the matters being studied. It may be, for example, that many factors besides MTV are involved in the attitudes male college sophomores have toward women. In addition, there are often ethical problems in scientific experimentation. We see this in the case of medicine, in which the experimental group is given some new drug and the control group is denied the drug. Is it ethical to deny people a drug that may affect their health—or even save their lives? Of course, dealing with the media doesn't involve life-and-death matters, but it is possible that certain experiments might disturb people psychologically. For example, many of the people involved in the Milgram "obedience" experiment (discussed later in this chapter) suffered from psychological problems caused by their participation in it and needed extensive counseling and therapy. That is why universities all have research boards that review potential experiments to make sure that the people being experimented on are not disturbed or harmed in any way.

❖ THE "BLACK RATS" CASE AND EXPERIMENTAL FRAUD

David Goodstein (1991) described a famous example of scientific fraud:

> In 1974 William Summerlin was doing research at the Sloan-Kettering Institute in Minnesota that required nature to produce for him some rats with black patches on their skin. Since nature was not sufficiently cooperative, he helped her along with a black, felt-tip pen and was caught in the act. (p. 11)

Goodstein's article, "Scientific Fraud," calls our attention to the fact that some researchers fake their data. In some cases, these researchers teach in world-famous "publish or perish" institutions and thus are motivated to tamper with data to produce "results" and get their papers published. In other cases, famous researchers use their elevated status to commit fraud. This behavior is facilitated by editors who want to publish papers by famous scholars. As a result, to avoid being duped, many scientists argue that if an experiment can't be replicated, they cannot accept the results found, regardless of the stature of the experimenters or the institutions at which they teach.

❖ A CHECKLIST ON EXPERIMENTAL DESIGN

The following checklist is adapted from John W. Creswell's *Research Design: Qualitative and Quantitative Approaches* (1994). He described this list as offering "key decisions" that experimental researchers have to make when designing their research. I have made some adaptations because I've not covered certain topics and kinds of experiments that he dealt with.

1. Who are the subjects (what population are they from) in your experiment?

2. How were the subjects selected? Was it randomly done?

3. Will the subjects be randomly assigned to groups?

4. How many subjects will be in the experimental group and the control group?

5. What is the dependent variable in the study? How will it be measured? How many times will it be measured?

6. What instrument(s) will be used to measure the outcome in the experiment? Why was it chosen? Is it reliable?

7. What steps will you take in this experiment?

    (a.) A random assignment of your subjects

    (b.) Collection of demographic information

    (c.) Administration of a pretest

    (d.) The experiment itself (introduction of the independent variable, also known as the treatment or factor)

    (e.) Administration of a posttest

8. What threats are there to the internal and external validity of your experiment? How will you deal with them?

9. Are you going to do a pilot test of your experiment?

10. What statistical methods will be used to analyze your data?

11. Are there any ethical questions you must consider when designing your experiment?

This list offers a useful guide for those planning and conducting experiments in that it provides an overview of the process of experimentation. Of course, there is a big difference between knowing the "theory" of experimentation and implementing that theory—that is, actually conducting an experiment.

❖ WHAT'S AN EXPERIMENT AND WHAT ISN'T?

In experiments involving humans, it's difficult, in some cases, to determine what is an experiment and what isn't. In this respect, let us consider social psychologist Stanley Milgram's research. Strictly speaking, one could argue that Milgram's research was not an experiment because he didn't have a control group. But is it that simple?

Milgram (1965) described his study as follows:

> Two persons arrive at a campus laboratory to take part in a study of memory and learning. (One of them is a confederate of the experimenter.) Each subject is paid $4.50 upon arrival and is told that payment is not affected in any way by performance. The experimenter provides an introductory talk on memory and learning processes and then informs the subjects that in the experiment one of them will serve as teacher and the other as learner. A rigged drawing is held so that the naive subject is always assigned the role of teacher and the accomplice becomes the learner. The learner is taken to an adjacent room and is strapped into an electric chair.
>
> The naive subject is told that it is his task to teach the learner a list of paired associates, to test him on the list, and to administer punishment whenever the learner errs in the test. Punishment takes the form of electric shock, delivered to the learner by means of a shock generator controlled by the naive subject. The teacher is instructed to increase the intensity of the electric shock one step on the generator for each error. The generator contains 30 voltage levels ranging from 15 to 450 volts, and verbal designations ranging from "Slight Shock" to "Danger: Severe Shock." The learner, according to plan, provides many wrong answers, so that before long the naive subject must give him the strongest shock of the generator. Increases in shock levels are met by increasingly insistent demands from the learner that the experiment be stopped because of growing discomfort to him. However, the experimenter instructs the teacher to continue with the procedure and disregard the learner's protests. (p. 128)

After conducting his controversial research, Milgram gave lectures in which he displayed photographs of the naive subjects. These photographs showed the incredible amount of strain on their faces, as many of them proceeded (so they thought) to shock the person strapped in the electric chair. He was investigating obedience and wanted to find out the degree to which people would be obedient in a difficult situation.

Milgram, who was a personal friend of mine, told me that he had asked many deans of schools of social and behavioral science how far they thought naive subjects would go up the electronic console, and most of the deans said they doubted that people would go beyond the third level. To Milgram's surprise, a considerable number of people went all the way to the most severe level on their shock-generating consoles.

This research was very controversial—as might be expected. It led to the decision to have all research involving humans examined by university panels dedicated to preventing abuses in experimentation.

Let me suggest that there are other ways of looking at experimentation that would suggest that Milgram did, in fact, conduct an experiment. I know he certainly thought he did. Here is a slightly different definition of experimentation, from James A. Schellenberg in *An Introduction to Social Psychology* (1974):

> **Experimentation**—the observation of phenomena under controlled conditions. In *laboratory experiments* the investigator himself creates the setting for his observations, where *in field experiments* he manipulates only some of the variables in an established social setting. A third category of *natural experiments* is sometimes used to refer to cases where the investigator actually controls nothing, but where events happen to occur in a way similar to that which an investigator might wish to create through controlled conditions. (p. 348)

Schellenberg's definition of an experiment suggests that Milgram's research was a laboratory experiment but one that did not have a control group. The control group, in a sense, was the population not involved in the experiment.

❖ ETHICS AND THE FACEBOOK EXPERIMENT

On June 30, 2014, the *Wall Street Journal* featured an article by Reed Albergotti, "Furor Erupts Over Facebook's Experiment on Users," on the now infamous Facebook experiment. Albergotti described the uproar over the experiment on 700,000 unsuspecting social media users as follows:

> A social-network furor has erupted over news that Facebook Inc.. . . . in 2012, conducted a massive psychological experiment on nearly 700,000 unwitting users.
>
> To determine whether it could alter the emotional state of its users and prompt them to post either more positive or negative content, the site's data scientists enabled an algorithm, for one week, to automatically omit content that contained words associated with either positive or negative emotions from the central news feeds of 689,003 users.

The research, published in the March issue of the *Proceedings of the National Academy of Sciences*, sparked a different emotion—outrage—among some people who say Facebook toyed with its users' emotions and used members as guinea pigs. In a blog post at Animalnewyork .com, the Facebook experiment was described as follows: "What many of us feared is already a reality: Facebook is using us as lab rats, and not just to figure out which ads we'll respond to but actually change our emotions" (Weiner, 2014).

What bothers many people about the experiment is that hundreds of thousands of Facebook users, without their being aware of what was happening, were used in an experiment to study how Facebook posts could lead to mood changes and "emotional contagion."

On the same morning, an article by Vindu Goel in the *New York Times* was headlined "Facebook Tinkers with Users' Emotions in News Feed Experiment, Stirring Outcry":

> To Facebook, we are all lab rats.
>
> Facebook routinely adjusts its users' news feeds—testing out the number of ads they see or the size of photos that appear—often without their knowledge. It is all for the purpose, the company says, of creating a more alluring and useful product.
>
> But last week, Facebook revealed that it had manipulated the news feeds of over half a million randomly selected users to change the number of positive and negative posts they saw. It was part of a psychological study to examine how emotions can be spread on social media.

The lab rat metaphor is striking. It points to the problem people have with the experiment: The Facebook users getting certain kinds of content did not realize they were part of an experiment, which violates the rules of ethics when it comes to the use of human subjects in experiments.

Facebook argued that it has implied consent since everyone who joins Facebook gives the company permission to do experiments of one kind or another, as a condition of using the service. However, as some commentators have suggested, toying with the emotions of unsuspecting users of Facebook may have had some serious consequences for some people. On a Twitter post on the subject, a privacy activist named Lauren Weinstein wrote, "I wonder if Facebook KILLED anyone with their emotion manipulation stunt?" (Goel, 2014).

The leader of the Facebook experiment, Adam D. I. Kramer, apologized, saying he and his team were sorry for any anxiety the experiment caused in people (Goel, 2014). He suggested that the results were insignificant and not worth the anxiety that reports of the experiment generated. That fact that Facebook was successful in manipulating the emotions of its users has caused many privacy advocates to wonder about the power social media has to shape people's moods and maybe even beliefs and behavior. Katy Waldman of Slate.com (2014) attacked the experiment as "unethical" and wrote, "Facebook intentionally made thousands upon thousands of people sad." The fact that Facebook can toy with people's emotions so easily is scary to some media scholars, who wonder whether this experiment has, somehow, opened a Pandora's box to other experimentation by social media sites and to greater willingness to manipulate users. For Marxist theorists, this experiment is just one more example of their argument that social media exploit the people who provide the content that makes these sites interesting to others, all at no cost to the social media companies.

❖ EXPERIMENTS: APPLICATIONS AND EXERCISES

1. Critique an article in a scholarly journal on media and communication that describes an experiment. Use the checklist on experimental design in your discussion of the article. Make a copy of the first page of the article to turn in with your analysis.

2. Design a simple experiment involving media effects that you can make with your classmates, with half of them as the control group and the other half as the group involved in the experiment. What do you want to find out? How will you discover what you want to find out? What problems do you face in conducting this experiment? Compare the experiments your classmates created to see if there are any commonalities among them. Did anyone have an experimental idea that strikes you as truly ingenious?

3. Investigate the response of academics and others to the Facebook experiment. What are the different perspectives on this experiment? What impact did the discovery of this experiment have on social media?

❖ CONCLUSIONS

We can see that defining experiments is difficult (because there are a number of different kinds) and conducting them is even more difficult (because people are so complicated and hard to figure out). Nevertheless, many experiments dealing with the media and related matters have been and will continue to be conducted by researchers from fields such as psychology, **sociology,** and communication. This research, reported in a variety of journals, is of great interest to commercial media organizations, the government, and the scholarly community.

This chapter provides an overview of experimentation that enables readers to analyze the methods used in experiments and to determine how well experiments are carried out. It also provides a means for students to devise their own experiments. These experiments will be simpler than those carried out by well-funded researchers, but nothing prevents students with imagination and initiative from doing some experimentation on their own.

❖ FURTHER READING

Boruch, R. F. (1997). *Randomized experiments for planning and evaluation: A practical guide.* Thousand Oaks, CA: SAGE.

Campbell, D. T., & Russo, M. J. (1999). *Social experimentation.* Thousand Oaks, CA: SAGE.

Christensen, L. B. (2006). *Experimental methodology* (10th ed.). Boston, MA: Allyn & Bacon.

Goos, P., & Jones, B. (2011). *Optimal design of experiments: A case study approach.* Hoboken, NJ: Wiley.

Keppel, G. (1991). *Design and analysis: A researcher's handbook* (3rd ed.). Englewood Cliffs, NJ: Prentice Hall.

Montgomery, D. C. (1997). *Design and analysis of experiments* (4th ed.). New York, NY: John Wiley.

Rosenthal, R., & Rosnow, R. L. (1991). *Essentials of behavioral research: Methods and data analysis* (2nd ed.). New York, NY: McGraw-Hill.

Ryan, T. P. (2007). *Modern experimental design.* Hoboken, NJ: Wiley.

What gave Comte and his followers so much confidence was the discovery that statistics, invented much earlier but new in use, disclosed interesting regularities. It appeared, for instance, that suicides did not occur haphazardly but kept to certain numerical proportions depending on sex, age, occupation, and the like. Similarly, it was discovered after the establishment of the modern postal service that the number of letters mailed without stamp or address did not vary at random but in relation to the time of day, the total number of letters sent, and so on. This made it seem likely that the notion of accident in individual or social behavior was simply a cloak for our ignorance of the hidden "laws."

Between Comte's beginnings and Marx's later works, the march of the Industrial Revolution had brought forth a greatly increased supply of statistics. Marx fashioned his elaborate attack on the capitalist system out of the famous "blue books" published by the British government on every phase of life, from the sanitation of factories and the accidents in coal mines to the incidence of alcoholism and infant diseases. A new image of society began to emerge from these serried ranks of figures . . . the older conception of the social order as a group of individuals endowed with free will and moved by ideas, customs, and creeds, appeared less and less believable.

—Jacques Barzun and Henry F. Graff,
The Modern Researcher (1957, pp. 204–205)

15

A Primer on Descriptive Statistics

With Felianka Kaftandjieva

CHAPTER 15 FOCUS QUESTIONS

- What are the levels of measurement?
- What are the central concepts used in descriptive statistics?
- What are the three measures of central tendency? Define *mean*, *median*, and *mode*.
- What are the measures of dispersion?
- How do we define standard deviation?
- What is a bell-shaped curve?
- What cautions should we keep in mind with statistics?
- What do the statistics on media use reflect about America?
- What was said about smartphones?

Statisticians use mathematical methods to analyze, summarize, and interpret numerical data. The research methods discussed in this book—content analysis, surveys, questionnaires, and experiments—yield these kinds of data. But numerical data do not mean very much until they have been analyzed and interpreted, using statistical methods.

The choice of statistical method of analysis depends on the data to be analyzed. Statisticians differentiate four kinds of data, depending on so-called levels of measurement.

❖ LEVELS OF MEASUREMENT

Nominal level. Typical examples of data on this level are demographics such as sex, nationality, and marital status. For each analyzed object, the only thing we are able to determine is to which of a few categories it belongs. We can code these categories with numbers, but they are used only as signs without any mathematical meaning.

For example, we can code sex as 0 for females and 1 for males, but nothing will be changed if we use 0 for males and 1 for females. We cannot use these numbers for any mathematical operation. We could equally well use such symbols as ▶)- for males and *§& for females. From the point of view of statistics, nominal data are the simplest kind because of the limited number of operations that can be applied to them.

Ordinal level. Data belong to this level when they can be ordered according to some criterion. Examples of such data are educational level or rank in the army. Based on this data, you can compare objects and say who has a high school diploma, 2-year college degree, 4-year college degree, or graduate degree or a higher rank in the military, but you cannot determine how big the difference is between levels. In other words, the only possible operation with data on the ordinal level is comparison (although any data transformation that maintains the order of the data can be applied).

Interval level. Temperature is a typical example of an interval level of measurement. Not only can we compare two days (or two bodies), finding out which one is warmer, but we also can determine the magnitude of the difference. The interval scales, however, have no naturally defined zero point. The zero points for Fahrenheit or Celsius scales are subjectively determined, and they can be changed if a new temperature scale is invented. Because of the lack of an intrinsically defined zero point with interval data, it is meaningless to make statements such as "Today is twice as warm as yesterday."

Ratio level. Salaries, height, weight, and number of children (or wives) are data that belong to the ratio level of measurement, and all mathematical operations valid for real numbers can be applied to such data.

❖ DESCRIPTIVE STATISTICS

There are two kinds of statistics—descriptive and inferential. This primer deals with descriptive statistics. *Descriptive statistics* refers to methods used to obtain, from raw data, information that characterizes or summarizes the whole set of data. That is, descriptive statistics allow us to make sense of the data more easily. (Inferential statistics allow us to generalize from the data collected to the general populations they were taken from.) The following are some of the most popular concepts from descriptive statistics.

Frequency Distribution

Statisticians are strange people. They tend to count everything—births and birds, deaths and debts, and so on. If we look at the beginning sentence of this chapter from the point of view of a statistician, it would not look like a set of words but like a set of numbers such as the following:

4	4	5	3	3	9	2	4
10	3	3	9	4	10	8	4
7	3	3	2	3	9	11	12

In fact, this numerical set represents the length of the words (as a number of letters) used in the following sentence: "What gave Comte and his followers so much confidence was the discovery that statistics, invented much earlier but new in use, disclosed interesting regularities."

We are lucky that the sentence was not too long—only 24 words. (In statistical language, this can be written as $N = 24$, and statisticians would say that "the size of our sample is (equal to) 24.") Fortunately, we did not decide to count the length of the words in the whole paragraph. But even when we have only 24 words, the numbers cannot reveal too much because they are not organized. The organization of the data in a form that is comprehensive and easier for analysis and interpretation is usually called *data tabulation,* and the data are presented as either a frequency table or a chart. The frequency table for the length of the words in the first sentence is presented in Table 15.1.

In the first column of this table, all observed values are given in ascending order. The numbers in the second column show how many times a value was observed in the analyzed sample. This is called a *frequency distribution,* and we can conclude, based on it, that most of the words in this sentence are short (3–4 letters). Taking into consideration that the length of the words is closely connected with the readability of the text, we also can assume (even without reading the sentence!) that it is easily understandable.

Table 15.1   Frequency Distribution of Length of Words in Example Sentence

Length of Words (in letters)	Frequency (f)
2	2
3	7
4	5
5	1
6	0
7	1
8	1
9	3
10	2
11	1
12	1
Total	24

It is also obvious that the words used differ very much in length. There are 2-letter words as well as 12-letter words. The frequencies also vary; as can be seen, there are no 6-letter words in the sentence, whereas there are seven 3-letter words.

The information in Table 15.1 can also be presented as a graph, as shown in Figure 15.1. From this chart, it is even easier than from a frequency table to see that most of the words are located in the left part of the distribution.

For small samples, as in this case, it is possible to have no examples for some of the categories (for example, 6-letter words). The more values there are in the data set, the bigger the probability of empty cells (with $f = 0$) in the frequency table. In such cases, it is better to group data in broader intervals with equal size. However, combining data leads to losing information on the one hand, and on the other hand, depending on the number of intervals used and their width, makes it possible to interpret the same information in different ways.

This can be easily demonstrated with the distributions, shown in Figure 15.2(a) and Figure 15.2(b). Both charts present a frequency distribution of the length of the words in the same sentence, but they look different. The first distribution has two peaks, whereas the second has only one—on the left side. The reason for these differences is that the distributions are based on different interval groupings—in the first case there are six intervals with a length of 2, while in the second case the intervals are fewer (four) but broader (with a length of 3).

That is why it is preferable, first, to prepare a frequency table (or a chart of frequency distribution) for raw (nongrouped) data and then, after their analysis, to proceed to grouping data into intervals if needed.

There are three main descriptive characteristics for each distribution:

1. *Location.* Where on the axis is the distribution positioned?

Figure 15.1   Frequency Distribution—Length of Words

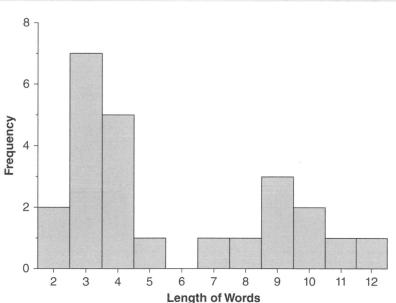

2. *Dispersion.* How broad is the distribution?

3. *Shape.* What is the form (appearance, pattern) of the distribution?

Figures 15.2(a) and 15.2(b)   Frequency Distribution of the Length of the Words in the Same Sentence

(a)

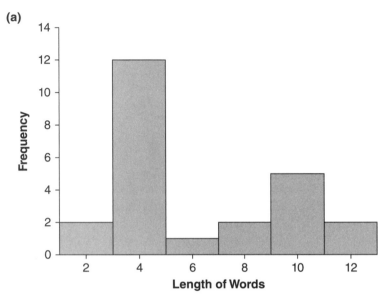

(b)

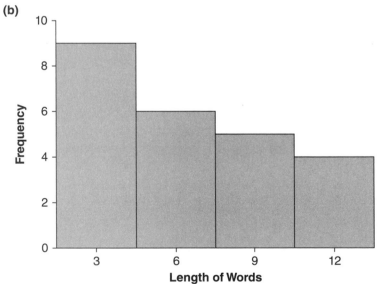

There are different statistical measures for each of these characteristics, each with its own advantages and disadvantages. The main reason for choosing a statistical measure, here, is the kind of data we have to analyze.

❖ MEASURES OF CENTRAL TENDENCY

The statistics describing the location of the distribution are usually called *measures of central tendency* because they indicate the central point of distribution on the scale. There are three more commonly used statistics: mean, median, and mode.

The Mean

The mean (the arithmetic average) is the sum of all observed data values divided by the sample size. In the example of our sentence, all we have to do to get the mean is add all observed values and divide the sum by 24:

$$\frac{4+4+5+3+3+9+2+4+10+3+3+9+4+10+8+4+7+3+3+2+3+9+11+12}{24}$$

The result of these calculations is 5.625. In other words, the average length of the words in the analyzed sentence is between 5 and 6 letters. Of course, statisticians like symbols and formulas, so in their language it looks like the following:

$$\overline{X} = \frac{\sum_{i=1}^{N} X_i}{N},$$

where

$\overline{X}$ is the symbol for the mean;

X_i is the symbol for each one of the observed values (that is why i can vary between 1 and N);

N is the size of the sample, 2; and

Σ is a symbol for the sum (Greek letter sigma).

One of the main disadvantages of the mean is that of all the measures of central tendency, it is most profoundly affected by extreme scores.

For example, let's imagine the following situation: A very bad surgeon had to do five surgeries in one day. Unfortunately, all the patients except one died, either during surgery or a few hours later. The lucky (or the most stubborn) patient not only survived but lived 45 years after the operation. So if we present the life expectency of all patients as the number of years they lived after the operation, we would have this: 0, 0, 0, 0, 45 or, on average, $(0 + 0 + 0 + 0 + 45)/5 = 9$ years, which is quite a good average result for any surgeon. The question, however, is, Would that surgeon be your first choice if you needed an operation? My answer is definite: No!

This disadvantage of the mean usually manifests when the sample size is comparatively small ($N < 30$), but the mean sometimes leads to wrong conclusions even with bigger samples. Did you hear about the statistician who drowned in a lake averaging only 2 inches in depth? The main reason for this problem is that the mean takes into account all observed values, and they affect the final result to the same degree. The last warning concerning the mean is that it is a valid measure of central tendency only for interval and ratio data.

The Median

The median (Me) is the point in the distribution that divides it into two halves. The median can be used as a measure of central tendency for all kinds of data except nominal data. The easiest way to find the median for raw data is to order them from the lowest to the highest. If we do this for the words in our sentence, the result is as follows:

$$2\ 2\ 3\ 3\ 3\ 3\ 3\ 3\ 3\ 4\ 4\ \boxed{4}\ |\ \boxed{4}\ 4\ 5\ 7\ 8\ 9\ 9\ 9\ 10\ 10\ 11\ 12$$

Because of the even number of words in the analyzed sentence, the midpoint is between two values, and then the median is equal to the average of these two nearest values:

$$Me = \frac{4+4}{2} = 4$$

In odd-numbered values, the median is equal to the value in the middle point of the ordered data.

Let's edit the analyzed sentence, skipping the second *much* (perhaps it is a bit too much to use *much* twice in the same sentence). The modified sentence is "What gave Comte and his followers so much confidence was the discovery that statistics, invented earlier but new in use, disclosed interesting regularities."

The change in the sentence leads to a change in the observed values—they are one fewer (N_1 = 23), and the number of 4-letter words is also one fewer. The ordered values are as follows:

2 2 3 3 3 3 3 3 3 4 4 4 4 $\boxed{4}$ 5 7 8 9 9 9 10 10 11 12

The middle point in this case is on the 12th observed value, and it is again 4 (Me = 4). In other words, the two versions of the sentence (with two or with one *much*) have equal medians.

The median does not depend on the extreme values because it does not take them into account. For example, the median for length of life of patients of the inept surgeon is equal to zero (0, 0, 0, 0, 45), and it is a much better indicator of the central tendency than the mean, which equals 9 years. That is why, especially for small samples, median is a better measure of central tendency than mean.

The Mode

The third measure of the central tendency, the mode (Mo), can be applied to all kinds of data. The mode is the most frequently observed value in the frequency distribution. In the case of our initial sentence, the mode is 3 because more words consist of 3 letters (7 words do so) than have any other length. In statistical language, it appears this way: Mo = 3.

Each frequency distribution has only one mean and median, but some distributions have more than one mode. The mode does not take into account the whole picture of the distribution, and it is not a very stable estimator of the central tendency. That is why it is the least-used measure of central tendency—used mainly in cases when the other measures cannot be applied (nominal data). If we compare the three measures of the central tendency for our case, we notice that they differ considerably:

$$X = 5.625; Me = 4; Mo = 3$$

Someone can reasonably ask, "Then, what is the *real* central tendency?"

The answer is that all three are real, but they mean different things. Which of them to use depends on the following:

- The level of measurement

- The sample size

In our case, the best estimator of the central tendency (the data are interval, but the sample size is small) is the median. Moreover, its meaning is very clear—half of the words are below, and the other half are above (50/50). In any case, when any measure of the central tendency is reported, we have to be aware of its meaning before making any interpretations and conclusions.

Let me offer an example taken from Brant Houston's *Computer-Assisted Reporting* (1996), which discusses the salaries of baseball players:

> Neill Borowski, head of computer-assisted reporting at *The Philadelphia Inquirer* . . . said that baseball fans were outraged by players' salaries because they always heard the average salary was $1.2 million. But the median salary was $500,000 and the mode, or the most frequent salary, was $109,000. These numbers indicate that there are a few players making really, really big money. The middle value, the salary amount that half the salaries exceed and half the salaries fall below, was $500,000. If you asked all baseball players for a count of hands for each salary, the largest number (the mode, not a majority) of the hands would go up for $109,000. (Okay, it's still a lot, but not as much as you thought. And it's being made by people who have to make all their money in 10 years or less.) (p. 75)

These figures are probably low because the salaries of baseball players have skyrocketed in recent years, but his point is well made. Most baseball players don't make the gigantic salaries that a relatively small and select group of ballplayers make.

❖ MEASURES OF DISPERSION

The statistics describing how broad the interval is on the measurement scale covered by the frequency distribution are usually called *measures of dispersion*. There are many such measures, but we describe here only two of them—the easiest one (range) and the most frequently used one (statistical deviation).

Range

The range (R), as a statistical concept, can be used for all kinds of data except nominal. It is equal to the difference between the maximum and the minimum observed values. That is why it cannot be applied to nominal data: They cannot be ordered, and consequently, the minimum and maximum values do not exist.

In the case of our initial sentence, the minimum value is 2 and the maximum value is 12, so the range is equal to 10 ($R = 12 - 2 = 10$). This statistic is easily calculated, and its meaning is very clear—the range is the distance between the two endpoints of the frequency distribution. The range, however, depends very much on the extreme values, and this is the main reason why the range is not used often as a measure of the dispersion.

Standard Deviation

The standard deviation (SD or s) is a measure of variability indicating the degree to which all observed values deviate from the mean. The mathematical formula used for calculation of the standard deviation is given here:

$$SD = \sqrt{\sum_{i=1}^{N} \frac{(X_i - \overline{X})^2}{N-1}},$$

where

SD is the symbol for the standard deviation;

$\overline{X}$ is the symbol for the mean;

X_i is the symbol for each one of the observed values (that is why i can vary between 1 and N);

N is the size of the sample; and

Σ is a symbol for the sum (Greek letter sigma).

It is obvious that the calculation of the standard deviation is much more complicated than the calculation of the range. Moreover, the standard deviation can be used only for interval and ratio data.

Despite these disadvantages, the standard deviation is the most frequently used statistic as a measure of dispersion because it takes into account all observed values and because the dispersion is expressed in the same units as the observed values.

❖ THE NORMAL OR BELL-SHAPED CURVE

In most cases, when the sample size is big enough ($N > 100$), the three measures of the central tendency are the same and are exactly in the middle of the frequency distribution. This kind of distribution is so often met that it is called "normal." Its graphical presentation looks like a bell (see Figure 15.3), and it is called the "normal curve" or "bell-shaped curve." It can be seen from this graph that if the distribution is normal, most of the cases are concentrated around the center of the distribution, and only a small number are distributed at the ends.

The normal distribution is also symmetrical. If we draw a vertical line through the middle point (mean-median-mode), the distribution will be split into two identical parts. Most of the characteristics (physical, chemical, biological, psychological, sociological) of the subjects or objects in a sample are approximately normally distributed. For example, beauty, intelligence, money, children, and lovers have normal distribution, and most of us are somewhere in the middle:

- Neither too beautiful nor very ugly

- Neither a genius nor a fool

- Neither very rich nor starving

At the same time, only a small percentage of people (and usually their names are well-known) are really beautiful or geniuses or billionaires. Fortunately, people at the opposite end of the scales of beauty, intelligence, or money are also few in number; most people are in the

Figure 15.3   Normal Distribution

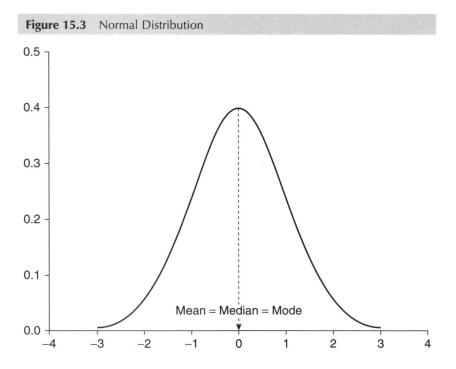

middle. In other words, the chance of ending up in the middle (in every-thing) is greater than the chance of being on the top. You might conclude that it isn't fair. And you will be correct. It is not fair, but it is "normal."

For example, let's have a look at the results of the 1991 US General Social Survey about educational levels shown in Figure 15.4. In this graph, raw data are grouped into 2-year intervals, and as can be seen, the distribution is close to the bell shape, but it is slightly asymmetrical, and its peak is a little higher than the top of the theoretical normal distribution. The two measures of the central tendency are identical (the mode and the median), at 12 years of education, and the mean is a little higher, at 12.88 years. Statisticians might be a bit disappointed with the fact that the distribution is not ideally bell shaped, but educa-tors would be happy with this asymmetry because it shows there are more people with a higher educational level than people with only a primary education. It is not "normal," but it is a hopeful sign.

The normal distribution is well studied from a theoretical point of view, and all its characteristics are well-known. For example, if the frequency distribution is approximately normal, we can conclude immediately that about 68% of the observed values fall into the interval $X - 1\ SD$; $X + 1\ SD$ and 95% of the observed values fall into the interval $X - 2\ SD$; $X + 2\ SD$, as shown in Figure 15.5.

A lot of statistical tests and inferential statistics are based on the assumption of normally distributed data, but they may be applied only

Figure 15.4   Frequency Distribution for US Educational Levels

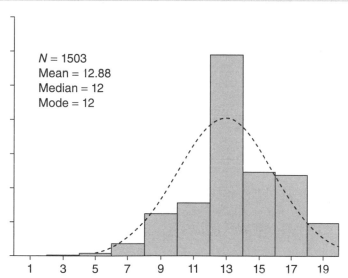

$N = 1503$
Mean = 12.88
Median = 12
Mode = 12

Figure 15.5   Normal Distribution

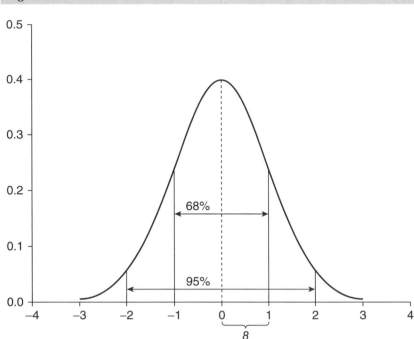

if the data gathered meet this assumption. That is why before applying any statistical method (valid only for normally distributed data), we have to test the hypothesis that our data are normally distributed. Otherwise, the results of the analysis will be meaningless.

A SHORT THEATRICAL PIECE ON STATISTICS

Arthur:	Statistics are very important. Perhaps you've heard the expression "There are lies, damned lies, and statistics."
Grand Inquisitor:	*I've always felt that statistics can be used any way you want to use them.*
Arthur:	There's another saying, "Figures don't lie, but liars figure."
Grand Inquisitor:	*Why do people love statistics so much?*

Arthur:	There's comfort in numbers. You get a sense of certainty and seriousness from numbers that you don't get from words or logical arguments.
Grand Inquisitor:	*I read recently that half of the marriages end in divorce now. Why don't people choose, when they get married, to be in the other 50% that doesn't get divorced?*
Arthur:	Everyone who gets married thinks that they are in the other 50%. Remember, this is a country where we all think we're above average. When people get married, they should also get divorced at the same time but not put the date on the divorce papers. That would make things a lot easier.

❖ THE PROBLEMS WITH RATINGS

A cautionary note: People can use statistics selectively to prove all kinds of things. As the folk saying goes, "Figures don't lie, but liars figure." For example, you might want to look carefully at the statistics used by radio and television stations, networks, and other media organizations because their data might be accurate as far as they go but neglect to deal with certain important matters (such as the demographic makeup and buying power of a show's audience), or they might put an unwarranted positive spin on figures about audiences and the popularity of programs. And there is reason to believe that the figures Nielsen and other ratings companies use may not be accurate due to the methods of data collection used (see the quotation from Barry Sherman, 1995, in Chapter 13).

Joseph R. Dominick (1993) listed a number of reasons to question the accuracy of ratings in *The Dynamics of Mass Communication:*

> First, it is possible that the type of person who agrees to participate may have viewing habits different from those of the viewer who declines to participate. Second, in the case of both Arbitron and Nielsen reports (based on about 55 percent of the diaries sent out) it is possible that "returners" behave differently from "non-returners." Third, people who know that their viewing is being

measured may change their behavior. A family might watch more news and public affairs programs than usual in order to appear sophisticated in the eyes of the rating company. Fourth, both ratings companies admit that they have a problem measuring the viewing of certain groups. Minorities, particularly blacks and Hispanics, may be underrepresented in the ratings companies' samples. Lastly, the stations that are being measured can distort the measurement process by engaging in contests and special promotions or by running unusual or sensational programs in an attempt to "hype" the ratings. (p. 516)

Despite these problems, ratings are useful and necessary—because the prices stations can charge for commercials are, in large measure, determined by the ratings their programs get.

❖ A CAUTIONARY NOTE ON STATISTICS

It's a good idea to be skeptical whenever statistics (and any research data) are given. You might ask yourself questions such as these:

- Who collected the data?

- How accurate are the data?

- How timely are the data?

- How complete are the data? (Did the researchers fail, for one reason or another, to obtain important data?)

- Are there other data that raise questions about the accuracy of (or that contradict) the data being dealt with?

- Are useful comparisons of data made?

- Are the methods used in the analysis appropriate for this kind of data?

- How have the data been interpreted?

❖ STATISTICS AND COMPARISONS

Often, data are presented using comparisons. Comparisons may be odious, but they are often very useful. Generally two kinds of comparisons are made:

Historical (before and after)

Spatial (here and there)

But there are other kinds as well. Here are some fascinating historical statistics from the Harper's Index found in the November 2012 issue of *Harper's* magazine:

- Percentage of Americans in 1992 who believed gun laws should be stricter: 78

- Percentage who believe so today: 43

- Percentage change since 1988 in US teen pregnancy rates: −36

- Factor by which US cases of West Nile virus have increased since the virus was first detected here in 1999: 51

In some cases, a statistic by itself is interesting in that it gives an idea of the size or scope of some activity. Here are some more examples from the same issue of the Harper's Index that are not comparative but are fascinating:

Percentage of Democrats who have an "unfavorable" opinion of Muslims: 29

Percentage of Republicans who do: 57

Percentage of Ohio Republicans who say Obama is more responsible than Romney for the death of Osama bin Laden: 38

Who say Romney is more responsible than Obama: 15

Who say they aren't sure which man is more responsible: 47

Number of "known cracks and breaks" in the dome of the US Capitol building: 1,300

Portion of Americans who don't walk for at least 10 continuous minutes at any point in an average week: 2/5

In 1987, Harper's Index reported that seven condoms are used every second in the United States. The figure is much higher now, no doubt, since the population is much larger. A condom company estimated that 87 condoms were used every second on Valentine's Day one year, but there's no way to verify that figure. The figure for condom usage is interesting, but it doesn't tell us a great deal. It would be much more useful to know what percentage of the American population uses condoms, which would enable us to determine how many people who use condoms are having intercourse in America every second. (How sociologists get these figures is another matter; our knowledge of statistics and problems with sampling might make us a bit skeptical about the accuracy of some research, although there are some methods that are very reliable if applied in the proper way.)

❖ DATA ON MEDIA USE IN AMERICA

Statistics tell us about the growth of new media technology in American culture. The figures in Table 15.2 about the time US adults spent with various electronic media in 2014 offer information that has important implications for anyone interested in the role of media in societies. In addition, the Kaiser Family Foundation (2010) estimated that children from 8 to 18 years spend nearly 8 hours a day—53 hours a week—looking at computer screens.

Obviously, we live in a media-saturated society that dominates our leisure time and has a profound impact on our society and culture as well as our individual lives. Today 98% of Americans have high-speed Internet access, and many families have more than one Internet-enabled device in their homes (Evans, 2015). Smartphones, which are actually powerful computers, are now prevalent. And Apple's iPad

Table 15.2   Average Time Spent per Day With Major Media by US Adults in 2014

5:04	Television
2:46	Radio
1:07	Smartphone
1:01	Internet on a personal computer
0:32	Time-shifted television
0:12	Game console
0:09	DVD/Blu-ray
0.02	Multimedia device

Source: Nielsen.

and other brands of tablet computers have made major changes in the way people use computers and consume media.

❖ SMARTPHONES

Here are some statistics on the penetration of smartphones in the United States from various recent studies cited by the Media Literacy Clearinghouse (n.d.):

Grade	Boys	Girls
Third grade	20%	18%
Fourth grade	25%	26%
Middle school	83%	84%
High school	86%	84%

Nearly half of all children age 12–17 years use their phones to send 100 or more text messages a day (Media Literacy Clearninghouse, n.d.). Statistics from the Nielsen Company (Fried, 2011) offer information on smartphone penetration by ethnicity:

> Its research shows that in the U.S., white consumers are less likely than blacks, Asians or Hispanics to have a smartphone. And that trend appears to be continuing, Nielsen said. According to its research, 42 percent of whites who purchased a mobile phone in the past six months chose a smartphone over a feature phone, compared with 60 percent of Asians and Pacific Islanders, 56 percent of Hispanics and 44 percent of African Americans. Among the ethnic groups, Asians and Pacific Islanders were most likely to have an iPhone, while the BlackBerry was particularly popular among African Americans.

❖ THE PROBLEM OF INTERPRETATION

When dealing with statistical data, there is the matter of interpretation. The data we get from research always have to be interpreted. Figures don't mean anything in and of themselves, and that's where problems often arise. If we don't find problems in the research methodology or means of data collection in research projects (or in both), we often find different points of view (and sometimes mistakes) in the interpretation of the data collected. So media stations and networks battle with one another, using statistics selectively, and we must be on guard and notice the qualifications they use and the way they "read" the data they have collected to suit their own purposes.

Statistics pose a dilemma. They must be interpreted, but the interpretations some people make are often highly speculative and based, in certain cases, on only those statistics that suit the purposes of the person(s) using the data and neglecting other data. Researchers should be honest and tell not only the truth but also the whole truth, to the extent they can. One problem is that researchers tend to see what they would like to see and very often unconsciously neglect some facts.

❖ STATISTICS: APPLICATIONS AND EXERCISES

1. Using the latest *Statistical Abstract of the United States*, find data on some aspect of media use in America that you find interesting. Print out the page with the data and turn it in with your discussion of what was interesting about the data. Then find data on media use in France, Japan, and Argentina to compare with the data about American media usage. What does this comparative data reveal about media usage in the countries involved? Did you learn anything interesting from making this comparative analysis?

2. Find statistical data on the amount of television young children (ages 3–10) watch daily in America, France, Japan, and Argentina and the amount of advertising to which they are exposed. Does using a comparative approach offer important insights about children and the media in America?

3. What do you make of the following statistics about televised football? A typical 3-hour game includes the following:

   11 minutes of action (a typical play takes 4 seconds)

   17 minutes of replays

   3 seconds devoted to cheerleaders

   67 minutes of players standing around, getting back to the huddle, lining up

   60 minutes of commercials

Given these statistics, why do you think televised football is so popular?

❖ CONCLUSIONS

This primer on descriptive statistics covers some of the more commonly used concepts to help you interpret data better and make sense of some of the articles you might be reading about media usage and related concerns. There are many books on statistics that can further your knowledge of this useful and interesting subject. Two of the most widely used software programs are SPSS (formerly Statistical Package for the Social Sciences; now Statistical Product and Service Solutions) and SAS (Statistical Analysis System). These programs greatly facilitate statistical analyses—and bigger mistakes (than made before their usage) if not properly used.

❖ FURTHER READING

Bluman, A. (2011). *Elementary statistics: A step-by-step approach* (8th ed.). New York, NY: McGraw-Hill.

Burdess, N. (2010). *Starting statistics: A short, clear guide.* Thousand Oaks, CA: SAGE.

Freedman, D., Pisani, R., & Purves, R. (1997). *Statistics* (3rd ed.). New York, NY: Norton.

Gonick, L., & Smith, W. (1993). *The cartoon guide to statistics.* New York, NY: HarperCollins.

Healy, J. F. (2015). *The essentials of statistics: A tool for social research.* Independence, KY: Cengage.

Kanji, G. K. (2006). *100 statistical tests* (3rd ed.). Thousand Oaks, CA: SAGE.

Kremelberg, D. (2011). *Practical statistics: A quick and easy guide to IBM SPSS Statistics, STATA, and other statistical software.* Thousand Oaks, CA: SAGE.

Moore, D. S. (1997). *The active practice of statistics: A text for multimedia learning.* New York, NY: W. H. Freeman.

Pearson, R. W. (2010). *Statistical persuasion.* Thousand Oaks, CA: SAGE.

Salkind, N. J. (2014). *Statistics for people who (think they) hate statistics* (5th ed.). Thousand Oaks, CA: SAGE.

Sirkin, R. M. (2006). *Statistics for the social sciences* (3rd ed.). Thousand Oaks, CA: SAGE.

Vogt, W. P., & Johnson, R. B. (2011). *Dictionary of statistics and methodology: A nontechnical guide for the social sciences* (4th ed.). Thousand Oaks, CA: SAGE.

Wright, D. B., & London, K. (2009). *First (and second) steps in statistics* (2nd ed.). Thousand Oaks, CA. SAGE.

Part V

Putting It All Together

What's the difference between capitalism and communism?

In capitalism, man exploits man. In communism, it's just the opposite.

—An old joke

He was in LOGIC a great critic,

Profoundly skill'd in Analytic;

He could distinguish, and divide

A hair 'twixt south, and south-west side:

On either which he would dispute,

Confute, change hands, and still confute,

He'd undertake to prove, by force

Of argument, a man's no horse.

He'd prove a buzzard is no fowl,

And that a Lord may be an owl.

A calf an alderman, a goose a justice,

And rooks, Committee-men and Trustees;

He'd run in debt by disputation,

And pay with ratiocination.

All this by syllogism, true,

In mood and figure, he would do.

—Samuel Butler, *Hudibras*
(1663–1678/2004, Part 1, Canto 1)

16

Nineteen Common
Thinking Errors

CHAPTER 16 FOCUS QUESTIONS

- What are the most common fallacies?
- Which fallacies are the easiest to commit?

This chapter lists and briefly explains some of the more common thinking errors we make—including errors known, in philosophical parlance, as *fallacies*. There is a strong relationship between logical and correct thinking and designing research projects. So it is important that we examine our thinking for mistakes we inadvertently might be making. I assume, of course, that all of the thinking errors discussed here are made by accident and are due to carelessness or not recognizing the error.

Researchers must be honest and report the results of their research; that is part of the ethics of research. But occasionally, researchers inadvertently make mistakes of one sort or another. That's to be expected. All anyone can ask when doing research is that you do the best job you can in designing your research and carrying it out and that you report your results—even if your findings surprise you or are, for some reason, distasteful to you.

A SHORT THEATRICAL PIECE ON CORRECT THINKING

Grand Inquisitor:	*Are people bald because they have no hair, or is it that they have no hair because they are bald?*
Arthur:	Isthay estionqway isway absurdway. Pons asinorum, post hoc ergo propter hoc, petitio principii, ad populam. Quid nunc.
Grand Inquisitor:	*Why is it that newspapers give the age of people when they die but not when they are born?*
Arthur:	I don't know. That's a very profound question. Probably because there is a bias in this country against babies. The elderly have great political power, but who cares about babies, since they don't vote?
Grand Inquisitor:	*What's the difference between an alligator?*
Arthur:	I give up!
Grand Inquisitor:	*An alligator can swim in the ocean but not on the land.*

Arthur:	Did you ever study critical thinking?
Grand Inquisitor:	*I'm naturally very critical—especially of others. I prefer not to think, except when it is absolutely necessary. With all the great computer programs now, one needn't do so.*

❖ COMMON FALLACIES

1. *Appealing to false authority.* We often use authorities when supporting our arguments—people who have expertise in certain areas—but we must be certain that the authorities we cite can speak with legitimacy on our subject. An authority on medicine is not an authority on education, for example. Some commercials for health products have used actors who play doctors in television programs as "authorities"; these individuals are, of course, actually actors or perhaps other celebrities.

2. *Stacking the deck (selected instances).* When we make arguments, we must be careful that we do not neglect information that negates our position and cite only data, statistics, and other information that support our position. We must be scrupulously honest when doing research and deal with all data. The other side of this fallacy is to use examples that are not generalizable.

3. *Overgeneralizing (allness).* This error involves assuming that what is true of some X is true of all X. The term *generalization* comes from the Latin *genus* (kind, class, genre) and refers to a statement that is true for every member of the group or class. If there is one contrary instance, it negates the generalization. Therefore, it is generally a good idea to qualify generalizations so that one contrary instance will not invalidate them. Not everyone in England speaks the kind of English the queen does or that certain members of the upper classes do (what is known as "the received pronunciation"). Actually, a relatively small proportion of the people in England does. So we have to be careful to avoid making generalizations about how "the English" speak. We cannot assume that what is true of some is true of all. (This is the kind of thinking that is behind stereotyping.)

4. *Imperfect analogies and comparisons.* When we make an analogy, we compare two things and allege that they are similar in some important way or ways. In ancient days, supporters of royalty

asserted that a country was like a body and needed a head (the monarch) to rule; otherwise, there would be chaos. This notion is silly, because a country is not like a body, which may explain why there are so few kings and queens nowadays. And when there were kings, there also was a great deal of chaos and confusion.

There are two kinds of analogies: metaphors, which state equivalence ("My love is a red rose") and similes, which use "like" or "as" and state similarity ("My love is like a red rose"). When you make analogies, you must be certain that the analogy is correct and fitting.

5. *Misrepresenting ideas of other people.* We often inadvertently misrepresent people's ideas because we are in a hurry or careless. We must be careful, for example, that when we quote people, we do so accurately. Leaving off a word can alter the meaning of the material quoted to a considerable extent. And the same applies to leaving out sentences that qualify previously discussed material. Misrepresenting people's ideas is also known as creating "straw men" that are easy to knock down.

6. *Pushing arguments to absurd extremes.* We do this when we take a reasonable statement by someone and greatly exaggerate it so that it loses any semblance of credibility. When we do this, we fail to notice any qualifications that might have been made or any limitations made by the person whose ideas we are distorting. This kind of thinking—pushing arguments to absurd extremes—is quite common and is done because we do not like an idea, have an emotional reaction to a statement, or want to generate an emotional reaction to an idea. Thus, for example, advocates for the National Rifle Association often argue that any attempt to limit the sales of guns means the government (or whoever) will "end up taking everyone's guns away."

7. *Before, therefore because of* (post hoc ergo propter hoc). This argument reasons that if X occurs before Y, X causes Y. Just because something takes place before something else does not mean it caused it. Determining what causes anything is very difficult. For example, suppose a person goes to a restaurant for lunch. Later that night, he has an upset stomach. It is possible, but not necessarily the case, that the lunch led to the upset stomach. The cause might have been dinner or a snack or not anything the guy ate but by a flu bug or something else. So we have to be very careful about assigning causes to phenomena.

8. *Misleading percentages.* Sometimes percentages can be misleading. You must give an absolute number so the percentages can be

interpreted correctly. In some cases, a 50% increase in the sale of books in a given period (from 100 to 150 copies sold) looks impressive when you see the percentage but turns out to be trivial when you see the raw data. You must always mention the raw numbers on which the percentages are calculated. In *Thinking, Fast and Slow* (2011), Daniel Kahneman talked about "Framing Effects." He explained, "Different ways of presenting the same information evoke different emotions. The statement 'the odds of survival after one month are 90%' is more reassuring than the equivalent statement that 'mortality within one month of surgery is 10%'" (p. 88). Not only can we mislead people with percentages, but also the way we use them shapes people's emotional responses to the information.

9. *Using seemingly impressive numbers.* Quoting numbers without giving the reader a sense of what percentage of the base the numbers represent is also a means of misleading people. Suppose one were to say that a survey shows that 500 economists believe that the economy is at risk of inflation. That figure means a lot if there are 1,000 economists in the country but not very much if there are 20,000. This mistake is the reverse of the preceding one, using percentages without giving absolute numbers. You should always know the percentages that lead to the numbers and the numbers that lead to the percentages.

10. *Misleading use of the term* average. We saw, in Chapter 15 on statistics, that there are three ways of figuring out averages: the mean, the median, and the mode. The mean is defined as the total divided by the number. Suppose we are dealing with salaries in the United States. You get a considerably different figure if you use the median—the figure halfway between the lowest and the highest salary—rather than the mean. That's because very high salaries will skew the median considerably. If there are a lot of millionaires and billionaires in a given population, the median salary will be skewed upward and will not give us a true picture of most people's salaries.

11. *Incorrect assumptions.* You have to make sure that what you assume to be the case is correct. If you begin your research with incorrect assumptions, your research—which builds on these assumptions—will be deeply flawed. It's a wise policy to always check on your assumptions because they may be incorrect. For example, many people assume that murderous violence in high schools is an urban phenomenon. What we've seen in the United States, however, is that many killings and massacres in our high schools have occurred in the suburbs.

12. *False conclusions.* Let us suppose that a class satisfaction survey is taken of 200 students and 8 people complain that they do not like the class. That does not allow you to argue that 192 people "liked" the class; all you know is that they did not complain. Many students in the class might not have liked it but did not indicate their feelings, for one reason or another.

13. *Mistaking correlation and causation.* Just because there is a correlation between X and Y does not mean that X causes Y. For example, there may be a correlation between the amount of higher education and small families, but it does not mean that the amount of education causes small families. There may be other factors involved, such as the age at which people with higher education get married. We have to distinguish between some factor causing something to happen and that factor contributing to something's happening.

14. *Diversion of attention by using emotional language.* There is a wonderful joke about what a minister scribbled in the margin of one of his sermons: "Argument weak—yell like crazy." The point is that people who feel very strongly about some issue may become very emotional about it, and their use of emotion often blinds them and their audience to the weakness in their argument. Sometimes people use "red herrings" (any means of distracting people from the issue at hand) to avoid dealing with a question.

Father: Why did you come home after midnight when I told you to be back by 11:00 p.m.?

Son: You're always picking on me.

The issue is why the son came home late, but the son has tried to divert it to why the father is "always picking on" him.

Let me offer this famous Jewish joke, which is another red herring—but in this case, more literally, a pink salmon.

A beggar named Cohen meets a wealthy person and pleads for some money for his starving family. The wealthy person gives Cohen some money. A short while later, the wealthy man goes to a restaurant and sees Cohen eating a very expensive dish there—salmon and mayonnaise. When the man asks Cohen about it, he says, "When I don't have money, I can't eat salmon and mayonnaise. When I do have money, I shouldn't eat salmon and mayonnaise. So when can I eat salmon and mayonnaise?"

Cohen has shifted the argument from why he isn't spending money to feed his hungry family to when he can eat salmon and mayonnaise.

15. *Begging the question* (petitio principii). In Latin, *petitio* means request or petition, and *principii* means beginning or at the start. So *petitio principii* is an argument that assumes its conclusion. That is, we accept as true what we are supposed to prove. When we argue correctly, the premises and conclusions must be separate. We beg the question by assuming that the answer to the question we are asking is obvious because it is in the conclusion; thus, by using different words, we "answer" the question. For example, the statement "Smoking marijuana is good for you because it is healthful," really begs the question. Saying it is "healthful"—the conclusion—is used to support the argument that "smoking marijuana is good for you."

16. *Oversimplification.* When dealing with complicated issues, to make ourselves clear or do the best we can with a weak position, we sometimes oversimplify things. Often, elements of the reasoning error discussed in 5 above, misrepresentation, are at work here. When we have oversimplified arguments made by others and weakened them by doing so, it generally is much easier to claim support for our own position.

17. Ad hominem *arguments*. The term *ad hominem* comes from the Latin for attacking the person—literally "to the man." We don't focus our attention on the argument being made but on the person who has made it. And by insulting or casting doubt on the "good name" of that person, we indirectly attack his or her ideas. We focus on "who" is making the argument and not on "what" argument is being made.

18. Ad populum *arguments*. In Latin, *ad populum* means appealing to the populace. These arguments usually take the form of "everyone knows . . ." or "everyone believes . . ." This kind of argument is really an appeal to be guided by so-called public opinion, but the appeal is spurious. When you say "everyone knows," you cannot possibly know what everyone knows. What you are probably doing is taking your

assumptions and generalizing from them—assuming that everyone agrees with you. These "everyone knows" arguments imply that they are based on common sense, but as "everyone knows," common sense tells us that the world is flat.

19. *Pooh-poohing arguments.* Pooh-poohing involves ridiculing other people and failing to take their ideas seriously. It is a means of avoiding logical argument and often uses the "everyone knows" tactic to suggest that an idea is so absurd it shouldn't even be considered. Pooh-poohing is a common evasive technique.

❖ CONCLUSIONS

It's very easy to make some of the mistakes discussed here. In part, this is because we often drop our guard when involved in a research project and don't examine our thinking processes as carefully as we should. There is no "perfect" research project; every kind of research has strong points and weak points, and there are almost always methodological problems that affect what we do and find. And then there is interpreting what we've found; different people may "read" the same data differently. Economists, for example, are notorious for interpreting the same data about the economy in wildly different ways.

That's why it is always a good idea to have other people look at your research design to offer suggestions. They may help you avoid making some of the thinking errors discussed in this chapter or other kinds of mistakes discussed in previous chapters. Although you might be able to discover thinking errors in the work of others, it is generally very difficult to see these errors in your own work. We all suffer from this problem—because we are so intimately involved in our research that we don't, or can't, see it objectively. It's a good idea to put your work aside for a short time so you can look at it more objectively. You wouldn't want to have your research attacked for appealing to false authorities, overgeneralizing, stacking the deck, making imperfect analogies, arguing on the basis of incorrect assumptions, or any of the other errors discussed here.

❖ FURTHER READING

Barnet, S., & Bedau, H. (2010). *Critical thinking, reading and writing: A brief guide to argument* (7th ed.). New York, NY: Bedford/St. Martin's.

Conway, D. A., & Munson, R. (1990). *Elements of reasoning*. Belmont, CA: Wadsworth.

Corbett, E. P. J. (1991). *The elements of reasoning*. New York, NY: Macmillan.

Darner, T. E. (1995). *Attacking faulty reasoning: A practical guide to fallacy-free arguments* (3rd ed.). Belmont, CA: Wadsworth.

Dowden, B. H. (1993). *Logical reasoning*. Belmont, CA: Wadsworth.

Kahneman, D. (2011). *Thinking, Fast and Slow*. New York, NY: Farrar, Straus, and Giroux.

Kelley, D. (1994). *The art of reasoning* (2nd exp. ed.). New York, NY: Norton.

Kirby, G., & Goodpaster, J. R. (1995). *Thinking*. Englewood Cliffs, NJ: Prentice Hall.

Moore, B. N., & Parker, R. (2011). *Critical thinking* (10th ed.). New York, NY: McGraw-Hill.

Russow, L-M., & Curd, M. (1989). *Principles of reasoning*. New York, NY: St. Martin's.

Wilson, D. C. (1999). *A guide to good reasoning*. New York, NY: McGraw-Hill.

Wright, L. (2012). *Critical thinking: An introduction to analytical reading and reasoning*. New York, NY: Oxford University Press.

Rules of Good Riting

1. *Verbs has to agree with their subjects.*

2. *Prepositions are not words to end sentences with.*

3. *And don't start a sentence with a conjunction.*

4. *It is wrong to ever split an infinitive.*

5. *Avoid cliches like the plague. (They are old hat.)*

6. *Be more or less specific.*

8. *Parenthetical remarks (however relevant) are (usually) unnecessary.*

9. *Also, too, never, ever use repetitive redundancies.*

10. *No sentence fragments.*

11. *Don't use no double negatives.*

12. *Proofread carefully to see if you any words out.*

—From Steve Wheeler, *Learning With e's* (2010)

17

Writing Research Reports

CHAPTER 17 FOCUS QUESTIONS

- Why is it useful to keep a journal?
- What trick was offered for organizing reports?
- What was said about outlines, first drafts, and revisions?
- What hints were offered for writing research reports?
- What is the IMRD structure of quantitative research reports?
- What are the most common problems found in writing?

After you've done your research, whether qualitative or quantitative (or both), you have to write a report on your findings. That is, you have to communicate what you discovered to others. The quality of your writing will play an important role in the way people respond to your research. Your report should be well organized, grammatically correct, and well argued. Academic papers observe basic scholarly conventions dictating appropriate content and style. These matters are discussed here.

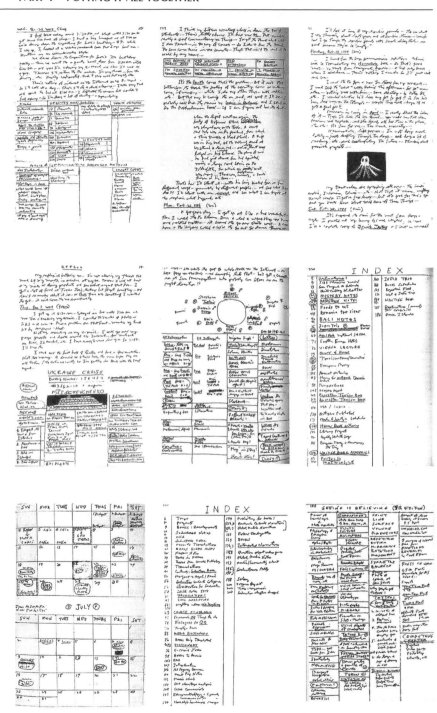

Pages from my journals, which I use to plan my books and conduct research.

❖ KEEPING A JOURNAL

In 1956, one of my professors suggested I keep a journal. At the time, the idea struck me as silly. "I don't have anything to write about," I thought. But later that year, for one reason or another, I bought a bound book and started keeping a journal. I use Canson Basic Sketch Books, which cost around $12. You can get them at most art supply stores or on the Internet. Since then, I have written 92 journals, and this book, like all my others, originated and took shape in my journals. For researchers and writers, journals are invaluable. They are also therapeutic. One reason **personal journals** are useful is that when writing in a journal, ideas pop into your head that would disappear if you didn't write them down, and the very act of writing in a journal tends to generate new ideas. On the basis of more than 50 years of journal keeping, let me offer some suggestions to help you make use of this valuable tool.

- The journal must be a bound volume.

- Number all the pages.

- Make the last page an index of the journal.

- Use the first four pages for drawing in monthly calendars.

- Write in dark ink.

- Write the date for each day's entries.

- Reserve some pages for brainstorming on topics you are working on.

- Use the bottom of your pages to write down email and website addresses.

I often draw four lines down a page for brainstorming on some topic. By indicating in the index the page numbers of the topics you cover on a given page, you can access them more easily. I also like to make little drawings in my journals, every once in a while, to give them more visual interest. You can write about ideas, hopes, thoughts, things that happened to you, and all kinds of other things. In a sense, you are creating a documentary about your life and ideas to access in later years. I sometimes use journal material I wrote a number of years ago in my writings. You never can tell when an idea will come in handy.

A SHORT THEATRICAL PIECE ON WRITING REPORTS

Grand Inquisitor:	*Why force poor, overworked students to write reports on their research? Why not let them dictate their reports on their smartphones? They could have music in the background, do some rapping . . . it would be cool.*
Arthur:	Because the written word lives! You can read over something that's been written and see how good the research is. There's also the quality of the writing. We live in an increasingly electronic age, but it's still important to be able to write.
Grand Inquisitor:	*I'm developing a software program. You just tell it what your subject is and it writes the paper. It also takes tests for you.*
Arthur:	We now have programs that automatically grade papers on the quality of the writing and the research.
Grand Inquisitor:	*Are professors really necessary nowadays?*
Arthur:	We're going to be replaced by holograms, Internet courses, and paper-grading machines.
Grand Inquisitor:	*Why not give students degrees when they enter? It would save them a lot of stress. And we wouldn't need any professors.*
Arthur:	Are you, by chance, a university president?

❖ A TRICK FOR ORGANIZING REPORTS

Here's an anecdote with an important moral. A number of years ago, I attended a conference at Stanford University. There were three speakers and a fourth person, a "respondent," who was there to offer his assessment of the research reports given. This is a common practice at conferences; the respondent assesses the reports, gives context, offers critiques, and so on.

Before the session started, I noticed him doing what seemed rather strange. He took four sheets of 8.5" × 11" paper, folded them in half, and tore them so he had eight half sheets of paper. Then he took those sheets and folded them in half and tore them. He did this a few times and ended up with a stack of small slips of paper. One sheet of 8.5" × 11" paper yields 16 slips, so he ended up with 64 little pieces—approximately 2" × 3"—of paper.

Then, as the speakers gave their reports, he'd write something down on a slip of paper. I noticed that he used one slip of paper for each idea. After the third speaker had given his report, there was a short break. The respondent spent the time assembling his small slips of paper and then gave a remarkably (since he had so little time to organize his talk) logically structured analysis of the reports he had heard, with comments, criticisms, and suggestions.

The Secret: One Idea per Slip of Paper

This methodology of one idea per piece of paper for organizing reports is worth using. If you have one idea per piece of paper, it is easy to physically move the pieces when you start making your report outline. If you have two ideas on a slip of paper, you can't move your ideas around easily.

This notion of one idea per slip of paper is at the heart of some computer programs designed to help writers organize their ideas. It's much easier to manipulate slips of paper (that is, single ideas) as you plan your report than it is to rewrite a poorly organized report. I have used this method of organizing material in many of my books. After I've got my stacks of paper, I set them down on a table. Then I start trying out different ways of organizing them until I've got what seems to me to be the best way of structuring things.

Of course, as you write, ideas suddenly arise in your head—probably from the unconscious—that help you flesh out ideas or explain them in interesting ways. In *Writing the Australian Crawl*, poet William Stafford (1978) said that "a writer is not so much someone who has something to say as he is someone who has found a process that will bring about new things he would not have thought of if he had not started to say them" (p. 17). There's no reason why research reports can't be written in an interesting manner, even if there are some rather formal rules for the way these papers should be organized.

❖ OUTLINES, FIRST DRAFTS, AND REVISIONS

I've already suggested that you use little pieces of papers to organize your thoughts. You can arrange them and rearrange them until you have a logically coherent outline for your paper. Remember that when making an outline, if you have subtopics, you must have at least two of them. That is, if you have an A, you have to have a B. The next important thing to do is write a first draft as quickly as you can and print it out. Then you can start going over it and revising it, because all writing is rewriting. Very few writers get things right the first time, which is why rewriting plays such an important role in writing.

Your revisions should be done on hard copy—that is, printouts of your first draft. For some reason, it is much better to make revisions on printouts of written material than on monitor screens. Then, after you've made your revisions to your printout, enter your revisions into your computer draft and print it out again. You can then revise the second-draft printout and put your new revisions into your computer draft. As a rule, you should plan on making three revisions of your written work to get it into acceptable condition. Hemingway is rumored to have written the closing sentence of one of his novels 30 times. You don't have to do that many revisions, but you do need to make at least three.

❖ WRITING RESEARCH REPORTS

Research reports conventionally have the following stylistic attributes:

Formal style. Reports do not use colloquial language and usually generate an air of seriousness about themselves.

Third person. Reports are written in the third person (*one*) rather than the first-person singular (*I*), although some journals are much more casual about things nowadays.

Gender-neutral language. Reports use gender-neutral language. This is most easily accomplished by avoiding *he* and *she* and using the plural.

Awkward: Each respondent took his or her questionnaire . . .

Better: The respondents took their questionnaires . . .

Transitions to guide readers. Transitions are important guides to readers to cue them into what is coming. The following chart lists some of the more important kinds of transitions:

Causes	Effects	Sequences	Meaning
Because	Therefore	First	We find, then
This leads to	As a result	Next	This suggests
Since	Accordingly	Finally	This implies
Examples	**Contrasts**	**Conclusions**	**Time**
For example	But	Therefore	Before
For instance	Nevertheless	Thus	After
To show this	In contrast	We find, then	At the same time

Active voice. Some writers use the passive voice to give their research an air of authority, but I think the passive voice, which uses some form of the verb "to be," tends to deaden the prose rather than enliven it.

Active voice: We *found* in our research . . .

Passive voice: It *was discovered* by us in our research . . .

What gives research authority is the quality of the thinking and of the research, not using the passive voice.

Verb usage. In writing your reports, it is important that you follow conventions about which verb tense should be used in each part of the report. Let me suggest you do the following:

Part of Report	Verb Tense to Use
Review of literature in introduction	Past
Discussion of procedures followed	Past
Discussion of meaning of research	Present
Discussion of future research	Future

These rules about verb tense usage are conventions that most researchers follow in their reports.

Jargon. Do not use jargon (that is, highly specialized terms) to the extent that you can avoid it. A good way to accomplish this is to write for an imaginary audience of readers who are intelligent but do not have any knowledge about your subject. Define all terms that might be difficult for your readers and avoid abbreviations and acronyms (words formed from the initial letters of a name, such as *NATO*).

Undeveloped writing. Undeveloped writing lacks detail and color. It tends to be vague, overly general, and abstract. You can avoid this style by doing things such as offering examples, defining your terms, dealing with causes and effects of the phenomena you discuss, and contrasting and comparing things.

❖ THE IMRD STRUCTURE OF QUANTITATIVE RESEARCH REPORTS

Conventionally, quantitative research reports are divided into four sections: an introduction, a description of the methodology employed, a report on the findings, and a discussion section. This is known as the IMRD structure. Qualitative research reports can employ this design as well. Let's look at each section.

Introduction. In this section, you offer your readers a discussion of the background of the study, deal with why you made the study or conducted the research and why it is relevant, and generally, offer a brief review of relevant literature on the subject. (See Chapter 2 on library searches to get details on this topic.) It is customary to offer a statement of your hypothesis in this section and to deal with the theories and research that have led you to make your hypothesis. The introduction, then, supplies readers with a sense of context and locates the research within a general area of knowledge. It also provides readers with information to help them understand the report.

Method. This section deals with the design of the research or with the methodology employed. It is detailed and very specific for two reasons: first, so your readers will see exactly what you did and, second, so your research can be replicated. Research methods must be described so other researchers can replicate your research should they wish to do so—perhaps because your findings are remarkable or they conflict with previous research on the same subject. In other words, in the method section you deal with the operationalization (the activities carried out) in your research. You delineate the methods used to prove (or disprove) your hypothesis or discover answers to questions you have raised. You have to define all your terms carefully and describe how you went about collecting your data and answering the research question you posed in the introduction.

What follows are things you might be doing that require an explanation and elaboration in your methodology section:

- Are you testing a theory?

- Are you testing competing theories?

- Are you testing a methodology?

- Are you replicating a study to test its findings?

- Are you trying to correct earlier research you did that had problems such as inconsistent results?

- Are you trying to find the answer to some question of interest?

- Are you trying to solve some social or political problem?

This section is often long and very detailed and usually draws the careful scrutiny of readers because your methodology is of crucial importance. If people can find flaws in your methodology, your findings will be considered useless. Many battles among scholars involve conflicting ideas about methodological matters.

Results. The findings are reported in the results section. If you have numerical data, present them as charts and graphs in which results and relationships are easy to see. Usually, the results section is fairly brief because it doesn't take as much space to report what you found as it does to describe how you found what you found.

In this section, offer your data and analysis of this data. In addition, discuss your results and their relation to your data.

Discussion. In this section, you discuss what you found, talk about any problems you faced in doing the research, describe any unexpected things that happened, deal with the relation between your findings and research by other scholars, offer suggestions for those doing research in the same area, and mention plans you might have for future research.

Here are some questions to consider for your discussion:

- Was your hypothesis supported by your research?

- Can you generalize from your findings?

- Were the questions you asked yourself at the beginning of your research answered?

- Did your findings lead you to ask other questions that might require new research?

- Were there ethical problems that presented themselves in your research? Or did your findings lead to ethical problems?

You may think of other questions to consider in addition to these.

For good examples of the IMRD structure, see these articles: "Playing Violent Video and Computer Games and the Adolescent Self-Concept" (Funk & Buchman, 1996) and "Sexual Humor on Freud as Expressed in Limericks" (Kantha, 1999).

❖ WRITING CORRECTLY: AVOIDING SOME COMMON PROBLEMS

Your report may be well organized, but it is also crucial that your writing be grammatically correct. If you write a report full of spelling errors, punctuation errors, and unclear and awkward passages, your credibility as a researcher will be very suspect. Here are some of the most common errors people make when they write.

Awkwardness. Awkward passages are ungainly and stiff and not well formed, for example, "The humanity of the death penalty is a problem that has long been a debate in many societies." Writing that uses the same sentence structure over and over again is also considered awkward.

Coherence problems. Your sentences should flow together, using transitions to guide your readers. Short sentences that follow one after another, without transitions—that is, choppy writing—is sometimes called "primer style" writing. An example follows.

> My research involved making a content analysis. I selected some comic books to study. I decided to look for how much violence was in the comics I chose. I had trouble defining *violence.*

You can see that the writer offers a string of short, simple sentences with no transitions between them.

Dashes and hyphens. Many writers mistake dashes for hyphens.

Dash: —

Hyphen: -

A dash (—) is made of two hyphens. Hyphens are used to link compound words (son-in-law) and cannot be used as dashes. Dashes are used to suggest a pause, longer than that suggested by a comma, in a sentence or to set off an important phrase.

Comma faults. Commas cannot be used to set off two independent clauses (that is, two complete ideas) without a conjunction (e.g., *and, but*). You must use a semicolon or make some other kind of a change, such as inserting a transition. For example,

Comma fault: John loved research, he really enjoyed interviews.

Correct: John loved research; he really enjoyed interviews.

Correct: John loved research because he really enjoyed interviews.

Fragments. In writing reports, make sure you use complete sentences and do not have sentence fragments—incomplete thoughts you think are sentences. In other kinds of writing, such as personal essays, you can use fragments for emphasis as long as you know what you are doing and use them sparingly.

Fragment: You've learned about research. *But wait!*

Padding or wordiness. This is writing that is too wordy, using many words where just a few would do.

Wordy: I am of the opinion that . . .

Correct: I think . . . or I believe . . .

Spelling errors. If you are not certain about the way a word is spelled, you should check its spelling in the dictionary. Spell-checkers in computer programs are useful, but sometimes they make mistakes because they don't recognize that a word that is spelled correctly does not fit the sentence in which it is found.

Following are words writers commonly confuse.

Word	Function	Example
To	Connective	I'm going to Paris . . .
Too	Excess	Too many errors . . .
Two	Number	You made two errors . . .
Their	Possession	They took their books . . .
There	Place	Are you going there?

(Continued)

(Continued)

Word	Function	Example
They're	They + are	They're too snobbish . . .
Who's	Who + is	Who's coming to the party?
Whose	Possession	Whose radio is that?
Its	Possession	The car lost its power . . .
It's	It + is	It's too late for tears . . .

Its causes many problems because it doesn't follow the rule usually found for possession in which possession is indicated by *'s*. *Its* is an anomaly, an exception. I should also point out that none of the possessive pronouns (*his, her, mine, theirs, ours, yours, its*) uses an apostrophe.

Clarity problems. Passages that readers find hard to understand, for one reason or another, are described as unclear. They are usually ambiguous and sometimes unintelligible. Frequently, these passages are also awkward and full of grammatical mistakes. One reason people write unclearly is that they know in their minds what they mean, but they don't express what they know in their writing. Another reason people write unclearly is that their thinking is unclear. It's an excellent idea to read your paper aloud (or have someone else read it to you). This will help you catch awkward and unclear passages and recognize ideas that need development or clarification (or both).

Pronoun reference problems. A pronoun is a word used in place of a noun or another pronoun that precedes it. The first rule of pronouns is that there must be agreement between pronouns and their antecedents in number. For example, the term *everyone* is singular and takes *his* or *her*, and not *their*, in the sentences in which *everyone* is used. The second rule of pronouns is that they refer to the noun or pronoun that immediately precedes them. If this rule is not followed, bizarre things can happen. For example, the following sentence involves incorrect pronoun reference:

Clutching his fried chicken, Bill got in his car and proceeded to eat it.

As written, the *it* here refers to the car, not the chicken. The sentence has to be reconstructed for it to make sense. A suitable revision of the sentence is this:

Bill got in his car clutching his fried chicken and started eating it.

Repetitiveness. Some writers seem to know only one construction for a sentence, and when you read their reports, almost every sentence has the same basic structure. You must vary the structure of your sentences so you don't bore your readers. Also, you should vary their length. If all of your sentences have the same structure and same length, people will find what you have written to be tedious and monotonous. You've got to consider the rhythm of your writing.

Verb agreement problems. Verbs have to agree with their subjects. A singular subject takes a singular verb form. A plural subject takes a plural verb.

I love Mary.	We love Mary.
You love Mary.	You love Mary.
He/she loves Mary.	They love Mary.

❖ ACADEMIC WRITING STYLES

Because of scholarly journal requirements, many scholars incorporate their literature reviews into their articles, using parentheses and the names of authors and dates of their publications, as the following example shows. This passage is taken from the article "Living on the Edge" by Robert McKercher and Candace Fu. It appeared in a 2006 issue of the *Annals of Tourism Research*, one of the most important journals in the field of tourism studies:

> Much of the published material on tourism and the periphery has focused on Fringe destinations such as Pacific Islands, arctic regions, or rural communities (Brown and Hall 2000; Gets and Nilsoon 2003; Hall 1994; Pearce 2002; Prideaux 2002; Wanhill 1995; Weaver 1998). Only a few studies have examined the periphery of existing destinations. These have explored such themes as attributes-based approaches toward periphality (Pearce 2002), residents' perceptions of the rural urban fringe (Weaver and Lawton 2001) and the periphery as a possible urban ecotourism venue (Dwyer and Edwards).

This style of using parentheses to cite relevant articles turns these scholarly articles, in a sense, into annotated bibliographies and makes the articles difficult to read. But these citations demonstrate that an author is up-to-date on the relevant literature and provide a service to readers by pointing out articles of importance. Papers by students do not need to adopt this style of writing.

❖ A CHECKLIST FOR PLANNING RESEARCH AND WRITING REPORTS

This checklist draws on one found in a guidebook for student anthropologists edited by Conrad Kottak, *Researching American Culture* (1982, p. 33), and other works:

- Choosing your research topic
  - o Find a subject you are interested in that can be researched in the time available to you.
  - o Narrow your topic as much as you can. The narrower your focus, the better chance you have of being able to do your research.

- Designing your research project
  - o Determine what topic you'll be investigating or what group of people you'll be studying.
  - o Figure out how to obtain a representative sampling of text (for content analyses, for example), a representative group of people (for surveys), or a place to observe (for participant observations).

- Determining the appropriate method for your project
  - o For textual analysis, consider semiotic analysis, ideological analysis, rhetorical analysis, content analysis, or some combination of these methods.
  - o For subcultural group analysis, consider participation observation.
  - o For opinion and attitude research, consider interviewing, questionnaires, and surveys and focus groups.
  - o For field studies, consider ethnomethodology, participant observation, and interviewing.
  - o For events in the past, consider historical analysis and content analysis.
  - o For studying human behavior, consider experimentation and literature searches of the topic you are investigating.

- Organizing your data for presentation
  - o Put quantitative data into charts and tables.
  - o Use qualitative data to support or reject an argument or affirm some position or thesis.

- Using the correct format for your reports

  o Use the IMRD structure.

  o Make sure you give a detailed bibliography of your sources following whatever style your instructor requires. (When doing research, it is vitally important to write down all the bibliographic information you might need for your references. The best way to do this is to use an index card for each reference or approximate index cards on the computer.)

A PRIMER ON AMERICAN PSYCHOLOGICAL ASSOCIATION (APA) STYLE

The APA style is the one used by most academics in the writings. There is also a website, www.apastyle.org that contains answers to questions you may have about the style to use in your papers and reports and another site, http://flash1r.apa.org/apastyle/basics/index.htm?, that has a tutorial on formatting that will be of use to you. It is a good idea to bookmark the www.apastyle.org page so you can refer to it if you have any questions about formatting. Below I offer a summary of the most important points to follow when writing papers and reports using the APA style.

1. The structure of research papers is:

   Title Page on its own page

   Abstract or summary of procedures and findings

   Introduction that sets the stage for the reader, provides context

   Methods used in research

   Results obtained from research

   Discussion of difficulties involved in research, ideas for future research, etc.

   References used in the research

   Appendixes

(Continued)

(Continued)

2. Use a 12-point Serif typeface (such as Times New Roman) for the for the text and 12-point San Serif such as Ariel san serif typeface for figures.

3. Double space everything in the manuscript and references.

4. Indent the first line of each paragraph one half inch.

5. The margins should be one inch on the left and one inch on the right.

6. The left margin should be aligned (straight) and the right margin should be ragged.

7. Indent the left margin for each paragraph one half inch.

8. Avoid bias, sexism in your use of language.

9. Write in a formal style; informal writing is not appropriate for academic discourse.

10. Call people what they want to be called in your writing.

11. Give the names of people whose ideas you are using in quotations and paraphrases. It's a good idea to give the first name and last names of authors, the title of their book or article, the date of its publication, and its page number the first time you cite them. After that, you can use their last name. The APA style is to give the author's surname, year of publication, and page number (or location on the Internet or wherever).

12. In your references section, you always use the author's surname and then initial (or with many authors, their surnames and initials, and then the title of the book or article, date of publication, publisher, etc.

13. The APA style for references involves hanging indents, in which the first line is flush left and other material is indented.

14. With journal articles, type the title of the article in regular typeface and the journal *title* and volume *number* in italics.

It is always a good idea to use your spell-checker to go over anything you write, to catch careless typing errors and other errors.

❖ CONCLUSIONS

The material discussed in this chapter is meant to guide you both in conceptualizing your research and in writing up your findings. There is a connection between thinking and writing: The quality of your writing reflects the quality of your thinking—and your knowledge of the rules of grammar is a key component of your writing.

The rules of grammar can be thought of as similar to the rules of the road. If you don't know what a stop sign or a red light means or which side of the road to drive on, you'll cause all kinds of confusion and chaos when you're driving and probably won't live very long. You have to know the rules of the road (and the laws in the particular state in which you're driving) to drive, and you have to know the rules of grammar to communicate with others clearly and effectively.

You must write correctly if your readers are to take your research seriously. It's a shame the way some students do excellent research and then write reports full of spelling, punctuation, and grammatical errors that make readers question their findings and even their intelligence. Some students think that just because their papers *look* good—that is, the quality of the printing is good and they've used some attractive typefaces—that their papers *are* good. That isn't the case. It isn't the quality of the uniforms of a football or baseball team that's important; it's the quality of the players wearing the uniforms.

The moral of this little disquisition is to be very careful about your writing. It's a good idea to use your spell-checker and grammar-checker if you are using a computer program that has these features. *You must use the dictionary to look up the correct spelling for any word that you don't know, because the spell-checker misses things.* Probably the best book (and also the shortest, at 92 pages) to help you learn to write correctly is Strunk and White's (1999) *Elements of Style.* It is a classic work.

Print out your research paper and make your corrections on the hard copy. That is what professional writers do. Then transfer your corrections from the hard copy to your computer file. (You cannot do a good job of revising a paper on your monitor; it simply doesn't work. You're more likely to catch errors when you look at a hard copy, and you need to see what the printed pages look like so you can correct spacing and formatting problems.) If you repeat this process a few times, your reports will be much better. You must assume that you'll need to write several drafts to do a good job of presenting your findings to readers.

❖ FURTHER READING

Ballinger, B. (1999). *The curious researcher: A guide to writing research papers* (2nd rev. ed.). Boston, MA: Allyn & Bacon.

Barzun, J., & Graff, H. (1992). *The modern researcher* (5th ed.). Boston, MA: Houghton Mifflin.

Becker, H. S. (1986). *Writing for social scientists: How to start and finish your thesis, book, or article.* Chicago, IL: University of Chicago Press.

Berger, A. A. (1993). *Improving writing skills: Memos, letters, reports, and proposals.* Newbury Park, CA: Sage.

Berger, A. A. (2008). *The academic writer's toolkit: A user's manual.* Walnut Creek, CA: Left Coast Press.

Emerson, R. M., Fretz, R. L., & Shaw, L. L. (1995). *Writing ethnographic fieldnotes.* Chicago, IL: University of Chicago Press.

Lamott, A. (1995). *Bird by bird: Some instructions on writing and life.* New York, NY: Anchor Books.

Lesley, J. D., Jr. (1998). *The essential guide to writing research papers.* White Plains, NY: Longman.

Queneau, R. (1981). *Exercises in style.* New York, NY: New Directions.

Rivers, W. L., & Harrington, S. L. (1988). *Finding facts: Research writing across the curriculum.* Englewood Cliffs, NJ: Prentice Hall.

Strunk, W., Jr., & White, E. B. (1999). *Elements of style* (4th ed.). New York, NY: Longman.

Turabian, K. (2010). *Student's guide for writing college papers* (4th ed.). Chicago, IL: University of Chicago Press.

Williams, J. M. (1990). *Style: Toward clarity and grace.* Chicago, IL: University of Chicago Press.

Glossary

Aberrant decoding This refers to the notion that audiences decode or interpret texts in ways that differ from those the creators of these texts expected. Aberrant decoding is the rule rather than the exception when it comes to the mass media, according to semiotician Umberto Eco (1976).

Aesthetics When applied to the media, aesthetics involves the way technical matters such as lighting, sound, music, kinds of shots and camera work, editing, and related matters in texts affect the way audience members react to texts.

America In my discussion of focal points in Chapter 4, I use America because the alliteration helps readers remember the focal points, but I could have used any country. America is one of the focal points along with art (text), audience, artist (creator), and medium.

Archetype According to Jung, archetypes are images found in dreams, myths, works of art, and religions all over the world. They are not transmitted by culture but are passed on, somehow, genetically, in a collective unconscious. We are not conscious of them directly, but they reveal themselves in our dreams and works of art. One of the most important archetypes is the hero.

Art One of the focal points I discuss in Chapter 4, this refers to any kind of creative expression—any text carried by a medium.

Artist An artist is not only someone who creates paintings or sculptures or plays musical instruments but anyone involved in the creation or performance of a text.

Attitude An *attitude*, as social psychologists use the term, refers to an enduring state of mind in a person about some phenomenon or aspect of experience. Generally, attitudes are either positive or negative; have direction; and involve thoughts, feelings, and behaviors (tied to these attitudes).

Audience An audience is generally defined as a collection of persons who watch a television program, listen to a radio program, or attend a film or some kind of artistic performance (symphony, rock concert). Members of the audience may be together in one room, scattered, or, in the case of television, watching from their own sets. In technical terms, an audience is made up of addressees who receive mediated texts sent by an addresser.

Binary oppositions According to linguist Roman Jakobson (Culler, 1986), seeing things according to binary oppositions (e.g., hot/cold, on/off) is the fundamental way humans find meaning in the world. Oppositions are different from negations. *Healthy/well* is an opposition; *healthy/unhealthy* is a negation.

Broadcast A broadcast is a text made available over wide areas through radio or television signals. Broadcasting differs from other forms of distributing texts such as cablecasting, which uses cables, and satellite transmission, which requires "dishes" to capture signals sent by satellites.

Class From a linguistic standpoint, a class is any group of things that has something in common. We use the term to refer to social classes or, more literally, socioeconomic classes: groups of people who differ in terms of income and lifestyle. Marxist theorists argue that there is a ruling class that shapes the ideas of the proletariat, the working classes.

Codes Codes are systems of symbols, letters, words, sounds, and so on that generate meaning. Language, for example, is a code. It uses combinations of letters that we call words to mean certain things. The relation between the word and the thing the word stands for is arbitrary, based on convention. In some cases, the term *code* is used to describe hidden meanings and disguised communication.

Cognitive dissonance The term *dissonance* refers to sounds that clash with one another. According to psychologists, people wish to avoid ideas that challenge the ones they hold or that create conflict and other disagreeable feelings. *Cognitive dissonance* refers to ideas that conflict with people's views and generate psychological anxiety and displeasure.

Communication There are many ways of understanding and using this term. For our purposes, communication is a process that involves the transmission of messages from senders to receivers. We often make a distinction between communication using language—verbal communication—and nonverbal communication that uses facial expressions, body language, and other means.

Communications The plural of *communication* refers to what is communicated in contrast to the process of communication.

Concept A concept is a general idea or notion that explains or helps us understand some phenomenon or phenomena. I make a distinction in this book among theories, concepts, and the application of concepts.

Connotations This term deals with the ideas or cultural meanings associated with a term, an object, or some phenomenon. *Connotation* comes from the Latin term *connotare*, "to mark along with." It is different from *denotation*, which refers to the literal meaning of a term.

Content analysis This is a methodology for obtaining statistical data from a collection of texts that are similar in some respect. Content analysis is a nonintrusive way of conducting research.

Control group In experiments, the control group is left alone and doesn't experience any kind of intervention, in contrast to the experimental group, to whom something is done. Then the two groups are compared to see whether significant differences are found in the experimental group, which can then be attributed to the intervention.

Critical discourse analysis A form of discourse analysis that focuses on the use of language by powerful groups in societies to dominate other groups and on the strategies of resistance by subjugated groups. In addition to style, it considers how stories are framed, how readers are positioned relative to the texts they consume, and how the use of language leads readers to make certain interpretations of the text.

Cultural imperialism (also media imperialism) This theory describes the flow of media (such as songs, films, and television programs) and popular culture from the United States and a few other capitalist countries in Western Europe to developing countries. Along with these texts and popular culture, it is alleged that values and beliefs (and bourgeois capitalist ideology) are also transmitted, leading to the domination of the receiving people.

Cultural studies This multidisciplinary approach (using concepts from literary theory, semiotic theory, sociology, psychoanalytic theory, political theory, and other social sciences and humanities) is used to analyze and interpret phenomena such as the media, popular culture, literature, social movements, and related matters.

Culture There are hundreds of definitions of this term. Generally speaking, from an anthropological perspective, it involves the transmission from generation to generation of specific ideas, arts, customary beliefs, ways of living, behavior patterns, institutions, and values. When applied to the arts, it is generally used to specify "elite" artworks such as operas, poetry, classical music, and serious novels.

Culture codes According to Clotaire Rapaille (2006), young children from the time they are born until age 7 become "imprinted" with certain codes distinctive to where they grow up, and these codes shape their tastes, behavior, and attitudes.

Data (plural of *datum*) Data are conventionally understood to be forms of information, frequently numerical, that can be organized, tabulated, and used as the basis for decision making.

Defense mechanisms These are methods used by the ego to defend itself against pressures from the id—or impulsive elements in the psyche—and superego elements such as conscience and guilt. Some of the more common defense mechanisms are repression (barring unconscious instinctual wishes and memories from consciousness), regression (returning to earlier stages in one's development), ambivalence (a simultaneous feeling of love and hate), and rationalization (offering excuses to justify one's actions).

Demographics This refers to similarities found in selected groups of people on factors such as race, religion, sex, social class, ethnicity, occupation, place of residence, and age.

Denotation When we give the literal or explicit meaning of a word or a description of an object, we give its denotation. *Denotation* is the opposite of *connotation*, which deals with the cultural meanings of a term or object.

Desexualization This refers to the argument by Charles Winick (1995) and others that differences between males and females are lessening, with men getting weaker and women getting stronger, and that American society is becoming desexualized—that is, the sexes are losing their distinctive characteristics and a unisex culture is evolving.

Discourse analysis A qualitative methodology that helps us understand social interactions and how social reality is produced through our spoken, written, and visual texts. The focus is on how authors of texts convey their ideas rather than on what those ideas are.

Ego In Freud's theory of the psyche, the ego functions as the executant of the id and as a mediator between the id and the superego. The ego is involved with the perception of reality and the adaptation to reality.

Emotive functions According to Roman Jakobson (Culler, 1986), messages have a number of functions. One of them is the emotive function, which involves the sender expressing feelings. (Other functions are referential and poetic.)

Ethnomethodology A branch of sociology that studies the everyday activities of people, seeing these activities as phenomena worth investigating in their own right. The focus is on how people make sense of the world and on commonsense attitudes, as revealed in conversation and behavior.

Evidence Evidence is material that a reasonable person would find worth considering that supports some contention or theory. Evidence can be qualitative or quantitative.

Facial expression According to Ekman and Sejnowski (1992), there are eight universal facial expressions showing emotions: anger, determination, disgust, fear, neutral (no expression), pouting, sadness, and surprise. Paul Ekman developed a Facial Action Coding System that deals with the 43 muscles in the human face used to show emotions.

False consciousness In Marxist thought, *false consciousness* refers to mistaken ideas people have about their class, status, and economic possibilities. These ideas help maintain the status quo and are of great use to the ruling class, which wants to avoid changes in the social structure. Marx argued that the ideas of the ruling class are always the ruling ideas in society.

Feminist criticism Feminist criticism focuses on the roles given to women and the way they are portrayed in texts of all kinds. Feminist critics argue that women are typically used as sexual objects and are portrayed stereotypically in texts, resulting in negative effects on both men and women.

Focal points These refer to the five general topics or subject areas of mass communication: the work of art or text, the artist, the audience, America or the society, and the media.

Focus groups Focus groups involve relatively small numbers of people, usually around 8 or 10 people, who are selected to participate in group discussions on topics of interest to marketers. They have been criticized for not getting at people's deepest thoughts and feelings and for providing ideas that offer little value to the companies paying for the focus groups.

Functional In sociological thought, the term *functional* refers to the contribution an institution makes to the maintenance of society. Something functional helps maintain the system in which it is found.

Gender This term refers to the sexual category of an individual, masculine or feminine, and to behavioral traits connected with each category.

Genre *Genre* is a French term that means "kind" or "class." As we use the term, it refers to the kind of formulaic texts found in the mass media: soap operas, news shows, sport programs, horror shows, detective programs, and so on. I have dealt with this topic at length in my book *Popular Culture Genres* (1992).

Grid-group theory Based on the work of social anthropologist Mary Douglas (1970), this theory argues that in modern societies, there are four mutually antagonistic lifestyles that shape people's choices in consumption and other areas of social and political life. Group involves the strength of the bounds in the units in which people find themselves (strong or weak), and grid involves the number of rules that they must obey (many or few).

Hawthorne effect This term is used to describe an experiment in which the observers have an impact on the results of the study.

Hypothesis A hypothesis is something assumed to be true for the purposes of discussion, argument, or further investigation. It is, in a sense, a guess or supposition about what factor may explain some phenomenon.

Icon In Peirce's (1977) trichotomy, an icon is a sign that conveys meaning by resemblance. Photographs are iconic, and so are the stylized drawings used in airports to help people find toilets or luggage.

Id The id in Freud's theory of the psyche (technically known as his structural hypothesis) is that element of the psyche representative of a person's drives. Freud (1965b) called it, in *New Introductory Lectures on Psychoanalysis*, "a chaos, a cauldron of seething excitement." It also is the source of energy, but lacking direction, it needs the ego to harness it and control it. In popular thought, it is connected with impulse, lust, and "I want it all now" kind of behavior.

Ideology An ideology refers to a logically coherent, integrated explanation of social, economic, and political matters that helps establish the goals and direct the actions of some group or political entity. People act (and vote or don't vote) on the basis of some ideology, even though they may not have articulated or thought about it.

Image Defining *image* is extremely difficult. In my book, *Seeing Is Believing: An Introduction to Visual Communication*, I define an image as "a collection of signs and symbols that we find when we look at a photograph, a film still, a shot of a television screen, a print advertisement, or just about anything" (Berger, 2012). The term is used for mental as well as physical representations of things. Images often have powerful emotional effects on people as well as historical significance. Two books that deal with images in some detail are Kiku Adatto's (1993) *Picture Perfect: The Art and Artifice of Public Image Making* and Paul Messaris's (1994) *Visual Literacy: Image, Mind and Reality.*

Index For Peirce (1977), an index is a kind of semiotic sign that conveys meaning based on a cause-and-effect relationship. Smoke is indexical in that it signifies fire.

Internet The Internet is a system of interlinked computer networks that enables people to send email (electronic mail) and access sites on the World Wide Web.

Interpretation We distinguish between interpretation and analysis. Interpretation involves applying concepts and methods from one or more disciplines to a literary text or to some phenomenon of interest. Analysis involves studying something by separating it into its components.

Intertextuality In literary theory, the term *intertextuality* is generally used to deal with borrowings by one text of other texts. This borrowing can involve content and style. In some cases, intertextual borrowings are not consciously made, whereas in other cases, such as parody, the borrowing is done on purpose.

Jokes Jokes are conventionally defined as short narratives, meant to amuse and create laughter, that have a punch line.

Lifestyles This term—which means, literally, style of life—refers to the way people live, from the decisions they make about how to decorate their homes (and where they are located) to the kind of car they drive, the clothes they wear, the kinds of foods they eat and the restaurants they visit, where they go for vacations, and what kind of pets they have.

Likert scale Likert scales enable respondents to indicate degrees or strength of attitude by using (most commonly) a numerical 5- or 7-point scale.

Marxism This system of thought developed by Karl Marx (and elaborated on by many others) deals with the relationship between the economic system in a country (the base) and the institutions that develop out of this economic system (the superstructure). Marxist media critics focus on the role of the media in capitalist societies, especially on the way the media help prevent class conflict and defuse alienation by generating consumerist cultures.

Mass For our purposes, *mass* as in *mass communication* refers to a large number of people who are the audience for some communication. There is considerable disagreement about how to understand the term *mass*. Some theorists say it is comprised of persons who are heterogeneous, do not know one another, are alienated, and do not have a leader. Others attack these notions, saying they are not based on fact or evidence but on incorrect theories.

Mass communication This term refers to the subject of this book—the transfer of messages, information, and texts from a sender to a large number of people, a mass audience. This transfer is done through the technologies of the mass media, such as newspapers, magazines, television programs, films, records, and the Internet. Often, the sender is a person in some large media organization, the messages are public, and the audience is large and varied.

Medium (plural: media) A medium is a means of delivering messages, information, and texts to audiences. There are different ways of classifying the media. Some of the most common are print (newspapers, magazines, books, billboards), electronic (radio, television, computers), and photographic (photographs, films, videos).

Metaphor A metaphor is a figure of speech that conveys meaning by analogy. Metaphors are not confined to poetry and literary works but, according to some linguists, are the fundamental way in which we make sense of things and find meaning in the world.

Metonymy According to linguists, metonymy is a figure of speech that conveys information by association and is, along with metaphor, one of the most important ways people convey information to one another. We tend not to be aware of our use of metonymy, but whenever we use association to create an idea about something (e.g., Rolls-Royce = wealthy), we are thinking metonymically.

Mimetic desire This theory of French literary theorist René Girard (1991) argues that people often imitate the "desire" of celebrities, sports heroes, and others when they purchase things, not their behavior.

Model A model, in the social sciences, is an abstract representation that shows how some phenomenon functions. Theories are typically expressed in language, but models tend to be represented graphically or by statistics or mathematics. Denis McQuail and Sven Windahl (1993) defined *model* as "a consciously simplified description in graphic form of a piece of reality. A model seeks to show the main elements of any structure or process and the relationships between these elements" (p. 2).

Modernism This term is used in art criticism for the period from approximately the turn of the century until around the 1960s. The modernists rejected narrative structure for simultaneity and montage and explored the paradoxical nature of reality. Some of the more important modernists were T. S. Eliot, Franz Kafka, James Joyce, Pablo Picasso, Henri Matisse, and Eugene Ionesco.

Multimodal critical discourse analysis This form of multimodal discourse analysis considers the ideological import of texts containing both words and images. Ideologies may be expressed consciously or unconsciously, and practitioners of critical discourse analysis hold that discourse is often used by a dominant group in society to maintain its position over other groups.

Multimodal discourse analysis This is the form of discourse analysis used to consider texts containing both words and images. The basic methodology used in multimodal discourse analysis is semiotics.

Neuropsychoanalysis This is an approach to studying phenomena that uses a mixture of neuroscience and psychoanalytic theory.

Paradigmatic analysis The paradigmatic analysis of texts involves finding the pattern of binary oppositions found (allegedly, some would argue) there. These oppositions enable people to find meaning in texts.

Participant observation Participant observation is a qualitative form of research in which a researcher becomes a member (to varying degrees) in some group or entity being studied. Being a participant enables a researcher to gain a better sense of the views and objectives of the group being studied.

Personal journal This is a record of one's ideas, thoughts, and speculations used to play with and think up new ideas to be used in scholarly research. Journals should be kept in bound notebooks, with the pages numbered and an index on the last page to facilitate access to ideas and thoughts that may be of interest and use when involved in scholarly writing.

Phallic symbol An object that resembles either by shape or function the penis is described as a phallic symbol. Symbolism is a defense mechanism of the ego that permits hidden or repressed sexual or aggressive thoughts to be expressed in disguised form. For a discussion of this topic, see Freud's (1900/1965a) *The Interpretation of Dreams.*

Phallocentric theory This term is used to suggest that societies are dominated by males and that the ultimate source of this domination, that which shapes our institutions and cultures, is the male phallus. In this theory, a link is made between male sexuality and male power. A more detailed discussion of this concept is found in my book *Cultural Criticism: A Primer of Key Concepts* (Berger, 1994).

Pilot study This term is used to refer to a small-scale test study made to determine whether the questions in a survey or questionnaire are easily understood. More generally, a pilot study refers to any small study that helps researchers refine their techniques and gain a sense of whether a full-scale study might be effective.

Poetic functions In Jakobson's theory, poetic functions are those that use literary devices such as metaphor and metonymy. Poetic functions differ, Jakobson suggested, from emotive functions and referential functions (Culler, 1986).

Political cultures According to Aaron Wildavsky (1982; Thompson, Ellis, Wildavsky, 1990), all democratic societies have four political cultures and need these cultures to balance one another. These political cultures are individualists, hierarchical elitists, egalitarians, and fatalists. A political culture is made up of people who share similar political values and beliefs and, for Wildavsky, similar group boundaries and observed rules and prescriptions. For an example of how Wildavsky's theories are applied to mass media and popular culture, see my book *Agitpop: Political Culture and Communication Theory* (Berger, 1990).

Political theory Political theory is the branch of philosophy (or political science) that deals with the nature of government and the role of the state.

Popular *Popular* is one of the most difficult terms used in discourse about the arts and the media. Literally speaking, the term means appealing to a large number of people. It comes from the Latin term *popularis,* "of the people."

Popular culture *Popular culture* is a term that identifies texts that appeal to a large number of people, that is, texts that are popular. But mass communication theorists often identify (or should we say confuse) *popular* with *mass* and suggest that if something is popular, it must be of poor quality, appealing to some mythical "lowest common denominator." Popular culture is generally held to be the opposite of *elite* culture—that is, arts that require sophistication and refinement to be appreciated, such as ballet, opera, poetry, classical music, and so on. Many critics now question this popular culture–elite culture polarity.

Postmodernism We are, some theorists suggest, all living in a postmodern era and have been doing so since the 1960s. Literally speaking, the term means "after modernism," the period from approximately 1900 to the 1960s. As a leading theorist of the subject, Jean-Francois Lyotard (1984), put it, postmodernism is characterized by "incredulity toward metanarratives" (p. xxiv). By this, he meant that the old philosophical belief systems that had helped people order their lives and societies are no longer accepted or given credulity. This has lead to a period in which, more or less, anything goes. See my books *Postmortem for a Postmodernist* (a mystery novel that explains postmodernism; Berger, 1997) and *The Postmodern Presence* (a reader; Berger, 1998b) for more on this subject.

Power Power is, politically speaking, the ability to implement one's policy wishes. When we use the term to discuss texts, it describes their ability to have an emotional impact on people—readers, viewers, or listeners.

Primary research Primary research is research personally done by someone investigating a subject of interest. Primary research differs, then, from secondary research, which is research done using and citing the work (often the primary research) of others.

Psychoanalytic theory Psychoanalytic theory is based on the notion that the human psyche has what Freud called the "unconscious," which, ordinarily speaking, is inaccessible to us (unlike consciousness and the preconscious) and which continually shapes and affects our mental functioning and behavior. We can symbolize this by imagining an iceberg: The tip of the iceberg, showing above the water, represents consciousness. The part of the iceberg we can see, just below the surface of the water, represents the preconscious. And the rest of the iceberg (most of it, which cannot be seen but we know is there) represents the unconscious. We cannot access this area of our psyches because of repression. Freud also emphasized sexuality and the role of the Oedipus complex in everyone's lives.

Public Instead of the term *popular culture,* we sometimes use the terms *public arts* or *public communication* to avoid the negative connotations of the terms *mass* and *popular.* A public is a group of people, a community. We can contrast public acts, those meant to be known to the community, with private acts, which are not meant to be known to others.

Qualitative research Qualitative research techniques are those (such as semiotic analysis, psychoanalytic criticism, ideological criticism, rhetorical interpretation, interviewing, and participant observation) designed primarily to yield nonquantitative or nonnumerical data. As such, they differ from quantitative research methods, although in some kinds of research, both approaches can be used.

Quantitative research Quantitative research techniques are those (such as content analysis, surveys and questionnaires, and experiments) designed to yield numerical data.

Questionnaire A questionnaire is a self-administered survey with specific questions that respondents answer.

Random sample This term refers to a sample generated by using a table of random numbers designed to select representative samples for surveys and questionnaires.

Ratings In media research, ratings refer to the percentage of households or of people in an area who have tuned their televisions or radios to a specific station, program, or network. Ratings differ from shares, which refer to the number of people or households tuned to a station, program, or network correlated with sets in use.

Rationalization In Freudian thought, a rationalization is a defense mechanism of the ego that creates an excuse to justify some action (or inaction when an action is expected). Ernest Jones (1908), who introduced the term, used it to describe logical and rational reasons people give to justify behavior actually caused by unconscious and irrational determinants.

Reactivity We use this term to describe the impact or effect of researchers on those studied. When people are being studied, they often behave differently than they do under ordinary circumstances.

Referential functions In Jakobson's theory, the referential function of speech deals with the way it helps speakers relate to their surroundings. Jakobson contrasted this with emotive and poetic functions of speech (Culler, 1986).

Representative samples In this book, I define representative samples as small groups of people held to have the same attributes as larger populations. In general terms, a sample is a part that is representative of some larger whole.

Research In this book, I define *research* as the use of qualitative or quantitative methods to obtain desired information about some group of people or subject of interest. Sometimes this information is in the form of numerical data, but not always.

Rhetoric In essence, rhetoric is the study of effective expression and of style in language. Rhetoric is also used to deal with the means by which people are persuaded. In recent years, rhetoric has also been used to study the mass media and popular culture.

Role Sociologists describe a role as a way of behavior learned in society that is appropriate to a particular situation. A person generally plays many roles with different people during a given day, such as parent (family) and worker (job).

Secondary research This term is used for research done by others that is cited by researchers to make some point or provide information. Secondary research differs, then, from primary research, which is original research done by a person or group.

Semiotics The term *semiotics* means, literally, the science of signs. *Semion* is the Greek term for sign. A sign is anything that can be used to stand for something else. According to C. S. Peirce (1977), one of the founders of the science, a sign "is something which stands to somebody for something in some respect or capacity" (Peirce, 1955, p. 99). My book *Signs in Contemporary Culture: An Introduction to Semiotics* (Berger, 1999) discusses many of the more important semiotic concepts and shows how they can be applied to popular culture.

Shadow In Jungian thought, the shadow represents the dark side of the psyche, which we attempt to keep hidden. It contains repressed and unfavorable aspects of our personalities as well as normal instincts and creative impulses. Thus, in all people, there is a continual battle between shadow aspects of our personalities and our egos, which also contain some negative features.

Share Share is used to designate the number of people or households tuned to a specific program, station, or network correlated with sets in use. It differs from ratings, which are tied to households tuned to a specific program, station, or network in a certain area.

Sign In semiotics, a sign is defined as anything that can be used to stand for something else. Semiotics is the science of signs and studies how they are used to generate meaning. As Umberto Eco (1976) explained, if signs can be used to tell the truth, they can also be used to lie.

Simile Similes are weak forms of metaphor that use *like* or *as*. The statement "My love is like a rose" is a simile; the statement "My love is a rose" is a metaphor.

Social media The social media are those Internet organizations, such as Facebook, Twitter, and YouTube, that enable people to communicate, at no cost, texts, images, and videos to large numbers of other people.

Socialization This term refers to the processes by which societies teach people how to behave: what rules to obey, roles to assume, and values to hold. Traditionally, socialization was done by the family, educators, religious figures, and peers. The mass media seem to have usurped this function to a considerable degree, with consequences that are not always positive.

Sociology Sociology is a social science that studies groups, institutions, and collectivities—that is, the social behavior of human beings. As such, it differs from psychology, which focuses on the mind, psyche, and individual behavior.

Subculture A subculture is a cultural subgroup whose religion, ethnicity, sexual orientation, beliefs, values, behaviors, and lifestyle varies from those of the dominant culture. In any complex society, it is normal to have a considerable number of subcultures. Some subcultures are deviant and others criminal.

Superego In Freud's typology, the superego is the agency in our psyches related to conscience and morality. The superego is involved with processes such as approval and disapproval of wishes on the basis or whether they are moral or not, critical self-observation, and a sense of guilt over wrongdoing. The functions of the superego are largely unconscious and are opposed to id elements in our psyches. Mediating between the two, and trying to balance them, is the ego.

Surveys Surveys generally take the form of lists of questions (technically known as "instruments") addressed to representative samples of some population to obtain valid numerical data about the larger population as a whole.

Symbol In Peirce's (1977) trichotomy, a symbol is anything that has a conventional meaning—that is, whose meaning must be taught to others and is not natural. Saussure (1966) disagreed with this notion, seeing the symbol as only partially conventional.

Synecdoche Synecdoche is a weak form of metonymy in which, generally speaking, a part is used to stand for the whole and vice versa. Thus, we use the term *Pentagon* to stand for the armed forces and military establishment of the United States.

Syntagmatic analysis A syntagmatic analysis of a text deals with its linear structure. The term *syntagm* means "chain," and thus, a syntagmatic analysis looks at the sequence of actions in a text. It differs from a paradigmatic analysis, which seeks out the binary oppositions that inform the text.

System 1 A type of thinking that occurs automatically, with little or no voluntary control.

System 2 A type of thinking that involves effortful mental activity, agency, choice, and concentration.

Text For our purposes, a text is, broadly speaking, any work of art in any medium. The term *text* is used by critics as a convenience so they don't have to name a given work all the time or use various synonyms. There are problems in deciding what the text is when we deal with serial texts, such as soap operas or comics.

Theory A *theory*, as I use the term, is expressed in language and systematically and logically attempts to explain and predict phenomena being studied. Theories differ from concepts, which define phenomena being studied, and from models, which are abstract, usually graphic, and explicit about what is being studied.

Typology A typology is a classification scheme or system of categories that someone uses to make sense of some phenomena. My list of 45 humor techniques in Chapter 8 is a typology.

Values Values are abstract and general beliefs or judgments about what is right and wrong, what is good and bad, that have implications for individual behavior and for social, cultural, and political entities. There are a number of problems with values from a philosophical point of view. First, how does one determine which values are correct or good and which aren't? That is, how do we justify values? Are values objective or subjective? Second, what happens when there is a conflict between groups, each of which holds central values that conflict with one another?

Values and Lifestyles (VALS) This refers to a typology of groups in America based on a survey of American values and lifestyles developed by the Stanford Research Institute. The VALS typology was used by advertising agencies seeking to understand what motivated consumers.

Violence This term is extremely difficult to define. Conventionally, it is used to describe the use of physical force by a person or group to hurt or harm someone or prevent someone from hurting or harming a person or group. Many media researchers are interested in the relation that may exist between watching television and violent behavior in people, and there have been many studies on this subject.

References

Adatto, K. (1993). *Picture perfect: The art and artifice of public image making.* New York, NY: Basic Books.

Alasuutari, P. (1995). *Researching culture: Qualitative method and cultural studies.* Thousand Oaks, CA: SAGE.

Albergotti, R. (2014, June 30). Furor erupts over Facebook study. *The Wall Street Journal,* B1. Retrieved from http://www.wsj.com/articles/furor-erupts -over-facebook-experiment-on-users-1404085840/

Allen, H. (1991). Everything you wanted to know about specs. *San Francisco Chronicle.* (Reprinted from the *Washington Post*)

Bakhtin, M. (1981). *The dialogic imagination: Four Essays.* Austin: University of Texas Press.

Barthes, R. (1972). *Mythologies* (A. Lavers, Trans.). New York, NY: Hill & Wang.

Barthes, R. (1977). *Image, music, text* (S. Heath, Trans.). New York, NY: Hill & Wang.

Barzun, J., & Graff, H. F. (1957). *The modern researcher.* New York, NY: Harcourt, Brace.

Benchley, R. (1920, February). The most popular book of the month: An extremely literary review of the latest edition of the New York City telephone directory. *Vanity Fair,* 69.

Berger, A. A. (Ed.). (1989). *Political culture and public opinion.* New Brunswick, NJ: Transaction Books.

Berger, A. A. (1990). *Agitpop: Political culture and communication theory.* New Brunswick, NJ: Transaction Books.

Berger, A. A. (Ed.). (1991). *Media USA: Process and effect* (2nd ed.). White Plains, NY: Longman.

Berger, A. A. (1992). *Popular culture genres.* Newbury Park, CA: SAGE.

Berger, A. A. (1994). *Cultural criticism: A primer of key concepts.* Thousand Oaks, CA: SAGE.

Berger, A. A. (1995). *Essentials of mass communication theory.* Thousand Oaks, CA: SAGE.

Berger, A. A. (1997). *Postmortem for a postmodernist.* Walnut Creek, CA: AltaMira.

Berger, A. A. (1998a). *Media research techniques* (2nd ed.). Thousand Oaks, CA: SAGE.

Berger, A. A. (Ed.). (1998b). *The postmodern presence.* Walnut Creek, CA: AltaMira.

Berger, A. A. (1999). *Signs in contemporary culture: An introduction to semiotics* (2nd ed.). Salem, WI: Sheffield.

Berger, A. A. (2011). The branded self: On the semiotics of identity. *American Sociologist, 42*(2/3), 232–237.

Berger, A. A. (2012). *Seeing is believing: An introduction to visual communication* (4th ed.). New York, NY: McGraw-Hill.

Berger, J. (1972). *Ways of seeing.* London, UK: British Broadcasting System and Penguin Books.

Berkhofer, R. F., Jr. (1969). *A behavioral approach to historical analysis.* New York, NY: Free Press.

Bernard, H. R. (1994). *Research methods in anthropology* (2nd ed.). Walnut Creek, CA: AltaMira.

Best, S., & Kellner, D. (1991). *Postmodern theory: Critical interrogations.* New York, NY: Guilford Press.

Bogdan, R. C., & Biklen, S. K. (1992). *Qualitative research in education: An introduction to theory and methods.* Boston, MA: Allyn & Bacon.

Braudel, F. (1981). *The structures of everyday life: Civilization and capitalism, 15th–18th century* (Vol. 1). New York, NY: Harper & Row.

Brenner, C. (1974). *An elementary textbook of psychoanalysis.* Garden City, NY: Doubleday.

Brummett, B. (2011). *Rhetoric and popular culture* (3rd ed.). Thousand Oaks, CA: SAGE.

Brunskill, D. (2013). Social media, social avatars and the psyche: Is Facebook good for us? *Australian Psychiatry, 21*(6), 527–532.

Butler, J. (1999). *Gender trouble: Feminism and the subversion of identity.* New York, NY: Routledge.

Butler, S. (2004). *Hudibras.* Retrieved from http://www.gutenberg.org/ebooks/4937/ (Originally published 1663–1678 in England)

Cameron, D. (2001). *Working with spoken discourse.* London, UK: SAGE.

Cameron, D., & Panović, I. (2014). *Working with written discourse.* London, UK: SAGE.

Cashmore, E., & Rojek, C. (1999). *Dictionary of cultural theorists.* New York, NY: Oxford University Press.

Chase, M. (1982, June 16). Your suit is pressed, hair neat, but what do your molars say? *Wall Street Journal,* 1.

Cirksena, K. (1987). Politics and difference: Radical feminist epistemological premises for communication studies. *Journal of Communication Inquiry, 11*(1), 19–28.

Creswell, J. W. (1994). *Research design: Qualitative and quantitative approaches.* Thousand Oaks, CA: SAGE.

Culler, J. (1976). *Structuralist poetics: Structuralism, linguistics, and the study of literature.* New York, NY: Cornell University Press.

Culler, J. (1986). *Ferdinand de Saussure* (Rev. ed.). Ithaca, NY: Cornell University Press.

Deacon, D., Pickering, M., Golding, P., & Murdock, G. (1999). *Researching communications: A practical guide to methods in media and cultural analysis.* London, UK: Arnold.

de Certeau, M. (1984). *The practice of everyday life* (S. Rendall, Trans.). Berkeley: University of California Press.

Dickey, M. (2006, April 27). Resources and tips for conducting online surveys. *The Chronicle of Philanthropy.* Retrieved from http://philanthropy.com/ article/ResourseTips-for/52521/

Dominick, J. R. (1993). *The dynamics of mass communication* (4th ed.). New York, NY: McGraw-Hill.

Douglas, M. (1970). *Natural symbols.* London, UK: Barrie & Rockliff, Cresset Press.

Dundes, A. (1968). Introduction. In V. Propp, *Morphology of the folktale* (2nd ed.; L. A. Wagner, Ed.; L. Scott, Trans.). Austin: University of Texas Press. (Original work published in 1928)

Durham, M. G., & Kellner, D. (Eds.). (2001). *Media and cultural Studies: Key works.* Malden, MA: Blackwell.

Eco, U. (1976). *A theory of semiotics.* Bloomington: Indiana University Press.

Eidelberg, L. (1968). *Encyclopedia of psychoanalysis.* New York, NY: Free Press.

Ekman, P., & Sejnowski, T. J. (1992, August 1). *Facial expression understanding.* Report to the National Science Foundation, Arlington, VA. Retrieved from http://face-and-emotion.com/dataface/nsfrept/exec_summary.html

Erikson, E. (1963). *Childhood and society.* New York, NY: W. W. Norton.

Evans, C. (2015, March 24). 98 percent of Americans are connected to high-speed wireless Internet. *The White House Blog.* Retrieved from https://www.whitehouse.gov/blog/2015/03/23/connecting-america-high-speed-broadband-internet

Freud, S. (1953). *A general introduction to psychoanalysis.* Garden City, NY: Doubleday.

Freud, S. (1963a). The antithetical sense of primal words. In *Character and culture: Vol. 9. The collected works* (P. Rieff, Ed.). New York, NY: Collier. (Original work published 1910)

Freud, S. (1963b). *Character and culture: Vol. 9. The collected works* (P. Rieff, Ed.). New York, NY: Collier. (Original work published 1910)

Freud, S. (1965a). *The interpretation of dreams.* New York, NY: Avon. (Original work published 1900)

Freud, S. (1965b). *New introductory lectures on psychoanalysis* (J. Strachey, Ed. & Trans.). New York, NY: Norton.

Fried, I. (2011, February 1). Nielsen: Ethnic minorities more likely than whites to buy smartphones. *Wall Street Journal.* Retrieved from http://allthingsd.com/20110201/nielsen-ethnic-minorities-more-likely-than-whites-to-buy-smartphones/

Fuchs, C. (2014). *Social media: A critical introduction.* London, UK: Sage.

Funk, J. B., & Buchman, D. D. (1996). Playing violent video and computer games and the adolescent self-concept. *Journal of Communication, 46*(2), 19–32.

Garfinkel, H. (1967). *Studies in ethnomethodology.* Englewood Cliffs, NJ: Prentice Hall.

Garfinkel, H. (2006). *Seeing sociologically: The routine grounds of social action.* Boulder, CO: Paradigm.

Gerbner, G. (with Signorielli, N). (1988). *Violence and terror in the mass media: An annotated bibliography.* Lanham, MD: UNIPUB (distributor).

Gibaldi, J. (1995). *MLA handbook for writers of research papers* (4th ed.). New York, NY: Modern Language Association of America.

Girard, R. (1991). *A theater of envy: William Shakespeare.* New York, NY: Oxford.

Goel, V. (2014, June 29). Facebook tinkers with users' emotions in news feed experiment, stirring outcry. *The New York Times,* B1. Retrieved from http://www.nytimes.com/2014/06/30/technology/facebook-tinkers-with-users-emotions-in-news-feed-experiment-stirring-outcry.html

Goodstein, D. (1991, Winter). Scientific fraud. *Engineering & Science.* Retrieved from http://calteches.library.caltech.edu/615/2/Goodstein.pdf

Gottdiener, M. (1997). *The theming of America: Dreams, visions, and commercial spaces.* Boulder, CO: Westview.

Grotjahn, M. (1957). *Beyond laughter.* New York, NY: McGraw-Hill.

Grotjahn, M. (1971). *The voice of the symbol.* New York, NY: Delta Books.

Hart. M. (2006–2007). *The Hawthorne experiments: Management takes a new direction.* Retrieved from http://mh-lectures.co.uk/hawth_0.htm

Heritage, J. (1984). *Garfinkel and ethnomethodology.* Cambridge, UK: Polity Press.

Hinsie, L. E., & Campbell, R. J. (1970). *Psychiatric dictionary* (4th ed.). New York, NY: Oxford University Press.

Hoesterey, I. (Ed.). (1991). *Zeitgeist in Babel: The postmodernist controversy.* Bloomington: Indiana University Press.

Houston, B. (1996). *Computer-assisted reporting.* New York, NY: St. Martin's Press.

Jameson, F. (1991). *Postmodernism, or, The cultural logic of late capitalism.* Durham, NC: Duke University Press.

Jones, E. (1908). Rationalization in every-day life. *Journal of Abnormal Psychology, 3,* 161–169

Jung, C. G. (with von Franz, M-L., Henderson, J. L., Jacobi, J., & Jaffe, A.). (1968). *Man and his symbols.* Garden City, NY: Doubleday.

Kahneman, D. (2011). *Thinking fast and slow.* New York, NY: Farrar, Straus, and Giroux.

Kaiser Family Foundation. (2010, January 20). *Generation M2: Media in the lives of 8- to 18-year-olds.* Retrieved from http://kff.org/other/event/generation-m2-media-in-the-lives-of/

Kantha, S. S. (1999). Sexual humor on Freud as expressed in limericks. *Humor, 12*(3), 288–299.

King, N., Jr. (2012, November 3–4). Obama holds lead in Florida and Ohio polls. *The Wall Street Journal,* A5.

Kottak, C. (1982). *Researching American culture.* Ann Arbor: University of Michigan Press.

Lakoff, G., & Johnson, M. (1980). *Metaphors we live by.* Chicago, IL: University of Chicago Press.

Lazere, D. (1977). Mass culture, political consciousness and English studies. *College English, 38,* 755–756.

Liberman, K. (2007). *Dialectical Practice in Tibetan Philosophical Culture: An Ethnomethodological Inquiry into Formal Reasoning.* Rowman & Littlefield Publishers.

Lifton, R. (1974). Who is more dry? Heroes of Japanese youth. In A. Berger (Ed.), *About man.* Dayton, OH: Pflaum.

Livingston, E. (1987). *Making Sense of Ethnomethodology.* Routledge.

Lodge, D. (Ed.). (1988). *Modern criticism and theory.* New York, NY: Longman.

Lotman, J. M. (1977). *The structure of the artistic text.* Ann Arbor: Michigan Slavic Contributions.

Lowenthal, L. (1944). Biographies in popular magazines. In P. F. Lazarsfeld & F. N. Stanton (Eds.), *Radio research 1942–1943.* New York, NY: Essential Books.

Lyotard, J-F. (1984). *The postmodern condition: A report on knowledge* (G. Bennington & B. Massumi, Trans.). Minneapolis: University of Minnesota Press.

Machin, D., & Mayr, A. (2012). *How to do critical discourse analysis.* London, UK: Sage.

Malinowski, B. (1961). *Argonauts of the western pacific.* New York, NY: E. P. Dutton.

Mannheim, K. (1936). *Ideology and utopia: An introduction to the sociology of knowledge* (L. Wirth & E. Shils, Trans.). New York, NY: Harcourt Brace.

Marx, K. (1964). *Selected writings in sociology & social philosophy* (T. B. Bottomore & M. Rubel, Eds.; T. B. Bottomore, Trans.). New York, NY: McGraw-Hill.

Matsumoto, D., & Hwang, H. S. (2013). *Nonverbal communication: Science and applications.* Thousand Oaks, CA: Sage.

McGowan, K. (2014, April). The second coming of Sigmund Freud. *Discover.* Retrieved from http://discovermagazine.com/2014/april/14-the-second-coming-of-sigmund-freud/

McKeon, R. (Ed.). (1941). *The basic works of Aristotle.* New York, NY: Random House.

McKercher, R., & Fu, C. (2006). Living on the edge. *Annals of Tourism Research, 33*(2), 508–524.

McQuail, D., & Windahl, S. (1993). *Communication models for the study of mass communication* (2nd ed.). New York, NY: Longman.

Medhurst, M. J., & Benson, T. W. (Eds.). (1984). *Rhetorical dimensions in media: A critical casebook.* Dubuque, LA: Kendall/Hunt.

Media Literacy Clearinghouse. (n.d.). *Media use statistics.* Retrieved from http://www.frankwbaker.com/mediause.htm

Merriam-Webster's collegiate dictionary (11th ed.). (2006). Springfield, MA: Merriam-Webster.

Messaris, P. (1994). *Visual literacy: Image, mind and reality.* Boulder, CO: Westview.

Milgram, S. (1965). Liberating effects of group pressure. *Journal of Personality and Social Psychology, 1,* 127–134.

Mitchell, A. (1983). *The nine American lifestyles: Who we are and where we are going.* New York, NY: Macmillan.

Mitchell, S. A., & Black, M. J. (1996). *Freud and beyond: A history of modern psychoanalytic thought.* New York, NY: Basic Books.

Musil, R. (1965). *The man without qualities* (Vol. 1). New York, NY: Capricorn.

Peirce, C. S. (1955). *Philosophical writings of Peirce.* J. Bachler (Ed.). New York, NY: Dover.

Peirce, C. S. (1977). Epigraph. In T. A. Sebeok (Ed.), *A perfusion of signs* (p. vi). Bloomington: Indiana University Press.

Phifer, G. (1961). The historical approach. In C. W. Dow (Ed.), *An introduction to graduate study in speech and theatre.* East Lansing: Michigan State University Press.

Phillips, N. & Hardy, C. (2002). *Discourse analysis: Investigating processes of social construction.* London, UK: SAGE.

Pines, M. (1982, October 13). How they know what you really mean. *San Francisco Chronicle.*

Priest, S. H. (2010). *Doing media research: An introduction* (2nd ed.). Thousand Oaks, CA: SAGE.

Propp, V. (1968). *Morphology of the folktale* (2nd ed.; L. A. Wagner, Ed.; L. Scott, Trans.). Austin: University of Texas Press. (Original work published in 1928)

Queneau, R. (1958). *Exercises in style.* New York, NY: New Directions. (Originally published in France in 1947 as *Exercises de style*)

Radway, J. (1991). *Reading the romance: Women, patriarchy, and popular literature.* Chapel Hill: University of North Carolina Press.

Rapaille, C. (2006). *The culture code: An ingenious way to understand why people around the world live and buy as they do.* New York, NY: Broadway Books.

Riessman, C. K. (1993). *Narrative analysis.* Thousand Oaks, CA: SAGE.

Root, R. L., Jr. (1987). *The rhetorics of popular culture: Advertising, advocacy, and entertainment.* New York, NY: Greenwood.

Sacks, H. (1992). *Lectures on conversation. Victoria: Vol. 1.* Oxford, UK: Polity Press.

Said, E. W. (1978). *Orientalism.* New York, NY: Pantheon.

Saussure, F. de. (1966). *Course in general linguistics* (W. Baskin, Trans.). New York, NY: McGraw-Hill. (Original work published 1915)

Schegloff, E. A. (2007). *Sequence organization in interaction: A primer in conversation analysis: Vol. 1.* Cambridge, UK: Cambridge University Press

Schellenberg, J. A. (1974). *An introduction to social psychology* (2nd ed.). New York, NY: Random House.

Schutz, A., & Luckmann, T. (1974). *Structures of the life world.* Amsterdam, Netherlands: Heinemann Education.

Sebeok, T. A. (Ed.). (1977). *A perfusion of signs.* Bloomington: Indiana University Press.

Sherman, B. (1995). *Telecommunications management: Broadcasting/cable and the new technologies* (2nd ed.). New York, NY: McGraw-Hill.

Shiv, B., & Fedorikhin, A. (1999). Heart and mind in conflict: The interplay of affect and cognition in consumer decision making. *Journal of Consumer Research, 26*(3), 278–292.

Silver, N. (2012, November 12). Google or Gallup? Changes in voters' habits reshape polling world. *New York Times*, A8.

Stafford, W. (1978). *Writing the Australian crawl: View on the writer's vocation.* Ann Arbor: University of Michigan Press.

Stearns, P. N. (1998). *Why study history?* American Historical Association. Retrieved from http://www.historians.org/pubs/free/WhyStudyHistory.htm

Steeves, H. L., & Smith, M. C. (1987). Class and gender in prime-time television entertainment: Observations from a socialist feminist perspective. *Journal of Communication Inquiry, 11*(1), 43–63.

Strunk, W., Jr., & White, E. B. (1999). *Elements of style* (4th ed.). New York, NY: Longman.

Sudnow, D. (1979). *Ways of the Hand. The Organization of Improvised Conduct.* New York: Bantam.

Thompson, M., Ellis, R., & Wildavsky, A. (1990). *Cultural theory.* Boulder, CO: Westview.

Time. (1999, March 29).

Treadwell, D. (2011). *Introducing communication research: Paths of inquiry.* Thousand Oaks, CA: SAGE.

Turner, R. (Ed.). (1974). *Ethnomethodology.* Baltimore, MD: Penguin.

van Dijk, T. A. (Ed.). (1997). *Discourse as structure and process: Discourse studies: A multidisciplinary introduction.* London, UK: SAGE.

van Dijk, T. A. (2001). A linguistic study of ideology. In I. F. Outkhtanova-Shmygova (Ed.), *Perspectives and methods of political discourse and text research* (Vol. 2). Minsk: Minsk Media Group, Belarusian State University.

Vattimo, G. (1991). The end of (hi)story. In I. Hoesterey (Ed.), *Zeitgeist in Babel: The postmodernist controversy* (pp. 132 141). Bloomington: Indiana University Press.

vom Lehn, D. (2014). *Harold Garfinkel: The creation and development of ethnomethodology.* Walnut Creek, CA: Left Coast Press.

Waldman, K. (2014, June 28). Facebook's unethical experiment. *Slate.* Retrieved from http://www.slate.com/articles/health_and_science/science/2014/06/facebook_unethical_experiment_it_made_news_feeds_happier_or_sadder_to_manipulate.html

Watson, J., & Hill, A. (1997). *A dictionary of communication and media studies* (4th ed.). New York, NY: Arnold.

Weiner, S. (2014, June 27). Facebook experiment manipulates 600,000 users [Blog post]. *Animal.* Retrieved from http://animalnewyork.com/2014/facebook-experiment-manipulates-emotions-600000-users/

Wheeler, S. (2010, April 28). 12 simple writing rules. *Learning with e's: My thoughts about learning technology and all things digital.* Retrieved from http://steve-wheeler.blogspot.com/2010/04/12-writing-rules.html

Wildavsky, A. (1982). *Conditions for a pluralist democracy, or cultural pluralism means more than one political culture in a country.* Unpublished manuscript, University of California—Berkeley, Department of Political Science.

Winick, C. (1995). *Desexualization in American life.* New Brunswick, NJ: Transaction.

Wiseman, J. P., & Aron, M. S. (1970). *Field projects for sociology students*. Cambridge, MA: Schenkman.

Wright, C. R. (1986). *Mass communication: A sociological perspective* (3rd ed.). New York, NY: Random House.

Zaltman, G. (2003). *How customers think: Essential insights into the mind of the market*. Cambridge, MA: Harvard University Business School Press.

Zeman, J. J. (1977). Peirce's theory of signs. In T. A. Sebeok (Ed.), *A perfusion of signs*. Bloomington: Indiana University Press.

Author Index

Subject Index

About the Author

Arthur Asa Berger is professor emeritus of broadcast and electronic communication arts at San Francisco State University, where he taught from 1965 to 2003. He has published more than 100 articles, numerous book reviews, and more than 70 books. Among his latest books are *Understanding American Icons* (2012), *Media Analysis Techniques* (5th ed.; 2014), *Ads, Fads and Consumer Culture: Advertising's Impact on American Character and Society* (5th ed.; 2015), and *Messages: An Introduction to Communication* (2015). He has also written a number of academic mysteries such as *Durkheim Is Dead: Sherlock Holmes Is Introduced to Sociological Theory* (2003) and *Mistake in Identity: A Cultural Studies Murder Mystery* (2005). His books have been translated into 10 languages, and a dozen of his books have been translated into Chinese. Professor Berger is married, has two children and four grandchildren, and lives in Mill Valley, California.

His email address is arthurasaberger@gmail.com.